PUBLICATIONS OF
THE MANCHESTER CENTRE FOR ANGLO-SAXON STUDIES

Volume 7

Britons in Anglo-Saxon England

The number of native Britons, and their role, in Anglo-Saxon England has been hotly debated for generations; the English were seen as Germanic in the nineteenth century, but the twentieth saw a reinvention of the German 'past'. Today, the scholarly community is as deeply divided as ever on the issue: place-name specialists have consistently preferred minimalist interpretations, privileging migration from Germany, while other disciplinary groups have been less united in their views, with many archaeologists and historians viewing the British presence, potentially at least, as numerically significant or even dominant.

The papers collected here seek to shed new light on this complex issue, by bringing together contributions from different disciplinary specialists and exploring the interfaces between various categories of knowledge about the past. They assemble both a substantial body of evidence concerning the presence of Britons and offer a variety of approaches to the central issues of the scale of that presence and its significance across the seven centuries of Anglo-Saxon England.

NICK HIGHAM is Professor of Early Medieval and Landscape History at the University of Manchester.

PUBLICATIONS OF
THE MANCHESTER CENTRE FOR ANGLO-SAXON STUDIES
ISSN 1478–6710

Editorial Board

Donald Scragg

Richard Bailey
Timothy Graham
Gale R. Owen-Crocker
Alexander Rumble
Leslie Webster

Published Titles

1. *Textual and Material Culture in Anglo-Saxon England: Thomas Northcote Toller and the Toller Memorial Lectures*, ed. Donald Scragg
2. *Apocryphal Texts and Traditions in Anglo-Saxon England*, ed. Kathryn Powell and Donald Scragg
3. *King Harold II and the Bayeux Tapestry*, ed. Gale R. Owen-Crocker
4. *The Place of the Cross in Anglo-Saxon England*, ed. Catherine E. Karkov, Sarah Larratt Keefer and Karen Louise Jolly
5. *Writing and Texts in Anglo-Saxon England*, ed. Alexander R. Rumble
6. *Anglo-Saxon Royal Diplomas: A Palaeography*, Susan D. Thompson

Britons in
Anglo-Saxon England

edited by
NICK HIGHAM

THE BOYDELL PRESS

© Contributors 2007

All Rights Reserved. Except as permitted under current legislation no part of this work may be photocopied, stored in a retrieval system, published, performed in public, adapted, broadcast, transmitted, recorded or reproduced in any form or by any means, without the prior permission of the copyright owner

First published 2007
The Boydell Press, Woodbridge

ISBN 978-1-84383-312-3

Transferred to digital printing

The Boydell Press is an imprint of Boydell & Brewer Ltd
PO Box 9, Woodbridge, Suffolk IP12 3DF, UK
and of Boydell & Brewer Inc.
668 Mt. Hope Avenue, Rochester NY 14620, USA
website: www.boydellandbrewer.com

A CIP record for this title is available
from the British Library

This publication is printed on acid-free paper

Contents

List of Illustrations	vii
List of Tables	viii
Contributors	ix
Acknowledgements	xi
Abbreviations	xii

1 NICK HIGHAM — 1
   Britons in Anglo-Saxon England: An Introduction

Part I: Archaeological and Historical Perspectives

2 CATHERINE HILLS — 16
   Anglo-Saxon Attitudes

3 HOWARD WILLIAMS — 27
   Forgetting the Britons in Victorian Anglo-Saxon Archaeology

4 LLOYD LAING — 42
   Romano-British Metalworking and the Anglo-Saxons

5 HEINRICH HÄRKE — 57
   Invisible Britons, Gallo-Romans and Russians: Perspectives on Culture Change

6 NICK HIGHAM — 68
   Historical Narrative as Cultural Politics: Rome, 'British-ness' and 'English-ness'

7 GALE R. OWEN-CROCKER — 80
   British Wives and Slaves? Possible Romano-British Techniques in 'Women's Work'

8 DAMIAN J. TYLER — 91
   Early Mercia and the Britons

9 MARTIN GRIMMER — 102
   Britons in Early Wessex: The Evidence of the Law Code of Ine

10 ALEX WOOLF — 115
    Apartheid and Economics in Anglo-Saxon England

| 11 | C. P. Lewis | 130 |

Welsh Territories and Welsh Identities in Late Anglo-Saxon England

| 12 | David E. Thornton | 144 |

Some Welshmen in Domesday Book and Beyond: Aspects of
Anglo-Welsh Relations in the Eleventh Century

Part II: Linguistic Perspectives

| 13 | Peter Schrijver | 165 |

What Britons Spoke around 400 AD

| 14 | Richard Coates | 172 |

Invisible Britons: The View from Linguistics

| 15 | Hildegard Tristram | 192 |

Why Don't the English Speak Welsh?

| 16 | O. J. Padel | 215 |

Place-Names and the Saxon Conquest of Devon and Cornwall

| 17 | Duncan Probert | 231 |

Mapping Early Medieval Language Change in South-West England

Index   245

Illustrations

4.1	Map: distribution of Anglo-Saxon metalwork employing enamel	45
4.2	Types of pennanular brooches found in pagan Anglo-Saxon contexts	48
4.3	Map: distribution of Class C pennanular brooches found in Anglo-Saxon contexts	50
5.1	The Marlboro Cowboy in Russia	63
5.2	Russian rubbish: packaging favours the visibility of imported goods	64
11.1	Map: the Welsh borders in the late Anglo-Saxon period	131
12.1	Map: Domesday Wales	151
12.2	Genealogies of Rhys Sais and Roger de Powis	156
12.3	The family of Owain ab Edwin	159
12.4	Map: Domesday Archenfield	162
15.1	Map of English regional dialects	206
15.2	Map of the present participle in Middle English	210
16.1	Map: distribution of the place-name element *tre* in South-West England	216
16.2	Map: distribution of the place-name element *bod* in South-West England	218
16.3	Map: distribution of the place-name element *tūn* in South-West England	220
16.4	Map: distribution of the place-name element *cot* in South-West England	222
16.5	Map: Cornish and Old English place-names in eastern Cornwall	224
17.1	Map: borrowings of Brittonic /ū/ and /ü/ into Old English as preserved in place-names	236
17.2	Map: borrowings of Brittonic /m/>/μ/>/v/ into Old English as preserved in place-names	238
17.3	Map: evidence for Brittonic 'pretonic reduction' and 'internal i-affection' preserved in English place-names	241

Tables

9.1	Comparative *wergilds* of Saxons and Britons in Ine's Law Code	105
12.1	Welshmen in Domesday Book	146
12.2	Welsh (and possible Welsh) names in Domesday Book	152

Contributors

Prof. Richard Coates, University of the West of England

Dr Martin Grimmer, University of Tasmania, Hobart, Australia

Dr Heinrich Härke, University of Reading

Prof. Nick Higham, University of Manchester

Dr Catherine Hills, University of Cambridge

Dr Lloyd Laing, University of Nottingham

Dr C. P. Lewis, Institute of Historical Research, University of London

Prof. Gale R. Owen-Crocker, University of Manchester

Dr O. J. Padel, St Neot, Cornwall

Dr Duncan Probert, University of Birmingham

Prof. Peter Schrijver, Universiteit Utrecht

Dr David E. Thornton, Bilkent University, Ankara, Turkey

Prof. Dr Hildegard L. C. Tristram, Freiburg, Germany

Dr Damian Tyler, Manchester Metropolitan University

Dr Howard Williams, University of Exeter

Mr Alex Woolf, University of St Andrews

This volume is dedicated to
the memory of Patrick Wormald,
who was a key contributor and participant at
the conference at Easter 2004 at which these papers were first
given, but who was prevented by his untimely death from himself
contributing to the published volume. Patrick was one of the
outstanding Anglo-Saxonists of his generation, and
ever generous with his own time and energies to support the
endeavours of others in the field. He is already and will
long continue to be sorely missed.

Acknowledgements

I am most grateful to The British Academy for financial support towards the attendance at the conference at Manchester in 2004 of several contributors based overseas. The conference also benefited enormously from a grant from the University of Manchester. Organisation rested heavily upon the expertise and hard work of Mary Syner and Margaret Worthington, and the staff of Hulme Hall. Hana Videen checked the manuscript in draft for consistency against the style sheet and also began to prepare the index, to my enormous benefit. I am also grateful to the editorial committee of the Manchester Centre for Anglo-Saxon Studies for their championship of the volume, to the anonymous external reader whom they prevailed upon to review the papers and whose many helpful comments have contributed greatly to the end product, and lastly to the professionalism and care for detail of Caroline Palmer and her colleagues at Boydell & Brewer.

Abbreviations

Ant	*Antiquity*
AntJ	*Antiquaries Journal*
Arch	*Archaeologia*
ArchJ	*Archaeological Journal*
Arnold, *FRBSE*	Christopher J. Arnold, *From Roman-Britain to Saxon England* (London, 1984)
ASE	*Anglo-Saxon England*
ASSAH	*Anglo-Saxon Studies in Archaeology and History*
BAR, BS	British Archaeological Reports, British Series
BAR, IS	British Archaeological Reports, International Series
Dark, *BERE*	Kenneth R. Dark, *Britain and the End of the Roman Empire* (Stroud, 2000)
DB	Domesday Book
EHR	*English Historical Review*
HE	Bede: Historia Ecclesiastica Gentis Anglorum: *Bede: Ecclesiastical History of the English People*, ed. Bertram Colgrave and R. A. B. Mynors (Oxford, 1969)
Higham, *RBAS*	Nicholas Higham, *Rome, Britain and the Anglo-Saxons* (London, 1992)
Hills, *Origins*	Catherine Hills, *Origins of the English* (London, 2002)
Hodges, *ASA*	Richard Hodges, *The Anglo-Saxon Achievement* (London, 1989)
Jackson, *LHEB*	Kenneth H. Jackson, *Language and History in Early Britain* (Edinburgh, 1953)
MedArch	*Medieval Archaeology*
RS	Rolls Series
S	Peter H. Sawyer, *Anglo-Saxon Charters: An Annotated List and Bibliography*, Royal Historical Society Guides and Handbooks 8 (London, 1968), followed by the listed number of the document
Stenton, *ASE*	Sir Frank M. Stenton, *Anglo-Saxon England*, 3rd edn (Oxford, 1971)
TRE	*Tempore regis Edwardi*: 'in the time of King Edward', 1066 (a short form used in Domesday Book)

1

Britons in Anglo-Saxon England: An Introduction

NICK HIGHAM

THE presence, or absence, of significant numbers of Britons in Anglo-Saxon England has recently been the subject of considerable debate, with scholars in several disciplines offering conflicting opinions. There are a number of key questions to which we would very much like answers. Whether or not there were many Britons within Anglo-Saxon England is just the starting point: if there were large numbers, how did they come to be there, what roles did they perform and what eventually happened to them? If there were only very few, then what became of the sub-Roman population of the lowland zone of the old diocese, and how should we explain particular instances when the presence of Britons is indicated very much later, for example, by place-name or literary evidence? And just what should we understand by the term 'Britons', both at different points in the past, and in our present?[1] Should we define this term in racial, ethnic, linguistic and/or religious terms, and what baggage is it carrying? What should we read into *Brittones* in Bede's *Historia ecclesiastica*, for example,[2] or *Bretwalas* and *Brettas* in the *Anglo-Saxon Chronicle*? What does *walh* signify in such place-names as Walton? And when we read in Domesday Book that one *Grifin* (the Welsh personal name Gruffudd) held Weston (Ches.) in 1066,[3] should we suppose that he was an immigrant from Wales or were 'Welsh' names used in the eleventh-century western Midlands, much as they seem to have been in late seventh-century Northumbria and Wessex?[4] Was there a significant flow of slaves from external British communities into Anglo-Saxon England, and, if so, did this create an identifiable and self-perpetuating underclass? Did Welshmen often follow Asser's example in the late-ninth century and, of their own volition, take

---

[1] See now Walter Pohl, 'Ethnic Names and Identities in the British Isles: A Comparative Perspective', in *The Anglo-Saxons from the Migration Period to the Eighth Century*, ed. John Hines (Woodbridge, 1997), pp. 7–40. The modern discussion of early medieval ethnicity was initiated by Patrick Geary, 'Ethnic Identity as a Situational Construct in the Early Middle Ages', *Mitteilungen der Anthropologischen Gesellschaft in Wien* 113 (1983), 15–26.

[2] The term occurs in forty-one chapters of the *HE*, including both singular and plural instances, so in around 29% of all chapters.

[3] Domesday Book 266b

[4] As the occurrence of such names as Chad, Cædwalla and Cædmon in apparently 'English' contexts in Bede's *HE*.

service with English lords and so secure estates? Or were Britons already present and primarily a left-over from Roman Britain?

Like many other historical debates concerning a comparatively distant past, this is one which has complex inter-connections with recent, popular culture.[5] The 'German-ness' of early England was considered an unassailable 'fact' by most nineteenth-century scholars.[6] However, 'German-ness' seemed less attractive in Britain following two World Wars and an ethnically cleansed past became increasingly disturbing to generations familiar with the 'Final Solution'. Anti-German popular culture mushroomed in the 1940s and was followed by a real effort to establish a 'British' origin for the nation independent of Germanic immigrants,[7] largely built around the highly suspect figure of 'King Arthur',[8] whose popularity has never since really waned on either side of the Atlantic.[9] Yet, in the most general terms, the English have generally retained the belief that they descend not from the Romano-Britons but from the tribes whom Bede described as migrating from Germany.[10]

Bede did not, of course, actually assay what happened to the indigenes: indeed, his key chapter on this theme (I, 15) ends with the Britons slaughtering their enemies at Mount Badon. He had little in the way of literary sources beyond the story he had from Gildas,[11] which told of death and destruction combined with warfare, enslavement and emigration. However, some ten generations after the *adventus*, 'English-ness' was for Bede a fact in need of an explanation and his references to both divine approbation and mass migration provided that to his

---

[5] See recent exploration of this issue by Heinrich Härke, 'Archaeologists and Migrations: A Problem of Attitude?', *Current Anthropology* 39,1 (1998), 19–24, and Hills, *Origins*, *passim*.

[6] Among archaeologists, J. S. Kemble, *The Saxons in England* (London, 1849) was particularly strongly connected with current German scholarship, but see Howard Williams, this volume. Among historians, the 'Germanist' tradition was established as the dominant historical narrative primarily by Edward Freeman (*Old English History*, London, 1878), J. R. Green (*History of the English People*, 4 vols., London, 1879–81) and William Stubbs (*The Constitutional History of England in its Origins and Development*, 3 vols., Oxford, 1891).

[7] Resulting in particular in the highly influential works of Leslie Alcock (*Arthur's Britain: History and Archaeology AD 367–634*, Harmondsworth, 1971) and John Morris (*The Age of Arthur*, Chichester, 1973). Both authors had highly distinguished war records.

[8] Concerning whose historicity as a fifth/sixth century figure and whose subsequent role as an historical icon, I refer to my own recent study, *King Arthur: Myth-making and History* (London, 2002).

[9] As demonstrated most recently by the production in 2004 of the Hollywood blockbuster, 'King Arthur', directed by Antoine Fuqua for Touchstone Pictures and Jerry Bruckheimer Films, that claims to tell 'the heroic true story behind one of the world's greatest legends', but in fact merely fleshes out a highly speculative theory advanced initially by H. Nickel 'The Dawn of Chivalry', *Metropolitan Museum of Art Bulletin* 32 (1975), 150–2, then elaborated by C. S. Littleton and L. A. Malcor, *From Scythia to Camelot: A Radical Reassessment of the Legends of King Arthur, the Knights of the Round Table and the Holy Grail* (New York, 1994).

[10] Bede, *HE*, I, 15.

[11] *De Excidio Britanniae*, XXIII–XXVI: *Gildas: The Ruin of Britain*, ed. M. Winterbottom (Chichester, 1978).

satisfaction, if not necessarily ours.[12] When he wrote briefly of King Æthelfrith's conquests of the Britons, Bede used the verb *exterminare*,[13] but it is unclear what he intended. In Classical Latin *exterminare* meant 'to drive out', rather than 'to destroy', and he offered the alternative of enslavement, suggesting more conquest than genocide, but this was the starting point for a general and long-lived assumption that the Britons had been quite literally wiped out. Victorian reconstructions of England's foundations conceived of the Britons as equivalent to the indigenous peoples who were then being destroyed and/or displaced by colonial settlement,[14] and the growing realisation that pre-existing languages had been replaced by Old English with unusual efficiency seemed to sustain this view. However, modern scholars have felt less comfortable with large-scale immigration combined with 'ethnic cleansing', amounting to genocide of a kind likely today to be condemned unilaterally.[15]

Increasing hesitancy concerning the 'German-ness' of Anglo-Saxon England and a disinclination to see its founders as mass-murderers has contributed, therefore, to reinterpretations of England's origins and a preference for processes of accommodation in the historical record, over and against genocide or mass-replacement. But modern reviews have also been stimulated by broader shifts in the way that archaeologists think about changes in the material record. British Prehistory was long interpreted as conditioned primarily by successive waves of 'peoples', each bringing with them their own material culture and displacing earlier arrivals, who fell victim or took refuge further west.[16] This 'invasion hypothesis' was challenged and ultimately overthrown in the 1960s,[17] giving way to a 'post-processual' view of cultures adapting to a variety of stimuli, including environmental change, long-distance contacts of various kinds and/or the devel-

---

[12] Divine approbation of the incomers closes *HE* I, 23; their large numbers are central to I, 15. Bede originated both these facets of the migration story.

[13] *HE* I, 34 but it recurs in I, 16, III, 24 and IV, 16. In each case the subject of the verb (the Saxon army, Æthelfrith, Penda then Cædwalla) was pagan and its force was to an extent rhetorical, connected to the barbarism of the agent: in all instances, Bede actually makes it clear that he did not envisage that a complete destruction of the population occurred, although that may have been what he was suggesting that Penda, at least, was attempting in III, 24.

[14] As Freeman, *Old English History*, p. 28: 'they had killed or driven out all the former people, save those whom they kept as mere slaves'. Compare this with the brutal dispossession and genocidal treatment of, for example, Tasmanian aborigines by European settlers. Charles Dickens' vision was markedly less bloodthirsty, suggesting that 'The poor Britons ... retired into Wales and the adjacent country; into Devonshire and into Cornwall', but he was writing for children: *A Child's History of England*, first serialized in *Household Words*, 1851–3; first edition London 1868.

[15] See, for example, recent reactions to the warfare which accompanied the break-up of Yugoslavia, ethnically polarized bloodshed in Rwanda in the 1990s, and current ethnic conflict in southern Sudan.

[16] Such a vision of the archaeological record was characteristic, for example, of the thinking of prehistorians immediately post-war: e.g. Jacquetta and Christopher Hawkes, *Prehistoric Britain* (London, 1947).

[17] Most particularly by Graham Clark, 'The Invasion Hypothesis in British Archaeology', *Antiquity* 40 (1966), 172–89. Thereafter, see Irving Rouse, *Migrations in Prehistory: Inferring Population Movements from Cultural Remains* (New Haven, 1986).

opment of new technologies. Although migration was still acknowledged in passing,[18] it became marginal as an explanation: whether even the 'Neolithic Revolution' should be put down exclusively to immigrants has become, therefore, a moot point.[19]

Such thinking questioned the centrality of migration as a determinant of cultural change in the historic era. The Romanization of Britain had long been interpreted as a military conquest followed by only limited immigration, so largely in terms of cultural and societal changes within the endogenous community,[20] and the Norman Conquest had been viewed similarly, though perhaps on a lesser scale.[21] However, the Scandinavianization of large parts of northern and eastern England was generally thought a consequence of large-scale immigration, until the development of a new, minimalist model of Viking activity by Peter Sawyer.[22] While this, in turn, has been criticised as understating the size of the Viking armies of the later ninth and early eleventh centuries, Sawyer has at least necessitated that Scandinavianization now be explored via more nuanced models than were implicit in earlier visions of the arrival of 'hordes' of savage northerners.[23]

Similar down-sizing was applied to the barbarian hosts which had swept into the Roman Empire during the late fourth and fifth centuries, which shrank in the later twentieth century to groups numbered at most in tens of thousands.[24] And these were now bound together in groups the identities of which were provisional, rather than absolute, and negotiated *in situ* in Late Antiquity rather than merely

---

[18] As is obviously essential, given the first appearance of *Homo sapiens* in Africa but its subsequent spread to every continent of the world: see e.g. Paul Mellars, 'The *Homo Sapiens* Peopling of Europe', in *The Peopling of Britain: The Shaping of a Human Landscape*, The Linacre Lectures, ed. Paul Slack and Ryk Ward (Oxford, 2002), pp. 39–67.

[19] See, for example, the shift of attitudes between Stuart Piggott, *The Neolithic Cultures of the British Isles* (Cambridge, 1954) and Paul Ashbee, 'A Reconsideration of the British Neolithic', *Ant* 56 (1982), 134–8.

[20] F. Haverfield, *The Romanization of Roman Britain*, 2nd edn (Oxford, 1912); Martin Millett, *The Romanization of Britain* (Cambridge, 1990). It is generally agreed that the army of occupation numbered initially between 40,000 and 60,000 men and that perhaps a comparable number of immigrants should be envisaged, so a total immigrant community of some 100,000.

[21] Early twentieth-century writers assumed a Norman army, then an immigration from Normandy following 1066, both to be numbered in several tens of thousands, although these are now generally scaled down, with an army estimated at 5–8,000, not all of whom remained, and comparatively few other incomers.

[22] Peter H. Sawyer, *The Age of the Vikings* (London, 1962).

[23] Contrast recent collections of papers on this issue, such as *Cultures in Contact: Scandinavian Settlement in England in the Ninth and Tenth Centuries*, ed. Dawn M. Hadley and Julian D. Richards (Brepols, 2000); *Land, Sea and Home*, ed. John Hines, Alan Lane and Mark Redknap, Society for Medieval Archaeology Monographs 20 (Leeds, 2004), with the assumption in favour of 'hordes' of Scandinavians made by e.g. Frederick T. Wainwright, 'The Scandinavians in Lancashire', *Transactions of the Lancashire and Cheshire Antiquarian Society* 58 (1945–6), 71–116 at p. 71.

[24] As Walter Goffart, *Barbarians and Romans, A.D. 418–584: The Techniques of Accommodation* (Princeton, 1980).

derivative of pre-migration communities.[25] In such circumstances, reappraisal of the Anglo-Saxon *adventus* was clearly to be expected, but this was a settlement process which had special significance. While scholarship had long given considerable weight to both Scandinavian and Norman contributions to early England, it was the Anglo-Saxon settlement which was fundamental to the very idea of 'English-ness' and which was responsible for planting a version of the Old German language in Britain, from which developed English. This was a very different phenomenon to the bulk of the remainder of the western Empire, where incomers generally shed their pre-existing languages in favour of provincial Latin. The very success of English has long been thought to have required a large number of users,[26] while the comparative lack of loan words or other linguistic features from either Latin or British suggested that comparatively little contact had occurred with the pre-existing population (as Coates, this volume) and that those (few) Britons who had acculturated and learned the language of the immigrants had done so with unusual levels of competence, entirely discarding their own tongues in the process.[27]

Not only language specialists were responsible, however, for an early insistence on large-scale Germanic colonisation, since a small quantity of near-contemporary written source material has long allowed this to be viewed as an historical event, in which historians could claim a central role. Despite occasional challenges,[28] the dominant vision across the middle decades of the twentieth century remained wedded to the notion of a large-scale settlement pushed home by successful warfare, as witness Sir Frank Stenton:

> The English conquest of Sussex proceeded slowly from west to east against a steady British resistance. The massacre which followed the storming of Anderida [the Roman Saxon Shore Fort at Pevensey] does not imply a war of extermination in the open country, but the extreme rarity of British place-names in Sussex points to English colonization on a scale which can have left little room for British survival.[29]

---

[25] The seminal work was that of Patrick Geary, 'Ethnic Identity as a Situational Construct', but see also his *Phantoms of Remembrance* (Princeton, NJ, 1994), and Walter Pohl with Helmut Reimitz (eds.), *Strategies of Distinction: The Contstruction of Ethnic Communities, 300–800* (Leiden, 1998).

[26] The case was made succinctly by Margaret Gelling, 'The Evidence of Place-Names', in *Medieval Settlement*, ed. Peter H. Sawyer (Chichester, 1976), pp. 200–11, particularly at pp. 201–3, and continues to be persuasive: Martin Welch, *Anglo-Saxon England* (London, 1992), p. 12; Margaret Gelling, 'Why Aren't We Speaking Welsh?', *ASSAH* 6 (1993), 51. John Hines, 'The Becoming of the English: Identity, Material Culture and Language in Early Anglo-Saxon England', *ASSAH* 7 (1994), 49–56, at p. 58; Edward James, *Britain in the First Millennium* (London, 2001), p. 114.

[27] Jackson, *LHEB*, p. 245.

[28] As R. Lennard, 'The Character of the Anglo-Saxon Conquests: A Disputed Point', *History* 18 (1933–4), 204–14.

[29] Stenton, *ASE*, p. 18.

While Stenton had retreated, therefore, from explicit genocide, large-scale immigration could still be allowed to have quietly evicted the Britons, and it was still felt to be appropriate to discuss early England with little reference to the indigenes other than in occasional pockets. Archaeologists at this date were interpreting Anglo-Saxon cemeteries as if capable of demonstrating the progress of a long and drawn out campaign of conquest leading to the expulsion of the earlier population.[30]

The Anglo-Saxon immigration had, therefore, long been viewed as exceptional by the standards of fifth-century Europe, in terms both of the sheer numbers involved and its inclusion of a mass of peasantry.[31] This picture of mass migration squeezing out the Britons became less credible, however, as new answers began to emerge to the question: How many Britons were there? From the 1960s onwards, aerial photography and archaeological survey revealed hitherto unsuspected numbers of new sites and population estimates for Roman Britain, which centred on a mere million or so in the 1930s,[32] climbed to two to four million for the fourth century,[33] with some estimates significantly higher.[34] Britain was beginning to look very full of people indeed in the later Roman period: indeed, such figures approximate to the sixteenth century, which was a period of marked population pressure. For the Britons to have been overwhelmed numerically by continental immigrants who had ferried themselves across the Channel in small boats was looking ever less plausible. Scholars needed either to embrace the mechanics of demographic collapse on a massive scale, or rethink the role of migration as an explanation of cultural change.

To complicate matters, outward migration does seem to have occurred, leading to the establishment of the Brittonic language in the Armorican peninsula,[35] and a British bishopric in exile in northern Spain. While this entire process is only very poorly understood, migration of Britons to Gaul may have increased in the later fifth to the seventh century, bringing a significant flow to the west of what had been Roman *Lugdunensis II*, to whom Procopius famously referred in the mid-

---

[30] See, for example, Edward T. Leeds, *The Archaeology of the Anglo-Saxon Settlements* (Oxford, 1913); Leeds, 'The Distribution of the Angles and Saxons Archaeologically Considered', *Arch* 19 (1945), 1–106.

[31] There is a useful discussion with references in Michael Jones, *The End of Roman Britain* (Ithaca, NY, 1996), pp. 10–12. The most recent overview, by Chris Wickham in his *Framing the Early Middle Ages: Europe and the Mediterranean, 400–800* (Oxford, 2005), agrees that the dominance of the English language implies the settlement of a contingent at least of incoming peasant farmers: p. 312.

[32] As R. G. Collingwood and J. N. L. Myres, *Roman Britain and the English Settlements* (Oxford, 1936), p. 180.

[33] Millett, *Romanization*, pp. 182–5; Jones, *End of Roman Britain*, p. 13; Barry Cunliffe, 'Tribes and Empires c.1500 BC – AD 500', in *The Peopling of Britain*, pp. 115–38, at p. 136.

[34] As Peter Salway, *Roman Britain* (Oxford, 1981), p. 544: 'four to six million'; Peter Fowler, *Farming in the first Millennium AD* (Cambridge, 2002), p. 17, suggests 5 million as a maximum likely population in late Roman Britain, with 4 million as a conservative estimate.

[35] Most recently, see Pierre-Roland Giot, Philippe Guigon and Bernard Merdrignac, *The British Settlement of Brittany* (Stroud, 2003).

sixth century.[36] However, contemporary authors attached little ethnic meaning to the terms *Britannia* and *Francia*.[37] The extent of immigrant settlement is very unclear and even the area where the Celtic language was established was too small to have accommodated more than a small proportion of the diocesan population at comparable densities.[38] Additionally, these immigrants were presumably speakers of Brittonic, not Latin. While it remains unclear how prevalent Latin was in the lowland zone of late fourth-century Britain, current thinking favours this being an area of Romance speakers, closely akin to Gaul,[39] in which case emigration necessarily derived from western Britain, not from the east, where Germanic immigration began. In other words, the creation of Brittany may not be an entirely satisfactory solution to the problem: What happened to the Britons of the eastern lowlands when the Anglo-Saxon Settlement occurred?

Traditional views of Germanic immigration, of course, face comparable difficulties of scale. Bede informs us that three tribes were involved, among which the Angles derived from the area known in his day as *Angulus*,[40] which can be identified with some confidence as the narrow isthmus of the Danish peninsula, around Schleswig and Flensburg. Thence Bede claimed that the East Angles, Middle Angles, Mercians and Northumbrians, plus other tribes which he failed to name, had migrated. A homeland approximating in scale to East Anglia and beset by numerous wetlands was therefore supposed to have populated two thirds of England, throwing up serious challenges to Bede's credibility.

Across the late twentieth century, palaeobotanical research was also massively revising views of the early English landscape. It had long been a matter of faith among historians that Anglo-Saxon England was heavily wooded and the story of the English Settlement was told against a regionalized backdrop of vast forests,[41] the gradual clearance of which, documented by place-names, occurred as the

---

[36] Procopius, *Gothic Wars* IV, 20, 8, on which see Averil Cameron, *Procopius* (London, 1985), pp. 214–16.

[37] For a recent reappraisal, see Julia M. H. Smith, 'Confronting Identities: The Rhetoric and Reality of a Carolingian Frontier', in *Integration und Herrschaft: Ethnische Identitäten und soziale Organisation im Frühmittelalter*, ed. Walter Pohl and Max Diesenberger (Vienna, 2002), pp. 169–84.

[38] Western Brittany approximates in size to the south-west peninsula of England. Giot *et al.*, *The British Settlement*, p. 50, guesstimate the Roman period population of all Armorica, so not just the 'British' part, at 300,000–600,000, so at a mere seventh of contemporary Britain. In the last resort, the nature of the 'British' migration into Armorica is as problematic as the Anglo-Saxon settlement in Britain and is at least as capable of a minimalist interpretation, with perhaps some survival of Gaulish in the region providing fertile ground for the development of Breton.

[39] Peter Schrijver, 'The Rise and Fall of British Latin: Evidence from English and Brittonic', in *The Celtic Roots of English*, ed. Markku Filppula, Juhani Klemola and Heli Pitkänen, University of Joensuu, Studies in English 37 (Joensuu, Finland, 2002), pp. 87–110, and this volume.

[40] *HE*, I, 15.

[41] The classic statement of this thesis comes in the beautifully coloured maps which illustrate the English Settlement in volume one of R. H. Hodgkin's *A History of the Anglo-Saxons*, 2 vols. (Oxford, 1935), which have the legend 'Dense Woodland' against the bright green which pervades so much of England.

English population rose during the mid- to late Anglo-Saxon period, from the very low levels of the initial *adventus*. A problem has long been that pollen analysis has been easier to undertake in the north and the west of Britain, where suitable deposits are commonest.[42] There the recognition that Roman-period clearance was often maintained into and even through the early Middle Ages caused little concern to historians:[43] indeed, continuing clearance had some potential to accommodate refugees from the south and east. The realisation that open landscapes also persisted across much of the lowland zone came later and provides a new means of examining the whole issue of the British/Anglo-Saxon interface in a new light. It is generally agreed that woodland was no more than about 20% of the total land surface in the late Roman period.[44] That it failed to advance to, say, 40–50% across lowland England in the sub-Roman period,[45] surely makes it unlikely that the existing workforce was either exterminated or expelled: could a massed Anglo-Saxon takeover of the countryside have been achieved with the comparative lack of disruption required by this evidence?[46]

That said, an overall decline of population from the very high levels postulated in the fourth century is compatible with the evidence, since the pollen record does suggest a widespread switch to less intensive modes of production. A similar switch out of cultivation characterized England in the post-plague Middle Ages and the late fifteenth-century population was arguably less than 50% of its high point c.1300 – perhaps as low as 30–40%.[47] Supposing the palaeobotanical evidence relating to the fifth and sixth centuries to be pointing towards a similar decline, we might envisage numbers falling to one to two million by around 600. Such is little more than a guesstimate, of course, but supposing it to be even approximating this level it still leaves a substantial problem for those envisaging Germanic incomers in numbers capable of overwhelming and replacing the existing population. Anglo-Saxon incomers did not in general come across an empty landscape but a well-worked one, arguably dotted with rural communities.

---

[42] See, for example, the early work of Winifred Pennington, 'Vegetational History in the North West of England: A Regional Synthesis', in *Studies in the Vegetational History of the British Isles*, ed. D. Walker and R. G. West (Cambridge, 1970), pp. 41–79.

[43] Except around Hadrian's Wall, where reforestation seems to have been widespread.

[44] Oliver Rackham, *Trees and Woodland in the British Landscape* (London, 1976).

[45] Martin Bell, 'Environmental Archaeology as an Index of Continuity and Change in the Medieval Landscape', in *The Rural Settlements of Medieval England*, ed. Mick Aston, David Austin and Chris Dyer (Oxford, 1989), pp. 269–86; Petra Dark, *The Environment of Britain in the First Millennium AD* (London, 2000), *passim*.

[46] The case was most recently made by Edward A. Thompson, *Saint Germanus of Auxerre and the End of Roman Britain* (Woodbridge, 1984), pp. 95–7

[47] The lay subsidy returns of 1524–5 suggest a population total at that date of around two and a quarter million: E. A. Wrigley and R. S. Schofield, *The Population History of England 1541–1871: A Reconstruction* (London, 1981), pp. 566–8; reconstructions of population levels around 1300 offer figures of five and a half to six and a half million: Richard Smith, 'Plagues and Peoples: The Long Demographic Cycle, 1250–1670', in *The Peopling of Britain*, pp. 177–210, at p. 181.

Anglo-Saxon archaeologists were not slow to recognize the challenge: in 1976 Philip Dixon interpreted the insular cemetery evidence in terms of very small groups of immigrants,[48] while Catherine Hills' review of current debates in 1979 embraced the notion of significant numbers of Britons and was willing to at least consider their burial in 'Anglo-Saxon' cemeteries.[49] In 1982, James Campbell posited Britons persisting even in eastern England into the sixth century, perhaps in positions of power.[50]

It was at this point that several scholars began to propose alternative models of cultural contact, which were designed to reinterpret the archaeological data without recourse to theories based on folk movements. Chris Arnold's was the earliest monograph to centre on the issue and the most dependent in theoretical terms on current thinking about prehistory.[51] Arnold sought to move the debate away from the culture-historical approach, and away from preoccupations with the date at which the English Settlement began,[52] which was threatening to engulf the subject. He envisaged the construction of Anglo-Saxon England as a broad process of cultural change within a long-cleared landscape, focusing specifically on the archaeological data, virtually ignoring literary sources, and treating the period as if prehistoric, so exploring the material remains to isolate evidence of patterning in the archaeological record. His book is about constructing and testing models, therefore, under a series of headings already tried and tested in prehistoric archaeology, but cognisant also of those specific to this particular period. Arnold concluded that there was no archaeological evidence capable of supporting a large-scale migration westwards from the eastern lowlands, opting rather for a generally static population. His explanation rested heavily on the economic collapse of Romanized Britain, which he envisaged brought down large-scale farming, villa-occupation, the monetary economy, mass production and urban markets, all well before Germanic migrants arrived.[53] He then postulated a small-scale immigration, largely of males, leading to a mixed-race society with both immigrant and indigenous sections present in 'Anglo-Saxon' cemeteries.[54]

A very different work was offered by Richard Hodges,[55] whose racy reappraisal of early England was stimulated in part by a desire to apply the ideas

---

[48] Philip Dixon, *Barbarian Europe* (Oxford, 1976), p. 54.
[49] Catherine Hills, 'The archaeology of Anglo-Saxon England in the pagan period: a review', *ASE* 8 (1979), 297–329, at 312–13.
[50] James Campbell, 'The Lost Centuries: 400–600', in *Anglo-Saxon England*, ed. James Campbell (London, 1982), pp. 20–44, at p. 29.
[51] Arnold, *FRBSE*.
[52] Largely as a consequence of the thesis of J. N. L. Myres in favour of a Saxon settlement on the Saxon Shore of late Roman Britain, on the basis very largely of his interpretation of a particular type of late Romano-British pottery as designed for a Saxon market: 'Romano-Saxon Pottery', in *Dark Age Britain: Studies presented to E. T. Leeds*, ed. D. B. Harden (London, 1956), pp. 16–39; *Anglo-Saxon Pottery and the Settlement of England* (Oxford, 1969), *passim*.
[53] Arnold, *FRBSE*, pp. 159–61.
[54] Arnold, *FRBSE*, pp. 122–41.
[55] Hodges, *ASA*.

of Alan Macfarlane concerning a particularly English Individualism to a more distant insular past.[56] Hodges concentrated primarily on the countryside, which he viewed as characterised from the third century by numerous small-scale farmers but thereafter in steep retreat, alongside rapid urban decline, leading inexorably in the late fourth century to wholesale economic collapse and with it the whole fabric of Roman Britain, which 'degenerated to a uniform (as opposed to a sporadic) state of aboriginal power', in association with large-scale demographic decline and political fragmentation.[57] This countryside was then re-organized with new 'so-called Anglo-Saxon settlement' in the early to mid fifth century, in association with small numbers of graves in what would later become long-lived cemeteries, in response to stimuli which Hodges postulated primarily in terms of contacts with Frankia in the 'age of Clovis'.[58] Although he noted the claims on an *adventus* as offered by both Gildas and Bede, Hodges' model of cultural change obviated the need for an Anglo-Saxon Settlement of any scale, leaving England and its 'British' neighbours to the west peopled by virtually the same biological communities as before, beefed up by the descendants of a few fifth-century immigrant mercenaries. On this model, the issue was not the presence or absence of Britons within Anglo-Saxon England but Anglo-Saxon England as just one of several successive cultural changes experienced by a comparatively static, island population.

Hodges offered, therefore, the vision of an early England which came into being following the dramatic demographic downturn and systems failure which had brought later Roman Britain to its knees, spear-headed by enterprising individuals becoming increasingly aware of changes in the way that social power operated in neighbouring parts of Europe. This study of early England rests on the politics and culture of early Merovingian Francia and new habits of, for example, cemetery organisation there,[59] and the putative expansion of Merovingian hegemony to the entire North Sea region.[60] This failed to explain, however, several key characteristics of early Anglo-Saxon England, such as the connections between insular Anglian culture, in particular, and Scandinavia,[61] and the markedly different behaviour in terms of language from Frankia, with the adoption of Anglo-Saxon in the British lowlands contrasting with Romance across most of Gaul.

---

[56] Hodges *ASA*, pp. xi, 1–3; Alan Macfarlane, *The Origins of English Individualism* (Oxford, 1978).
[57] Hodges, *ASA*, pp. 16–25, quotation at p. 19.
[58] Hodges, *ASA*, pp. 27–42, quotations at pp. 26, 34.
[59] As exemplified in the work of Edward James, 'Merovingian Settlement Studies, and Some Implications for Anglo-Saxon England', in *Anglo-Saxon Cemeteries,* BAR, BS 82, ed. Philip Rahtz, Tania Dickinson and Lorna Watts (Oxford, 1979), 35–55.
[60] As postulated by Ian Wood, initially in *The Merovingian North Sea* (Alingsås, 1983), on the basis of several rather ambivalent sixth-century texts: while Merovingian rulers clearly liked the notion of a regional hegemony centred upon themselves, a cautious approach might be to suggest that the evidence is currently insufficient to sustain a view of Frankish dominance of even lowland England for extended periods of the sixth century.
[61] John Hines, *The Scandinavian Character of Anglian England in the Pre-Viking Period*, BAR, BS 124 (Oxford, 1984).

Hodges' study was published while my own book-length study of the Roman/ Anglo-Saxon interface was in progress,[62] but its inception was very different. This work grew out of research on a peripheral region of Roman Britain and Anglo-Saxon England, the North West, where some characteristics of the evidence base were particularly accentuated. For example, Roman towns and villas barely took hold, leaving a settlement pattern consisting of forts, *vici* and farmsteads,[63] and rural settlements have proved notoriously difficult to identify archaeologically, not just in the fifth century but across the period *c.*300–*c.*1200.[64] A near total absence of 'Anglo-Saxon' graves contrasts with a pattern of place-naming in which Old English was clearly dominant from a comparatively early date.[65] Conventional explanations of the presence of Old English centred on Anglian immigration,[66] but failed to explain the apparent discard of characteristic artefacts and methods of disposing of the dead. If the absence of distinctive material culture here was no guide to the presence or absence of population, then it might be that the same should be envisaged of sub-Roman Britain more widely. With Landscape History increasingly highlighting continuities in terms of track-ways and field-systems across the Roman/Medieval divide,[67] and allied to new readings of several literary texts from the period, the result was a reinterpretation of the Anglo-Saxon Settlement in terms of elite dominance/emulation theory, postulating a high degree of biological continuity allied to cultural change triggered by a comparatively small number of incomers seizing power during a period of rapid cultural change consequent upon the collapse of empire.

Elite dominance theory has since tended to steer the debate in new ways and has exercised considerable influence on ensuing discussions.[68] A handful of

[62] Higham, *RBAS*.
[63] See most recently, *Living on the Edge of Empire: Models, Methodology and Marginality*, ed. Michael Nevell (Manchester and Chester, 1999).
[64] Excluding specific categories of monument such as carved stones of both Anglian and Scandinavian type. For the nature of Romano-British settlement, see Nicholas Higham, 'Native Settlements West of the Pennines', in *Rome and the Brigantes*, ed. Keith Branigan (Sheffield, 1980), pp. 41–7; *The Northern Counties to AD1000* (Harlow, 1986); Nicholas Higham and Terry Cane, 'The Tatton Park Project, Part 1: Prehistoric to Sub-Roman Settlement and Land Use', *Journal of the Chester Archaeological Society* 74 (1999, for 1996–7), 1–61.
[65] See particularly John McN. Dodgson, *The Place-Names of Cheshire*, English Place-Name Society volumes 44–8, 54 (Cambridge, 1970–81).
[66] E.g. John McN. Dodgson, 'The English Arrival in Cheshire', *Transactions of the Historical Society of Lancashire and Cheshire,* 119 (1967), 1–37.
[67] As the extensive fieldscapes then being identified in Essex and East Anglia: Warwick Rodwell, 'Relict Landscapes in Essex', in *Early Land Allotment*, ed. H. C. Bowen and Peter J. Fowler, BAR, BS 48 (Oxford, 1978), pp. 89–98; Tom Williamson, 'Early Co-axial Field Systems on the East Anglian Boulder Clays', *Proceedings of the Prehistoric Society* 53 (1987), 419–32.
[68] At the extreme, Richard Coates has coined the term 'Highamist' to describe interpretations of the Anglo-Saxon immigration based on comparatively small numbers of immigrants combining with indigines who became 'English' via acculturation: 'The Significance of Celtic Place-Names in England', in *The Celtic Roots of English*, ed. Filppula *et al.* (Joensuu, Finland, 2002), pp. 47–63, at p. 74.

works have sought to reinstate migration at the centre of the debate,[69] but many commentators now assume the Anglo-Saxon migration to have been small numerically,[70] and even of little short-term consequence,[71] and there is a real danger that an elite dominance interpretation of cultural change is becoming the new orthodoxy,[72] with the continuing presence of the indigenes talked up.[73] Archaeologists are now far less sure than they used to be concerning the relationship between the material culture evidenced in particular cemeteries and the ethnicity and/or biological origins of the local population,[74] and landscape archaeology seems to confirm that real continuities existed between Roman Britain and the early Middle Ages.[75] The latest monograph to focus on the issue, by Catherine Hills, is comfortable with, but not insistent on, the notion of Britons in some numbers in early Anglo-Saxon England, setting out the arguments both for and against and probing the several disciplinary approaches that have been attempted to assess their respective merits. Her judicious review offers three conclusions: mass migration remains unresolved both historically and archaeologically; our willingness to accept such has been much influenced by ideological positioning, but elite migration did occur, with or without larger population movement into Britain.

That said, the proponents of elite dominance theory have failed to persuade most linguists, and place-name scholars in particular, that it offers a credible mechanism for the spread of Old English across the British lowlands. As both Coates and Padel make clear in this volume, language adoption by one community from another generally retains far more from the preceding language than is evident in this instance, in which borrowing from either British or Latin is

[69] Martin Welch's *Anglo-Saxon England* (London, 1992) was published virtually at the same time as *Rome, Britain and the Anglo-Saxons*. More particularly, see Helena Hamerow 'Migration Theory and the Anglo-Saxon "Identity Crisis"', in *Migrations and Invasions in Archaeological Explanation*, ed. John Chapman and Helena Hamerow, BAR, IS 664 (Oxford, 1997), pp. 33–44, and G. Ausenda, 'Current Issues and Future Directions in the Study of the Early Anglo-Saxon Period', in *The Anglo-Saxons from the Migration Period to the Eighth Century: an Ethnographic Perspective*, ed. J. Hines (Woodbridge, 1997), pp. 411–51, at pp. 420–2.

[70] As, for example, Bryan Ward-Perkins 'Why did the Anglo-Saxons not become more British?', *English Historical Review* 115 (2000), 513–33; John Blair, *The Church in Anglo-Saxon Society* (Oxford, 2004), p. 8.

[71] Dark, *BERE*, *passim*, argued that the Britons retained control of most of even the lowlands of Britain up to the late sixth century and were the most successful heirs of the Empire anywhere in Western Europe.

[72] As Jones, *End of Roman Britain*, p. 37: 'numbering perhaps several tens of thousands'; Barry Cunliffe, 'Tribes and Empires', p. 136: 'in the period 1500BC–AD500 we have suggested that the population ... was refreshed by a constant trickle of new people arriving from the continent but never was it overwhelmed or even significantly modified by invaders in the manner that scholars used to imagine forty years or so ago'.

[73] See, for example, John Moorhead, *The Roman Empire Divided: 400–700* (Harlow, 2001), pp. 104–9; Edward James, *Britain in the First Millennium*, p. 121.

[74] See, for example, the survey offered by Jones, *End of Roman Britain*, pp. 19–28; Hills, *Origins*, pp. 95–9.

[75] Most dramatically in very recent years, Dominic Powlesland's as yet unpublished survey of the Vale of Pickering.

minimal. Unless very different perspectives take hold in this area (as Tristram argues herein), the outcomes of debate among linguists poses a very real challenge to the preferred interpretation of many archaeologists and some historians. I do not mean to suggest that elite dominance/emulation theory should be discounted from efforts to interpret the construction of Anglo-Saxon England: merely that we should accept that any hypothesis which testing shows to be wanting should give way to new (and arguably more complex) theories,[76] which repair its weaknesses and weld its strengths together with those derived from other explanations.

Additionally, fresh types of data are beginning to come on stream, with some potential for further exploration of the presence of Britons in Anglo-Saxon England. It has been suggested that 'English' skeletons can be distinguished from 'British' by the shape of their feet,[77] or by virtue of the different height typical of 'warrior graves' as opposed to male inhumations lacking weapons.[78] Other approaches include the analysis of teeth from graves of the period so as to explore the trace elements in the water drunk by the individual in their formative years,[79] and genetics as a tool of historical anthropology.[80] Most of these studies are, however, currently in their infancy, and the genetic approach, in particular, has so far produced somewhat conflicting interpretations.[81]

The meaning of Y chromosome research on the current population is also much affected by the assumptions being made concerning the genetic homogeneity of the British population *c*.400. Current visions of a comparatively uniform 'British-ness' may be illusory, given the regionalism likely to have been characteristic of populations in Late Prehistoric and Roman Britain. Indeed, Tacitus's writings might encourage us to think in terms of several comparatively distinct, tribal populations:

> ... physical appearances show variety, and that variation is suggestive. The reddish hair and great limbs of the Caledonians imply Germanic ancestry, the dark faces of the Silures [of south-east Wales], the tendency of their hair to curl and the fact of Spain lying opposite, all incline one to the belief that Spaniards migrated in olden days and settled the land. The tribes nearest to the Gauls are correspondingly similar to them.[82]

---

[76] As I have since argued: 'From sub-Roman Britain to Anglo-Saxon England: Debating the Insular Dark Ages', *History Compass* 2 (2004), 1–25.

[77] Phyllis Jackson, 'Footloose in Archaeology', *Current Archaeology* 144 (1995), 466–70.

[78] Heinrich Härke, '"Warrior Graves"? The Background of the Anglo-Saxon Weapon Burial Rite', *Past and Present* 126 (1990), 22–43.

[79] J. Montgomery, P. Budd and J. Evans, 'Reconstructing the Lifetime Movements of Ancient Peoples', *European Journal of Archaeology* 3(3) (2000), 370–85; Paul Budd, Andrew Millard, Carolyn Chenery, Sam Lucy and Charlotte Roberts, 'Investigating Population Movement by Stable Isotope Analysis: A Report from Britain', *Antiquity* 78 (2004), 127–41, for which see Hills, this volume.

[80] Both Martin Evison and Mark Thomas spoke at the conference but neither felt able to provide a contribution to the publication.

[81] Hills, *Origins* and this volume.

[82] Tacitus, *Agricola*, XI.

Tacitus was well-informed, since his father-in-law had served as governor (*c.* 78–83) and campaigned widely. While the association of physical stereotypes with peoples overseas is questionable, it may be that British tribal communities did display considerable regional difference, as did, for example, the inhabitants of late-Roman Spain.[83] It is, therefore, very difficult to establish what is being identified by research which identifies broad similarities between the genetics of modern populations in much of England and coastal communities in Holland, but dissimilarities with Wales.[84]

We are left, therefore, with a series of major disjunctions. There is a substantial lacuna in the archaeological record as we progress from the late fourth century into the mid-fifth, but this is not total and metalworking, at least, seems to have continued, in small quantities at least (as Laing's contribution), and in any case an absence of evidence which can be explained in terms of economic and structural change should not necessarily be construed as evidence for the absence of a substantial population. The pollen record does seem to imply that land-use generally continued, if not necessarily at the same intensity at least without consistent abandonment or reforestation. There is a growing body of evidence for the on-going use of tracks and field systems (but less so settlements) across the period, particularly in eastern England where they were most highly developed. There was a revival of material culture with the appearance of low levels of 'Anglo-Saxon' artefacts from the second quarter of the fifth century,[85] which rapidly increased thereafter to become widespread by the early sixth century, at least in the south and east of Britain. Both literary and artifactual evidence would seem to agree that this should be associated with incomers from southern Scandinavia and the North Germanic seaboard, initially perhaps as mercenaries but ultimately as conquerors. The loss of widespread 'Britishness' seems extreme: the collapse of pre-existing material culture, coin-use and settlement habits exceeds that observable in most parts of the Continent; the comparative lack of evidence for Christianity in the British lowlands in the later fifth and sixth centuries is difficult to explain without massive cultural change; and Old English drove out both Latin and Brittonic, which contrasts dramatically with the outcomes of barbarian settlements across much of the Continent. Yet we have evidence for the continuing presence of 'British' individuals and/or commu-

---

[83] Several different ethnicities, each with specific physical characteristics, were outlined by Isidore, *Etymologiae sive Origines*, XIX: see discussion by Dietrich Claude, 'Remarks about Relations between Visigoths and Hispano-Romans in the Seventh Century', in *Strategies of Distinction: The Construction of Ethnic Communities, 300–800*, ed. Walter Pohl and Helmut Reimitz (Leiden, 1998), pp. 117–30.

[84] Michael E. Weale, Deborah A. Weiss, Rolf F. Jager, Neil Bradman and Mark G. Thomas, 'Y Chromosome Evidence for Anglo-Saxon Mass Migration', *Molecular Biology and Evolution* 19.7 (2002), 1008–21.

[85] The dating of the initial appearance of Anglo-Saxon material to the period 425–50 is now comparatively well established: see John Hines, 'Philology, Archaeology and the *adventus Saxonum vel Anglorum*', in *Britain 400–600: Language and History,* ed. Alfred Bammesberger and Alfred Wollmann (Heidelberg, 1990), pp. 17–36; for sixth- and seventh-century dating of insular horizons, see *The Pace of Change: Studies in Early-Medieval Chronology*, ed. John Hines, Karen Høilund Nielson and Frank Siegmund (Oxford, 1999).

nities inside Anglo-Saxon England in specific places and at particular periods emanating from legal texts (Grimmer, Woolf), place-names (Probert) and even Domesday Book (Lewis, Thornton), particularly on the western margins where Britons do seem to have been more numerous (as Tyler). A significant British presence does, therefore, seem discernable right across the Anglo-Saxon period alongside evidence for large-scale discontinuity between Anglo-Saxon England and sub-Roman Britain, to the confusion of us all.

It is this conundrum which the Manchester conference in 2004 was designed to address. By bringing together archaeologists, place-name specialists and other linguists, historians and geneticists under one roof, the hope was to expose current research in each discipline to critical appraisal from a variety of different perspectives. In addition, the focus was not on just pre-Viking England, in the hope that insights from later periods might have considerable potential to advance discussions. Not all the papers given at the conference are published here: several had either already been promised elsewhere or were not available, for various reasons, but it is a pleasure to introduce such a substantial and varied collection, drawn from studies encompassing the fifth century through to the eleventh, all targeted on furthering our understanding of the Anglo-British interface. Much questioning and discussion occurred at the conference, which speakers were then invited to incorporate into their published papers. These therefore come to publication enriched by the context in which they were initially presented. Several key themes emerge, which might usefully be taken forward. For example, the Anglo-British interface clearly needs to be seen in highly variable terms across both space and time, and we should avoid a 'one rule fits all' approach. Yet the collapse of the Roman Empire, its culture and its political systems, does underlie the creation of England, with or without a British input (as paralleled by contemporary studies of the fall of the USSR: Härke, below). A sociological and economic perspective emerges as valuable, for example in terms of the consequences of legal differentiation of Anglo-Saxons and Britons and the possibility that wholesale enslavement of Britons may have occurred over time (as Woolf). Cultural valuation of Britons and Anglo-Saxons, by themselves and each other, offers new insights, while the study of place-names and language continue to provide major entrées to these issues. And contemporary cultural needs have clearly had a considerable impact on the ways that nineteenth and twentieth-century scholars have approached the issue of a British presence in Anglo-Saxon England (as Hills and Williams), as too does the recognition that Domesday Book reveals 'Welsh' individuals and families inhabiting 'English' named settlements (as Lewis). There is no simple solution provided to the central conundrum addressed here and no attempt to hide very real levels of disagreement between those who credit a significant British presence and those who do not, but the volume does provide a series of fresh viewpoints and new avenues, which it is hoped will both stimulate and contribute to fresh research over the next few decades.

2

Anglo-Saxon Attitudes

CATHERINE HILLS

I TAKE my title from the novel of that name by Angus Wilson,[1] who borrowed it from Lewis Carroll.[2] Debby Banham has also already used the title for an interesting paper which addresses a different, although related, topic from mine.[3] At the time of the conference I was, like most of us, excited by the find of a rich seventh-century burial at Prittlewell near Southend, excavated by the Museum of London archaeology service during the autumn of 2003.[4] Discussion of this find reflects current thinking about the relationship between religious belief and burial practice, specifically early medieval Christianity and paganism, which can be set against sixty years of evolving interpretations of the significance of Sutton Hoo, a site whose discovery influenced Angus Wilson's choice of theme for his novel. While writing this paper up for publication, I was struck by the contrast between two television programmes screened in 2004 within a few weeks of each other, both on Channel 4,[5] both purporting to present current knowledge of the Anglo-Saxon impact on Britain but presenting very different stories. The reasons for that difference seem to me to encapsulate the main theme of this paper, which revisits issues I have already discussed elsewhere.[6]

My contention is that our attitudes, whether Anglo-Saxon or not, arise from our multiple and changing individual and collective identities, which condition the ways in which we see and interpret the world, past or present. We need to try to understand those attitudes, in ourselves and in those whose works we are reading, viewing or hearing, before we can decide what, if anything, we really know, whether about the fifth century AD or anything else, across time. Embedded in the scholarship surrounding the debate over the respective roles played by Saxons, Britons and others in the transition from Roman Britain to

[1] Angus Wilson, *Anglo-Saxon Attitudes* (London, 1956).
[2] Lewis Carroll, *Through the Looking Glass* (London, 1871), chapter 7, ' "Not at all," said the King. "He's an Anglo-Saxon messenger – and those are Anglo-Saxon attitudes. He only does them when he's happy." '
[3] Debby Banham, 'Anglo-Saxon Attitudes: in Search of the Origins of English Racism', *European Review of History* 1.2 (1994), 143–56.
[4] Museum of London Archaeology Service, *The Prittlewell Prince* (London, 2004).
[5] Both programmes screened by Channel Four in the autumn of 2004: Monarchy, presented by David Starkey, director David Wilson, production Granada Bristol; Britain AD, presented by Francis Pryor, producer/director Timothy Copestake, Diverse Productions.
[6] Hills, *Origins*.

medieval England, Scotland and Wales are a great many assumptions, dictated as much or more by contemporary political, intellectual and social climates as by the evidence. Conclusions often depend partly on premises, and all of us cast our net in specific directions, looking where we expect to find support for our conclusions. Unravelling the bias in our own and others' work is further complicated by the fact that we are not consistent. Most of us change imperceptibly in our thinking in tune with current fashion, and we read things differently at different stages in our careers- and even select and present our findings differently to different audiences.

The novel *Anglo-Saxon Attitudes* by AngusWilson, published in 1956, has as its theme the cover-up of a hoax committed during the (fictional) excavation of an Anglo-Saxon burial which seems to me to be something like a conflation of the burial of St Cuthbert and Sutton Hoo mound 1. Wilson worked for years at the British Museum (or, rather in what is now the separate British Library) where he heard directly of the 1939 excavations at Sutton Hoo, and also of the Piltdown hoax.[7] His fictional holy saint Eorpwold was apparently buried with a pagan idol, a wooden phallic symbol, which caused great surprise and concern to its early twentieth-century excavators. (Later excavators would have been instantly suspicious at the preservation of a wooden object in the sandy soils of Suffolk.) When I first read this book I thought it very funny. It was widely thought the academics in the novel were based on people whom Wilson knew when he worked at the British Museum, names known to me as established scholars: Thomas Kendrick, for example, or Margaret Murray. As a graduate student I found the idea of an academic hoax and its concealment by a senior academic, albeit a fictional one, amusing, and I admired the pastiche of Bede and other medieval writers provided as an appendix by Wilson. When I returned to the book years later I found it a depressing story of wasted lives and unattractive characters, and I had ceased to find the hoax, which in any case occupies only a small part of the book, either funny or interesting. The contortions forced on the characters by contemporary attitudes towards marriage and homosexuality now seem as odd to me as those of Lewis Carroll's Anglo-Saxon messenger.

The idea that a Christian missionary might have been buried with a pagan object was presented as shocking to the early twentieth-century excavators, one of whom was an Anglican cleric, and still fairly devastating to the mid-twentieth-century academics revisiting the story, with by then some new evidence of a similar find elsewhere. Within the two periods of the novel there was a shift from widespread adherence to Christianity, and of a view of Bede and his contemporaries as practitioners of something like Edwardian Anglicanism, to a more detached view in which Christian belief was none the less still alive and important, although most of the characters seem anything but godly and one, Rose Lorimer, even professes pagan beliefs, but she is sinking into madness. It was expected that burials would be identifiable as Christian or pagan, largely through presence or absence of any grave-goods, or perhaps through the presence of identifiably 'Christian' or 'pagan' objects. The debate over Sutton Hoo

---

[7] Margaret Drabble, *Angus Wilson. A Biography* (London, 1995), pp. 199–205.

had however begun to complicate the picture. Over the years since Chadwick first posed the question 'who was he?',[8] that is, who was buried or commemorated in mound 1, the answer has changed, partly according to changes in the dating of the coins, but also in response to shifts in interpretation of burial practice. Although Chadwick already in 1940 pointed out that there were furnished burials on the continent which were accepted as Christian it has taken a long time to break down an expectation that a sharp dichotomy between pagan and Christian should be visible in the archaeological record, and to accept that belief may not be expressed in a simple, easily readable way in burial ritual. When gold foil crosses were found in the Prittlewell burial, otherwise apparently a rich 'pagan' grave, it attracted a great deal of interest. The exact significance of the crosses continues to be debated, but they are certainly comparable to crosses found in other richly furnished graves in south Germany and northern Italy, graves assumed to be those of Christians. On the whole we are no longer tied to preconceptions about the nature of early medieval religion, nor, mostly, committed to specific beliefs about the early Anglo-Saxon church. A range of interpretations now seems possible as to the extent and character of the Christian beliefs of those buried in either Sutton Hoo mound 1 or Prittlewell, and those who buried them. We are not starting from quite such firm premises as were the initial researchers at Sutton Hoo (except Chadwick), let alone Wilson's fictional excavators. Ideas do change discernibly over time.

However, it would be a mistake to imagine that all thinking evolves in some coherent and uni-directional manner. Many different views coexist, confidently presented simultaneously as accepted current wisdom. Exploring the roots of these ideas needs to go beyond scholarly works to the stories told in schools and films or on TV. These versions of events not only lay the foundations for the inspiration of future generations of students, academics and fieldworkers, they also form the views of decision makers, including funding bodies and government, whose support is vital for the future of the past. Popular presentations, because simplified for clarity, often show more immediately the outlines and implications of an argument which may be nuanced, modified, even fudged, in scholarly writing, so they can be important sources for analysis of the history of interpretation. In Victorian England historical paintings offer such insights: for the later twentieth century, and at least so far as 2005 into the twenty-first century, it is television to which we must turn. Presentation and personality may seem to provide a distracting filter in television – indeed sometimes they are the main point of the programme. But academic careers and so research are not unconnected to personality or presentation, so even this is relevant.

The two television programmes which struck me by their contrasting views (which must surely have confused the discriminating non-specialist viewer of both), were the first episode of Monarchy, presented by David Starkey, and Britain AD, presented by Francis Pryor. From the books of these series can be taken the following: '... it is scarcely possible to exaggerate the scale of the Saxon incursions ... DNA evidence shows that up to ninety percent of the male population

---

[8] H. Munro Chadwick, 'Who was He?' *Antiquity* 14 (1940), 76–87.

was displaced – driven west or killed ... ethnic cleansing at its most savagely effective',[9] and: 'I believe that the changes in the archaeological record of eastern and south eastern Britain are better explained by acculturation than migration.'[10] Adding the book of a third, earlier series, Schama's History of Britain, we find 'Romano-Britons and North Sea warriors must have lived alongside each other as neighbours rather than implacable foes'.[11] Personal confusion is added by the fact I am credited as an advisor in both of the first two books.[12]

Unravelling the sources of the different views presented above, which demonstrate neatly the need for continuing discussion of this topic, is an exercise with wider relevance. Although each of the three presenters is an established historian or archaeologist, none is a specialist in early medieval Britain, and so none is speaking directly from his own first-hand research. Moreover, even such weighty figures as these will not have had an entirely free hand in the content of programmes or even books: it is a popular misapprehension that presenters speak their own words. All programmes are the result of teamwork, technical production and research. Within that, the role of the presenter can range from real articulation of the original ideas of that presenter to being an actor reading a script to which they have had little or no input. Schama, Starkey and Pryor have certainly succeeded as presenters because they have strong personalities, and I am sure they were not ciphers in these programmes. However, which presenter is chosen will depend on the kind of programme, and perhaps the kind of message, the commissioning editor and the producer have decided, or been persuaded, to transmit. While Pryor did appear to be driving his programme, Starkey was outside his home territory of the Tudors, and really only engaged once King Alfred came in sight and the murky waters of archaeology could be left behind for the clarity of history.

The details of all of these programmes are of course reliant on the research of others. Here the question is which research and how are its conclusions presented. 'Research' in television terms seems different from at least the theory of academic research, if not the practice, in that it often starts from premises and looks for supporting evidence.[13] Many talking heads have been frustrated by the editing of their pieces to camera so that only the section where they are supporting the thesis of the programme is left, and any qualification – or downright contradiction – has disappeared. Heinrich Härke, for example, appeared in Britain AD discussing his work on material change in Soviet Russia, also

---

[9] David Starkey, *The Monarchy of England. The Beginnings* (London, 2004), p. 18.
[10] Francis Pryor, *Britain A.D. A Quest for Arthur, England and the Anglo-Saxons* (London, 2004), p. 149.
[11] Simon Schama, *A History of Britain. At the Edge of the World? 3000 BC – AD 1603* (London, 2000), pp. 45–6.
[12] And the editor of this volume appeared in the first episode of Pryor's series and is acknowledged in the book, while several other contributors also featured on screen.
[13] In fact my arguments in this paper tend to suggest academics often do the same thing. Also, it is unfair to suggest television producers are never open to persuasion: in the 1980s I was able to persuade Forbes Taylor to make a very different programme, 'Blood of the British', from the one he had had in mind.

presented at Manchester,[14] which supported the thesis that material change need not mean invasion, whereas all his arguments to the opposite effect in relation to Anglo-Saxons and Britons were left out. Also, however bright and keen the TV researchers may be there is no reason to expect their summaries of what you tell them, or they read, to be any more precise or exact than when they were writing essays or exam answers a few years previously. Nor, perhaps, should we assume that our exposition of our own research or synthesis of others, when speaking to TV researchers over the telephone or lunch, is any sharper or less ambiguous than it is in lectures or tutorials.

Why do these programmes present such different views of the process by which *Britannia* became England, Scotland, and Wales? Part of the answer is that they had very different briefs. Starkey's story of the English monarchy begins properly with Alfred (although only under Alfred's successors was there a kingdom of all England). Other periods are simply a prelude to the real matter in hand, and do not really concern him. With Pryor the reverse is true: prehistory ends with the Romans and/or the Anglo-Saxons during the first millennium AD. He is passionately determined to relate prehistory to later periods and to combat any impression that the prehistoric peoples of Britain have no connection to the modern population, and so can safely be forgotten. Waves of Romans, Saxons, Vikings and Normans did not obliterate all that went before, and the real roots of modern Britain lie deep in the past.

They also have superficially different styles of presentation. David Starkey is magisterial and authoritative, we hear only his voice in the programmes and his book, confident statements are presented without contradiction as currently accepted wisdom. Francis Pryor, on the other hand, interviewed assorted colleagues, mostly archaeologists, on and off screen, and their views were quoted extensively in his book. On the face of it this is a more inclusive and less authoritarian way of doing it. Actually, he has a strong message of his own, which the supporting cast were chosen to reinforce. Of wider significance is the fact that Starkey is an historian, Pryor a prehistorian. Despite much apparent interdisciplinary communication it seems to me that there is still a divide in the way historians and archaeologists see the first millennium AD, and that if anything we are currently tending to diverge more in our views. This may not be apparent to younger scholars who speak to others of like mind and may feel they can move on from battles fought in previous generations. I think the quotations with which I began this section show that is not so.

Historians, unsurprisingly, remain attached to the written word: however sophisticated their critique of texts and hotly contested their various interpretations they remain committed to the intrinsic value of written words. All academics, even archaeologists, share this commitment to some extent. Writing is the permanent form of what is often seen as one of the prime distinguishing characteristics of human beings, speech. It has also often been believed to be the medium for divine communication. Anglo-Saxon historians have often followed Stenton in thinking that between the end of Roman government and the late

---

[14] Heinrich Härke, this volume.

seventh century lay a period 'whose history could not be written',[15] and so little need be said of it. Deconstruction of Gildas, Nennius *et al.* as objective history has not improved the situation, though most historians would now add a chapter or more of discussion of archaeological evidence for the early period.

Even historians who are really conversant with archaeologists and their research still find much archaeological interpretation 'unprovable'. See for example the recent, excellent book by David Rollason on the history of Northumbria.[16] Rollason presents alternative models (essentially two versions of peaceful assimilation versus one of aggressive take-over) for the creation of Northumbria, and analyses the evidence for each. He takes account of the possibility that not all those buried with 'Anglo-Saxon' grave-goods need have been of Germanic ancestry, but his discussion of this lacks the broader context of archaeological and anthropological debate surrounding the nature of identities and the complexity of their material manifestation. He then presents a convincing account of hostility and conflict between Briton and Saxon drawn from written documents. A comparable account is given in Banham's paper of the same title as this one, in which she goes so far as to argue that the Anglo-Saxons were racists.[17] However balanced Rollason's presentation, it is clear that he believes the traditional account to be most convincing.

The historical account is clear, consistent and familiar, and rests on accepted modes of argument. The invading Anglo-Saxons took over much of what had been Roman Britain, and that process involved population change. I think younger archaeologists may not appreciate how strongly entrenched that version is, and how difficult it is to provide alternative arguments which will convince either historians or the general public. They are more likely to believe Starkey than experts on the period who offer a more problematic perspective.

It is of course difficult to deny some aspects of this historical record. That Anglo-Saxons thought of themselves as different from, and superior to, Britons does seem to be demonstrated by their own writings. By the late seventh century in most of southern and eastern Britain there were kingdoms ruled by dynasties whose descent was traced from Germanic gods. The recorded language and identity of their people was Anglo-Saxon and they themselves believed, if Bede carried as much weight in his own day as he has since, that they came from 'three very powerful Germanic tribes'.[18]

History is mostly written from the top down. We don't really know much about ordinary people in Anglo-Saxon England, except insofar as they impinged on authority, as sources of tribute, objects of miracles or lawbreakers. The 'Anglo-Saxon' population might indeed have been related to its leaders, descended from immigrants and speaking Germanic languages from the start, or they could have been descended from Britons who had taken on Anglo-Saxon identity because

---

[15] Stenton, *ASE*, p. 1.
[16] David Rollason, *Northumbria, 500–1100: Creation and Destruction of a Kingdom* (Cambridge, 2003).
[17] Banham, 'Anglo-Saxon Attitudes'.
[18] *HE*, I, 15.

people followed their lords and were their people, whatever their ancestry. I don't think the sources tell us which option is the truth, probably because that was not a matter which concerned their authors very much, and also because there may be no simple story, as the process may have varied from one place or time to another.

There is also a foreshortening effect which compresses history retrospectively. This affects accounts of language change as well as ethnic and political history. The situation as perceived by Bede and later writers was the result of processes, whether of assimilation or annihilation, which took place over several preceding centuries. We can in fact see this process continuing for centuries after the seventh century.

Archaeologists, especially prehistorians like Pryor, are more likely to take a bottom-up approach to the past. That is, they start from fields, huts and bones, not from kings and treasure. Pryor's contention is that the landscape, especially the agrarian landscape, does not show a break from 'Roman' to 'Saxon' and that there is no sign of a new population in the middle of the first millennium AD. He supports this by comparison with the start of the Roman period, which is widely accepted as the arrival of a military elite, who did not replace the farming population. The native farmers began to use wheel-thrown pottery and are thus described as 'Romano-British', although many of them took generations to give up other aspects of Iron Age culture, such as round houses, which, in the South West, endured throughout the Roman period. Other research into the archaeological landscape, farming and the environment, also tends towards interpretation in terms of continuity rather than sudden change. See for example Peter Fowler: 'there is nothing, culturally, technologically or environmentally, to indicate major agrarian change'.[19] Petra Dark sees a pattern of regional variation, with at most some decline in the intensity of landuse.[20] The evidence is patchy, especially in the east, but, so far, where detailed environmental studies have been carried out, they point towards continuity rather than dramatic change in landuse.[21] Dominic Powlesland has used both his large-scale excavation of West Heslerton and his astonishing geophysical survey of the Vale of Pickering to argue for continuing occupation and, indeed, continuity of population.[22]

---

[19] Peter Fowler, *Farming in the First Millennium AD* (Cambridge, 2002), p. 288.
[20] Petra Dark, *The Environment of Britain in the First Millennium AD* (London, 2000).
[21] See for example: Peter Murphy, 'The Anglo-Saxon Landscape and Rural Economy: Some Results from Sites in East Anglia and Essex', in *Environment and Economy in Anglo-Saxon England*, ed. James Rackham, Council for British Archaeology Research Report 89 (York, 1994), pp. 23–39; Ralph Fyfe and Stephen Rippon, 'A Landscape in Transition? Palaeoenvironmental Evidence for the End of the "Romano-British' Period in South-West England"', in *Debating Late Antiquity in Britain AD 300–700,* ed. Rob Collins and James Gerrard, BAR, BS 365 (Oxford, 2004), pp. 33–42; Rob Collins, 'Before "The End": Hadrian's Wall in the Fourth Century and after', in *Debating Late Antiquity*, ed. Collins and Gerrard, pp. 123-32.
[22] Dominic Powlesland, 'Early Anglo-Saxon Settlements, Structures, Form and Layout', in *The Anglo-Saxons from the Migration Period to the Eighth Century: an Ethnographic Perspective*, ed. John Hines (Woodbridge, 1997), pp. 101–24; Dominic Powlesland 'Early

On the whole, the admittedly incomplete and patchy evidence which we have suggests continuous use of fields, animals and crops, even occasionally the same buildings. Survival of some or most of the peasantry is more plausible than their wholesale replacement by incomers, who perhaps, as Schama suggests 'had no intention of stooping to farming themselves',[23] an interesting reversal of older ideas about free, democratic, German peasants hewing clearings from the forest. We should not forget, however, that whole regions of England have at times been laid waste in recorded history, notably by the Normans. That might have been the fate of some regions in the fifth to sixth centuries AD.

A key point is that much previous discussion, by archaeologists and historians, of the relationship between Roman and Saxon sites took insufficient account either of their scale and density of distribution, or of their contexts. In early accounts and maps a convenient blanket of trackless forest or marsh filled in the spaces between scattered farms, whereas now we can see most of lowland England has been more or less continuously exploited since at least the Iron Age. The size of the population is not clear: all that can be said is that population at the time of Domesday Book has been calculated as approximately two million, and comparison of settlement density then and at earlier periods suggests comparable, or significantly larger, populations at various times. It is usually stated that there was a considerable decline in population in the middle of the millennium, but this is based partly on the assumption that this must have happened, partly on the dramatic fall in the quantity of rubbish which happened to be both durable and visible. It is in fact difficult to calibrate this: each Romano-British peasant left far more trace of himself than his Anglo-Saxon successor, while the scale of rubbish produced by each of us now is several degrees of magnitude greater than anyone before the Industrial Revolution.

The traditional backbone of Anglo-Saxon archaeology is furnished burial. Views here also tend to differ, but not always split along disciplinary lines. Most historians, some archaeologists and much of the wider public probably still accept the attribution of ethnic significance to burial deposits, which is seen as supporting the traditional historical account of the relationship between Britons and Anglo-Saxons. At one time it seemed to historians that this would provide the answer to the gap in written sources. As more and more burials, pots and brooches were excavated and dated, the distribution maps filled up, and apparently put flesh (or at least bones) on the brief entries in the *Anglo-Saxon Chronicle*. The 'Anglian', 'Saxon' or 'Jutish' objects in graves showed how far those people had spread, and how densely they had settled, by dates calculated from artefact typology. The works of J. N. L Myres and John Morris are the high point of this optimistic approach: both are still in print, weighty and authoritative tomes by very learned men, still forming the ideas of the next generation of Anglo-Saxon scholars.[24]

Anglo-Saxon Settlement and Landscape in the Vale of Pickering', paper given at the 55th Sachsensymposium (given Cambridge, September 2004, publication pending).

[23] Schama, *History of Britain*, p. 46.

[24] J. N. L. Myres, *Anglo-Saxon Pottery and the Settlement of England* (Oxford, 1969); J. N. L. Myres, *The English Settlements* (Oxford, 1986); John Morris, *The Age of Arthur* (London, 1973).

But then archaeologists, now assisted by metal detectorists, began to find so much material that the patterns became fuzzy. There are simply too many Anglo-Saxon burials in the east of England to identify meaningful associations with any other kind of archaeological evidence, Roman settlements, for example, of which there are also a great number. The spots join up into a continuous blur across East Anglia: any gaps are more likely to denote the outlines of modern conurbations than anything ancient, while clear linear concentrations in the distribution are generally consequent on survey along the routes of modern motorways.[25]

The theoretical basis for a simple equation between pots and peoples was seriously undermined decades ago in prehistoric archaeology, and for some years now early medieval archaeologists have also doubted their ability to read ethnicity from grave-goods. But, as pointed out above, historians have difficulty with this approach, which does rather cut the conventional ground from beneath our feet. If these are not 'Anglo-Saxons' on ethnic or racial criteria, then who are they? And how can we say anything useful about them, especially anything useful towards constructing a narrative of events? It is also difficult to explain at a more practical level. Contacted the other day by excavators who thought they might have found some Anglo-Saxon graves, I ventured out into the freezing fen and confirmed that, yes, those bits of rusty iron were parts of Anglo-Saxon shield bosses and so they did indeed have some Anglo-Saxon burials. All those present knew what we meant. At some future date those burials can be interpreted as either incomers or locals adopting foreign habits, but life is too short to include such discussion in a proposal to a developer for extended time for excavation. Complicated messages confuse or lose any non-specialist audience, particularly school children, journalists or audiences for TV programmes.

It is interesting that Starkey makes reference to scientific evidence, the DNA which demonstrates ethnic cleansing: now it is science which will reveal the truth, to both historians and archaeologists. It is odd that highly critical academics who are happy to tear apart the work of colleagues in their own subject are willing to accept so much on trust from other disciplines. This is especially true of non-scientists' belief in science. The paper whose results Starkey is summarizing does indeed conclude: 'The best explanation for our findings is that the Anglo-Saxon cultural transition in Central England coincided with a mass immigration from the continent', and favoured Frisia as the main place of origin of the immigrants.[26] However, a later paper argues 'there is a clear indication of a continuing indigenous component in the English paternal genetic makeup'. In this paper it was also concluded that distinguishing between Anglo-Saxon and Danish Viking period immigration was not currently possible.[27] The teams carrying out this

---

[25] This sentence owes much to maps produced by Mary Chester-Kadwell, currently a PhD student in the Department of Archaeology, University of Cambridge.

[26] Michael E. Weale, Deborah A. Weiss, Rolf F. Jager, Neil Bradman, and Mark G. Thomas, 'Y Chromosome Evidence for Anglo-Saxon Mass Migration', *Molecular Biology and Evolution* 19.7 (2002) 1008–21.

[27] Cristian Capelli, Nicola Redhead, Julia K. Abernethy, Fiona Gratrix, James F. Wilson, Torolf Moen, Tor Hervig, Martin Richards, Michael P. H. Stumpf, Peter A. Underhill, Paul

research both included geneticists from University College London, including Mark Thomas as a contributor to both papers. He also spoke at Manchester, and explained clearly the problems involved in this kind of research, as did also Martin Evison.[28] Mark Thomas has used computer modelling to achieve his results, a powerful technique whose results do, however, depend on the premises set up at the start of the exercise. At another conference Thomas presented an alternative model, which might produce the same genetic results. Instead of a sudden destruction of male Britons by overwhelming numbers of invaders, a much smaller, but dominant, group of foreign men over generations would have preferential access to wives and greater survival rates for their sons.[29] In recent centuries mixed populations have emerged in colonial contexts, which show how that could have worked in early medieval Britain. It seems to me we are still some way from being able to make confident statements on the basis of genetic evidence, either about ethnic cleansing or continuity.

Pryor preferred the results produced by another scientific technique, stable isotope analysis. This was explained by Paul Budd and Sam Lucy, part of the team who have been applying the technique to skeletons from West Heslerton.[30] This uses the trace elements from drinking water, specifically stable isotopes of strontium and oxygen, preserved in tooth enamel, to show whether an individual grew up in the same area as that where they died and were buried. Results from a sample of twenty burials from West Heslerton suggest only seven were local, thirteen appear to have come from a more westerly region, across the Pennines, and only four seemed non-British, possibly from Scandinavia. This suggests regional mobility rather than immigration from overseas. However, this is a developing field of research, in which some basic questions as to the science still seem to be under discussion. Again we should not rush to accept all preliminary conclusions.

The point I want to make here is to note the alacrity with which proponents of differing views have seized on new scientific research which appears to support their own case, ignoring or playing down contradictory findings. Maybe further work in these directions will provide conclusive results: so far we have been following our prejudices and choosing the science which fits those best.

Possibly the strongest reason for taking up differing positions is the one least admitted, or even always appreciated. This is how we understand our own identity, and how, if we see ourselves as British in any way, we think we fit into the story.

Bradshaw, Alom Shaha, Mark G. Thomas, Neil Bradman and David B. Goldstein, 'A Y Chromosome Census of the British Isles', *Current Biology* 13 (2003), 979–984 .

[28] Martin Evison, 'All in the Genes? Evaluating the Biological Evidence of Contact and Migration', in *Cultures in Contact*, ed. Dawn Hadley and Julian Richards (Turnhout, 2000), pp. 277–90.

[29] Mark Thomas, 'Y Chromosome Evidence for a Substantial Anglo-Saxon Contribution to the Modern Gene Pool in Central England', paper given at the 55th Sachsensymposium (given Cambridge, September 2004, publication pending).

[30] Paul Budd, Andrew Millard, Carolyn Chenery, Sam Lucy, Charlotte Roberts, 'Investigating Population Movement by Stable Isotope Analysis: a Report from Britain', *Ant* 78 (2004), 127–41.

The equation of ethnicity with ancestry is a powerful mechanism for justifying group identity. Ancestry seems to provide an unavoidable, predetermined – and therefore guilt-free basis for group definition, which is what makes it dangerous, and so worth investigating with as much critical detachment as we can muster (not much, unfortunately, if you follow my arguments). It is relatively easy to trace attitudes to Anglo-Saxons from the fifth century to the twentieth,[31] and to work out how and why Bede, Geoffrey of Monmouth, Matthew Parker, even J. N. L. Myres, and all the rest saw them differently. But the debate is given force by the fact that it relates to the identities of people living today in Britain. Are the English quite different from the Scots, Welsh, Irish and Cornish because they are descended from Germanic invaders, whereas the others are 'native' inhabitants? Or does most of the population, including the 'English' have British ancestry, the very real regional differences coming from long-term, geographical, economic and political structures? Are we actually a mixture, a population whose ancestors moved within the British Isles and across the North and Irish Seas more freely than a romantic image of unchanging, ancient, rural life might suggest? Is this a country which has always absorbed new peoples and cultures and should continue to do so, or should we defend our national character(s) against Europe and immigrants from around the world? Many of these questions are not asked: we simply take up positions which fit our own world views. Implicit in all the stories told, by academics, teachers or TV presenters, are different answers to questions we do not always realize exist. And those stories are then used, selectively, by others, to support their own political arguments.

---

[31] Hills, *Origins*, chapter 2. Also Sam Lucy, *The Early Anglo-Saxon Cemeteries of East Yorkshire*, BAR, BS 272 (Oxford, 1998), chapter 2.

3

Forgetting the Britons in Victorian Anglo-Saxon Archaeology

HOWARD WILLIAMS*

We derive our antiquities of the period of Anglo-Saxon paganism from one source, the graves.[1]

How we explain the origins and development of furnished burial rites in southern and eastern England dated to the fifth and sixth centuries AD is the focus of ongoing debate and controversy. Currently, archaeologists and historians have various answers to this question, from the adoption of Germanic 'fashions' by indigenous Britons to a mass-migration of Germanic settlers. Many scholars opt for different points on a spectrum between these extremes, including the settlement, accommodation and interaction of Germanic groups with Britons on a local level and the invasion and subsequent imitation of Germanic warrior elites. In contrast, some writers opt out of the debate by arguing that furnished burial is unequivocally 'Germanic', whether this be in terms of biological origins, linguistic connections, cultural affiliations or political hegemony.[2] Yet even if archaeologists and historians sometimes have different answers, they share a common interest in the same question, but it is a question that has two sides. While traditionally we have used furnished graves to address the question 'When and where did the Anglo-Saxons settle?', the flip-side of the same question is 'What happened to the Britons?'

As a contribution to this ongoing historical and archaeological research, this paper aims to return to the very origins of this debate: the study of early medieval

---

* I would like to thank Elizabeth Williams for commenting on an earlier version of this paper. All errors remain my responsibility.
[1] Thomas Wright, *The Celt, the Roman, and the Saxon: A History of the Early Inhabitants of Britain down to the Anglo-Saxon Conversion to Christianity* (London, 1852), at p. 399.
[2] Discussions of furnished graves: e.g. Chris Arnold *The Archaeology of the Early Anglo-Saxon Kingdoms* (London, 1997, 2nd edn); Tania Dickinson, 'Review article: What's New in Early Medieval Burial Archaeology?', *Early Medieval Europe* 11(1), 71–87; Heinrich Härke, '"Warrior Graves"? The Background of the Anglo-Saxon Weapon Burial Rite', *Past & Present* 126 (1990), 22–43; Helena Hamerow, 'Migration Theory and the Migration Period', in *Building on the Past*, ed. B. Vyner (London, 1994), pp. 164–77; Higham, *RBAS*; Sam Lucy, *The Anglo-Saxon Way of Death* (Stroud, 2000); Martin Welch, *Anglo-Saxon England* (London, 1992).

graves by Victorian archaeologists. In recent years, several writers have pointed out that the attribution of early medieval graves to the 'Anglo-Saxons' says as much about the Victorian search for English national and racial origins and the desire to identify graves as material proof of Germanic settlement as it does about the nature of the material evidence.[3] However the specific treatment of Britons in Victorian interpretations of early Anglo-Saxon graves has received less attention. Although it was in the early- and mid-twentieth century that a political context of increasing Germano-phobia brought the fate of the Britons to the fore,[4] underlying attitudes and antipathies towards Britons can be recognised in nineteenth-century, Germano-philic descriptions and interpretations of early medieval graves.

By using the excavation reports and publications of graves discovered in the period from 1840 to 1870 as my source material, this paper intends to review the different ways in which commentaries upon archaeological discoveries in journals and books consciously used graves to create a narrative of English origins within which the Britons had no place.

Victorian Anglo-Saxonism and archaeology
Building upon the discoveries of the eighteenth-century antiquarians Bryan Faussett and James Douglas, the period from 1840 to 1870 saw a rapid increase in the excavation, identification and publication of early medieval graves.[5] The dissemination of excavation reports of early medieval cemeteries in society journals and books fuelled the growing middle- and upper-class enthusiasm for antiquarian, archaeological and historical knowledge of the Saxon past. Key figures in the study of early Anglo-Saxon graves and their contents included many of the leading archaeologists, historians and antiquaries of the period, notably Charles Roach-Smith, Thomas Wright, William Wylie, John Kemble and John Akerman. Their reports and syntheses of material evidence provide a fascinating

---

[3] Arnold, *Archaeology of the Early Anglo-Saxon Kingdoms*, pp. 1–18; Susan Content, 'The Text as Culture: the Making of the English', *Scottish Archaeological Review* 9 and 10 (1995), 36–40; Bonnie Effros, *Merovingian Mortuary Archaeology and the Making of the Early Middle Ages* (Berkeley, CA, 2003); Bonnie Effros, 'A Century of Remembrance and Amnesia in the Excavation, Display, and Interpretation of Early Medieval Burial Artifacts', in *Erinnerungskultur im Bestattungsritual*, ed. J. Jarnut and M. Wemhoff (Munich, 2003), pp. 75–96; Bonnie Effros, 'Memories of the Early Medieval Past: Grave Artefacts in Nineteenth-Century France and Early Twentieth-Century America', in *Archaeologies of Remembrance: Death and Memory in Past Societies*, ed. H. Williams (New York, 2003), pp. 255–81; Hills, *Origins*; Sam Lucy *The Early Anglo-Saxon Cemeteries of East Yorkshire: An Analysis and Reinterpretation* (Oxford, 1998), pp. 5–21; Sam Lucy, 'From Pots to People: Two Hundred Years of Anglo-Saxon Archaeology', in *'Lastworda Betst': Essays in memory of Christine E. Fell with her unpublished writings*, ed. C. Hough and K. A. Lowe (Donnington, 2002), pp. 144–69.

[4] S. Lucy, 'From Pots to People'.

[5] E.g. Michael Rhodes, 'Faussett Rediscovered: Charles Roach Smith, Joseph Mayer, and the Publication of *Inventorium Sepulchrale*', in *Anglo-Saxon Cemeteries: A Reappraisal*, ed. E. Southworth (Liverpool, 1990), pp. 25–64; Howard Williams, 'Heathen Graves and Victorian Anglo-Saxonism: Assessing the Archaeology of John Mitchell Kemble', *ASSAH* 13 (2006), 1–18.

insight into Victorian discoveries. Although these reports are often incomplete, imprecise and inaccurate by modern standards, archaeologists today continue to employ nineteenth-century archaeological publications as invaluable resources for their ongoing studies of early medieval mortuary practices and society. Yet the reports are, at the same time, a valuable source of historical information into the intellectual climate then current and its social and ideological context. Although Anglo-Saxonism as a discourse can be traced through earlier centuries,[6] and archaeological monuments had been employed in debates over English identity prior to the nineteenth century,[7] for the first time scholars believed they had identified direct evidence of the earliest Germanic settlers arriving on the shores of Britain in the latter days of Roman rule. Indeed, instead of seeing archaeology as just the handmaiden of history, scholars like Kemble and Roach-Smith were keen to advocate the value of early medieval graves as 'illustrating history' and as providing a more definitive proof of England's Teutonic heritage than the fragmentary and ambiguous historical and mythical sources.[8] As ideological products of their time, excavation reports of early medieval graves seem to have had a powerful impact upon contemporary attitudes towards the Anglo-Saxons as well as influencing subsequent thinking and research up to the present day.

Forgetting the Britons
In this light, how were early medieval Britons, those thought to have been vanquished or made subservient to the invading Anglo-Saxons, treated by these reports? To answer this question, I would like briefly to explore six themes discussed within the pages of Victorian archaeological reports of early medieval graves: Roman-inspired objects, Roman objects, burial rites, bones, monuments and landscape. Within each theme it is possible to identify how relations between Romans and Anglo-Saxons were perceived. Discussions of artefacts and burial rites appear to have been central to the interpretation of the graves as 'Teutonic' or 'Anglo-Saxon', and yet repeatedly discussions avoid any mention of the possibility of a British or Celtic connection. Rather than being merely a passive omission, it is argued that within the socio-political context of mid-nineteenth century Britain, this 'forgetting' of the Britons was integral to attribution of the graves to a Teutonic supremacy, which would then set the stage for the emergence of the distinctive Anglo-Saxon culture and society to which Victorian Britain looked for the foundations of its civilisation, at home and abroad.

Roman-inspired objects
The idea of period- and subject-specialisation would have been foreign to many Victorian antiquaries and archaeologists. Many of those digging and reporting discoveries of early medieval burials were equally familiar with Roman sites and

---

6   E.g. Allen Frantzen, *Desire for Origins* (New Brunswick, 1993).
7   E.g. the White Horse of Uffington: Philip Schwyzer, 'The Scouring of the White Horse: Archaeology, Identity, and "Heritage"', *Representations* 65 (1999), 42–62.
8   Charles Roach-Smith, *Inventorium Sepulchre: an Account of Some Antiquities dug up at Gilton, Kingston, Sibertswold, Barfriston, Beakesbourne, Chartham, and Crundale ... Kent, from AD 1757 to AD 1773, by Rev. Bryan Faussett* (London, 1856), at p. ix.

material culture.⁹ Regarding the artefacts recovered from Anglo-Saxon graves, many were regarded as distinctively 'Teutonic', such as weapons and pottery, but others were thought to demonstrate the transmission of craft skills and techniques from Romans to Saxons. For example, Wright and Roach-Smith noted similarities between Roman and Saxon pins, shears, tweezers, combs, mirrors and bracelets, while Anglo-Saxon glass vessels were regarded as owing a debt of 'origin and influence' to Roman glass-making.¹⁰ Some Anglo-Saxon metalwork was thought to follow Roman styles, with John Akerman even suggesting that Roman and Saxon brooches showed both similarities in form and also in their use as an element of female costume.¹¹ Overall, Roach-Smith believed that: 'it is not difficult to trace most of the Saxon and Frankish ornamental designs to a Roman origin ...'¹² He thought this was especially the case for the Anglo-Saxon graves of Kent, where the proliferation of 'Roman' inspired objects was interpreted as reflective of the comparatively high level of civilisation of this kingdom. For example, the garnet disc brooch from Faversham was described by Roach-Smith as demonstrating the 'superior wealth and refinement of the Kentish Saxons, and ... how much they had profited by Roman art and artists'.¹³ The material evidence thus identified Kent in particular as heir to Rome, so the more ready and willing to re-adopt Roman Christianity. In contrast, this author has been unable to find a single instance where Celtic or British influence was explicitly suggested regarding any object in an early medieval grave, nor were Britons referred to as potential bearers or transmitters of Roman art to the Saxons.

Re-used Roman objects

As well as identifying Roman-inspired objects, Victorian archaeologists recognised old Roman objects which had been re-used and interred in Anglo-Saxon graves. In some instances such objects were used to suggest dates for the graves. For instance, a late Roman brooch from a Saxon grave on Bowcombe Down (Isle of Wight) suggested to the excavators a 'transitional' date for the grave between

---

⁹ Indeed, Charles Roach-Smith is as renowned for his work on Roman sites as he is for his systematic reporting of Anglo-Saxon cemetery finds: see D. Kidd, 'Charles Roach Smith and his Museum of London Antiquities', in *Collectors and Collections*, ed. R. Camber (London, 1977), pp. 105–35.

¹⁰ Thomas Wright, *The Celt, the Roman, and the Saxon*, pp. 416–18; 'The real value of antiquities should be determined by the extent to which they are capable of being applied towards illuminating history', Charles Roach-Smith, *Inventorium Sepulchre*, at pp. xxx–xxxiii, xliv; T. M. Wright, 'On Anglo-Saxon Antiquities, with a particular reference to the Faussett Collection', in *Essays on Archaeological Subjects Volume 1*, ed. T. Wright (London: John Russell Smith, 1861), pp. 107–71, at p. 132.

¹¹ John Yonge Akerman, *An Archaeological Index to the Remains of Antiquity in the Celtic, Romano-British and Anglo-Saxon Periods* (London, 1847), at p. 127.

¹² Charles Roach-Smith, 'Anglo-Saxon Remains Recently Discovered in Kent, in Cambridgeshire, and in some other counties', *Collectanea Antiqua* 6 (1868), 136–72, at p. 142.

¹³ Charles Roach-Smith, 'On Anglo-Saxon Remains Recently Discovered at Faversham, at Wye, and at Westwell, in Kent', *Archaeologia Cantiana* 1 (1858), 42–49, at p. 46.

the Roman and the Saxon periods,[14] while the mixture of Roman and Saxon articles at Sandwich was regarded by Wright as evidence for the 'intermixture of the two peoples'.[15] Yet such comments are rare and most accounts demonstrate a clear awareness that most Roman artefacts in Anglo-Saxon graves were necessarily re-used, including bronze bowls, spoons, hairpins, and, most famously, the Roman intaglio re-set in a gold ring from the ship-burial at Snape.[16]

The re-use of Roman coins in either bag collections or pierced for suspension inspired the greatest amount of discussion, with some suggesting that they were amulets and others seeing them as evidence of some form of continuation of Roman currency.[17] In no cases was this seen as the continuity of Britons, since the very coins selected were thought to show a Germanic affinity. One fascinating spin on this perspective comes from Akerman's discussion of the coins from Kemble (Glouc.), arguing that the preference for coins of Carausius in Anglo-Saxon graves was because this emperor

> ... was a Batavian, a man of kindred race, who reigned several years in Britain, whose memory must have long survived his fall, and whose exploits in a previous age must have been long remembered with pride by every nation of Teutonic blood.[18]

Whenever possible, Roman objects were seen as evidence of the inheritance of Roman culture and power rather than the continuation of Roman people and institutions and in every case the 'Britons' were not mentioned.

Burial rites

As well as artefacts which betray some legacy of Roman Britain within a new Germanic context, Anglo-Saxon burial rites were sometimes regarded as influenced by Roman practice. The use of Roman pot sherds as grave goods was first interpreted in this light by James Douglas, later supported by John Akerman. At Harnham Hill (Wiltshire), Akerman identified water-worn and abraded Roman pottery sherds placed in Saxon graves and called up Hamlet Act V Scene I as

---

[14] E. Wilkins, E. Kell and J. Locke, 'Examination of an Anglo-Saxon Barrow on Bowcombe Down, Isle of Wight', *Journal of the British Archaeological Association* 106 (1860), 253–61.

[15] Thomas Wright, 'On Recent Discoveries of Anglo-Saxon Antiquities', *Journal of the British Archaeological Association* 2 (1847), 50–9, at p. 58.

[16] John Yonge Akerman, 'An Account of the Discovery of Anglo-Saxon Remains at Kemble, in North Wiltshire', *Arch* 37 (1857), 113–21, at p. 115; Septimus Davidson, '… account of the discovery … of Antiquities on Snape Common, Suffolk', *Proceeding of the Society of Antiquaries London*, 2nd Series 2 (1863), 177–82, at p. 182; Charles Roach-Smith, 'Anglo-Saxon Remains Recently Discovered in Kent, in Cambridgeshire, and in some other counties', *Collectanea Antiqua* 6 (1868), 136–72, at p. 164; Thomas Wright, *The Celt, the Roman, and the Saxon*, at p. 427.

[17] E.g. John Yonge Akerman, *Remains of Pagan Saxondom* (London, 1855); Thomas Wright, 'On Antiquarian Excavations and Researches in the Middle Ages', *Arch* 30 (1844), 438–57.

[18] John Yonge Akerman, 'An Account of the Discovery of Anglo-Saxon Remains at Kemble, in North Wiltshire', *Arch* 37 (1857), 113–21, at p. 114.

supporting evidence for their deliberate interment.[19] The practice of burying coins in graves was also seen as a continuation of Roman rites. Similarly John Brent interpreted the provision of vessels with the dead at Stowting (Kent) as reflective of lingering vestiges of Roman afterlife beliefs.[20] Apart from the Germanic choice for weapon-burial and cremation, the practice of placing vessels and personal possessions with the dead led Roach Smith to observe that:

> ... the sepulchral ceremonies of the two nations very closely resembled each other, with the exception of the interment of the weapon of war, which is the chief characteristic of the graves of the Teutonic peoples.

Both contrasts and comparisons between Roman and Saxon graves were facilitated by instances when graves of both periods were found on the same site. When George Rolleston excavated at Frilford (Oxfordshire), he found five types of grave; two distinctively Roman graves and three characteristically Saxon. The burial rites as described by Rolleston charted British history from the later Roman period, with high-status lead coffin burials and poorer graves with wooden coffins, through the Saxon pagan period, with cremation and furnished inhumation burials, to instances of poorly furnished graves that he regarded as transitional between pagan and Christian.[21]

A final example exemplifies how burial rites were used to infer both racial identities but also racial interactions, albeit concerning an object now thought to be of dubious authenticity. Charles Roach-Smith discussed a cinerary urn from Joseph Mayer's collection with typical 'Anglo-Saxon' decoration and containing cremated bone and Saxon artefacts but bearing the Latin inscription: 'Laelia Rufina, who lived thirteen years, three months and six days'. Although a clear forgery by modern standards, Roach-Smith thought the urn to be genuine and to derive from the well-known cremation cemetery at Spong Hill, North Elmham:

> If the urn came from the ancient cemetery at North Elmham, as most probably it did, it shows that in one instance, at least, a Roman family interred the remains of its dead conjointly with the Saxons, presuming the generality of the urns found there contain the bones of Saxons and not of Romans of a very late time. We have found the Saxons and the Romans reposing in other burial places side by side; and here they would seem to hold the same posthumous relationship. The inference that may be drawn from these facts is antagonistic to the popular idea that the advent of the Saxons into Britain was attended with hostility, and with carnage and extermination of the population of Britain.[22]

---

[19] John Yonge Akerman, 'An Account of Excavations in an Anglo-Saxon Burial-Ground at Harnham Hill near Salisbury', *Arch* 35 (1855), 259–78, at p. 265.

[20] John Brent 'An Account of Researches in an Anglo-Saxon Cemetery at Stowting, in Kent, during the autumn of 1866', *Arch* 41 (1867), 409–20 at p. 418.

[21] George Rolleston, 'Researches and Excavations carried on in an Ancient Cemetery at Frilford, near Abingdon, Berks, in the years 1867–1868', *Arch* 42 (1869), 417–83.

[22] Charles Roach-Smith, 'Inscribed Funereal Urn in the Museum of Joseph Mayer', *Collectanea Antiqua* V (1861), 115–21, at pp. 120–1.

Therefore, Roach-Smith's passion for Roman antiquities clearly encouraged his view that the Saxons interacted with and adopted Roman customs and beliefs.

Bones

So far we have seen how artefacts and burial rites were used to distinguish and infer interactions between the Roman and Saxon 'races' while excluding the Britons from the picture, but the skeletons were made to tell racial history as well. Throughout the period in question, craniological and skeletal examinations of selected material from Anglo-Saxon cemeteries increasingly took place alongside incidental observations. Skeletal age, sex, stature, robust-ness and dental condition, as well as skull size and shape, were among the attributes used to infer race, class and the civilising tendencies manifested by individual skeletons and whole cemetery populations.[23] For example, John Thurnam applied this approach to the skulls recovered during excavations at Lamel Hill near York.[24] As a rule, elongated rather than round skulls indicated Teutonic rather than Celtic origins,[25] while a tall stature was also considered an indication of Germanic rather than British descent.[26] As well as race, skulls were viewed in terms of an index of civilization, with the Lamel Hill skulls regarded as 'Teutonic' but inferior to modern skulls, indicating a lower order of culture.[27] Likewise, for skulls from Harnham Hill, Thurnam combined race, class and intellect in his assessment that they were Teutonic but did not show 'a high grade of intellectual endowment or mental cultivation', suggesting that they belonged to '... the lower ranks of the West Saxon settlers and conquerors'.[28]

A particularly important site used to contrast the bones of Romans and Saxons was unearthed by George Rolleston's excavations at Frilford, mentioned above. Rolleston was an Oxford Professor of Anatomy and his excavation report dedicated more attention to the bones of the 123 skeletons recovered than to the usual descriptions of grave goods. He noted a contrast between the age profiles of the Roman and Anglo-Saxon graves; with the Roman burials tending to be of older men while the Saxon graves contained younger individuals. He interpreted this difference using an analogy drawn from the contemporary imperial world of Britain's colonies overseas, as if between

> a civilized Christian village and that of an outlying station on the border-land between some gradually advancing empire, and the territories of some gradually receding but intermittently aggressive aborigines.

---

[23] M. Morse, 'Craniology and the Adoption of the Three-Age System in Britain', *Proceedings of the Prehistoric Society* 65 (1999), 1–16.

[24] John Thurnam, 'Description of an Ancient Tumular Cemetery, probably of the Anglo-Saxon Period, at Lamel-Hill, near York', *ArchJ* 6 (1849), 27–39, 123–36.

[25] Thurnam, 'Description', 128–30.

[26] Thurnam, 'Description', 132.

[27] Thurnam, 'Description', 130.

[28] John Thurnam in John Yonge Akerman, 'An Account of Excavations in an Anglo-Saxon Burial-Ground at Harnham Hill near Salisbury', *Arch* 35 (1855), 259–78, at p. 275.

Rolleston seems to be explicitly contrasting Roman with Saxon, therefore. Meanwhile he appears to implicitly admit the presence of Britons in early Saxon England, but consigned to the role of intransigent and faceless natives resisting the onslaught of Saxon 'progress'.[29]

Rolleston then used the shape of crania as evidence for the race, class and intellect of the skeletons. He identified different types of Roman skulls, explained by the fact that both Romans and Romano-Britons lived together and race did not define Roman citizenship.[30] Two skeletons in lead coffins were distinguished as strong and tall; one with a 'lofty' cranium was thought indicative of British birth and blood (a 'Romanised Celt') while the other was interpreted as broad and low and therefore of Mediterranean (Roman) origin.[31] The other crania were considered less impressive but still civilised, with only one skeleton seen as 'British' and assumed to have been a slave.[32] For Rolleston, and for other contemporaries like Thomas Wright, the fate of the Britons is explained not by genocide but by the fact that they had already fled, become extinct, enslaved or inter-bred with more civilised Romans by the time the Saxons had arrived, making their fate or presence then neither important nor relevant. Rolleston envisages Saxon incomers encountering 'Romans' in towns but no distinct group of 'Britons'. This in turn explains why Rolleston does not dwell on his inability to distinguish clearly between Roman and Saxon skulls and even suggests that Romans may have intermarried with the Anglo-Saxons. Such a view perhaps seemed the more acceptable to Rolleston as allowing the Anglo-Saxons to be seen as inheritors of the Roman civilised intellect but not the primitive traits of the British.[33] These examples illustrate that while bones were used to distinguish Romans from Teutons, 'Celtic' skull types were only to be found in prehistoric graves and no attempt was made to suggest the intermarriage or even the presence of Britons in Saxon cemeteries.

Monuments

Let us now move on to discuss how the monumental form of graves distinguished Britons and Romans from Saxons. The form of early Anglo-Saxon barrows was seen as evidence of their distinctive racial character. Although Victorian archaeologists were cautious in attributing date and race from the morphology of monuments alone, following the discoveries of Bryan Faussett and James Douglas as well as excavations by John Akerman, Saxon barrows were regarded as comparatively small but typically clustered in large cemeteries. In contrast, 'British' (i.e. prehistoric) and Roman barrows were deemed to be larger and of more distinctive character.[34] For instance, John Akerman was able to contrast his discovery

---

[29] Rolleston, 'Researches and Excavations', at p. 431.
[30] Rolleston, 'Researches and Excavations', at p. 449.
[31] Rolleston, 'Researches and Excavations', at pp. 450–52.
[32] Rolleston, 'Researches and Excavations', at p. 459.
[33] Rolleston, 'Researches and Excavations', at pp. 462–5.
[34] John Yonge Akerman, 'An Account of the Opening of a Considerable Number of Tumuli on Breach Downs, in the County of Kent, *Arch* 30 (1844), 47–56; Thomas Wright, 'On Recent Discoveries of Anglo-Saxon Antiquities', *Journal of the British Archaeological Association*

of Saxon barrows on Breach Down in Kent, with British barrows uncovered and reported in the pages of *Archaeologia*.[35] Indeed, the well-known conical barrows at the Bartlow Hills, Ashdon (Essex), were systematically excavated by John Gage and published in the pages of *Archaeologia*, seemingly indicating a link between the external form of the monument and the distinctly Roman burial rites they contained.[36]

Monuments emphasised racial distinctions in another way. The early medieval practice of re-using prehistoric and Roman monuments was identified by Victorian barrow-diggers at sites like Chavenage (Gloucestershire), Linton Heath (Cambridgeshire) and Oldbury (Warwickshire).[37] Similarly, the Peak District archaeologist, Thomas Bateman, uncovered innumerable examples of Anglo-Saxon graves inserted into British barrows.[38] Unlike Sir Richard Colt Hoare, who thought secondary barrow burials with iron implements were also 'British', many were now aware that these represented graves of separate periods and races.[39] Therefore, although the archaeological technique of stratigraphy was still in its infancy, prehistoric and Roman burial mounds re-used by Saxon graves offered to the nineteenth-century archaeologists a clear chronology of British history in microcosm. Each phase of the burial-mound's use offered a separate and successive phase of settlement by different races. Although this author is aware of few explicit, nineteenth-century interpretations of this monument re-use, it provided implicit support, at least, for the view that the British were 'pre-Roman' and had no place in the archaeology of Anglo-Saxon cemeteries. It may have also enhanced the idea that the Saxon invaders were the legitimate heirs to the British and Roman past.

Landscape

Although Victorian-period discussions of early medieval graves focus their attention upon the grave goods interred with the dead, we have seen how burial rites, bones and monuments were also considered. Even the location and landscape

---

2 (1847), 50–9; Thomas Wright, 'On Anglo-Saxon Antiquities, with a particular reference to the Faussett Collection', in *Essays on Archaeological Subjects Volume 1*, ed. Thomas Wright (London: John Russell Smith, 1861), pp. 107–71, at p. 109.

[35] For example, Lord Londesborough, 'An Account of the Opening of Some Tumuli in the East Riding of Yorkshire, *Arch* 34 (1852), 251–58.

[36] John Gage, '... a plan of barrows called the Bartlow Hills, in the parish of Ashdon, in Essex, with an account of Roman sepulchral relics recently discovered in the lesser Barrows', *Arch* 25 (1833), 1–23; John Gage, '... the recent discovery of Roman sepulchral relics in one of the greater Barrows at Bartlow ...', *Arch* 26 (1835), 300–17; John Gage, '... an account of further discoveries of Roman sepulchral relics at the Bartlow Hills', *Arch* 28 (1840), 1–6; John Gage, '... account of the final excavations made at the Bartlow Hills', *Arch* 29 (1842), 1–4.

[37] Richard C. Neville, 'Anglo-Saxon Cemetery Excavated, January 1853', *ArchJ* 11 (1854), 95–115; Charles Roach-Smith, 'Warwickshire Antiquities', *Collectanea Antiqua* 1 (1848), 33–48, at p. 35; Thomas Wright, 'Saxon Remains Found in Gloucestershire', *Journal of the British Archaeological Association* 4 (1849), 50–4.

[38] Thomas Bateman, *Ten Years' Diggings in Celtic and Saxon Grave Hills in the Counties of Derby, Stafford, and York, from 1848 to 1858* (London, 1861).

[39] Richard Colt Hoare, *The Ancient History of Wiltshire, Volume 1* (Salisbury, 1812).

context of cemeteries were drawn into the interpretations of the historical significance of furnished burials.

It became customary when discussing Saxon cemeteries to employ the British and Roman archaeology of the environs to provide an historical backdrop to the Saxon invasions. In these accounts, hillforts were regarded as possible refuges used by natives fleeing from the Saxons, while forests and uplands were inhabited by the dispossessed Britons.[40] Meanwhile, linear earthworks could have been raised by Britons as they retreated westwards under the onslaught of Teutonic hordes.[41] Ancient monuments like Wayland's Smithy illustrated the antiquity of the British presence in the landscape prior to the coming of the Saxons, but they also highlighted that this was a race unknown to the Saxons, a dead race of the past rather than a vibrant contemporary culture. These were monuments ripe for appropriation with new names, myths and associations by the invading Anglo-Saxons.[42] This view is clear in many of the excavation reports and archaeological accounts:

> When our forefathers came into this island, they found it covered with Roman towns and buildings, as well as with monuments of an earlier population, in the shape of cromlechs, vast entrenchments and other similar works. With the character and uses of the Roman buildings they were perfectly well acquainted; but they looked with greater reverence on cromlechs, and barrows, and indeed on all earthworks of which the origin was not very apparent, because their own superstitions had taught them to attribute such structures to the primeval giants of their mythology, who were objects of dread even to the gods themselves.[43]

According to this view, the Britons were already a thing of the past.

The location of Anglo-Saxon cemeteries was sometimes used to support the view of Germanic settlement at the expense of the indigenous population, drawing upon images of military conquest followed by settlement very much inspired by the written accounts of Gildas and Bede. When William Wylie explored the Saxon cemetery at Fairford,[44] he felt that its proximity to the present village implied continuity from a Saxon past to the Victorian present. Yet its location also implied dislocation from the British and Roman past. Wylie paints a picture of the local Britons, the *Dobunni*, displaced out of the fertile valleys of the Upper Thames region into the Cotswolds, echoing the imagery of Gildas's account of Britons fleeing into the wilderness:

---

[40] I.W., 'Berkshire Antiquities', *ArchJ* 5 (1848), 279–91, at p. 286.

[41] Edwin Guest, 'On the Early English Settlements in South Britain', *Proceedings of the Archaeological Institute* (1849), 28–72; Edwin Guest, 'On the boundaries that separated the Welsh and English races during the seventy-five years which followed the capture of Bath, AD 577, with speculations as to the Welsh Princes who during that period were reigning over Somersetshire', *Archaeologia Cambrensis*, third series 28 (1861), 269–92.

[42] John Yonge Akerman, 'Observations on the celebrated Monument at Ashbury, in the county of Berks, called "Wayland Smith's Cave"', *Arch* 32 (1847), 312–14; Thomas Wright, 'On the Legend of Weland the Smith', *Arch* 32 (1847), 315–24; William Wylie, *Fairford Graves* (Oxford, 1852).

[43] Wright, 'Weland the Smith', p. 315.

[44] Wylie, *Fairford Graves*.

> Some of them [the Britons] may have taken refuge, and maintained a precarious existence, among the (at that period) wild recesses and dense thickets of the Cotswold Hills, where the invader would scarcely care to follow them.[45]

Relationships between Saxon cemeteries and Roman sites also fuelled the imagination of early archaeologists. Many painted a picture of a late-Roman landscape of villas, towns and forts in various states of decay when the Saxons arrived, while others saw the proximity of Roman and Saxon burial sites as evidence of the succession of one race and another. Roach-Smith and Wright were both aware that Anglo-Saxon graves were sometimes found near Roman towns and fortresses and in different publications they came to varying explanations for these relationships, from the expedient use of Roman ruins for raw materials to a model of overlap in which continuities might be seen, particularly in the respect for the same burial grounds.[46] At Northfleet, the Saxons used localities for burial

> ... which had previously been used for like purposes by the Romans and the presence of Saxon urns in graves which contained skeletons indicates the partial adoption of usages which customs had stamped as sacred, after those usages had become superseded by others of a totally different character.[47]

Roach-Smith and Wright increasingly saw this as evidence for an 'amicable relationship' between Romans and Saxons,[48] with Wright even suggesting that Roman life may have survived in towns, while Saxon life flourished in the surrounding countryside, as evidenced by the rural locations of cemeteries, with both races contributing to the emergence of medieval England.[49] The replacement of Roman by Saxon in the towns was therefore seen as gradual. Moreover, Wright argues that this was a process that began in the Roman period itself with the stationing of barbarian mercenaries and federate troops, so that the 'Romans' were in effect Teutonic brothers of the Anglo-Saxons.[50] The funerary context of this connection between Romans and Saxons is also recognised. At Frilford, where, as we have seen, Roman and Saxon graves were uncovered, Rolleston noted that the 'rightful succession' of one race and another can be seen in the fact that 'The

---

[45] Wylie, *Fairford Graves*, at p. 8.
[46] Charles Roach-Smith, 'Warwickshire Antiquities', *Collectanea Antiqua* 1 (1848), 33–48, at pp. 45–6.
[47] Charles Roach-Smith, 'Discovery of Anglo-Saxon Remains at Northfleet, Kent', *Journal of the British Archaeological Association* 3 (1848), 235–340, at p. 238.
[48] Charles Roach-Smith, *Inventorium Sepulchrale*, p. xlix.
[49] *Ibid.*, p. xlix; Charles Roach-Smith, 'Anglo-Saxon Remains Found in Kent and Lincolnshire', *Collectanea Antiqua* 5 (1861), 129–40, at pp. 129–30; Thomas Wright, 'On Recent Discoveries of Anglo-Saxon Antiquities', *Journal of the British Archaeological Association* 2 (1847), 50–9, at p. 51.
[50] Thomas Wright, 'On the Ethnology of South Britain at the End of the Extinction of the Roman Government in the Island', in *Essays on Archaeological Subjects Volume 1*, ed. Thomas Wright (London, 1861), pp. 67–84; Thomas Wright, 'On Recent Discoveries of Anglo-Saxon Antiquities', *Journal of the British Archaeological Association* 2 (1847), 50–9.

Saxons ... had no reluctance against burying in the ground which held the bones of the former lords of the soil.'[51]

Discussion

How should we interpret this brief review of mid-nineteenth-century studies of early medieval graves? At one level, a short answer seems clear: Britons fail to make an appearance within Victorian interpretations of early medieval graves as an explicitly defined sub-Roman population. They are either assumed to be not present or not important. This is however, not to say that Victorian students of early medieval graves were racial purists. While some regarded furnished cremation and inhumation graves as purely Teutonic, those familiar with Roman material culture entertained the influence of Roman objects, culture and people in the Saxon period as a civilising force, particularly in Kent. Whether violent or peaceful, whether overlapping or discrete, the relationship of Romans and Saxons was successive, the latter replacing and inheriting the landscape of the former. This was a view that Richard Hingley has argued to have grown in importance in the later nineteenth century.[52] Yet this view could not and would not write Britons into the equation other than as subsumed within the Roman race and Roman culture, as the victims of Saxon weapons, or as refuges fleeing to the hills and to the west. Therefore, if as Bonnie Effros has recently argued, nineteenth-century discussions of early medieval graves and material culture constituted a material dimension to the construction of origin myths for nineteenth-century nation states,[53] then in an Anglo-Saxon context it was a myth that incorporated both remembering and forgetting. The key element that was 'forgotten' was the Britons, and with this strategic amnesia, early medieval graves could be regarded as indisputably Anglo-Saxon, through and through.

To provide a broader context for this 'forgetting' of the Britons, we can cite the development of racial theory and of 'Anglo-Saxonism', in particular, in contrasting the racial identities of the Celts (or Britons) with that of the Germans (or English) during the eighteenth and nineteenth centuries.[54] The origins of British archaeology should be referred to as 'imperialist' rather than purely 'nationalist', and the celebration of English origins was sustained through being contrasted with native 'savages' and 'primitives' encountered and subjugated both outside the British Isles and within it.[55] It could be used as evidence of an inherent racial bias predicated upon contemporary antagonism towards the 'Celts' of Wales, Scotland and Ireland among the middle and upper-class Victorian English, exhibited in historical and philological research as well as contemporary literature.

---

[51] Rolleston, 'Researches and Excavations', at p. 434.
[52] Richard Hingley, *Roman Officers and English Gentlemen* (London, 2000).
[53] Effros, 'Memories of the Early Medieval Past', p. 276.
[54] For definitions and discussions of Anglo-Saxonism, see *Anglo-Saxonism and the Construction of Social Identity*, ed. Allen Frantzen and John Niles (Gainsville, FL, 1997).
[55] Peter Bowler, 'From "Savage" to "Primitive": Victorian Evolutionism and the Interpretation of Marginalized Peoples', *Ant* 66 (1992), 721–9; Bruce Trigger, 'Alternative Archaeologies: Nationalist, Colonialist, Imperialist', *Man* 19 (1984), 355–70.

In contrast to eighteenth-century antiquarianism, the new emphasis upon racial theory could not suffer the idea of a mixed origin for the English.[56]

However, the rejection of the Britons may have other related contexts within the development of archaeological thought. The eighteenth- and early nineteenth-century 'imaginative' approaches epitomised by the druidical interpretations of prehistoric monuments by William Stukeley were deemed unacceptable 'failings' to the self-consciously 'scientific' archaeology of the 1840s and 1850s, the aim of which was the gradual accumulation of 'facts' rather than theory.[57] Therefore the 'forgetting' of the Britons by scholars of Anglo-Saxon graves may have been an attempt to justify current perspectives and distance themselves from attempts to root English culture in Celts and druids.

Equally, many of the scholars of Anglo-Saxon graves such as Thomas Wright and John Kemble were strong critics of the Danish Three Age System then being promoted in Britain by Jens Worsaae (splitting prehistory into ages of stone, bronze and iron), and were dismissive of the sophistication and longevity of prehistoric cultures prior to the Romans.[58] For these scholars, Britons was both a chronological and racial term which was increasingly refined as 'Celtic' in the mid-nineteenth century with reference to the pre-Roman Iron Age.[59] In this light 'Britons' simultaneously implied 'pre-Roman' chronology as well as a particular racial identity, neatly consigning the Britons to the comparatively distant past as well as to the outer edge of Britain. Conversely, it may have been a deliberate snub to these scholars that motivated Daniel Wilson, Britain's earliest proponent of the Three Age system, to be among those to challenge the Anglo-Saxon label applied to early medieval brooches and instead to suggest that they belonged to 'Romanised Britons'.[60]

A further influence may have been the increasing study of early medieval inscribed stones from the west and north of Britain. These 'Celtic crosses' seemingly provided distinctive material remains for the Britons that could not be more

---

[56] L. P. Curtis, Jr, *Anglo-Saxons and Celts. A Study of Anti-Irish Prejudice in Victorian England* (Berkeley, CA, 1968); Reginald Horsman, 'Origins of Racial Anglo-Saxonism in Great Britain before 1850', *Journal of the History of Ideas* 37 (1976), 387–410; H. A. MacDougall, *Racial Myth in English History – Trojans, Teutons, and Anglo-Saxons* (Montreal, 1982); Sam Smiles, *The Image of Antiquity: Ancient Britain and the Romantic Imagination* (London, 1994), pp. 113–28; D. White, 'Changing Views of the Adventus Saxonum for Nineteenth and Twentieth Century English Scholarship', *Journal of the History of Ideas* 32 (1971), 585–94.

[57] e.g. Thomas Bateman, 'On Early Burial-Places in the County of Nottingham', *Journal of the British Archaeological Association* 8 (1853), 183–92; Thomas Wright, 'On the Progress and Present Condition of Archaeological Science', *Journal of the British Archaeological Association* 22 (1846), 64–84.

[58] J. J. A. Worsaae, *The Primeval Antiquities of Denmark* (London, 1849); Judith Wilkins, 'Worsaae and British Antiquities', *Ant* 35 (1961), 214–20.

[59] Simon James, *The Atlantic Celts: Ancient People or Modern Invention* (London, 1999), pp. 44–58.

[60] Daniel Wilson, 'On the Advantages Derived from Archaeological Investigation', *Proceedings of the Archaeological Institute* (1852), 1–14 at p. 12; Thomas Wright challenges this assertion in Thomas Wright, 'On Anglo-Saxon Antiquities', p. 123.

different from the furnished graves of southern and eastern England.[61] Similarly, the early medieval sites of Ireland were different yet again, exemplified by the discoveries of crannogs such as Lagore,[62] and the passage grave tombs such as Newgrange that were assigned to a comparable chronology by writers in this period.[63] The juxtaposition of such reports with discussions of 'Anglo-Saxon' graves at the meetings of the national societies, and often published within the same journal, may have emphasised the distinctive material and racial identities of 'Celt' and 'Saxon'.

In turn, these arguments could be used to encourage wariness concerning the pervading influences of contemporary culture upon our interpretations of furnished, early medieval graves. We might cite the influence of these early studies upon our continuing willingness to impose ethnic and racial labels onto archaeological finds and graves. Indeed, it can be confidently suggested that the very desire to find the 'missing' Britons in twentieth-century, Anglo-Saxon archaeology is itself a century-long struggle to renegotiate the 'forgetting' of the Britons in the context of Anglo-Saxon graves by the generations of scholars who have gone before.

Conclusion

This is, perhaps, an unsurprising discussion given recent developments in archaeological theory that emphasise the self-critical analysis of our ideas, their origins and socio-political context. Yet we can augment previous studies by emphasising the variety of elements of early medieval graves that were drawn into the argument in nineteenth-century studies: not only grave goods but also burial rites, bones, monuments and landscape. Indeed, it is worthy of note that it is in the final theme, landscape, that we see most explicitly the fate of the Britons addressed. This finds a resonance with the contemporary geographical history of Edwin Guest who, while ignoring the evidence of Anglo-Saxon graves, used the *Anglo-Saxon Chronicle*, dykes and the British landscape to chart his vision of the settlement and expansion of the earliest English and the westward flight of the Britons.[64]

However, I would instead like to conclude with some further points that derive from this review which are highly relevant to contemporary discussions of the Britons in Anglo-Saxon England. If we can suggest that the application of the

---

[61] J. O. Westwood, *Lapidarium Walliae: the Early Inscribed and Sculptured Stones of Wales* (Oxford, 1876–9).

[62] F. W. Wakeman, 'Irish Antiquities of the Saxon Period', *Collectanea Antiqua* 3 (1854), 37–44; see also C. Stephen Briggs, 'A Historiography of the Irish Crannog: the Discovery of Lagore as Prologue to Wood-Martin's Lake Dwellings of Ireland of 1886', *AntJ* 79 (1999), 347–77.

[63] D. C. Harvey, '"National" Identities and the Politics of Ancient Heritage: Continuity and Change at Ancient Monuments in Britain and Ireland c. 1675–1850', *Transactions of the Institute of British Geographers*, new series 28 (4) (2003), 473–87.

[64] Edwin Guest, 'On the Early English Settlements in South Britain', *Proceedings of the Archaeological Institute* (1849), 28–72; D. White, 'Changing Views of the Adventus Saxonum for Nineteenth and Twentieth Century English Scholarship', *Journal of the History of Ideas* 32 (1971), 585–94.

label 'Anglo-Saxon' to early medieval graves has its origins in Victorian Anglo-Saxonism and, therefore, is not only tarnished by racial theories but also theoretically problematic for dealing profitably and meaningfully with early medieval archaeological remains, then we must equally challenge, and perhaps reject, the antithetical racial identity that was suppressed in Victorian writings. Until we do so, our debates concerning social and cultural change from the archaeological evidence will simply be discussions of how 'British' and how 'Germanic' was fifth- and sixth-century southern and eastern Britain. It is only when we realise that both terms, and the spectrum of possibilities between them, are based upon Victorian racial constructs, that we can begin to challenge the constellation of prejudices and biases that underpin our academic writing of early medieval archaeology and history. This author would argue that we should forget neither Britons nor Saxons, but equally challenge the meanings and origins of the labels we employ. The challenge then becomes to write new histories from the material evidence that are less obsessed with sustaining a racial and linguistic dichotomy of Britons and Saxons when studying early medieval graves.

4

Romano-British Metalworking and the Anglo-Saxons

LLOYD LAING*

THE decline in manufacturing which characterized late Roman Britain and the early post-Roman period has caused real difficulties in assessing the extent and degree of continuity which Anglo-Saxon workmanship exhibits with earlier Insular production, but metalworking is perhaps the one exception which can enable us to explore this interface. This paper will, therefore, seek to examine evidence for contact between Anglo-Saxon artificers and consumers of metalwork and traditions of production in late Roman and early post-Roman Britain. In the late Roman period in Britain, there is evidence for the development of distinctive types of personal adornment, which seem in general to be larger than their antecedents and to be made on occasion in silver, pointing to a new importance attached to these items as signifiers of social status. It may be pointed out that brooches, though ubiquitous in first- and second-century contexts in Britain, generally fell out of fashion in the third, the only types to remain in use being the crossbow, disc and penannular types. Crossbow brooches, which were particularly used as marks of rank,[1] do not seem to have been produced after the end of the Roman period, but their possible influence on the design of some Anglo-Saxon metalwork is discussed below. The use of brooches as insignia of office was well-established by the end of the Roman period and continued as late as the tenth century: Constantine Porphyrogenitos documents a ceremony in which the emperor pinned a fibula on the shoulder of a new official.[2]

Alongside brooches, long dress pins came into fashion: the immediate inspiration may have been some of the ornate pins found in late Roman contexts on the Continent, such as the Fécamp, Wijester and Muids types,[3] which are common in the Low Countries, and one of which comes from the Anglo-Saxon cemetery

---

* My thanks are due to Kevin Leahy, Nick Stoodley and Susan Youngs for information about particular finds which resulted in more complete distribution maps.
[1] E. Keller, *Die spätrömischen Grabfunde in Südbayern*, Veröffentlichungen der Kommission zur archaeologischen Erforschung des spätrömischen Raetien, Der Bayerischen Akademie der Wissenschaften 8 (Munich, 1972). See also Bruce N. Eagles, *The Anglo-Saxon Settlement of Humberside*, BAR, BS 68 (Oxford, 1979), p. 66.
[2] Edward James, *The Merovingian Archaeology of South-West Gaul* BAR, IS 251 (Oxford, 1977), p. 100.
[3] H. W. Böhme, *Germanische Grabfunde des 4. bis 5. Jahrhunderts. Zwischen unterer Elbe und Loire* (Munich, 1974), p. 35 and fig. 12.

at Gilton in Kent.[4] Previously, Romano-British pins had been intended for use in the hair, and had much shorter shanks.[5]

Surviving Romano-British Workshops

The workshops that produced these dress-accessories and other types of ornamental metalwork with their attendant art in the later fourth century seem to have continued in Britain in the fifth, if not the sixth century. The key area for demonstrating this has been the Bristol Channel/Severn Estuary area, though evidence is also forthcoming from further afield in Wiltshire. Here it would seem that various types of penannular brooch (particularly those of Fowler's Classes F and G) and pins (both proto-hand pins and large dress pins) were being produced at the time of the Anglo-Saxon settlements, and that enamelling was also in production, probably in the manufacture of hanging bowls and penannulars among other artefacts. Evidence of fifth/sixth century metalworking, including probably in enamel, is attested on a number of sites in the South West, notably the New Market Hall at Gloucester.[6] Other sites with evidence of continuing ornamental metalworking in the period under review include Cadbury Congresbury, where there was evidence for furnaces and gold, lead, enamel, non-ferrous scrap metal residues, molten glass and cullet,[7] Glastonbury Tor,[8] and Cannington (all in Somerset), where the cemetery produced an unfinished penannular brooch as well as two finished brooches of Fowler's Class G.[9] Although no working site was found at Cadbury Castle (Som.), scrap metal and an ingot pointed to industrial activity.[10] This continuing tradition of metalworking is most readily demonstrated in the South West, but there are indications that it was to be found in other parts of *Britannia*. There are now thirteen F penannular brooches from South Humberside, one enamelled, as well as a series of sixteen hanging bowls or their mounts.[11] Enamelled penannulars are now also documented from Norfolk and Yorkshire.

The art that characterizes hanging-bowl mounts and later so-called 'Celtic'

---

[4] W. A. van Es, 'Late-Roman Pins from Xanten/Dodewaard and Asselt', *Berichten van de Rijksdienst voor het Oudheikundig Bodemonderzoek* 17 (1967), 121–8.
[5] Hillary Cool, 'Roman Metal Hair Pins from Southern Britain', *ArchJ* 147 (1990), 148–82.
[6] M. Hassall and J. Rhodes, 'Excavations at the New Market Hall, Gloucester, 1966–67', *Transactions of the Bristol & Gloucester Archaeological Society* 92 (1974), 15–100, at p. 30.
[7] Philip Rahtz et al., *Cadbury Congresbury 1968–73: A Late/Post-Roman Hilltop Settlement in Somerset*, BAR, BS 223 (Oxford, 1992), p. 238.
[8] Philip Rahtz, 'Excavations at Glastonbury Tor, Somerset, 1964–6', *ArchJ* 127 (1971), 1–81, at p. 19.
[9] Philip Rahtz et al., *Cannington Cemetery* (London, 2000), p. 352.
[10] Leslie Alcock, *Cadbury Castle, Somerset* (Cardiff, 1995), p.125.
[11] Information by courtesy of Kevin Leahy, Scunthorpe Museum. Many of the hanging bowls are listed in Rupert Bruce-Mitford, 'Late-Celtic Hanging-Bowls in Lincolnshire and South Humberside', in *Pre-Viking Lindsey*, ed. Alan Vince (Lincoln, 1993), pp. 45–70.

art of the early medieval period originated from metalwork in the Roman period, where in the fourth century such ornamental devices as triskeles, peltas, confronted trumpets and dodo-heads or eyed scrolls abound. This art was developed in the fifth and sixth centuries and had an impact on the Anglo-Saxons, as did certain types of artefacts displaying it and some of the technological skills of the British workshops.

Romano-British Ornamental Techniques and the Anglo-Saxons

Enamelling

Enamelling was not practised by the Anglo-Saxons in their homelands but is found, albeit to a restricted extent, in England, where it was presumably acquired from the Britons. A series of square-headed brooches display this feature, five of which may come from south-east Cambridgeshire, but with others coming from Sleaford (Lincs.), near Beverley (Yorks.), Emscote (Warwicks.), and Lakenheath (Suffolk).[12] Enamelling also appears to have been employed on a disc brooch from Ebrington (Glos.), on a disk from Great Saxham (Suffolk),[13] on a disk mount from Hockwold-cum-Wilton (Norfolk), a saucer brooch and a cruciform brooch from Bury St Edmunds (Suffolk),[14] as well as, arguably, a disc from Barton (Suffolk).[15] I have expressed my doubts as to whether the Barton disc is in fact Anglo-Saxon,[16] but, to extend the distribution of Anglo-Saxon enamelling, mention may be made of the bucket with enamelled mounts from Great Chesterford (Essex),[17] the enamelled spearhead from the Anglo-Saxon burial at Lowbury (Berks.),[18] the sixth-century cruciform brooch fragment from Scopwith (Lincs.),[19] or the garnet and filigree disc brooch from Gilton (Kent), found by Faussett in 1771.[20] It has frequently been suggested that enamelling was a localized phenomenon in the north Suffolk/Cambridgeshire area (first mooted by Fox in 1923 and repeated subsequently), but the overall distribution, while not conflicting with this suggestion as one possible area for production, does not explain all the finds. The fairly

---

[12] John Hines, *A New Corpus of Anglo-Saxon Great Square Headed Brooches* (London, 1997), p. 220; Lloyd Laing, 'The Bradwell Mount and the Use of Millefiori in Post-Roman Britain', *Studia Celtica* 33 (1999), 137–53.

[13] Vera Evison, 'An Enamelled Disc from Great Saxham', *Proceedings of the Suffolk Institute of Archaeology and History* 34.1 (1977), 1–13.

[14] Christopher Scull, 'Enamelling on Early Anglo-Saxon Metalwork', *ASSAH* 4 (1985), 117–22, at p. 117: Cruciform brooch 118.

[15] David Brown, 'Swastika Patterns', in *Angles, Saxons and Jutes. Essays presented to J. N. L. Myres*, ed. Vera Evison (Oxford, 1981), pp. 227–35.

[16] Laing, 'Bradwell Mount'.

[17] Vera Evison, *An Anglo-Saxon Cemetery at Great Chesterford, Essex*, Council for British Archaeology Research Report 91 (York, 1994), pp. 22–4.

[18] Michael G. Fulford and Stephen J. Rippon, 'Lowbury Hill, Oxon: A Re-assessment of the Probable Romano-Celtic Temple and the Anglo-Saxon Barrow', *ArchJ* 151 (1994), 158–211, at p. 204.

[19] Kevin Leahy, *Anglo-Saxon Crafts* (Stroud, 2003), p. 160 and illus. 85.

[20] Ronald Jessup, *Anglo-Saxon Jewellery* (London, 1950), p. 37.

4.1 Distribution of Anglo-Saxon metalwork employing enamel, after Scull, 1985, with additions

wide distribution of enamelling might suggest that its presence on objects which might otherwise be considered of Anglo-Saxon derivation should not imply that they were necessarily produced by Romano-British survivors; this is particularly significant in the case of hanging bowls.

Niello

Niello, a black silver sulphide paste, was popular in late Saxon England in Trewhiddle Style metalwork. Long before this, however, it was employed on pagan Saxon disk brooches in filling in the zig-zag lines that made up the outer borders,[21] and appears on the gold buckle from Sutton Hoo (Suffolk). Niello was employed fairly widely in the Roman period but again like enamel did not enjoy much popularity among the Germanic peoples before the migrations. As with enamel, the niello found from the fifth century onwards is of somewhat different composition to that of the Roman, using silver/copper/sulphide.[22] Apart from on sixth-century disc brooches, it is found on Quoit Brooch Style metalwork.

Millefiori

Millefiori glass inlay is again a device commonly employed in Roman Britain, appearing on disc brooches from contexts as late as the fourth century. There is no evidence that the pagan Anglo-Saxons produced it, but they seem to have recycled Romano-British millefiori disc brooches and used sections as inlays, most notably in the Sutton Hoo shoulder clasps and purse lid. Recycled Romano-British millefiori was also used on three pendants, from Sibbertswold, Sarre and Milton Regis (all in Kent), and possibly on that from Woodyates (Dorset).[23] Millefiori was imitated using a paillon on the Kingston Brooch.

Punching

An ornamental technique current in late Roman Britain was the use of punches to build up decorative schemes. In his study of Quoit Brooch style metalwork, Inker has pointed out that the technique of having carved outlines and punched infill is a feature of Quoit Brooch style metalwork which is also found on the late Roman bracelets from Hoxne (Suffolk).[24] It is now fairly widely accepted that the origins of Quoit Brooch style metalwork in fifth-century Britain lie in a Romano-British past,[25] and indeed, the Quoit Brooch style represents *par excellence* the survival of Romano-British metalworking into the post-Roman period in the area of Anglo-Saxon settlement. It is worth noting, however, that the use of small punches to build up ornament is not confined to the Quoit Brooch style

---

[21] Michael Avent, *Anglo-Saxon Garnet Inlaid Disc and Composite Brooches,* BAR, BS 11 (Oxford, 1975), p. 13.

[22] Susan La Niece, 'Niello: an Historical and Technical Survey', *Antiquaries Journal* 63 (1983), 279–97.

[23] Laing, 'Bradwell Mount', 139–41.

[24] Peter Inker, 'Technology as Active Material Culture: The Quoit Brooch Style', *MedArch,* 44 (2000), 25–52, at p. 48.

[25] Seiichi Suzuki, *The Quoit Brooch Style and Anglo-Saxon Settlement* (Woodbridge, 2000), p. 109; Inker, 'Technology as Active Material Culture', p. 48.

but occurs also on many of the disc, cruciform and small-long brooches current in the later fifth and sixth centuries in England. As far as I am aware, although punches were used on occasion as part of the decoration on Migration Period pieces on the Continent, they were not used as the exclusive decorative device in the way in which they were on Anglo-Saxon brooches.

Romano-British Artefacts and the Anglo-Saxons

Brooches

Disc brooches were not taken up by Britons outside the former confines of *Britannia* in the centuries following the withdrawal of Roman rule, but there is certainly evidence that they were in production into the last years of the Roman period, and may well have continued to be produced thereafter, when they may have been the inspiration for the many types of disc brooch found in pagan Anglo-Saxon England, as Leeds first suggested.[26] Although disc brooches are found in later Frankish contexts, they seem to have been developed in England in the period 450–550. Tania Dickinson, in her studies of these brooches, has pointed out that they employ techniques which are characteristic of late Roman workshops, namely the use of stamps, nicked edges and rough casting.[27] She favoured the view that their production was concentrated in the Upper Thames region. Although disc brooches were fashionable in the second century, when many types were enamelled, the type favoured in the fourth had a central glass setting and concentric ornament, sometimes also displaying gilding. There are several examples from fourth-century contexts, including one from Nettleton (Wilts.), from a sealed context dated to around 360,[28] and two from the hoard of Valentinian and Theodosian *solidi* from Newgrange, Ireland.[29] Their association with this find is significant, since it implies their status value as offerings. There are a considerable number of these from Anglo-Saxon cemeteries: Roger White has listed sixteen,[30] although they may have been selected as substitutes on account of their similarity to Anglo-Saxon disc brooches.[31] It is certainly likely that they were around, if not in production, at the time of the Anglo-Saxon Settlements.

Various types of penannular brooch developed in the fourth century. A scheme for those brooches which were seen to survive into the fifth and sixth centuries

---

[26] E. T. Leeds, 'The Distribution of the Angles and Saxons Archaeologically Considered', *Arch* 91 (1945), 1–106, at p. 52.

[27] Tania Dickinson, 'On the Origin and Chronology of the Early Anglo-Saxon Disc Brooch', *ASSAH* 1 (1979), 39–80, at pp. 39–41, 51.

[28] William J. Wedlake, *The Shrine of Apollo at Nettleton, Wilts*, Society of Antiquaries of London Research Report 40 (London, 1982), p. 148, fig. 23/5.

[29] R. A. G. Carson and Claire O'Kelly, 'A catalogue of the Roman coins from Newgrange, Co. Meath', *Proceedings of the Royal Irish Academy* 77C (1977), 35–55, at p. 52.

[30] Roger White, *Roman and Celtic Objects from Anglo-Saxon Graves. A Catalogue and an Interpretation of their Use*, BAR, BS 191 (Oxford, 1988), pp. 26–8.

[31] Roger White, 'Scrap or Substitute: Roman Material in Anglo-Saxon Graves', in *Anglo-Saxon Cemeteries: A Reappraisal*, ed. E. Southworth (Stroud, 1990), pp. 125–52, at p. 146.

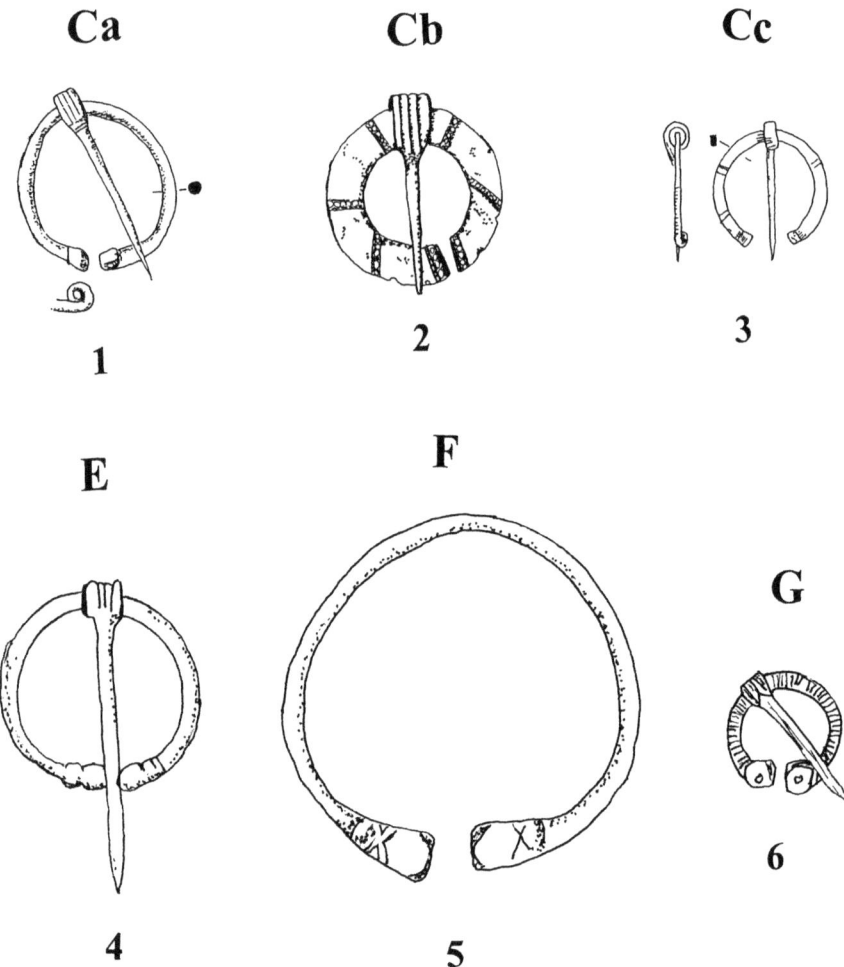

4.2 Types of pennanular brooches found in pagan Anglo-Saxon contexts. 1: Holywell Row 83, Cambs.; 2: Highdown 73, Sussex; 3: Winnall II 8, Hants; 4: Broughton Lodge 58, Notts.; 5: Bifrons 6, Kent; 6: Fairford 31, Glos.

was advanced by Elizabeth Fowler,[32] in which she defined in particular Classes E and F (the so-called 'zoomorphic' types), Classes G and H, and a number of others which are comparatively rare and which do not readily fit into her scheme. Of these Class H is a development of the sixth century which is not represented in Anglo-Saxon contexts and therefore not considered here. The remaining classes are, however, found in Anglo-Saxon graves, along with types which are not found in the 'Celtic West' or only very rarely. It is worth noting now that some of the brooch types found in late Roman and post-Roman Britain have relatively restricted distributions. Fowler's Class C is largely confined to the South East of England, Class G to the Severn Estuary, Class D7 to Hadrian's Wall (though examples are found as far south as Norfolk) and Class F to, again, the Severn region and to Humberside.

A particular type of penannular brooch is in fact the commonest in Anglo-Saxon contexts: Fowler's Class C. These are characterized by terminals which are rolled or turned over, and were for long seen as a pre-Roman type which survived into the later first century AD, but then disappeared. Since the publication of late Roman examples from Colchester (Essex),[33] it has been recognized that Class C brooches enjoyed a new vogue in the fourth century, during which three distinctive types were current. Like the Iron-Age examples, the late occurrences enjoy a distribution which is largely confined to south-east Britain. Ca has a round-sectioned or D-sectioned hoop and curled over terminals, Cb has a flattened, rectangular-sectioned hoop, sometimes with linear engraving, and curled-over terminals, and Cc has flattened, folded-over terminals rather than a coil. Ca was current at Colchester, AD 350–450,[34] Cb remained in use in the later fourth to early fifth century, as indicated by a find from Chichester (Sussex),[35] and Cc was still around in the early fifth century, as shown by an example from Verulamium (Herts.).[36] This was of the flattened hoop variety, but later fourth-century examples with circular hoops are known from Portchester (Hants),[37] again Verulamium[38] and Wroxeter (Salop).[39] That C brooches were finding their way into Anglo-Saxon graves in the fifth century is shown by the Cb brooch from Mucking II (Essex) grave 979, which was dated by Evison to the early fifth

---

[32] Elizabeth Fowler, 'Celtic Metalwork of the Fifth and Sixth Centuries AD', *ArchJ* 120 (1963), 98–160.
[33] Nina Crummy, *Colchester Archaeological Report 2: The Roman Small Finds from Excavations in Colchester, 1971–9* (Colchester, 1983), pp. 18–19.
[34] Crummy, *Colchester 2*, p. 18 and fig. 16/103.
[35] Donald F. MacKreth, 'The Roman Brooches from Chichester', in *Chichester Excavations 6*, ed. A. Down (Chichester, 1989), pp. 182–94, at 192.
[36] Shepherd S. Frere, *Excavations at Verulamium*, III (Oxford, 1984), p. 31 and fig. 9/55.
[37] Barry Cunliffe, *Excavations at Portchester Castle*, I, *Roman*, Society of Antiquaries of London Research Report 32 (London, 1975), pp. 199, fig. 109/7.
[38] Frere, *Verulamium*, III, p. 31 and fig. 9/56.
[39] Donald MacKreth, 'Penannulars', in *The Roman Baths and Macellum at Wroxeter, Excavations by Graham Webster 1955–85*, ed. P. Ellis (London, 2000), pp. 155–9, at p. 157, no. 41.

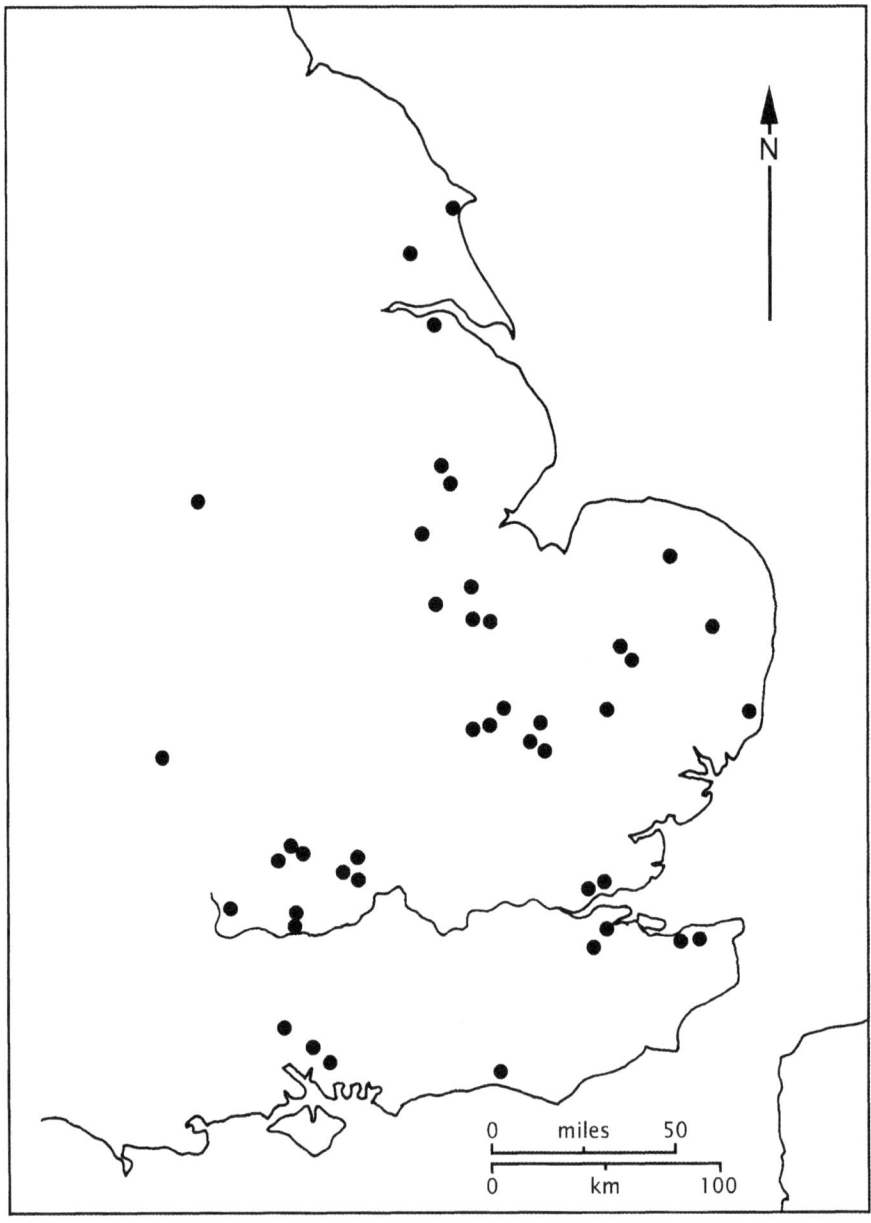

4.3 Distribution of Class C pennanular brooches found in Anglo-Saxon contexts, after White, 1988, with additions

century,[40] and by a series of other examples from graves dated to the late fifth to early sixth centuries.[41]

Iron was a material not frequently used for brooches in Roman Britain but is commonly represented in the penannular brooches from Anglo-Saxon cemeteries. There are twenty-four flat-hooped brooches listed from Anglo-Saxon cemeteries in White's survey, three of iron,[42] to which may now be added further examples. White lists thirty-five round-hooped brooches from Anglo-Saxon cemeteries, of which fourteen were of copper alloy, one of silver and the rest of iron.[43] Apart from the Cc brooches, which seem to have been frequently of iron (all the Wroxeter examples are of this material), iron was not as commonly represented in the Romano-British C brooch series. The Cb and Cc brooches from Anglo-Saxon graves are virtually identical to the late Roman types, but the frequency of iron among the Ca brooches suggests a different pattern. Were the Cb brooches acquired from surviving Romano-British smiths, and the Ca brooches mostly Anglo-Saxon copies? In this context it might be noted that annular or quoit brooches current in the sixth century closely resemble the penannulars with flattened hoops and may have been inspired by them.

Turning to the other categories of penannular, Class G is a group which is not known from contexts that pre-date the end of the Roman period. The only dubiously-stratified example was represented in rubbish including very late Roman pottery from the Roman fort of Castell Collen (Radnor.).[44] There are no other instances of stratified G brooches from secure Roman contexts, though those from Lydney (Glos.) are arguably late Roman rather than post-Roman, and Rahtz has pointed out that if Gs were in production in the fourth century one would have been likely to have been found in contexts of this period in the South West.[45] The conclusion must be that they developed at the very end of the Roman period and continued in production in Romano-British workshops in the fifth century, from which they were obtained by the Anglo-Saxons. The distribution of the G1 brooches (the type found in Anglo-Saxon contexts) is clearly concentrated in the Bristol Channel region, suggesting that this was a major area of production in the fifth and sixth centuries.[46] A few of Dickinson's complex categories of Class G brooch are found only in Anglo-Saxon contexts, namely her Group G1:3 (partially-ribbed hoop/plain terminals), G1:5 (ribbed hoop, single dot on terminals), G1:8 (plain hoops/plain terminals) and G1:6 (ribbed hoop, plain terminal), though in this case there is a variant from Caerwent in south Wales which may have been of the eighth century and does not belong with the main series. The

---

[40] Vera Evison, 'Distribution Maps and England in the First Two Phases', in *Angles, Saxons & Jutes*, ed. Vera Evison (Oxford, 1981), pp. 126–67, at p. 139.
[41] White, *Roman and Celtic Objects*, pp. 12–14.
[42] White, *Roman and Celtic Objects*, pp. 12–14.
[43] White, *Roman and Celtic Objects*, pp. 9–12.
[44] H. Evelyn-White, 'Excavations at Castell Collen, Llandrindod Wells', *Archaeologia Cambrensis*, 6th series 14 (1914), 1–58 at p. 43.
[45] For a discussion of dating, see Tania Dickinson, 'Fowler's Type G Penannular Brooches Reconsidered', *MedArch* 26 (1982), 41–68, at p. 53.
[46] Map: 'Fowler's Type G Brooches', fig. 2.

absence of these from non-Saxon contexts might argue that they represent variants made for or by Anglo-Saxon smiths.

The E/F brooches are those known as 'zoomorphic', and the two categories have been distinguished on account of size differential: Class E are comparatively small, Class F large. E brooches seem to have been in widespread production in the fourth century and continue until the beginning of the fifth: an example from Frocester (Glos.) was dated to the 'fifth century or later',[47] but as far as I am aware there are no other examples from a certainly-dated later context except in Anglo-Saxon cemeteries. By the same token it is difficult to point to examples of the larger F brooches that come from contexts before the end of the Roman period. The example from Frocester was associated with a coin of Arcadius and was apparently nearly new: the context was dated to late fourth to early fifth century.[48] The Frocester F penannular was transitional in size between the Es and the more developed Fs and had a pseudo-barrel pin head, which has been argued as pre-dating the evolved barrel type found for example in Ireland. At Witcombe Villa (Glos.) the F penannular came from Lysons' excavations in the nineteenth century, but the site has produced very late material, including a 'Totworth' strap end and a zoomorphic, barred, composite bone comb of the fifth century.[49] The examples of F brooches from the Roman forts at Kirkby Thore (Cumbria), Corbridge (Northumb.) and Caernarvon (Gwynedd), along with the example from Caerwent (Mont.) are all unstratified and could have come from very late occupation; claims that Kirkby Thore has no late occupation[50] are somewhat disproved by the occurrence of Huntcliff ware and other very late pottery in Charlesworth's excavations.[51]

It might be argued that some of the E and F brooches from Anglo-Saxon cemeteries are Anglo-Saxon copies of British prototypes. The E brooch from Broughton Lodge (Notts.) seems a simplistic rendering without any of the characteristic features of the type, as does the brooch from Barrington A (Cambs.). The same might be argued for the F brooches from Bifrons 6 (Kent), and Staxton 4 (Yorks.), the latter of which certainly has a replacement pin. A brooch from Kempton seems to be a hybrid, with the flattened hoop of a C brooch. That leaves few 'imported' brooches from Anglo-Saxon graves: the E brooches from Brighthampton (Oxon.) grave 25 and Glaston (Rut.) grave 12, and the F brooches from Stratford and Alveston (Warwicks.) and Abingdon (Berks.) grave 2 are the only convincing Romano-British products, while the pin from Highdown (Sussex) never adorned a Romano-British brooch. The other penannulars in Anglo-Saxon contexts are without convincing parallels in late Roman Britain or in the post-Roman West, with the exception of the brooch from Highdown grave 74, a large

---

[47] Eddie Price, *Frocester. A Romano-British Settlement, its Antecedents and Successors* (Gloucester, 2000), p. 41 no.72.
[48] Price, *Frocester*, p. 41 no.74.
[49] Elsie Clifford, 'The Roman Villa at Witcombe, Glos.', *Transactions of the Bristol & Gloucester Antiquarian Society* 73 (1954), 5–69.
[50] Stephen Johnson, *Later Roman Britain* (London, 1980), p. 86.
[51] Dorothy Charlesworth, 'Recent Work at Kirkby Thore', *Transactions of the Cumberland & Westmorland Antiquarian and Archaeological Society* 64 (1964), 63–75.

A5 brooch that appears to be Irish but has an odd hinge mechanism (possibly a later repair?) on the hoop which is without parallel in the Celtic world.

The conclusion that should probably be drawn from this assemblage is that the penannular brooch series from Anglo-Saxon graves are almost all Anglo-Saxon interpretations of the penannular brooch idea, which may have spread to the Anglo-Saxons through contacts with western workshops.

Hanging bowls

It is now apparent that the occurrence of hanging bowls in Anglo-Saxon graves is the outcome of a fashion for burying metal vessels in the 'Final Phase' burials of the seventh century.[52] The fact that they were not buried until this period does not, however, convince that they were not produced in the previous two centuries in British workshops, and the case for some of these workshops being in the South West has been suggested above. The fact remains that not all hanging bowls or their mounts that have been found in Anglo-Saxon contexts are necessarily British products rather than Anglo-Saxon. Some clearly display design elements which are purely Germanic, such as the circle of animals on the mounts from Benty Grange (Derbys.),[53] which appear to be fish in the style of those on the Crundale sword pommel.[54] Other animals in Saxon style appear on a disc found with the Lullingstone (Kent) hanging bowl[55] (itself arguably Anglo-Saxon, not Celtic, in the light of what is now known of Anglo-Saxon pottery stamps),[56] a now lost silver disc from Kent once in Liverpool,[57] and a mount from Faversham (Kent) with yapping animals.[58] Other bowls with animal ornament in a Saxon style are those from Willingdon (Sussex),[59] or Sutton Hoo 2.[60] The latter employs die-stamped foils, which appear to be a Germanic device in origin. In addition to these hanging bowl mounts, there are a few others. There is nothing that is not in place in an Anglo-Saxon context in the ornament of ring-and-dot that appears at Caistor (Lincs.),[61] which has an escutcheon that looks like a disc brooch, or some sixth-century quoit brooches such as those from Risley grave 94, Eastry and Bifrons grave B16 (Kent),[62] or Capheaton (Northumb.),[63] while that on the

---

[52] Helen M. Geake, 'When were Hanging Bowls Deposited in Anglo-Saxon Graves?', *MedArch* 43 (1999), 1–8.
[53] Jane Brenan, *Hanging Bowls and their Contexts*, BAR, BS 220 (Oxford, 1991), no. 9.
[54] George Speake, *Anglo-Saxon Animal Ornament* (Oxford, 1980), pl.14b.
[55] Françoise Henry, 'Hanging Bowls', *Journal of the Royal Society of Antiquaries of Ireland* 66 (1936), 209–46, fig. 9e.
[56] Catherine Hills, 'Animal Stamps on Anglo-Saxon Pottery in East Anglia', *Studien zur Sachsenforschung* 4 (1983), 93–110.
[57] Henry, 'Hanging Bowls', fig. 9b.
[58] Henry, 'Hanging Bowls', fig. 9a; Brenan, *Hanging Bowls*, nos. 23 and 24.
[59] Brenan, *Hanging Bowls*, no. 70.
[60] Brenan, *Hanging Bowls*, no. 55.
[61] Brenan, *Hanging Bowls*, no. 11.
[62] Barry Ager, 'The Smaller Variants of the Anglo-Saxon Quoit Brooch', *ASSAH* 4 (1985), 1–58, e.g. fig. 5g.
[63] Brenan, *Hanging Bowls*, no. 13.

Banstead Down (Surrey) bowl[64] is so simple it could probably have been done by anyone, Celt or Saxon. The Basingstoke (Hants) bowl[65] has a design which appears to have been a poorly understood rendering of a pelta-pattern, a feature shared by the Castle Yard (York) bowl.[66] The interlace on the Bekesbourne (Kent) disc[67] is not in keeping with Celtic style. There is nothing 'Celtic' about the two escutcheons from Whitby,[68] and the design of a cross of arcs that appears on one of the Faversham (Kent) bowls[69] and on a disc from Camerton (Som.),[70] is one which is not unknown in Anglo-Saxon art but is not readily matched in Celtic ornament prior to the late seventh or eighth century. Other bowl mounts which could as easily be Anglo-Saxon as British in manufacture include those from Barham, Coddenham and Badleybridge, Needham Market (all Suffolk), and Bawsey (Norfolk).

Other Connections

Apart from that on hanging bowls, it is clear that ornament of Romano-British derivation was taken up in the Anglo-Saxon world, probably during the seventh century.

For example, the cruciform brooch, though a purely Germanic introduction, acquired in Britain a horse-head footplate. The later forms have exaggerated nostrils and other features, but those on the earlier types have very stylized zoomorphic features. Longley saw the influence of F brooches and possibly bucket ox-head escutcheons of the type represented at Mount Sorrel (Leics.) on their design.[71] A more likely origin is the footplates of some crossbow brooches such as some from Richborough (Kent),[72] which are virtually indistinguishable from the footplates on some early Class I cruciforms, such as those from Mildenhall or Ixworth (Suffolk).[73]

A happy marriage of British and Anglo-Saxon styles is apparent on the *press-blech* foils on the bag mount from Swallowcliffe Down (Wilts.).[74] Here the purely Anglo-Saxon is combined with trumpet pattern and yin-yang scrolls derived from

---

[64] Brenan, *Hanging Bowls*, no. 2.
[65] Brenan, *Hanging Bowls*, no. 6.
[66] Brenan, *Hanging Bowls*, no. 15.
[67] Brenan, *Hanging Bowls*, no. 7.
[68] Brenan, *Hanging Bowls*, no. 68.
[69] Brenan, *Hanging Bowls*, no. 25.
[70] Brenan, *Hanging Bowls*, no. 12.
[71] David Longley, *Hanging-Bowls, Penannular Brooches and the Anglo-Saxon Connexion*, BAR, BS 22 (Oxford, 1975), p. 35.
[72] Barry W. Cunliffe, *Excavations at Richborough V*, Society of Antiquaries of London Research Report 23 (London, 1965), pp. 130–31, pl. XXXVIII.
[73] Nils Aberg, *The Anglo-Saxons in England in the Early Centuries after the Invasion* (Uppsala, 1928), figs. 44 and 48.
[74] George Speake, *A Saxon Bed Burial on Swallowcliffe Down. Excavations by F de M Vatcher* (London, 1989), pp. 75–80.

Romano-British tradition. It is probably not coincidental that this product is to be found in Wiltshire, which we have already seen is crucial to an understanding of the British legacy to early medieval metalwork. Yet Swallowcliffe does not stand alone. The pin set from Roundway Down (Wilts.) is a fine example of hybrid style.[75] These linked pins with their gold-and-garnet work are in the mainstream of Anglo-Saxon metalworking, but the artefact type is of Romano-British derivation. In the centre of the linking chain is a blue glass stud with raised cruciform design, similar to another found in a Saxon burial at Camerton (Som.), some twenty-five miles away.[76] Linked pins of simpler type were found in the cemetery at Winnall II (Hants) in graves 7 and 8, in the latter case still with their chains. These were in silver, and from the same grave came a pair of Class Cb brooches.[77] The glass studs are best matched in the Celtic world, being of a type produced at Garryduff (Co. Cork)[78] and Lagore (Co. Meath) in Ireland,[79] though moulds for similar studs are known from Iona so there is no real reason to see them as specifically Irish. The linked pins are a dress accessory which makes its appearance in Final Phase burials of the seventh century; there are thirteen such sets, distributed from Derbyshire to Kent,[80] and Roman inspiration must surely lie behind their use. Two Class E zoomorphic dress pins (a type which developed in Roman Britain) from Skaill (Ork.) appear to have come from a linked set and were dated to the late fourth to fifth centuries.[81]

Conclusions

The evidence might seem to suggest that continuing traditions of Romano-British metalworking in the fifth century and beyond had some small influence on pagan Saxon England, contributing ornamental techniques and artefact types to the Anglo-Saxon repertoire. Through these the Anglo-Saxons probably also acquired the vocabulary of so-called 'Celtic' art that came to its full fruition in such later masterpieces as the Lindisfarne Gospels.

The reverse flow of techniques and ideas, from the Anglo-Saxon areas to the Celtic, is outside the scope of this paper. The evidence suggests that this was a later phenomenon which did not commence until the later-sixth and seventh centuries when Germanic metalworking techniques seem to have transformed Celtic skills.

---

[75] Audrey Meaney and Sonia C. Hawkes, *Two Anglo-Saxon Cemeteries at Winnall*, Society for Medieval Archaeology Monograph 4 (London, 1970), pp. 48–9.
[76] William J. Wedlake, *Excavations at Camerton, Somerset* (Taunton, 1958), 255.
[77] Meaney and Hawkes, *Winnall*, p. 11.
[78] Michael J. O'Kelly, 'Two ring-forts at Garryduff, Co. Cork', *Proceedings of the Royal Irish Academy* 63C (1962), 17–125, at pp. 72–4 and pl. lx.
[79] Hugh O'N. Hencken, 'Lagore crannog. An Irish Royal Residence of the 7th to 10th centuries AD', *Proceedings of the Royal Irish Academy* 53C (1950), 1–247, at 129.
[80] Geake, 'When were Hanging Bowls Deposited?', p. 35.
[81] Simon Buteux, *Settlements at Skaill, Deerness, Orkney*, BAR, BS 260 (Oxford, 1997), p. 103.

It is very much apparent from the workshops at the Mote of Mark (Kirk.)[82] and Dunadd (Argyll),[83] and the culmination can be seen in the Hunterston Brooch from Ayrshire, one of the finest creations of the so-called 'Celtic' tradition.

[82] David Longley, 'The Mote of Mark: The Archaeological Context of the Decorated Metalwork', in *Pattern and Purpose in Insular Art*, ed. M. Redknap *et al.* (Oxford, 2001), pp. 75–89.

[83] Alan Lane and Ewan Campbell, 'Celtic and Germanic Interaction in Dalriada: the 7th Century Metalworking Site at Dunadd', in *The Age of Migrating Ideas*, ed. Michael Spearman and John Higgitt (Edinburgh, 1993), pp. 52–63.

5

Invisible Britons, Gallo-Romans and Russians: Perspectives on Culture Change

HEINRICH HÄRKE

SINCE the 1980s a new consensus has emerged in British early medieval archaeology according to which a substantial proportion of the native Romano-British population survived into the Anglo-Saxon period.[1] This view is usually associated with a 'minimalist' perspective on the Anglo-Saxon immigration. It is also worth pointing out that this new consensus is mainly based on new thinking, not new evidence. The key problem for this new consensus has been the near-invisibility, in archaeological terms, of the postulated sub-Roman, British population. This is, of course, one of the main reasons why the traditional 'ethnic cleansing' model, derived from the written sources,[2] has persisted for so long in Anglo-Saxon archaeology.

The aim of this paper is not to support any particular model of post-Roman population stability or change, but rather to explore the nature of post-empire culture change and its implications for archaeology. The approach is theoretical and comparative: a recapitulation of the nature of the archaeological problem, complemented by comparative observations from Gaul, and followed by a discussion of a modern case of 'empire collapse' and its consequences for material culture, settlement patterns, and other aspects relevant to the archaeological debate. The focus here will be entirely on material culture because other types of evidence will be covered by other contributors to this volume.[3]

---

[1] Arnold, *FRBSE*; Hodges, *ASA*; Higham, *RBAS*; Dark, *BERE*. For an overview, see now Hills, *Origins*.
[2] Stenton, *ASE*; J. N. L. Myres, *The English Settlements*, Oxford History of England, IB (Oxford, 1986).
[3] For an earlier survey of the question of Britons in early Anglo-Saxon England, see Heinrich Härke, 'Briten und Angelsachsen im nachrömischen England: Zum Nachweis der einheimischen Bevölkerung in den angelsächsischen Landnahmegebieten', *Studien zur Sachsenforschung* 11 (1998), 87–119.

Post-Roman Culture Change in Britain: The Nature of the Problem

The archaeological sequence of the first half of the first millennium AD in England is, in itself, reasonably clear and unambiguous: (1) Roman material culture up to the beginning of the fifth century; then (2) a black hole ('post-crash gap'[4]) in the first half of the fifth century, first punctuated, and then followed, by (3) Anglo-Saxon material culture from the second half of the fifth century.

That much is not in dispute, nor is the absence, implied in this sequence, of unambiguous evidence for a post-Roman, native, non-Anglo-Saxon material culture in England. The few types of possibly British (or rather more generally, Celtic) artefact types in post-Roman England have been discussed at length several times.[5] Such artefacts (penannular brooches, hanging bowls and enamelled items) have been recovered exclusively from Anglo-Saxon cultural contexts, and for this and other reasons, they cannot be considered firm proof of the existence of a British population. Even if they were, the native population suggested by the 'British' artefacts need not have been large: there are some eighty-five hanging bowls and 110 penannular brooches from Anglo-Saxon contexts (mostly graves), and another forty items with enamel are known from all of post-Roman Britain.[6] This compares with some 30,000 graves from sites with diagnostically Anglo-Saxon material culture of the fifth to seventh centuries. What is in dispute is the interpretation of the 'black hole' in relation to the fate of the native Romano-British population. The situation essentially allows for three possible explanations.

The first of these (proposition 1) takes the absence of evidence to be evidence of absence (or largely so, at any rate). This has always been considered a defensible proposition because the archaeological sequence appears to be so clear-cut, and it appears to have the support of other types of evidence, most notably that of written sources and linguistic evidence (including place-names). This so-called 'traditional' explanation which assumes large-scale 'ethnic cleansing' of the native population has had few recent defenders because the weight of the debate of the last decade or so has swung against it. But it may have been given a new lease of life by studies of modern Y-chromosome DNA, one of the few pieces of new evidence recently brought into this debate.[7]

---

[4] After Simon Esmonde Cleary, 'Approaches to the Differences between Late Romano-British and Early Anglo-Saxon Archaeology', *ASSAH* 6 (1993), 57–63.

[5] The key publications are: Elizabeth Fowler, 'Celtic Metalwork of the Fifth and Sixth Centuries AD: A Re-appraisal', *ArchJ* 120 (1963), 98–160, and 'Hanging Bowls', in *Studies in Ancient Europe*, ed. John M. Coles and Derek D. A. Simpson (Leicester, 1968), pp. 289–310; David Longley, *Hanging Bowls, Penannular Brooches and the Anglo-Saxon Connexion*, BAR, BS 22 (Oxford, 1975); J. D. Bateson, *Enamel-working in Iron Age, Roman and Sub-Roman Britain*, BAR, BS 93 (Oxford, 1981); Roger H. White, *Roman and Celtic Objects from Anglo-Saxon Graves: A Catalogue and an Interpretation of their Use*, BAR, BS 191 (Oxford, 1988); Jane Brenan, *Hanging Bowls and their Contexts*, BAR, BS 220 (Oxford, 1991); and see Lloyd Laing in this volume.

[6] Figures distilled from the publications cited above in note 5.

[7] Michael E. Weale *et al.*, 'Y Chromosome Evidence for Anglo-Saxon Mass Migration', *Molecular Biology and Evolution* 19 (2002), 1008–21.

If, however, you believe for whatever reasons that there must have been post-Roman Britons, there are two possible explanations for the absence of a British material culture: the evidence has not survived (proposition 2), *or* the evidence has survived, but has not been recognized (proposition 3).

For the evidence not to have survived in the archaeological record (proposition 2), it would have had to be made entirely of perishable materials. There is, in fact, just such a case from this period: the largely aceramic and organic material culture of early medieval Ireland where vessels, tools and even decorations (such as hair-pins) were made of wood and leather, and houses were built in a light wickerwork construction which left few, if any, traces in the ground.[8] Such material has been found in waterlogged conditions in culturally diagnostic, datable contexts (crannogs and raths).[9] If we assume that post-Roman, British, material culture was of this type, then we can hypothesize that Britons were almost completely 'invisible' in the first half of the fifth century; that Britons in early Anglo-Saxon England may have lived in 'invisible' enclaves recognizable only by the presence of Roman, and absence of early Anglo-Saxon, material culture; and further, that such enclaves may later have become visible by acculturation, i.e. the gradual adoption by these Britons of Anglo-Saxon material culture. This is exactly the explanation which West has suggested for the archaeological sequence on the Suffolk clay-lands.[10]

The third proposition (that Britons were present, but their evidence has not been recognized, at least not initially) has probably attracted most attention and interest in the recent debate. Proponents are able to point to a small number of archaeological cases which seem to support this idea. Radiocarbon dates show that the cemetery of Queenford Farm (Oxfordshire) continued from the Late Roman into the sub/post-Roman period, perhaps as late as the sixth century.[11] The evidence here was so undiagnostic (inhumation without grave-goods, no grave markers) that this would not have been recognized without radiocarbon dates. The settlements of Coombe Down and Chisenbury Warren (Salisbury Plain) seem to have continued in their Iron Age to Romano-British form into the post-Roman period.[12] This was only recognized from a few sherds of grass-tempered ware spotted by a pottery specialist familiar with Anglo-Saxon as well

---

[8] General overviews in Nancy Edwards, *The Archaeology of Early Medieval Ireland* (London, 1990); Lloyd Laing, *The Archaeology of Late Celtic Britain and Ireland* (London, 1975).

[9] Hugh Hencken, 'Lagore Crannog: an Irish Royal Residence of the 7th to 10th Century A.D.', *Proceedings of the Royal Irish Academy* 53 C (1950), 1–247; Chris Lynn, 'Deer Park Farms: a Visit to an Early Christian Settlement', *Current Archaeology* 113 (1989), 193–8; overview in Kieran Denis O'Conor, *The Archaeology of Medieval Rural Settlement in Ireland* (Dublin, 1998).

[10] Stanley West, *West Stow: The Anglo-Saxon Village*, East Anglian Archaeology Report 24 (Ipswich, 1985), p. 168.

[11] R. A. Chambers, 'The Late- and Sub-Roman Cemetery at Queenford Farm, Dorchester-on-Thames, Oxon', *Oxoniensia* 52 (1987), 35–69.

[12] Roy Entwistle, 'The Prehistoric and Romano-British Settlement of Salisbury Plain', *Sanctuary (The MOD Conservation Magazine)* 24 (1995), 26–7.

as Romano-British pottery.[13] In these two cases the key to recognition was dating because the cultural diagnostics pointed to the Roman period, if anywhere.

Other evidence is less certain but also highlights the nature of the problem. Early Anglo-Saxon houses may be hybrid Germanic-Roman types, implying the presence of Britons among the builders.[14] Men buried without weapons in early Anglo-Saxon inhumation cemeteries may have been Britons living in Anglo-Saxon communities.[15] Early Anglo-Saxon dress ornaments with enamel decoration in eastern England may have been made and worn by acculturated Britons.[16] The early Anglo-Saxon cemetery of Wallingford may have been a burial place of acculturated Britons: the place-name suggests the presence of Britons, not Anglo-Saxons.[17] The key to recognition here is the assumption or identification of mixed cultural diagnostics, largely resting on the theoretical expectation of British survival and acculturation.

While proposition 1 is a straightforward *conclusio e silentio*, and proposition 2 similarly so but with a different starting assumption and, therefore, a different conclusion, proposition 3 is logically on firmer ground, since it rests on the partial observation of likely reasons for the 'invisibility' of the postulated Britons. So, either we take the evidence at face value and accept that there were no, or very few, post-Roman Britons, *or* we have to assume that the Britons were initially (i.e. after the end of Roman Britain, but before the large-scale appearance of Anglo-Saxon material culture) largely invisible, and then rapidly adopted Anglo-Saxon culture so that they appear as Anglo-Saxons in the archaeological record.[18]

---

[13] Pers. comm. Michael Fulford (University of Reading).
[14] Brian Hope-Taylor, *Yeavering: An Anglo-British Centre of Early Northumbria*, Department of Environment Archaeological Report 7 (London, 1977); Philip Dixon, 'How Saxon is the Saxon House?', *Structural Reconstruction: Approaches to the Interpretation of the Excavated Remains of Buildings*, ed. P. J. Drury, BAR, BS 110 (Oxford, 1982), pp. 275–87; Simon James *et al.*, 'An Early Medieval Building Tradition', *ArchJ* 41 (1984), 182–215; Anne Marshall and Garry Marshall, 'Differentiation, Change and Continuity in Anglo-Saxon Buildings', *ArchJ* 150 (1993), 366–402.
[15] Heinrich Härke, '"Warrior Graves"? The Background of the Anglo-Saxon Weapon Burial Rite', *Past & Present* 126 (1990), 22–43, and *Angelsächsische Waffengräber des 5. bis 7. Jahrhunderts*, Zeitschrift für Archäologie des Mittelalters Beiheft 6 (Cologne and Bonn, 1992).
[16] Chris Scull, 'Further Evidence from East Anglia for Enamelling on Early Anglo-Saxon Metalwork', *ASSAH* 4 (1985), 117–24.
[17] For the cemetery, see E. Thurlow Leeds, 'An Anglo-Saxon Cemetery at Wallingford, Berkshire', *Berkshire Archaeological Journal* 42 (1938), 93–101; for the place-name, see Margaret Gelling, *The Place-names of Berkshire*, II, English Place-Name Society volume 50 (Cambridge, 1974), pp. 535–6.
[18] The latter is by now the more widely accepted assumption; see Heinrich Härke, 'Population Replacement or Acculturation? An Archaeological Perspective on Population and Migration in Post-Roman Britain', in *The Celtic Englishes* III, ed. Hildegard L. C. Tristram, Anglistische Forschungen 324 (Heidelberg, 2003), pp. 13–28.

Culture Change on the Continent: Comparative Observations

A similar problem is presented by the archaeological situation in other parts of Western Europe affected by Roman collapse and Germanic immigration. The question of the native Gallo-Roman population in northern France, the Rhineland and Moselle valley, and north-west Switzerland has been studied and discussed by Continental colleagues since the 1940s and '50s.[19]

In northern France, an area of sparse Germanic settlement, there is some archaeological evidence of continuity from the fourth to the sixth century.[20] Towns were partially deserted but may have continued in use for defensive and other purposes. The construction of rural villa buildings switched from stone to timber. In addition new types of timber-built settlements and houses of Germanic type appeared. Some pottery types (decorated Argonne ware and rough 'kitchen ware') continued from the Late Roman to the post-Roman period. Thus, the 'Black Hole' in native material culture and datable contexts is less pronounced than in Britain, but it still exists to some extent. Then the scatter of intrusive Germanic (Frankish) material culture disappeared by the end of the sixth century, suggesting an acculturation process in which the immigrant Frankish minority became Gallo-Romans,[21] unless the Frankish evidence in northern France actually represented the adoption of a new elite material culture by Gallo-Romans in the first place.[22]

The situation in the Rhineland, the Moselle valley and north-western Switzerland was more like post-Roman England, both in the suggested scale of Germanic settlement (Franks on the Middle and Lower Rhine and the Moselle, and Alamanni on the Upper Rhine and northern Switzerland) and in the archaeological invisibility of the native Gallo-Roman population.[23] There was continuity of settlement in some towns, primarily Cologne and Trier, dated mostly by Frankish material culture. There is virtually no rural settlement evidence for

---

[19] See Herrmann Ament, 'Franken und Romanen im Merowingerreich als archäologisches Forschungsproblem', *Bonner Jahrbücher* 178 (1978), 377–94; Edward James, 'Cemeteries and the Problem of Frankish Settlement in Gaul', in *Names, Words and Graves: Early Medieval Settlement*, ed. Peter H. Sawyer (Leeds, 1979), pp. 55–89; and Edward James, *The Franks*, The Peoples of Europe (Oxford, 1988).

[20] Paul van Ossel, 'Die Gallo-Romanen als Nachfahren der römischen Provinzialbevölkerung', in *Die Franken: Wegbereiter Europas. Vor 1500 Jahren: König Chlodwig und seine Erben* (exhibition catalogue, Reiss-Museum Mannheim), vol. 1 (Mainz, 1996), pp. 102–9.

[21] Volker Bierbrauer, 'Romanen im fränkischen Siedelgebiet', in *Die Franken: Wegbereiter Europas. Vor 1500 Jahren: König Chlodwig und seine Erben* (exhibition catalogue, Reiss-Museum Mannheim), vol. 1 (Mainz, 1996), pp. 110–20.

[22] Suggested by E. James, 'Cemeteries and the Problem of Frankish Settlement in Gaul', in *Names, Words and Graves*, ed. Sawyer, pp. 55–89, *contra* Horst W. Böhme, *Germanische Grabfunde des 4. bis 5. Jahrhunderts*, Münchener Beiträge zur Vor- und Frühgeschichte 19 (Munich, 1974).

[23] See overviews by H. Ament, 'Franken und Romanen im Merowingerreich als archäologisches Forschungsproblem', *Bonner Jahrbücher* 178 (1978), 377–94; V. Bierbrauer, 'Romanen im fränkischen Siedelgebiet', in *Die Franken: Wegbereiter Europas. Vor 1500 Jahren: König Chlodwig und seine Erben* (exhibition catalogue, Reiss-Museum Mannheim), vol. 1 (Mainz, 1996), pp. 110–20.

the native population; what is there is of Frankish type. The best evidence for early medieval Gallo-Romans is provided by a small number of suburban and *vicus* cemeteries of Late Antique type which continued in use from the fourth to the sixth/seventh centuries,[24] much like Queenford Farm in England. They are characterized by the inhumation rite, an absence or near-absence of grave goods, the use of sarcophagi and inscribed gravestones, and the frequent occurrence of multiple burials. From the later fifth and sixth centuries, Germanic-style graves (single inhumations with grave goods but no sarcophagi or grave markers) appeared in these cemeteries, and in new, separate 'row-grave cemeteries', seen as the result of Frankish and Alamannic immigration and the adoption by Gallo-Romans of the dominant Germanic culture.

There is, then, some evidence for the native population and its acculturation. However, the main type of evidence is not material culture but a burial rite marked more by the absence of Germanic features and artefacts than by its own diagnostic features. The archaeological near-invisibility of the natives is conspicuous in the Moselle valley where historical and linguistic evidence document the continuity of a Romance-speaking population for several centuries after the end of Roman provincial administration.[25]

The parallel problem on the Continent highlights that the partial or total 'invisibility' of native populations in the wake of the collapse of the Western Roman Empire is a wider issue, not a purely insular one. This, in turn, should focus our attention on the process of post-collapse material culture change which produces such a situation. One of the best ways to study such a process may be to look at a modern case of 'empire collapse'.

Culture Change after the Collapse of the Soviet Empire

The disintegration of the 'Soviet Empire' (a term with which our Russian colleagues are understandably unhappy, in the same way that most students of the Late Roman Empire do not like it being compared to the Soviet Union) began in the late 1980s, with the first 'province' lost in 1989 (East Germany). Thereafter, disintegration was fast, reaching the core of the 'empire' in 1991 with the end of Communist rule in the Soviet Union itself, rapidly followed by political fragmentation as constituent republics declared independence. This, in turn, accelerated the processes of economic and social change which had been under way since the *perestroika* of the later 1980s. Material culture change started later and more

---

[24] In the Rhineland: Krefeld-Gellep and the various cemeteries of and around Cologne; in the Moselle valley: Gondorf and Kobern; in Switzerland: Kaiseraugst.

[25] See the references cited in Ament, 'Franken und Romanen', *passim*. Compare any Roman distribution maps of the Moselle valley area with its striking emptiness on the maps of Germanic male and female grave-goods of the fourth/fifth centuries in H. W. Böhme, *Germanische Grabfunde des 4. bis 5. Jahrhunderts*, Münchener Beiträge zur Vor- und Frühgeschichte 19 (Munich, 1974).

5.1 The Marlboro cowboy in Russia: the native symbolic system is swamped with Western cultural messages (hoarding in central Moscow, 1998)

slowly; it was noticeable in Russia by 1993 but took off dramatically over the following two or three years.[26]

This process has been marked by the rapid adoption of elements of Western consumer culture ('Western' meaning North American, West European, Turkish, and Far Eastern) which was virtually nonexistent in the USSR. Bottled and canned drinks and cigarettes of Western brands were the first to appear, with packaged food, fruits, sweets and pet foods not far behind. The change in dress styles has been massive, with tracksuits and baseball caps now as much in evidence as in the West. These, and carrier bags, are the most prominent means of displaying Western logos; Western carrier bags have become status items which can be bought from specialist stalls. The market for toys and electrical and electronic goods (both categories rare and expensive in the Soviet Union) has been completely taken over by Western imports. Cars have become a key element of the material culture change, with up to fifty percent of cars in the streets of Moscow now being Western marques. Russian-made vehicles have become totally unfashionable; any second-hand, foreign-made car conveys more prestige and higher status.

[26] See Heinrich Härke, 'Collapse of Empire and Material-culture Change: The Case of the Soviet Union', *MedArch* 43 (1999), 183–5.

5.2 Russian rubbish: packaging favours the visibility of imported goods (household rubbish container, Stavropol 1998)

Closely associated with this influx of Western goods is the widespread use of Latin script and English language, which has spread to Russian shops and services. By 1993, there were kiosks called SHOP in small provincial towns, and by 1997 English names and logos were used by major Russian firms (e.g. LUKoil and Rokada). Perhaps even more significantly, graffiti are found in English as often as in Russian, demonstrating that Latin script and English language have entered popular culture. Soviet-style political murals have all but disappeared and been replaced with advertising hoardings which show Latin-script logos and scenes of Western consumerism (e.g. the Marlboro cowboy). Icons of Western culture (e.g. Mickey Mouse, Daisy Duck etc.) have superseded, if not totally replaced, Soviet-period symbols.

Russian towns have undergone even more dramatic changes. Since right after the collapse of the Soviet Union, a new type of house has been built in large numbers: the detached family home, which was not built in the Soviet period. Models for this innovation were initially taken from Western films and TV series; by 1997 architect-designed, Western house types were becoming available in Russia. Perhaps even more significantly, new family homes are concentrated in new suburbs which have sprung up outside all Russian towns and are now reaching staggering sizes.

Funerary rites and grave monuments have so far undergone only modest changes. One of the main reasons for this appears to be that the generation being buried now are veterans of the Soviet period who have often stipulated a wish to be buried in the rite familiar to them. Observable changes include the increasing use of religious symbols (particularly the Orthodox cross) in funerals and on grave monuments, and a slow increase in the proportion of cremations (hampered by the lack of crematoria). As a consequence Soviet funerary rites show continuity into the post-Soviet period.[27]

The Russian process of culture change includes other elements which are usually thought to be associated with empire collapse. Economic change has been signalled by the collapse of the Soviet heavy industry, which has resulted in a horizon of abandoned factories. This was partly caused by foreign imports, but the unavailability of Russian-made goods and products has further fuelled the spread of Western equivalents and replacements.

Population decline and increased mobility, whilst less relevant to the issue of material culture change, have been prominent features of the post-Soviet epoch. There was a temporary but marked drop in the birth rate right across Eastern Europe in the late and post-Soviet periods. In Russia this phenomenon has been so marked and persistent that her population is still declining by 800,000 each year.[28] This problem dates back to the Soviet period but has become more pronounced since 1991.

Increased mobility has partly been caused by the political and social changes, partly made possible by the end of stifling controls on movement and travel. Examples of internal migration include the return of the 'Soviet Mobile Field Army' from the 'lost provinces' to Russia; the abandonment of marginal settlements, particularly in Siberia; and ethnic population shifts such as those of the Crimean Tartars, Caucasian refugees and Russian civilians expelled from central Asia. Emigration from Russia has been on an even larger scale: 650,000 Jews have moved to Israel, and some 2.5 million ethnic Germans to Germany.[29] In addition, Russians are now traveling abroad in increasing numbers for business, sport, education, and recreation, quite a few of them settling either temporarily or permanently outside Russia. There have been far fewer people traveling or moving to Russia, but there has been a marked increase in tourism to Russia in recent years.

Where does that leave the question of material culture 'invisibility'? Russian natives, too, have become temporarily 'invisible' in the process of culture change outlined above. The heavy packaging of imported Western goods and foods has led to their being overrepresented in the archaeological record. Russian goods tend to be sold in neutral, re-usable packaging without logos or lettering (clear glasses or plastic bags), and Russian produce arrives in the markets and shops in neutral crates or without any packaging. In the case of houses, typological dating would assign blocks of flats to the Soviet period, and Western-style family homes and new suburbs to the post-Soviet period, making 'native' buildings disappear in the transition (until they are refurbished with Western fittings, that is). US dollars are Russia's second currency and the preferred currency for savings; and

---

[27] See Catherine Merridale, *Night of Stone: Death and Memory in Russia* (London, 2000).
[28] *Daily Telegraph*, 15 May 1997, quoting a report of President Yeltsin's Commission on Women, the Family and Demography.
[29] The figure for immigration into Germany was supplied by the Statistisches Bundesamt, Wiesbaden, Germany; the one for Israel is from the *Daily Telegraph*, 10 May 1999.

because Russians do not trust Russian banks, such savings are kept at home, creating a horizon of post-Soviet hoards exclusively in US dollars.

Script and symbols are less clear-cut: Latin script is heavily overrepresented on shop signs and hoardings, but Cyrillic script continues to be used in books and newspapers (with a curious smattering of Latin-script words and logos incorporated into the Cyrillic text). Whilst this should be taken as reasonably clear evidence of the survival of some Russian natives into the post-Soviet period, a more recent process of 'indigenisation' (since about 1997–8) is making natives more visible in material culture and settlements. Native food styles are making a comeback; imported foods and goods are tailored for the Russian market, with Russian text on their packaging (in addition to Western logos which remain *de rigueur*); international magazines are published in Russian editions now, with just the cover showing the English or German title in Latin script; and houses are built or decorated in a 'neo-traditionalist' style drawing on pre-Soviet, Russian architectural elements.

Conclusions

It is tempting to speculate that future archaeologists of, say, the mid-fourth millennium AD will conclude that the collapse of the Soviet Empire was followed by massive immigration from Western Europe, the USA, Turkey and the Far East, with immigrants arriving in their own vehicles, building their own houses in their own separate settlements, and bringing their own food, tools and toys. But it is doubtful if the post-Soviet analogy can be used in this way to highlight suggested fallacies in the study of the post-Roman period. After all, the conditions for the spread of cultural ideas and goods are very different today from those pertaining in the middle of the first millennium AD. One and a half millennia before TV and the internet, before advertising and glossy magazines, before planes and container ships, the spread of ideas and goods required a higher degree of personal interaction; and it is arguable that massive shifts of ideas and material culture in non-state (or post-empire) societies may often have required population shifts on a commensurate scale. The case of post-Soviet Russia may, therefore, be of little help in solving the question of the scale of the Anglo-Saxon immigration, except to confirm that higher group and individual mobility may be typical of post-empire situations.

In other aspects, too, post-Soviet Russia is not an exact analogy for post-Roman Britain. For a start, the modern case involves the collapse of a supposedly inferior culture and its replacement by the superior one, instead of the other way round (although relative assessments of inferior and superior cultures may be profoundly misleading). Secondly, Russia is the former centre of the collapsed 'empire', not its periphery (although culture change on the periphery of the former Soviet Union closely mirrors the one described above for Russia herself). And thirdly, though less relevant here, observed migrations of the last decade or so have been mostly out of the 'empire', not into it.

But the post-Soviet case may provide a contemporary case to reflect on the contexts and consequences of 'systems collapse'.[30] In particular, it provides an argument for the 'invisibility' (if temporary) of native material culture to be a regular consequence of rapid political, social and economic collapse. This invisibility would seem to result from material culture change which itself is the consequence partly of economic and social change, partly of psychological factors. Certainly in post-Soviet Russia, it is clear that the loss of political and cultural self-confidence and the search for new cultural models has been a major factor in the adoption of foreign material culture. The main implication for post-Roman England appears to be that the invisibility of the native population is not really surprising; it should be expected.[31]

This general point does not prove, of course, that there were large numbers of post-Roman Britons; it only implies that, if they were there, they would most likely be archaeologically invisible. The evidence on the Continent and the Russian case also suggest where one might look for them: in apparently Late Roman settlements and cemeteries; in areas with a high population density in Roman times which appear to be virtually empty in the post-Roman period; and in apparently Anglo-Saxon settlements and cemeteries.

---

[30] As defined by Colin Renfrew, 'Systems Collapse as Social Transformation: Catastrophe and Anastrophe in Early State Societies', in *Transformations: Mathematical Approaches to Culture Change*, ed. Colin Renfrew and Kenneth L. Cooke (New York, 1979), pp. 481–506.

[31] The recognition of migrations poses a similar problem: migrants regularly go through their own processes of culture change during and after their migrations, whilst archaeologists are all too often looking for a simple, one-to-one transfer of the original (i.e. emigration area) material culture to the new settlement areas.

6

Historical Narrative as Cultural Politics: Rome, 'British-ness' and 'English-ness'

NICK HIGHAM*

IT HAS often been remarked that the British indigenes had only a minimal impact on the culture of the barbarian successor states which emerged across the lowland heartlands of the old Roman diocese.[1] In contrast, Gaul is generally considered to have retained far more from its Roman past, as regards all of settlement continuity, spoken language, place-names and Christianity, and the comparison has had a profound effect on interpretations of early Anglo-Saxon England. The barbarian settlement of Gaul is generally seen as an elite phenomenon characterised primarily by assimilation of the culture of the indigenes. Traditional explanations of the English settlement have centred rather on mass migration coupled with displacement and/or extermination of the existing population.[2] This model has been challenged recently, of course, with alternative theories posited on acculturation,[3] but such have struggled to explain the very different outcomes on each side of the Channel.

To take a specific example, a recent paper by Bryan Ward-Perkins contrasted Frankish interaction with Late Antique Gaul and Anglo-Saxon contact with the Britons, concluding that:

> If the Anglo-Saxons had encountered among the Britons a late Roman and Latin culture as powerful as that which the Franks found in Gaul, the cultural history of what was to become England might have been very different.[4]

Instead, he argued, many Britons chose to become Anglo-Saxons, primarily because, in the incomers' view, native culture was 'inferior'. However, the generally sophisticated Latinity of the Briton Pelagius, a trained rhetor who preached

---

* I am grateful to both Paul Fouracre and Martin Ryan for comments on an early draft of this paper. The opinions expressed, however, and all errors, remain exclusively my own.
1 Ever since Edward Freeman, *Old English History* (London, 1878), 2nd edn.
2 Although the explicitly racial explanations of Freeman, *Old English History*, at p. 28, and William Stubbs, *Select Charters* (Oxford, 1870), at pp. 1–3, were substantially moderated by R. H. Hodgkin, *A History of the Anglo-Saxons*, 2 vols. (Oxford, 1935), I, 68–73.
3 Arnold, *FRBSE*; Hodges, *ASA*; Higham, *RBAS*.
4 Bryan Ward-Perkins, 'Why did the Anglo-Saxons not become more British?', *English Historical Review* 115 (2000), 513–33 at pp. 519–20.

his own version of Christianity in Rome before its sack in 410, of Patrick, the Briton who headed a mission to Ireland most probably in the first half of the fifth century, and of Gildas himself, whose use of language mirrored closely that of writers within mid- to late-fifth-century Gaul,[5] leads inevitably to some doubt concerning the poverty of insular Latin culture. Much of lowland Britain, at least, probably had Latin-speaking elites in the early fifth century,[6] who had been educated on a diet of Virgil, grammar and rhetoric, perhaps with the Bible thrown in.[7] Their recent ancestors had in many cases commissioned the mosaics, including some with Latin texts, which adorned the villas of late Roman Britain, even if many of them, perhaps, could still speak the British tongue. Indeed, it is a commonplace today to argue that early fifth-century Britain was rather more like contemporary Gaul, Italy and Spain than has hitherto been imagined.[8]

That said, the greater the *Romanitas* with which we endow sub-Roman Britain, the more problematic are explanations of the comparatively complete disappearance of that very 'Roman-ness', unless we resort to mass migration from Germany and the extermination or expulsion, equally en masse, of the provincials. The fact of a Germanic immigration should not be at issue, but notions of it as so massive as to have constructed England virtually without other processes at work, certainly are. Neither the migration of one to two million nor the mass expulsion or genocide of similar numbers of indigenes seems likely, given contemporary transport systems, logistics, communications and weapons. Against such hypotheses must be set the view that a rural proletariat had considerable value to Germanic warriors, few of whom are likely to have set out on the great adventure of resettlement overseas with the intention of becoming peasants.[9] Early Anglo-Saxon England, like Francia, Bavaria or later Iceland, was arguably based to a considerable extent on un-free labour, and some part at least of this labour force was probably indigenous: there is a thin but persistent scatter of evidence, in all of Law Codes, hagiography, narratives of one kind or another, personal and place-names, for a widespread British presence in Anglo-Saxon England, albeit largely at comparatively low levels of society.[10]

So were the experiences of Britain and Gaul so very different in the sub-Roman period, and if so, in what ways and why? Our first response must be that it depends very much which parts of Gaul you examine. The fourth-century Prefecture of the Gauls divides into four dioceses, from the south the *Hispaniae, Viennensis, Galliae* and *Britanniae*. These had very different experiences over the

---

[5] See François Kerlouégan, *Le De Excidio Britanniae de Gildas: Les Destinées de la Culture Latine dans l'Ile de Bretagne au VIe Siècle* (Paris, 1987).

[6] Peter Schrijver, 'The Rise and Fall of British Latin: Evidence from English and Brittonic', in *The Celtic Roots of English*, ed. Markku Filppula, Juhani Klemola and Heli Pitkänen (Joensuu, 2002), pp. 47–85.

[7] Gildas had also certainly read Orosius, *Seven Books against the Pagans*.

[8] Paul Barnwell, 'Britons and Warriors in Post-Roman South-East England', *ASSAH* 12 (2003) 1–8.

[9] As pointed out long since by H. P. R. Finberg, *The Formation of England: 550–1042* (London, 1974), at p. 32.

[10] Hence the derivation of 'Welsh' from *wealh,* meaning 'foreigner' or 'slave'.

following two centuries, with Late Antique culture far less pressured in the south than the north. Provincial Latin survived in central and southerly parts of the *Galliae* but was replaced by Brittonic in the Armorican peninsula, apparently as a consequence of migration from Britain, and by versions of Germanic in a discontinuous 100–200 km wide zone along the Rhine, which continued eastwards, into Roman Illyrium and Pannonia. Likewise, some Roman sites witnessed the construction of 'German' type buildings such as are found in England.[11] To take a second indicator, aligned and generally unfurnished inhumation continued from the Roman period across southern France and Spain.[12] In the Rhineland march of Gaul, however, furnished inhumations with evidence of social ranking offer parallels with southern Anglo-Saxon England,[13] while the cremation cemeteries, burial mounds and horse burials of central eastern England are paralleled by contemporary practices north and east of the Rhine,[14] on the edges of the old Roman world. Paganism was perhaps as widespread in Belgic Gaul as eastern England in the fifth century and probably long survived the conversion of the Frankish court under Clovis (481–511).

The contrast between lowland Britain and Gaul works best, therefore, for the *Viennensis*, below the Loire. Further north the fifth and sixth centuries witnessed a degree of dilution and/or replacement of Late Antique culture throughout parts of the frontier region of the Gallic Prefecture. Anglicisation of the heartlands of the British diocese occurred as part of a larger process of cultural retrenchment and barbarian intrusion which affected considerable parts of what are now the Low Countries, north-eastern France, Switzerland and Bavaria. In this context, what seems to have been happening was a wholesale realignment of cultural boundaries in Late Antiquity, with the north shedding *Romanitas*, temporarily at least, in favour of more 'Germanic' or transitional cultures of one kind or another, even while the cultural heartlands of the Empire in the far West, in Spain and Aquitaine, survived virtually intact, despite their absorption into new Germanic kingdoms. But even during the fourth century these frontier areas were arguably far less 'Roman' in many respects than the southern hinterland, as regards embedded social hierarchies and Latin culture, and far more used to, and influenced by, a barbarian presence. Only the long arm of Imperial armies kept Roman authority dominant on the edge, and these increasingly consisted of barbarians by the later fourth century, with several groups settled inside the Empire. In some senses, all we are seeing is the working out of a social and political model, based on the twin concepts of core and periphery, which was undergoing rapid cultural and political change. Britain was a particularly exposed salient of this

---

[11] Such as the sunken-featured buildings and halls found on the former villa site at Neerharen-Rekem on the Maas, although these halls are far larger than the vast majority of English examples.

[12] Edward James, *The Merovingian Archaeology of South-West Gaul*, BAR, IS 25, 2 vols. (Oxford, 1977); Roger Collins, *Visigothic Spain* (Oxford, 2004), pp. 174–86.

[13] Edward James, *The Franks* (Oxford, 1988), pp. 44–64.

[14] Cremated remains also form a small minority of graves in some fourth and fifth century cemeteries in northern Gaul, as at Vron and Hordain, but these are far out-numbered by inhumations.

long northern frontier, which, when its garrisons became inoperative, was peculiarly vulnerable to barbarian raids and land-taking from both land and sea, open to attack from any direction by virtue of its island status. Its social and economic core in the south and east were particularly vulnerable to seaborne migrants and so to cultural change. Within this model, it would be surprising if Britain had not experienced a comparatively extreme version of cultural and social processes common across much of the old frontier region.

That said, the British diocese should not be seen just as a part of the wider border zone of the Empire but also as a social and cultural entity in its own right, with its own unique position within the later Roman Empire and its own particular characteristics.[15] Britain entered the Empire late and left it early relative to neighbouring regions, and without the gradual cessation of Roman management which typified fifth-century Gaul. Also, it was surrounded by the ocean, rather than by other provinces, in a way that no other Roman territories were outside the Mediterranean. In the fourth century government was often by punitive expedition and political pogrom, with lengthy periods in which central government was in abeyance. Although there was considerable Romanization of parts at least of Britain, it always lay on the edge of the Roman world, and astride the margins of the climatic and environmental conditions which that world required, with important consequences for the economy. It was, in winter particularly, to an extent cut off whenever the weather was bad in the Channel. Britain was, therefore, marked out as different in the Roman period: it was in some respects less 'Roman' than other provinces, and it may be that its *Romanitas* was comparatively fragile.[16]

Over time the robustness of a particular identity is influenced by several factors:[17] one is its perception by others; a second is the value it was accorded internally; a third is the comparative attractiveness of proximate identities; a fourth is the dynamic factor – major political or ideological crises may have the capacity to stimulate dramatic shifts in a system of group identity which had hitherto been comparatively robust and subject only to gradual change. A fifth factor is the permeability of ethnic boundaries, which can be highly variable.[18]

The cultural identities of both Britain and Gaul in the fifth century were rooted in their experiences of the Empire, so that is the next issue to explore, to see whether or not dissimilarities here may have had some potential to affect the interaction between indigenous culture and Germanic incomers. I propose for this purpose to focus on textual evidence, even though this poses considerable

---

[15] As argued particularly by Michael Jones, *The End of Roman Britain* (Ithaca, NY, 1996), *passim*.

[16] The survival of the British language is a case in point, and Britain was certainly the only island in the late Roman world with an internal land frontier beyond which lay unconquered tribes. For comparison, see the several essays in *Dialogues in Imperialism: Power, Discourse and Discrepant Experience in the Roman Empire*, Journal of Roman Archaeology, Supplementary Volume 23, ed. David Mattingly (Portsmouth, 1997).

[17] R. Jenkins, *Rethinking Ethnicity: Arguments and Explorations* (London, 1997); *Archaeological Approaches to Cultural Identity*, ed. S. Shennan (London, 1994).

[18] The classic study is by Fredrik Barth, *Ethnic Groups and Boundaries: The Social Organization of Culture Difference* (Oslo, 1969). Barth's study highlighted the comparative impermeability of Pathan group identity in comparison with their neighbours.

problems in this period, given the comparatively elite status of literacy. That said, Edward Said has helpfully underlined the centrality of narrative to the construction of identity:

> stories ... become the method colonized people use to assert their own identity and the existence of their own history. The main battle in imperialism is over land, of course; but when it came to who owned the land, who had the right to settle and work on it, who kept it going, who won it back, and who now plans its future–these issues were reflected, contested, and even for a time decided in narrative. As one critic has suggested, nations themselves *are* narrations.[19]

Crucial to our assessment of post-Roman, 'British' cultural identity is the recognition that it was undertaken in ways and for purposes which differed fundamentally from those of continental provinces of the Empire. In Spain and southern Gaul, *Romanitas* survived as an overriding group identity that was valued by local elites. Authors such as Cassiadorus and Salvian thought of themselves as 'Roman', and aristocrats recalled with pride the senatorial status of their families within the old Roman world. In Britain, in contrast, the sub-Roman period witnessed an assertion of 'British-ness' and the reversion of *Romanitas* to a form of 'Otherness'. This contrast arguably reflects differences between the insular and continental experiences of empire and, in particular, very different opinions of the Britons and the Gauls by continental authors.

The 'Otherness' of Britain was already a feature of Mediterranean literature before its conquest. Its island status characterised it for early geographers and ethnographers. In his *De bello Gallico* Caesar represented the Gauls as rapidly assimilating to civilised behaviour and Roman rule.[20] In contrast, Britain was an 'Other' land, out in the furthest Ocean, whose inhabitants, like the Germans, he consistently termed *barbari*;[21] Druidism, centred in Britain, was presented as an anti-civilising force, contesting the Romanisation of Gaul;[22] British warriors aided Gaulish 'rebels', opposing benevolent, Roman rule;[23] Britons dyed themselves with woad, and wore their hair and moustaches long; those in the hinterland were utter savages, who 'live on milk and flesh and clothe themselves in skins',[24] comparable to those archetypal 'Others' in Germany, where 'fierce and barbarous nations' who ate only fish and the eggs of birds inhabited other coastal islands.[25]

The Britons were, therefore, stereotypically barbaric and 'Other'. Their insularity perhaps made it inevitable that this 'Otherness' would remain a standard idiom, but it is important to stress that the notion of British savagery was deeply rooted in Roman culture. So, in his *Ad Furium et Aurelium*, Catullus used India,

---

[19] Edward Said, *Culture and Imperialism* (London, 1993) at p. xiii, in the context of modern European imperialism
[20] Julius Caesar, *De bello Gallico*.
[21] Caesar, *De bello Gallico*, IV, 21, 24, 25, 32, 34.
[22] Caesar, *De bello Gallico*, VI, 13.
[23] Caesar, *De bello Gallico*, IV, 20–30.
[24] Caesar, *De bello Gallico*, V, 14.
[25] Caesar, *De bello Gallico*, IV, 1, 10.

the Arabs, the Parthians and the Nile to express an exotic and valued 'Otherness' towards the east, but his western counterweight was 'the beast-like Britons [who] live at Earth's remotest gate'.[26] This stereotype was not to change thereafter, despite conquest and Romanization. Tacitus emphasised the Ocean as a divide between Britain and the civilised world, and told a story of the conquest of these *barbari*, which remarked in disparaging terms on their savagery, cruelty and cowardice.[27] In contrast, Transalpine Gauls were contemporaneously entering the Senate.[28] A Vindolanda writing-tablet of 98–104/5 disparaged the *Brittunculi* – British recruits who were being trained by Roman (or Batavian) officers.[29] Ausonius later laboured the point that a good Briton was a contradiction in terms: 'Silvius is called *Bonus* and also called *Britannus*. Who would believe a *bonus* citizen had sunk so low?'[30] And here is the panegyrist Claudian writing for Stilicho *c*.400, remarking on the greatness of Rome: 'Nor did Ocean bar her way; launching upon the deep she sought in another world for Britons to be vanquished.' Rutilius Namatianus, returning home to Gaul from Italy in 416, wrote *De reditu suo*, in which occur the lines, 'The Ocean can bear witness, Thule can bear witness, And every field the savage Briton ploughs'.[31]

There was, therefore, an entrenched stigmatisation of the Britons within normative continental elite culture, which emphasised their 'Otherness' and their cultural inferiority. Other frontier communities were not treated in quite this way. How Roman attitudes were received in Britain before the fifth century is unclear, but the consistency and depth of this cultural prejudice presumably made it difficult for Britons to gain acceptance, for example, as men of letters, intellectuals, artists, clerics or administrators elsewhere in the Empire. Indeed, there is a noticeable lack of such advancement. Before 400 there were no British emperors, no certain instances of British provincial governors, and no other identifiable senior figures of British extraction in the Senate or imperial administration. While several generals held Britain as a breakaway empire, none before 400 were British in origin and all, before 406–10, were put down by invading armies. The violent suppression of insular revolts may on occasion even have enhanced this sense of 'Otherness'.[32]

While the more southerly Gaulish provinces clearly owned membership of the Empire and its institutions from a comparatively early date, the British experience was very different. Late incorporation, cultural prejudice and both social and geographical marginality seem to have encouraged the retention and reinforcement of an insular 'British-ness' as something which was separate from and even opposed to, or by, 'Roman-ness'. Local naming strategies survived: although the several Britons who headed up the breakaway state from 406 onwards had Roman

---

[26] C. Valerius Catullus, *Carmen* XI: *ad Furium et Aurelium*, line 9.
[27] Cornelius Tacitus, *Agricola*, 11.
[28] Cornelius Tacitus, *Annales*, XI, 23.
[29] Alan K. Bowman and J. D. Thomas, *The Vindolanda Writing Tablets*, II (London, 1994), p. 343.
[30] D. Ausonius, *Epigrammata* cix.
[31] Lines 499–500.
[32] As described by Ammianus Marcellinus, *Res gestae*, XIV, 5.1–7.

names,[33] the last of them, Constantine, appointed the British-named Gerontius as his principal military commander, and although two of Gildas's British leaders were named in Latin, three had British names.[34] In the sub-Roman era, at least, a very particular, insular identity emerged in opposition to Rome. That there was some causal link between this unique phenomenon and the preceding tension between 'British-ness' and 'Roman-ness' cannot be proven but it at least seems plausible.

This emphasis on British identity as something separate from and in some sense opposed to Rome is visible earliest in the writings of Patrick, then becomes cast in stone via Gildas. Both authors valued the Roman world and saw its people as a prestigious and particularly moral community,[35] but their narratives make it quite clear that the British elite owned a separate identity which was constructed, in part at least, against Rome. That ethnicity was defined for Gildas by reference to the Old Testament Israelites, by-passing 'Romanity' as a form of cultural identity even while it was constructed within a profoundly Romano-Judaic context.[36] Whereas Roman history foregrounded conquest and imperial destiny, the Bible offered a model characterised by successive experiences of brutal assault, devastation and colonisation. It was this vision of a colonised people, as opposed to an imperial race, that Gildas adopted, depicting the Britons as morally opposed to the Romans, so as inherently cowardly and rebellious against both God and just rulers.[37] He illustrated these themes by reference to successive historical incidents, some of which he grossly misrepresented, in order to model Britain on Israel. By so doing he insisted that his people depended completely on their relationship with God and so claimed the Old Testament positioning of the Chosen People as a model for his own fatherland, his *patria*, in the present. Gildas interpreted the recent past in terms of divine warnings and then punishments by the Lord of the immorality of His people that only deep-rooted moral reform could stave off. The Saxon arrival and rebellion were, therefore, divine punishments consequent upon the culpable blindness of the British tyrant and his inept and wicked councillors.[38]

Gildas's vision must have been extremely uncomfortable for those of his

---

[33] Marcus, Gratian, Constantine.
[34] Ambrosius Aurelianus was identified as if a Roman by Gildas: *De Excidio Britanniae*, XXV, 3, in *Gildas: The Ruin of Britain*, ed. Michael Winterbottom (Chichester, 1978), at p. 98, but the *praenomen* may be figurative and his own addition, given that it means 'heavenly'; his kings are the Latin Constantine (*DEB*, XXVIII) and Aurelius Caninus (*DEB*, XXX), but this last *cognomen* is perhaps a latinisation of a British name form (meaning 'doglike'), plus the British named Vortipor (*DEB*, XXXI), Cuneglasus (*DEB*, XXXII) and Maglocunus (*DEB*, XXXIII). British personal naming gradually became dominant in the 'British' West thereafter.
[35] Patrick, *Epistola*, 2, in *St. Patrick, His Writings and Muirchu's Life*, ed. A. B. E. Hood (Chichester, 1978).
[36] Gildas, *De Excidio Britanniae*, I, 13; IV, 4; V–XX.
[37] Witness his repetitive use of Jeremiah's *Lamentations* as a context for his own introduction, and the attacks of the Assyrians on Judaea as a parallel for the Saxon rebellion and devastation of Britain: *DEB*, I, 5; XXIV, 2.
[38] In *DEB*, XXIII.

fellow countrymen who accessed his work. Quite apart from those whom he specifically attacked by name, that is the five British kings, or by profession, the British clergy virtually *in toto*, he portrayed the vast majority of his fellow *cives* in the present as steeped in sin and destined for hell.[39] His text was not easily bounded in time, and the logic of his narrative implies that the British people should be deemed to have remained disobedient to the Lord until such time as His protection had been re-established. If Britain was as if Jerusalem under sack by the Babylonians and Chaldeans, then only the destruction of the enemies of God's people (the Saxons) could signal a restoration of divine favour. Yet Gildas depicted the Britons as unwarlike, while martial qualities were accredited to every other people, be they Romans, Picts, Scots or Saxons. Once the *De Excidio Britanniae* had become established as the formative narrative of post-Roman Britain,[40] then ownership of the 'British-ness' which was defined therein carried with it the implication of cowardice, the illegitimacy of internal hierarchies and admission of gross immorality. This cannot be described as a culture with high internal valuation, or as one which was likely to attract outside emulation in the way that *Romanitas* could.

On the other hand, Gildas's portrayal of others, the Romans excepted, offered his own people considerable value by comparison. The Picts and Scots were barely-human barbarians, brutal and worm-like savages, whose facial hair and exposed bodies reflected their bestiality.[41] The Saxons were 'the whelps of the barbarian lioness', an 'abomination', devious and conniving and the Assyrians of the Old Testament.[42] By contrast, the Britons remained God's people in the present, in error admittedly, but still capable of regaining divine favour. The metaphors of the lion preying on the defenceless Christian and the wolf on the sheepfold are used repeatedly and aptly encapsulate Gildas's vision of a fundamentally Christian people beset by barbarians. His principal method of constructing his work is also relevant here: it was to amass long verbatim quotations from holy text, barely connected by a few lines of his own, to hammer home the message that, through the Bible, God was speaking directly to the Britons. By this means Gildas was asserting his own people's particular claims upon the one Christian God and His Scripture as a type of national cult. They were, in the present day, the 'latter-day Israel',[43] the people of the Book. Excepting only 'Romanity', which belongs in this text and in an insular context to the distant past, any other group identity was portrayed by Gildas as utterly valueless. 'Saxon-ness' was worst of all, implicitly at least being excluded from the human race and explicitly as being an abomination, incapable of redemption. The contrast is between the latter-day Israel and the 'Other', those who might enter heaven, should they repent, and those certainly destined for hell.

---

[39] *DEB*, I, 13–14.
[40] Which may have been Bede's doing, whose *HE* clearly designated Gildas as the *historicus* of the Britons and used so much of his moral framework as served his own purposes: *HE*, I, 22.
[41] *DEB*, XIX, 1.
[42] *DEB*, XXIII, 3; XXIII, 1; XXIII, 4–5; XXIV, 2.
[43] *DEB*, I, 13.

The frailties of this ideological self-positioning in the longer term were, however, considerable. While the Britons successfully exported Christianity to Ireland, they seem to have been less enthusiastic when it came to missionary work among these 'abominable' incomers from Germany, for whom Christian 'British-ness' was presumably neither attainable nor much sought after, compared with either a form of 'German-ness' or the 'Roman-ness' eventually on offer via St Augustine. The vision of a sinful and cowardly nation which was not actively evangelising its neighbours and in some respects out of touch with current Catholic traditions could be exploited with ease by rival narrators and would be in particular, of course, by Bede. His prejudicial positioning of the Britons as disobedient to the Lord may have had some impact on British opinion. The *Historia Brittonum* seems to have been written in part at least to contest his valuation, claiming martial virtues for the Britons vis-à-vis invaders, as well as laying claim to a centrality for the Britons within God's purposes within Britain, via the Moses-type figure of St Patrick, and Arthur, who was represented, implicitly at least, as a Joshua-like figure. Therein, the entire Hengest story was retold to the advantage of the Britons, being re-thought by non-Saxons contesting the right of the incomers to tell their version of the 'fall of Britain'.[44] This work illumines what the author felt to have power in the cultural, ideological and ethnic battleground of his own day, but by then lowland Britain had been lost to 'British-ness'. When, two generations later, Asser wrote his *Vita* of King Alfred, he treated the Britons as synonymous with the Welsh.[45]

This British group identity would prove vulnerable on several fronts. Firstly, the English conversion to Christianity seriously impaired the gate-keeping role which ownership of the Christian God as a kind of national or tribal deity served for Gildas's construction of British identity. If salvation were possible on either side of the divide, then 'British-ness' had lost much of its value. While some British clergies attempted to deny the legitimacy of the English church and police the boundary, only those protected by sympathetic secular elites in the far west could achieve this. Aldhelm's letter to Gerontius of *Dumnonia* provides the best illustration,[46] remarking on Dyfed's priests as aggressively hostile to English practices. However, across the lowlands, from c.600–670s, the patronage of convert kings gradually introduced bishops who were committed to Anglo-Roman practices and unsympathetic to clergy still adhering to British (or Ionan) traditions. The result was the marginalisation of 'British' Christianity, the 'reformation' of hitherto successful British cult centres (such as St Alban's and Whithorn) under new management and the exclusion of 'British' systems of Christian authority. Portrayal of the past, so construction of the present, was now

---

[44] See discussion in N. J. Higham, *King Arthur: Myth-making and History* (London, 2002), at pp. 98–166.
[45] Asser was himself from St David's, Pembrokeshire.
[46] *Aldhelm: The Prose Works*, ed. Michael Lapidge and Michael Herren (Cambridge, 1979), letter 4, pp. 155–60 at 158. Archbishop Lawrence had earlier noted the Irish Bishop Dagan's refusal to take food with, or even in the same space used by, the Italian clergy in early seventh-century Kent: *HE*, II, 4.

to be based on very different types of Christian narrative, which portrayed British Christianity as deviant and erroneous and claimed Roman authority in so doing.

Secondly, neither community was impervious to the facts of political power. The issue is raised in a similar context by Bishop Daniel's letter to Boniface.[47] If God had over generations granted barbarians *imperium* and success as colonial occupiers, what credibility did Gildas's vision of the Saxons as 'an abomination' retain? His construction of 'British-ness' was at its most robust as regards its power to denigrate others and exclude them from salvation, but it had been invalidated by the facts of power across the British lowlands throughout the sixth and seventh centuries, which, in any construct, were at least countenanced by God.

Lastly, 'British-ness' had initially been constructed in the context of cultural exclusion in the Roman period, then demilitarisation in the fifth century. What then emerged was a contest between two non-Roman origin myths, one British and one Anglo-Saxon, in which the indigenous story was excluded by the logic of its own construction from the great fount of authority and legitimacy which Rome and its imperial legacy provided for neighbouring provincial elites. When Germanic incomers and Gauls negotiated a new and common identity during the late fifth and sixth centuries, they did so via a language and religion which were valued by all parties. Anglo-Saxon immigrants to Britain encountered a Latin culture there, but one owned by an elite which had never been accommodated effectively within the supra-national community of Rome. Their British identity was, therefore, arguably very different to the 'Roman-ness' of Late Antique *Viennensis*, far less self-confident, and with Roman culture far less well embedded in either urban or villa society.

To sum up, therefore, Britain was a particularly exposed part of the northern frontier of the Empire, which underwent cultural changes in the sub-Roman period which were not dissimilar to parts of the Rhineland and Danube provinces. The contrast with Roman Gaul depends very much which part of Gaul one uses, for the frontier regions there experienced a comparable Germanisation to that in lowland Britain. That said, we also need to keep in mind the authority of 'British-ness' within and proximate to 'Roman-ness' and question the viability of British group identity when faced by barbarian conquest in the sub-Roman period. Continental Latin literature had tended to depict Britons as if excluded from full participation in the Roman cultural enterprise and this may help explain why sub-Roman Britain was characterised by a form of 'British-ness', as opposed to the 'Roman-ness' of other parts of the Prefecture. The low self-valuation and comparative fragility of this identity, modelled by Gildas on Israel, may well have had real consequences for the impact of the insular indigenes on the emerging cultures and identities of the post-imperial world in Britain. If we contrast the respective merits of British and Anglo-Saxon grand narratives of national origins, the comparison is very much to the disadvantage of 'British-ness'. Bede's portrayal of the English as a people of the Lord positioned within divine protection and in conformity with a Roman authority

---

[47] Dorothy Whitelock, *English Historical Documents* I (London, 1955), at pp. 795–7.

which the Britons opposed provides a powerful rationale for their geopolitical success. Ownership of the heroic foundation story of that colonial enterprise, that is the legend of Hengest and Horsa, acted as an effective gate to 'Englishness' in its broadest sense: for Bede it was the indigenes who were 'abominable' and 'barbarian'.[48] In contrast, Gildas's 'British-ness' had little value left by the mid-seventh century: its unique claim to God had been undermined; its vision of the Saxons as 'an abomination' had proved hollow; an unheroic and unmartial past merely compounded a present which was still manifestly conditioned, within this construct, by punishment by God. Communities or individuals who owned 'British-ness' were treated by their English neighbours as un-free and/or as heretics, to be variously exploited, punished and/or regained for God. Even thereafter in the British West, the *Historia Brittonum* sought to rid 'British-ness' of the pejorative traits embedded in the writings of Gildas and Bede.[49] Elsewhere, a low self-evaluation of group identity, external contempt and religious condemnation are likely to have led the indigenes to despair of their own identity and re-invest in the processes of Anglicisation. By the eighth century it seems likely that many who were biologically in large part Britons had substituted one narrative for another and elected to own the Hengest story as their own. The result was British ethnocide, as opposed to genocide, across lowland Britain and well into many upland regions, including most of Northumbria.

Our remodelling of the ways in which 'English-ness' began, therefore, does need to take account of migration, both of Germanic incomers and British emigrants, but it also requires that we construct more complex models of cultural change, to include processes of Anglicisation. It may be helpful to recognise the power of early writers to influence our debate. Let us turn, for an epilogue, to Bede's *Historia ecclesiastica*, IV, 2, where he was positioning the English around 669–70 at the pinnacle of their success as a people of God, under the guidance of Archbishop Theodore, who had, of course, been sent from Rome, and under the protection of the Northumbrian king of the day, Ecgfrith:

> Never had there been such happy times since the English first settled in Britain; for with such courageous Christian kings they were a terror to all the barbarian peoples [*barbaris nationibus*], and the desires of all men were directed to the new-found joys of the heavenly kingdom.

With Northumbrian kings briefly dominant, Bede was envisaging a Bernicia-centric Golden Age appropriate to the rhetoric of Rome, which conferred barbarity on 'Others'. Combining as it did political power with ideology, this challenge to other identities and the values invested in them was a powerful one,

---

[48] *HE*, II, 1, of the British King Cædwallon. For a recent review of this theme, see Alex Woolf, 'The Britons: from Romans to Barbarians', in *Regna and Gentes: The Relationship between Late Antique and Early Medieval Peoples and Kingdoms in the Transformation of the Roman World*, ed. Hans-Werner Goetz *et al.* (Leiden, 2003), pp. 345–80.

[49] By claiming, for example, an apostolic role in the Catholic tradition for Patrick (chaps. 52–55) and martial qualities for British leaders such as Vortimer, Arthur and Urien (chaps. 44, 56, 63).

and British ethnocide was arguably in part consequential on the potency of such attitudes.

The success with which the Franks incorporated others, such as the Gallo-Romans, across a great area, to form a new, 'confederate', Christian people, has been widely acknowledged. This 'Frankish-ness' eventually came to be expressed under the Carolingians as the new Israelites and as descendants of Troy, with 'Romans' now portrayed in terms of the pagan Empire responsible for killing the early martyrs. So, too, were the 'Angles or Saxons' markedly successful in incorporating various indigenous communities in Britain, in part by incorporating desirable forms of *Romanitas* within their own identity. The cultural mechanisms were very different assuredly, but so, too, were the circumstances. But, given the considerable differences in the ways that Britain and Gaul were positioned culturally throughout the later Roman period, we ought not to be surprised when we perceive dissimilarities in their post-colonial histories. Divergent experiences of Romanity, different types of imperial assimilation, different positions of self and of 'Other' over numerous generations, all impacted on the unfolding relationships between barbarian incomers and provincial communities, driving them down significantly different roads on the two sides of the Channel. That a much higher proportion of the population of the Anglo-Saxon kingdoms than that of the Frankish provinces was necessarily immigrant is not a safe deduction: while migration narratives are central to Anglo-Saxon perceptions of their own beginnings in Britain, we should be constructing more subtle narratives to explain the ensuing predominance of 'English' material and linguistic culture, which should consider a variety of factors capable of affecting the valuation of competing cultural identities, including the value attached to 'British-ness' across the Roman and Early Medieval periods by Britons as well as their several neighbours.

7

British Wives and Slaves? Possible Romano-British Techniques in 'Women's Work'

GALE R. OWEN-CROCKER

SPINNING and weaving are believed to have developed as women's crafts because they were compatible with child rearing; they were interruptible tasks, like food preparation and other domestic chores.[1] Given the high proportion of hours that must be spent spinning in order to support weaving, about 10:1, anyone available may have been recruited to spin, including children and old men no longer capable of heavy work. Nevertheless, textile implements from furnished Anglo-Saxon graves – spindle whorls and weaving beaters, shears and needles – are gendered, feminine possessions.[2] Weaving, from classical antiquity at least, is presented in art and text as women's work, until the introduction of the horizontal loom into western Europe about AD 1000. This loom was operated by treadles, and its inception marks the beginning of mechanization and industrialization. It was a man's instrument. Before that watershed, and even after the horizontal loom's introduction, women wove on a vertical loom, and their weaving was probably often communal. An illustration in the ninth-century, Carolingian *Utrecht Psalter*, copied more clearly in the twelfth-century, English *Eadwine Psalter*, shows this collaborative, women's world.[3] The woman on the left holds the end of a skein of thread on a forked stick, gesturing animatedly

---

[1] This argument (and my title) derives from Elizabeth Wayland Barber, *Women's Work: the First 20,000 Years. Women, Cloth and Society in Early Times* (London, 1994), pp. 29–33. For archaeologists' opinions on gender division of labour, see Jane Balme and Wendy Beck, 'Archaeology and Feminism – Views on the Origins of the Division of Labour', in *Women in Archaeology: a Feminist Critique*, ed. Hilary du Cros and Laurajane Smith (Canberra, 1993), pp. 61–74.

[2] Nick Stoodley, *The Spindle and the Spear: a Critical Enquiry into the Construction and Meaning of Gender in the Early Anglo-Saxon Burial Rite*, BAR, BS 288 (Oxford, 1999), pp. 33 and 31, fig. 26. I know only two possible instances of a man with a spindle whorl in an Anglo-Saxon cemetery; one was elderly (Mitcham, Greater London, No. 223; H. F. Bidder and John Morris, 'An Anglo-Saxon cemetery at Mitcham', *Surrey Archaeological Collections* 56 (1959), 51–131, at p. 74). The other had a small, amber whorl which might have functioned as a bag fastener (Finglesham, Kent, Grave K6; Helen Geake, *The Use of Grave-Goods in Conversion-Period England, c.600–c. 850*, BAR, BS 261 (Oxford, 1997), p. 60).

[3] Utrecht, Universiteitsbibliotheek 32, *Script. Eccl.* 484, fol. 84r; Cambridge, Trinity College MS R. 17. 1, fol. 263r.

to her companion who holds a pair of shears. Two women work at a two-beam vertical loom. They are probably preparing the warp: one woman, kneeling, spreads the warp threads with her fingers; she holds what looks like a comb with an angled handle in her other hand. Her companion holds shears. It was probably a world where a woman worked alongside her sister and her cousin, where techniques were passed down from mother to daughter.

The Manchester Medieval Textiles Project has documented over 4,000 textile fragments of the Anglo-Saxon period, mostly from fifth- to seventh-century graves. The majority of these grave-finds are mineralized, preserved as corrosion products of metalwork with which they were in contact, though it is often possible to distinguish fibre, spinning direction, weave and thread count. Occasionally rust has enclosed, and so preserved, textile in a flexible state, in which case more detailed analysis is usually possible, although as the fragments are tiny, often just a few millimetres across, a patterned weave may have to be reconstructed from a representative section. Many of the more sophisticated textiles may have gone unidentified because there is insufficient remaining to make deductions. The majority of textiles derive from the clothing in which bodies were buried, particularly from brooches which women wore at each shoulder.[4] Few textiles survive from lower down the body, from the skirts of garments, or trousers; and as men were buried with less body-jewellery than women, there is relatively little evidence from male graves. Non-clothing textiles are uncommon – they include wrappings for weapons and other grave-goods, and examples preserved by exceptionally waterlogged conditions and metalwork in the Sutton Hoo Ship Burial, deriving from bedding, a hanging and binding tape for the scabbard.

Broadly speaking, the textiles divide into loom-woven fabrics and narrow bands, usually tablet-woven. Tablet weaving produces strong, flexible bands used as girdles and garment edges, and as starting borders for cloth woven on the warp-weighted loom. The latter is a vertical loom with one horizontal beam, at the top. The warp threads – the fixed threads in weaving – are attached to this beam (often by means of a starting border) and hang down. They are kept taut by weights tied to groups of threads at the bottom of the loom. Round, clay loom weights are common on Anglo-Saxon settlement sites, sometimes found in isolation, but most importantly in rows, where they have dropped from abandoned looms.[5] The Anglo-Saxons definitely used the warp-weighted loom. The evidence of loom weights is confirmed by characteristic tools: the double-ended pin beater and the sword-shaped batten, which was used to compact the weft threads during weaving by beating upwards. Metal battens have been found in relatively rich female graves, evidently high-status possessions. There were probably utilitarian versions of wood or bone which have not survived.

The Anglo-Saxons were not the first peoples to introduce the warp-weighted

---

[4] Gale R. Owen-Crocker, *Dress in Anglo-Saxon England: revised and enlarged edition* (Woodbridge, 2004), pp. 42–3, 273–4.
[5] Notably from a very large loom at Grimstone End, Pakenham, Suffolk; Steven J. Plunkett, 'The Anglo-Saxon Loom from Pakenham, Suffolk', *Proceedings of the Suffolk Institute of Archaeology and History* 39 (1999), 277–98. Presumably a loom, particularly one set up for weaving, would only be abandoned in an emergency, such as fire.

loom to Britain. Finds of loom weights confirm that it was in use before and during the Roman occupation, though the Anglo-Saxons, who were more restricted in the form of weights they used, are more likely to have been following their continental tradition than copying what they found on arrival.

It is a distinguishing feature of this loom that if it is leaned against a wall, at an angle, work is more economical: a shed rod can be inserted between the warp threads, dividing them. Half the warp hangs down behind the rod; the other half, curved over the rod, hangs in front. This creates a 'shed', the space between the warp threads through which the bobbin of weft is passed. No other loom has this 'natural shed': with other equipment, each warp thread must be tied to a heddle rod, to raise and lower the thread for the weft to pass through. With the warp-weighted loom, only the back threads need to be tied to a heddle rod. Although more rods are needed for complex patterned weaves, the natural bipartite division of the warp is advantageous.

Most early Anglo-Saxon woven textiles are consistent with weaving on this loom. The simplest is tabby, or plain weave, which makes use of the natural shed with alternate throws of the weft. Characteristic of the warp-weighted loom is 2 x 2 twill, which uses an 'over two, under two' progression, and by moving along one thread each time produces a cloth with distinctive diagonal lines. This loom, because of its capacity for additional heddle rods, is particularly suited to weaving twill; and twill is particularly effective for weaving wool, as it increases the insulating capacity of the cloth by retaining air.[6] The most elaborate products of the warp-weighted loom are so-called four-shed twills, which utilize the natural shed plus three heddle rods, producing diamond and lozenge patterns, subtle woven designs often enhanced by spinning warp and weft in different directions (Z/S spinning). Tapestry weaving was still a foreign art at this stage.[7] Anglo-Saxon products were not, normally, subjected to finishing processes known to the Romans, and which were to become popular for woollen cloth later in the Middle Ages – fulling, teaseling and shearing,[8] procedures which create a soft finish. Such treatment would obscure any woven pattern, the essence of the most skilled weaving on the warp-weighted loom.

The majority of textile finds from Anglo-Saxon graves are tabbies and simple 2 x 2 twills; four-shed twills and tablet-weave constitute significant minorities. The tabbies and twills, like the warp-weighted loom which probably produced them, are consistent with Migration Age textiles from Scandinavia and continental Europe, although Anglo-Saxon England produces a more heterogeneous mixture, as it does in other artefacts, such as pottery, than the more regionalized

---

[6] Lise Bender Jørgensen, *North European Textiles until AD 1000* (Aarhus, 1992), p. 120.

[7] There is one example from the Sutton Hoo Ship Burial, SH 14; Elisabeth Crowfoot, 'The Textiles', in *The Sutton Hoo Ship Burial*, ed. Rupert Leo Scott Bruce-Mitford, 3 vols. (London, 1975–83), III.i, ed. Angela Care Evans (1983), 409–79 at pp. 428–33.

[8] See R. Patterson, 'Spinning and Weaving', in Charles Singer, E. J. Holmyard, A. R. Hall and Trevor I. Williams, *A History of Technology*, 7 vols. (Oxford, 1956–78), II (1956), 191–220 at pp. 214–17.

continent.⁹ Finds of tablet-weave are not common in the Netherlands and north German homelands,¹⁰ but are characteristic of Scandinavia which contributed Anglian, Jutish and other settlers to Anglo-Saxon England.¹¹

Apart from rarities from high status sites, which were probably luxury imports, the majority of early Anglo-Saxon textile fragments are consistent with the Scandinavian and north German/Frisian origin of the immigrants and the weaving techniques they imported. There are, however, a few fragments of textile which are not so easily explained. These are woven in so-called 'three-shed' twill, or 2 x 1 twill, in which the weft passes over two, then under one, thread of the warp. It has been suggested that this 2 x 1 weaving could be a survival of Romano-British technology in Anglo-Saxon England.¹² If so, 2 x 1 textiles may be the product of wives and slaves of native descent who had learned the technique at their mother's knee and continued to practise it.

Because of its asymmetry, 2 x 1 twill does not exploit the warp-weighted loom's natural shed. Therefore it has been assumed to have been made on a different loom.¹³ The only alternative for textiles of this date is the two-beam vertical loom.¹⁴ This loom-type existed in Scandinavia until about AD 200 when it was evidently supplanted by the warp-weighted loom,¹⁵ and it coexisted with the warp-weighted loom in Italy and the Mediterranean provinces of the Roman

---

[9] Regional distribution is discussed in Lise Bender Jørgensen, 'The Textiles of the Saxons, Anglo-Saxons and Franks', *Studien zur Sachsenferschung* 7 (1991), 11–23 and developed in her *North European Textiles until AD 1000*.

[10] This may be due to lack of survival.

[11] Lise Bender Jørgensen, 'Scandinavia AD 400–1000', in *The Cambridge History of Western Textiles*, ed. David Jenkins, 2 vols. (Cambridge, 2003), I, 132–8, at p. 132, notes that two thirds of Scandinavian textiles of the Migration Age are Z/Z-spun plain wool 2 x 2 twills and one sixth tablet-woven. The popularity of tablet weaving may have been related to the popularity of wrist clasps, which were introduced from Scandinavia in the sixth century; John Hines, *The Scandinavian Character of Anglian England in the Pre-Viking Period*, BAR, BS 124 (Oxford, 1984), pp. 35–109.

[12] Elisabeth Crowfoot, 'The Textiles', in Barbara Green and Andrew Rogerson, *The Anglo-Saxon Cemetery at Bergh Apton, Norfolk: Catalogue*, East Anglian Archaeology 7 (1978), 98–106, at 105; 'Textiles' in Care Evans, *Sutton Hoo* III.i, 438–42; 'Textiles', in Stanley E. West, *The Anglo-Saxon Cemetery at Westgarth Gardens, Bury St Edmunds, Suffolk: Catalogue*, East Anglian Archaeology Report 33 (1988), pp. 14–19 at p. 14; 'Textiles Associated with Metalwork', in Tim Malim and John Hines, eds., *Edix Hill (Barrington A), Cambridgeshire*, Council for British Archaeology Research Report 112 (York, 1998), pp. 235–46, at p. 239.

[13] This interpretation arises from Marta Hoffmann, *The Warp-weighted Loom: Studies in the History and Technology of an Ancient Implement*, Studia Norvegica 14 (Oslo, 1964), pp. 203, 251–3 where the author suggests that 2 x 1 twill was not devised for the warp-weighted loom and is more suited to a two-beam loom. John Peter Wild (*Textile Manufacture in the Northern Roman Provinces* (Cambridge, 1970), p. 70) states, 'The suggestion is theoretically attractive, but cannot as yet be shown to be true from archaeological material.' This caution is still valid today, and the theory itself has been challenged by John Hedges (see below). Nevertheless the two-beam loom and Romano-British origin have been repeated in textile reports when 2 x 1 twills are identified.

[14] This loom can weave either tubular or flat cloth. The tubular version is created by inserting a horizontal rod and winding the warp threads round it.

[15] Bender Jørgensen, *North European Textiles*, pp. 120–2.

Empire until at least the fifth century, eventually displacing it.[16] Being made entirely of organic materials, the two-beam loom does not leave any archaeological trace, unlike the warp-weighted, which is evidenced in many countries and cultures by its characteristic clay or stone weights.

2 x 1 twill is not typical either of the Germanic homelands of the Anglo-Saxon immigrants, nor of Frisia and the Rhineland with which they traded. In an encyclopaedic study of textiles from graves in north and west Europe, Lise Bender Jørgensen has demonstrated that 2 x 1 twill is completely absent from Frisia, the southern Netherlands, Saxon Germany, Austrasia (the Rhine Valley) and Baiuwaria;[17] nor is it characteristic of Scandinavia.[18] Instances may have been missed, however, since 2 x 1 twill can be unidentifiable unless the analyst is able to view both sides. Bender Jørgensen says:

> ... as most of the textiles from the Merovingian period graves have been found rusted on to metal artefacts so that only one side is visible, a number of 2/1 twills may have passed undetected. These are notoriously difficult to analyse, since one side looks deceptively like tabby and the other just like 2/2 twill.[19]

However, it seems that generally 2 x 1 twill is untypical of Germanic culture in north-west Europe.

It is then possible that the 2 x 1 twills in early Anglo-Saxon England are evidence of a pre-existing two-beam loom which continued to operate side by side with the more archaeologically apparent warp-weighted loom.[20] However,

---

[16] Wild, *Textile Manufacture*, p. 67; Penelope Walton Rogers, 'The Re-appearance of an Old Roman Loom in Medieval England', in *The Roman Textile Industry and its Influence: a birthday tribute to John Peter Wild*, ed. Penelope Walton Rogers, Lise Bender Jørgensen and Antoinette Rast-Eicher (London, 2001), pp. 158–71, at p. 160.

[17] Lise Bender Jørgensen, 'A Coptic Tapestry and other Textile Remains from the Royal Frankish Graves of Cologne Cathedral', *Acta Archaeologica* 56 (1985), 85–100, at p. 97, fig. 12. The only north-west continental regions where it is found are Thuringia and Alamannia.

[18] Jørgensen, 'A Coptic Tapestry', p. 99; Lise Bender Jørgensen, 'Scandinavia AD 400–1000', in Jenkins, *Cambridge History of Western Textiles*, p. 132.

[19] Lise Bender Jørgensen, 'The Continental Germans', in Jenkins, *Cambridge History of Western Textiles*, I, 118–24 at 121. However, a number of mineralized textiles have been so identified from Anglo-Saxon England. Elisabeth Crowfoot recognized two three-shed twills at Morning Thorpe by 'the passage of threads showing clearly on both at broken edges', Elisabeth Crowfoot, 'Textiles', in Barbara Green, Andrew Rogerson and Susan G. White, *The Anglo-Saxon Cemetery at Morning Thorpe, Norfolk. Volume I: Catalogue*, East Anglian Archaeology 36.i (1987), 171–188 at p. 172.

[20] The situation is complicated by the apparent revival of 2 x 1 twill, which was popular in England from the tenth to the fourteenth centuries onwards, this time in fine, smooth, Z-spun wool, often brightly coloured (Penelope Walton Rogers, 'The Anglo-Saxons and Vikings in Britain, AD 450–1050', in Jenkins, *Cambridge History of Western Textiles*, I, 124–32, at p. 130; see also Penelope Walton, in Dominic Tweddle, *Finds from Parliament Street and Other Sites in the City Centre*, The Archaeology of York, The Small Finds 17/4 (1986), pp. 233–4, at p. 233). The two-beam loom may have been reintroduced from France at this time (Walton Rogers, 'The Re-appearance of an Old Roman Loom', in Walton Rogers *et al.*, *The Roman Textile Industry*, pp. 163–4, 166) shortly before the introduction of the horizontal loom; Hoffmann, *Warp-weighted Loom*, p. 258.

the premise that, since 2 x 1 twills were not natural to the warp-weighted loom[21] they must have been woven on a different instrument, was questioned by John Hedges in 1982. Hedges pointed out that the assumption, made by Marta Hoffmann in her text-book study of the warp-weighted loom and since universally followed, that the loom was always set up slanted, was based on modern Scandinavia, and that earlier representations, for example Greek vase paintings, show it vertical. Without the slant, the natural shed – diagnostic in Hoffmann's argument – is absent. Hedges argued that a warp-weighted loom set upright without the natural shed was not unsuitable for weaving three-shed twills, citing Scandinavian 2 x 1 twills with starting borders as possible examples.[22] Penelope Walton Rogers subsequently wove 2 x 1 on a warp-weighted loom set vertically 'without great technical difficulties',[23] though Scandinavian textile specialists remain unconvinced that the loom was used this way in northern Europe.[24] Arguably, however, the early Anglo-Saxon 2 x 1 twills could have been made on the warp-weighted loom, so it is not necessary to assume that a non-Germanic, two-beam loom was in use; but the question remains: why would anyone in an Anglo-Saxon context weave 2 x 1 unless they were maintaining an aberrant cultural tradition? 2 x 1 twills are rare occurrences among the tabbies and 2 x 2 twills of Anglo-Saxon cemeteries.[25] The Manchester Medieval Textiles Project identifies that 2 x 1 twill is recorded from only twenty-one of the hundreds of Anglo-Saxon cemeteries with textile, though some have examples from more than one grave.[26] The majority are from Anglian areas, ranging from East Anglia up

---

[21] Hoffmann, *Warp-weighted Loom*, p. 248.

[22] John Hedges, 'Textiles', in *Anglo-Scandinavian Finds from Lloyds Bank, Pavement and other Sites*, ed. Arthur MacGregor, The Archaeology of York 17.3 (1982), pp. 102–27, citing examples from Lund, Sweden. The Lund examples, like one from Bryggen, Bergen, Norway, are much later than our Anglo-Saxon 2 x 1 fragments, from eleventh- to fifteenth-century and twelfth- to thirteenth-century levels respectively, and could, therefore, have been made on a horizontal loom, while one from Feddersen Wierde, Germany, is much earlier – 50 BC to AD 100; Märta Lindström, 'Textilier', in *Uppgrävt förflutet förPKbanken i Lund*, ed. Anders W. Mårtensson, Archaeologica Lundensia 7 (1976), pp. 279–92, at pp. 279, 288–92, figs 249–51. The Lund starting border could be described as transitional: it has only four thick warp threads and as such is 'only a short step' from abandoning the starting border 'in favour of a couple of setting-up strings'; Karen-Hanne Stærmose Nielsen, *Kirkes Væv: Opstadvævens historie og nutidige brug*, Forsøg med Fortiden 6 (Lejre, Historisk-Arkæologisk Forsøgscenter Lejre, 1999), pp. 100–101, fig. 56B, quoted from an unpublished translation loaned by Frances Pritchard. I am grateful to Lorna Dunn for help with Lindström's Swedish text and to Frances Pritchard for discussing the significance of the Lund finds with me.

[23] Walton, in Tweddle, *Finds from Parliament Street*, p. 233.

[24] Information from Frances Pritchard, to whom I am grateful for reading this article in draft and making several helpful suggestions.

[25] Distribution of cloth types in Anglo-Saxon England is shown in Bender Jørgensen, *North European Textiles*, pp. 27–30, figs 16–29. There is a histogram of the thread counts of 2 x 1 twills at p. 36, fig. 42, but no distribution map. This cloth, Bender Jørgensen Type 9, is discussed on pp. 35–6.

[26] Barrington A, Cambridgeshire; Bergh Apton, Norfolk; Broomfield Barrow, Essex; Buckland, Dover, Kent; Butler's Field, Lechlade, Gloucestershire; Cleatham, North Lincoln-

through Lincolnshire and East Yorkshire to Northumberland. Finds also include Petersfinger and Lechlade, in West Saxon areas, and Mucking and Buckland, which are in the south east, respectively East Saxon and Kentish territories; so the Anglian bias is as likely to reflect the distribution of burial sites with textile preservation as a geographical distribution of this weave.[27] Wherever it occurs, 2 x 1 twill is a minority find. If it represents a stratum of the population this would seem to be small, and if manufacture was contemporary with the people buried in the cemeteries, 2 x 1 appears to be a minority output of the textile workers. Even at Milfield, Northumberland (in the area of Anglian Bernicia where an Anglo-Saxon élite may have ruled a population largely of Celtic stock,[28] or at least where British and Anglo-Saxon coexisted[29] and hence where Celtic textiles might be manifested), 2 x 1s were rarities.[30]

Excluding examples from 'princely graves' at Sutton Hoo and Broomfield, which may have been imports, and focussing on finds from 'folk cemeteries', I have considered how these textiles functioned and if it is possible to distinguish the value that was put on them by their owners. They have been recovered from both male and female burials. An outstanding example from a female grave at Little Eriswell was woven in flax with a very fine thread count.[31] It was associated

---

shire; Fonaby, Lincolnshire; Little Eriswell, Suffolk; Milfield North, Milfield South, Northumberland; Morning Thorpe, Norfolk; Mucking, Essex; Oxborough, Norfolk; Petersfinger, Wiltshire; Sewerby, East Yorkshire; Sleaford, Lincolnshire; Spong Hill, Norfolk; Sutton Hoo Ship Burial, Suffolk; Wakerley, Northamptonshire; Wasperton, Warwickshire; West Garth Gardens, Bury St Edmunds, Suffolk. The database identifies tenth-century examples from Winchester, and tenth- to eleventh-century from Coppergate, York, which I have discarded for the present purpose (see note 20). Eighth-century examples from Fishergate and Parliament Street, York, may suggest continuity; but dearth of textile evidence from the Middle Saxon period, which offers neither furnished graves nor waterlogged occupation sites, makes continuity difficult to prove.

The Manchester Medieval Textiles Project is directed by Elizabeth Coatsworth, Manchester Metropolitan University, and the author. I am grateful to Dr Coatsworth for producing the data discussed in this paper.

27 In Bender Jørgensen's tables 2 x 1 twill is absent from the following 'Saxon' county groups: Berkshire, Oxfordshire; Warwickshire; Hampshire, Sussex and Surrey. The Manchester data confirms this.

28 Leslie Alcock, 'Quantity or Quality: the Anglian Graves of Bernicia', in *Angles, Saxons and Jutes: essays presented to J. N. L. Myres*, ed. Vera I. Evison (Oxford, 1981), pp. 168–86; Higham, *RBAS*, pp. 185, 205–6.

29 Roger Miket suggests 'the Bernician population was an amalgam of British and Anglo-Saxon stock'; Roger Miket, 'A Re-statement of Evidence from Bernician Anglo-Saxon Burials', in *Anglo-Saxon Cemeteries 1979: the Fourth Anglo-Saxon Symposium at Oxford*, ed. Philip Rahtz, Tania Dickinson and Lorna Watts, BAR, BS 82 (Oxford, 1980), pp. 289–305.

30 Milfield North, probably late sixth- to seventh-century: one out of twenty-four textile fragments (J. M. Cronyn, with contributions by P. Clogg and G. Turner-Walker, 'Textiles', in C. J. Scull and A. F. Harding, 'Two Early Medieval Cemeteries at Milfield, Northumberland', *Durham Archaeological Journal* 6 (1990), 1–29, at p. 9); Milfield South, late seventh- to eighth-century, and probably associated with the royal vill of *Maelmin* (Bede, *HE*, II, xiv), one out of four; P. Clogg 'Textiles', in Scull and Harding, 'Milfield', 21.

31 30 x 22 threads per cm.

with what was described as rabbit fur,[32] and attached to a lump of red sandstone placed under the head of the corpse. It is possible the cloth derived from a linen and fur headdress, but the most likely identification is a linen pillowcase. We can speculate that, having decided to prop up the woman's head with a stone, the mourners 'prettied it up' by putting a pillow case on it.[33] In the site publication it is suggested that this textile was imported from the Near East, but the burial was, in terms of quantity and quality of grave-goods, of average prosperity, not rich, and the same could be said of the site in general. It is not a context where one might expect exotic or luxurious textiles, but this might be a rare survival of a skilled domestic industry. The textile may have been old and consigned willingly to the grave for that reason, just as broken jewellery often accompanied a corpse.

In several cases 2 x 1 twills have been found on the brooches which are typical finds from women's graves, which suggests that the unusual textile was employed for the usual garment. At Butler's Field the cloth was identified as finely woven diamond twill,[34] a patterned weave, and skilled product. It was found on a saucer brooch, one of a pair with a female skeleton. This was not a rich grave: it contained no gold, for instance, though the woman had over 300 amber beads, an unusually large quantity. She may have been important in her community, which was one that demonstrated considerable continuity from Roman times. At Mitchell's Hill 2 x 1 twill attached to wrist clasps[35] could have derived from the undergown sleeve. In several cases 2 x 1 twill has been found attached to objects probably carried at the belt: chatelaines, a possible key, a knife, several buckles – one found at the sacrum of a skeleton, another found in the middle of a grave. In each case the textile might have derived from the skirts of a garment, but it is possible that it belonged to a pouch, which contained some of the equipment people carried with them, such as knives and keys. If so, it may be that the 2 x 1 twill was considered a good, strong material for a pouch, and so was specially woven for that purpose; alternatively, a bag may have been made from recycled textiles, obsolete garments or furnishings. At Butler's Field a fragment of three-shed twill was found on the outside of the metal grip of a shield.[36] Again circumstances invite conflicting interpretations of the textile's status. The shield grip was found at the centre of the skeleton's pelvis. The textile could simply derive from clothing. Alternatively it could have been wrapped around the shield grip to make it more comfortable to hold, and any old rag might have been used for that. If, on the other hand, it had wrapped up the shield for the grave, it might have

---

[32] There is no evidence that rabbits were known to the Anglo-Saxons and it is usually assumed that they were introduced to England by the Normans. However, a recent find from Lynford, Norfolk, confirms Marcus Terentius Varro's evidence that the Romans were farming rabbits for meat in Britain as early as the first or second century AD; David Sapsted, 'Romans Introduced the Rabbit', *The Daily Telegraph*, Thursday 14 April 2005, p. 12.
[33] There is precedent for a fine linen pillow case at Sutton Hoo, though it is not 2 x 1 twill.
[34] Threadcount recorded as 25 x 16. Threadcounts are unusually high (i.e. they suggest fine textiles) at this site.
[35] Grace M. Crowfoot, 'Anglo-Saxon Tablet Weaving', *AntJ* 82 (1952), 189–91 at p. 190.
[36] Grave 64.

been something more prized.³⁷ The young man in the grave was accompanied by this shield but had no sword, so his status was perhaps above average but not of the highest rank.

To question the possibility that 2 x 1 twill was a survival of Romano-British culture, I have looked for other evidence of Roman-British survival whenever 2 x 1 twill has appeared in recent publications, and have usually found it somewhere in the cemetery. Occasionally this evidence also concerns textile processing: finds from Sewerby, for example, included both three-shed twill and napped or teaselled fabrics,³⁸ and at Bergh Apton curled fibres on the 2 x 1 twill itself were likely to be the result of teaseling that textile, which was from a woman's brooch.³⁹ In other cases the evidence is in the form of artefacts, remains of pre-Anglo-Saxon pottery or metalwork. At Oxborough a Roman brooch was found in the same grave as the 2 x 1 twill. Pre-Anglo-Saxon artefacts in themselves are not conclusive evidence that the Romano-British and Germanic cultures co-existed; the Anglo-Saxons seem to have been acquisitive with regard to Roman coins and old Roman brooches, for example, which frequently appear in Anglo-Saxon graves. They were old, as much as hundreds of years, when buried. They may testify to Roman taste but are not a guide to ethnicity.⁴⁰ The issue is contentious. Some consider the Anglo-Saxons as no more than 'treasure hunters'. Roger White favours selective re-use:

> this material cannot be used to demonstrate the survival of the Romano-British population into Anglo-Saxon England. The material is not selected randomly but conforms to a pattern of usage which is related to, and mirrors the use of, contemporary Anglo-Saxon artefacts.⁴¹

This includes vessels as well as jewellery. White takes the view that these objects were used by people who could not afford the 'real thing', an opinion I would question.⁴² Helen Geake, however, in arguing that the 'conversion period' changes are a Roman revival rather than the Byzantine/Frankish influence which is usually suggested, hints at continuity:

> there are a number of objects of Roman manufacture which continue to find their way into graves throughout the migration period. ... There are slight indi-

---

37 It may have been customary to use special textiles as wraps: 2 x 1 twill wrapped weapons and the helmet at Sutton Hoo and a unique 'summer-and-winter' weave the Wollaston helmet.
38 Elisabeth Crowfoot, 'The Textiles', in *An Anglo-Saxon Inhumation Cemetery at Sewerby, East Yorkshire*, ed. Susan M. Hirst, York University Archaeological Publications 4 (York, 1985), pp. 48–54.
39 Manchester Medieval Textiles Project no. 011 003; Elisabeth Crowfoot, 'The Textiles; the Anglo-Saxon Cemetery at Bergh Apton', *East Anglian Archaeology* 7 (1978), 98–106.
40 Roger White, 'Scrap or Substitute: Roman Material in Anglo-Saxon Graves', in *Anglo-Saxon Cemeteries: a Reappraisal*, ed. Edmund Southworth (Stroud, 1990), pp. 125–52.
41 White, 'Scrap or Substitute', p. 146.
42 Owen-Crocker, *Dress*, pp. 41, 323.

cations that ... make it likely that knowledge of Roman-British tradition was a continuing trend.[43]

Many pre-Anglo-Saxon objects buried in Anglo-Saxon graves were evidently amuletic.[44] Audrey Meaney has identified the practice of carrying 'something old' as characteristic of the women accompanied by amulet bags with ivory ring frames. The ancient object may be in the pouch or elsewhere in the grave, like a Roman bead on the necklace of such a woman at Minerva Park.[45] The discovery of an ancient object in an Anglo-Saxon grave may or may not mean continuity of ownership, because a bead or a metal brooch will not deteriorate over a period during which it is 'lost';[46] but textile, being organic, is a different matter. It is perfectly possible to keep textile for a long time. I have linen in my cupboard that is over seventy years old, in excellent condition; but the key point is that it is in the cupboard. If exposed to damp or soil, organic materials will rot. If these 2 x 1 textiles are Romano-British survivals, we must posit either survival of the textiles themselves, carefully stored over a very long period of time and handed over from one custodian to another; or survival of women with the expertise to make them.

But are the textiles Romano-British? Certainly they are not characteristically Germanic, but there is little evidence to demonstrate that they are typically Romano-British either. Bender Jørgensen lists only two cases from Roman Britain: linen from Carpow, Perthshire, Scotland, and wool from Corbridge, Northumberland.[47] She falls back on the argument that examples may have been overlooked (see also p. 84, above), and makes an assumption hardly justified by the evidence: 'We must therefore content ourselves with the conclusion that 2/1 twills were among the Roman-Period cloth-types of northern Europe. Their precise proportion in the material can only be guessed at.'[48] 2 x 1 twill is equally rare in Celtic Britain, being confined to at most two survivals in Ireland,[49] though

[43] Geake, *Use of Grave-Goods*, p. 121. Evidence is negative – absence of earrings and pierced goldwork – as well as positive – presence of hanging bowls and penannular brooches in both Romano-Britain and conversion Anglo-Saxon graves. Geake is not concerned with Migration Age graves.

[44] Audrey L. Meaney, *Anglo-Saxon Amulets and Curing Stones*, BAR, BS 96 (Oxford, 1981).

[45] Owen-Crocker, *Dress*, p. 70.

[46] As Eckhardt and Williams argue, the fact that an artefact had been retrieved from a temporal and cultural context divorced from the circumstances of re-use might increase its amuletic value; Hella Eckardt and Howard Williams, 'Objects without a Past: the Use of Roman Objects in Early Anglo-Saxon Graves', in *Archaeology of Remembrance: Death and Memory in Past Societies*, ed. Howard Williams (New York, Boston, Dordrecht, London, Moscow, 2003), pp. 141–70. Continuity of use is most arguable when an object dates to late in the Romano-British period, but instances are uncommon.

[47] Both are Z/Z-spun; Bender Jørgensen, *North European Textiles*, p. 21. Wild identified only six examples from the north-west provinces of the Roman Empire, all in Mainz. Several were felted; all were fairly coarse weaves: 8–13/14 threads per cm.

[48] Bender Jørgensen, *North European Textiles*, p. 129 in the section titled 'The Textiles of the Roman Empire' where the 2 x 1 cloth is called 'Corbridge Type'.

[49] One example from Church Island, near Valencia, Co. Kerry, a sixth- to seventh-century site; Bender Jørgensen, *North European Textiles*, p. 20. Maria Amelia FitzGerald,

the lack of loom weights from Irish occupation sites may indicate that some loom other than the warp-weighted was used there.⁵⁰

However, the surviving Anglo-Saxon find spots are so distributed they do not indicate any obvious trade route, and, as noted, the textiles are often found on sites with some Romano-British associations; so perhaps they are indeed relics of Romano-British culture. That does not mean that Celtic ethnicity is represented by the aberrant textiles. Archaeological textile generally survives through contact with metal, and in the cases under consideration that metalwork is characteristically Anglo-Saxon. While grave-goods may show the ethnicity a person wants to display, they do not show genetics. We simply do not know if native Celts are present among the population of Anglo-Saxon cemeteries, 'disguised' in Germanic grave-goods or anonymous in graves without artefacts. Further, if those making the textile were a substratum of society, servants and slaves, they worked for masters and mistresses, and they themselves may not be the occupants of the graves that carry their product. In other words, the textile worn may not be a guide to the ethnicity of its owner, but to the cultural tradition of its maker. An ethnic Celt wearing Anglo-Saxon jewellery and an Anglo-Saxon wearing Romano-British cloth are both possible in Anglo-Saxon cemeteries.

Textile Production in Prehistoric and Medieval Ireland, 5 vols., unpublished PhD thesis, Manchester Metropolitan University, 2000, I, 133 adds a second from the crannog at Island Mac High, Co. Tyrone, previously considered Bronze Age, now possibly seventh-century.

⁵⁰ Hodkinson suggests that the two-beam vertical loom or possibly the backstrap loom was in use in Ireland; Brian Hodkinson, 'A Reappraisal of the Archaeological Evidence for Weaving in Ireland in the Early Christian Period', *Ulster Journal of Archaeology* 50 (1987), 47–53. Tools associated with the warp-weighted loom are rare in Ireland. FitzGerald dismisses three of the five possible double-ended pin beaters as 'not sufficiently robust to have functioned as pin-beaters' (*Textile Production in Ireland*, p. 153). There are only two definite and datable weaving battens, seventh- to eighth-century from Rathtinaun Lough Gara, Co. Sligo, and eighth- to ninth-century from Littleton Bog, Co. Tipperary; FitzGerald, p. 143.

8

Early Mercia and the Britons

DAMIAN J. TYLER

THIS essay considers some aspects of the ethnic composition of the Mercian kingdom and hegemony to the death of Penda, king of the Mercians *c*.633–*c*.655. The early Mercians appear in Bede's *Historia ecclesiastica* as an 'English' group; we are told that they are of Anglian stock,[1] and Bede treats them throughout as a part of the *gens Anglorum*, if often a morally dubious part. It will be argued here that the situation was rather more complex than Bede implies. Three zones of interaction between the Mercian kingship and the Britons will be proposed: firstly an 'outer zone' consisting of kingdoms which formed part of and contributed to Penda's hegemony; secondly, an 'inner zone' made up of groups more closely tied to the Mercian kingship; and finally, a 'core zone', the people of the early Mercian kingdom proper. It will be argued that as one moves from the periphery to the centre, British elite culture becomes less prominent, but that even in the heartland of the earliest Mercian kingdom there was in the early seventh century a British element among the elite.

The paucity of literary sources relating to Mercia is well-known and has long been an impediment to the study of this kingdom. Those texts which exist are mainly narratives, Bede's *Historia ecclesiastica* being the principal. Furthermore, the literary sources we possess are of an almost exclusively non-Mercian origin. Thus, we view Mercian kings through the eyes of outsiders (and frequently enemies), and our vision of them and their activities is inevitably distorted.[2] When the literary sources are considered alongside place-name and archaeological material, however, it is possible to make some tentative suggestions and to attempt to create a model of the ethnic dynamics of early Mercia.

Between his victory over Oswald, king of the Northumbrians, *c*.642,[3] and his own death in *c*.655,[4] Penda was the dominant king in southern Britain. Though we have few precise details, it is clear that during this period he created and maintained a very successful hegemony, and that his overkingship was acknowledged by many kings–as many as thirty if we can credit Bede's statement that on

---

[1] *HE*, II, 15.
[2] For a succinct discussion of the problems of early Mercian sources, see Barbara Yorke, *Kings and Kingdoms of Early Anglo-Saxon England* (London, 1990), pp. 100–1.
[3] *HE*, III, 9.
[4] *HE*, III, 24.

his final campaign Penda was accompanied by thirty *duces regii*.[5] The kingdoms embraced by this overkingship are here considered the 'outer zone'. This outer zone included Anglo-Saxon groups such as the East Angles and their king Æthelhere.[6] However, it also included the kingdom of Gwynedd in north Wales and other unnamed Welsh kingdoms.[7] The 'British-ness' of these groups is beyond question, and indeed, though we now use the terms *Cymry* or Welsh, that ethnic identity persists to the present. There are no records of conflict between the Mercians and the British kingdoms until the end of the seventh century.[8] Thus, in their dealings with the elites of this zone, Penda and his Mercians were clearly accustomed to positive interactions with Britons. This has long been acknowledged,[9] and there is no need to discuss this zone any further at this point.

In the seventh century several peoples who later came to form integral parts of the Mercian kingdom appear to have been semi-autonomous polities, albeit with close ties to Mercia. These polities are here designated the 'inner zone'. Penda made his son Peada king of one of these peoples, the Middle Angles of the south-east midlands, probably in the early 650s.[10] The groups under consideration in this chapter, however, lay between Mercia and the Welsh kingdoms. South-west of Mercia was the kingdom of the Hwicce, the outlines of whose territory are preserved by those of the medieval diocese of Worcester, and whose lands embraced Worcestershire, most of Gloucestershire and part of Warwickshire.[11] It is possible that Penda was instrumental in the creation of this kingdom, and that from its inception it was a dependency of Mercia.[12] To the north of the Hwicce lived the Magonsæte, who were ruled in the mid-seventh century by a King Merewalh, who may have been another son of Penda. The approximate

---

[5] *HE*, III, 24. On Penda's kingship and hegemony see Damian J. Tyler, 'Kingship and Conversion: Constructing Pre-Viking Mercia' (Unpublished University of Manchester PhD thesis, 2002), pp. 40–101; Damian J. Tyler, 'An Early Mercian Hegemony: Penda and Overkingship in the Seventh Century', *Midland History* 30 (2005), 1–19.

[6] *HE*, III, 24.

[7] *Historia Brittonum*, in *Nennius: British History and the Welsh Annals*, ed. and trans. John Morris (Chichester, 1980), chap. 65.

[8] Yorke, *Kings and Kingdoms*, p. 104.

[9] Stenton, *ASE*, pp. 82–3; H. P. R. Finberg, 'Mercians and Welsh', in *Lucerna – Studies of Some Problems in the Early History of England*, ed. H. P. R. Finberg (London, 1964), pp. 66–82 *passim*; Nicholas Brooks, 'The Formation of the Mercian Kingdom', in *The Origins of Anglo-Saxon Kingdoms*, ed. Steven Bassett (Leicester, 1989), pp. 159–70 *passim*; Yorke, *Kings and Kingdoms*, p. 104.

[10] *HE*, III, 21.

[11] On the Hwicce see, *inter alia*, H. P. R. Finberg, 'The Princes of the Hwicce', in H. P. R. Finberg, *The Early Charters of the West Midlands* (Leicester, 1961), pp. 167–80; Della Hooke, *The Anglo-Saxon Landscape: The Kingdom of the Hwicce* (Manchester, 1985*)*; Steven Bassett, 'In Search of the Origins of Anglo-Saxon Kingdoms', in *Origins*, ed. Bassett, pp. 3–27 *passim*; Patrick Sims-Williams, *Religion and Literature in Western England 600–800* (Cambridge, 1990), *passim*.

[12] See Stenton, *ASE*, p. 45; Finberg, 'Princes of the Hwicce', pp. 167–8; Margaret Gelling, *The West Midlands in the Early Middle Ages* (Leicester, 1992), p. 80; Hooke, *The Kingdom of the Hwicce*, p. 8; Wendy Davies and Hayo Vierck, 'The Contexts of Tribal Hidage: Social Aggregates and Settlement Patterns', *Frühmittelalterliche Studien* 8 (1974), 223–93, at pp. 238–9; Yorke, *Kings and Kingdoms*, pp. 108–9.

extent of this kingdom is shown by the medieval diocese of Hereford.[13] Northwards again, inhabiting northern Shropshire and possibly also Cheshire, were the Wreocensæte.[14] It will be argued that in the mid-seventh century these groups were ethnically British. This premise will be based on the probable existence here of a British Church structure.[15] Cases for the 'British-ness' of these groups have also been made by Patrick Sims-Williams and Steven Bassett.[16]

Some support for the existence of a British Church among the Hwicce can be found in Bede's account of Augustine of Canterbury's unsuccessful attempts to assert his authority over the British bishops. We are told that:

> Interea Augustinus adiutorio usus Aedilbercti regis conuocauit ad suum colloquium episcopos siue doctores proximae Brettonum prouinciae in loco ubi usque hodie lingua Anglorum Augustinaes Ác, id est Robur Augustini, in confinio Huicciorum et Occidentalium Saxonum appellatur, [...][17]

Nicholas Higham has argued that this passage suggests that both the West Saxons and the Hwicce were subject to the *imperium* of King Æthelberht of Kent.[18] It seems to the current writer more likely that the meeting occurred at the interface between Æthelberht's (and Augustine's) authority and that of the British bishops and their patrons. This in turn suggests that at the beginning of the seventh century the Hwicce were Christian and ethnically British.[19]

---

[13] On this group see H. P. R. Finberg, 'St Mildburg's Testament', in Finberg, *Early Charters of the West Midlands*, pp. 197–216; H. P. R. Finberg, 'The Princes of the Magonsæte', in Finberg, *Early Charters of the West Midlands*, pp 217–24; Finberg, 'Mercians and the Welsh', esp. pp. 70–7; Kate Pretty, 'Defining the Magonsæte', in *Origins*, ed. Bassett, pp. 171–83.

[14] On the Wreocensæte see *inter alia* Margaret Gelling, 'The Early History of Western Mercia', in *Origins*, ed. Bassett, pp. 184–201 *passim*; Nicholas J. Higham, *The Origins of Cheshire* (Manchester, 1993), pp. 68–98 *passim*.

[15] In making this argument it is not my intention to give support to popular misconceptions regarding 'the Celtic Church'. On this issue see Kathleen Hughes, 'The Celtic Church: Is this a Valid Concept?', *Cambridge Medieval Celtic Studies* 1 (1981), 1–20; Wendy Davies, 'The Myth of the Celtic Church', in *The Early Church in Wales and the West*, ed. Nancy Edwards and Alan Lane (Oxford, 1992), pp. 12–21.

[16] Sims-Williams, *Religion and Literature*, pp. 75–84; Steven Bassett, 'Church and Diocese in the West Midlands: the Transition from British to Anglo-Saxon Control', in *Pastoral Care before the Parish*, ed. John Blair and Richard Sharpe (Leicester, 1992), pp. 13–40; Steven Bassett, 'How the West was Won: the Anglo-Saxon Takeover of the West Midlands', *ASSAH* 11 (2000), 108–18.

[17] 'Meanwhile Augustine, making use of the help of King Æthelberht, summoned the bishops and teachers of the neighbouring British kingdom to a conference at a place which is still called in English *Augustinæs Ác*, that is Augustine's oak, on the borders of the Hwicce and the West Saxons'; *HE*, II, 2.

[18] N. J. Higham, *An English Empire – Bede and the Early Anglo-Saxon Kings* (Manchester, 1995), pp. 47–8.

[19] On the Augustine's Oak conference, see also *Venerabilis Baedae Opera Historica*, ed. Charles Plummer, 2 vols. (Oxford, 1896), II, 73–8; Eric John '"Orbis Britanniae" and the Anglo-Saxon Kings', in *Orbis Britanniae and Other Studies*, ed. Eric John (Leicester, 1966), pp. 1–63, at p. 15; J. M. Wallace-Hadrill, *Bede's Ecclesiastical History of the English People – A Historical Commentary* (Oxford, 1988), pp. 52–4. Plummer and John argue that

Also in his account of this conference, Bede tells us that in the early seventh century there was an important British monastery at Bangor-is-y-coed. Though Bede's characterization of the size and importance of this community have been called into question,[20] its existence is undoubted. Later in the same chapter, while describing the slaughter of British clergy at the battle of Chester (c.613), Bede states:

> Erant autem plurimi eorum de monasterio Bancor, in quo tantus fertur fuisse numerus monachorum, ut cum in septem portiones esset cum praepositis sibi rectoribus monasterium diuisum, nulla harum portio minus quam trecentos homines haberet, qui omnes de labore manuum suarum uiuere solebant.[21]

We may feel some doubts regarding the number of the inmates of this community, but it does seem likely that Bangor-is-y-coed was a house of at least local significance and a focus of wealth and authority. Bangor-is-y-coed is generally thought of as a 'Welsh' monastery. Its site does today lie on the Welsh side of the border, being in what was before the local government reorganization of 1974 the detached portion of Flintshire, but it is approximately seven kilometres (four miles) east of Wat's Dyke and may in the seventh century have lain in the territory of the Wreocensæte.[22] If so, this would tend to support the case for a British ecclesiastical structure in the western midlands in the early seventh century.

Archaeology can also shed light on the ethnic and religious identities of the peoples of the western midlands. The most prominent archaeological indicators of early-medieval British Christianity are inscribed stones,[23] while the most conspicuous archaeological evidence of Anglo-Saxon paganism is provided by furnished burials.[24] It is regrettable therefore that most of the western midlands

---

Bede here implies the Britons were subject to the *imperium* of King Æthelberht. Wallace-Hadrill disagrees, suggesting that the text merely demonstrates that the king's authority ran as far as the West Saxon–Hwiccan frontier. None of these authors consider the ethnicity of the Hwicce.

[20] Nicholas Higham has recently argued that Bede's rhetorical requirements led him to greatly exaggerate the importance of Bangor-is-y-coed, Nick Higham, '*Bancornaburg:* Re-visiting Bangor-is-y-coed', in *Archaeology of the Roman Empire – A Tribute to the life and works of Professor Barri Jones*, ed. N. J. Higham, BAR, IS 940 (2001), pp. 311–18 *passim*.

[21] 'Most of them were from the monastery of Bangor, where there was said to be so great a number of monks that, when it was divided into seven parts with superiors over each, no division had less than 300 men, all of whom were accustomed to live by the labour of their hands', *HE*, II, 2.

[22] For an opposite interpretation see Higham, '*Bancornaburg*', *passim*, where it is argued that the area centred on Bangor-is-y-coed, prior to annexation by the Mercians, formed part of the kingdom of Powys.

[23] See in the first instance Victor E. Nash-Williams, *The Early Christian Monuments of Wales* (Cardiff, 1950).

[24] On Anglo-Saxon burials see, *inter alia*, Audrey Meaney, *A Gazetteer of Early Anglo-Saxon Burial Sites* (London, 1964); Tania Dickinson, 'The Present State of Anglo-Saxon Cemetery Studies', in *Anglo-Saxon Cemeteries 1979*, ed. Philip Rahtz, Tania Dickinson and Lorna Watts, BAR, BS 82 (Oxford, 1980), pp. 11–34; Catherine Hills, 'The Archaeology of Anglo-Saxon England in the Pagan Period: a Review', *ASE* 8 (1979), 297–329; Helen Geake, 'Burial Practice in Seventh- and Eighth-Century England', in *The Age of Sutton*

falls outside the distribution areas of both these features. Inscribed stones are not found in eastern Wales either so their absence from the western midlands may have cultural, rather than religious, causes.[25] The absence of furnished burials from most of this region is rather more difficult to explain. With the exception of a possibly Anglo-Saxon cemetery at Bromfield, Shropshire,[26] no furnished Anglo-Saxon burials have been identified west of the Severn, and there are none at all known in northern Shropshire or Cheshire. Thus, in so far as we can tell, typical pre-Christian Anglo-Saxon burial customs were never practised among the Magonsæte or the Wreocensæte. There are some furnished burials known from the territory of the Hwicce, but these are geographically restricted to the peripheries of the kingdom, being found largely in the Cotswolds and the area of the Warwickshire Avon.[27] Furthermore, even in these areas such burials cease by the end of the sixth century, significantly earlier than elsewhere in England.

What are we to make of this disparity? Firstly, we should be wary of assuming a straightforward correlation between furnished burial and paganism, or unfurnished burial and Christianity, as the deposition of grave goods continued in England into the early eighth century.[28] The change may have had more to do with the spread of Mediterranean ideals than with Christianity *per se*,[29] though the dissemination of such ideals is likely to have been largely mediated by Christian clerics.[30] Nevertheless, without being too insistent on the pagan/Christian polarization, we can say that furnished burial seems to have been an Anglo-Saxon cultural practice and unaccompanied burial characteristically British. As noted above, there are no known furnished Anglo-Saxon burials at all in the likely territory of the Wreocensæte and only one dubious cemetery in that of the Magonsæte. It seems unlikely in the extreme that any Anglian incomers to

---

Hoo – The Seventh Century in North-Western Europe, ed. Martin Carver (Woodbridge, 1992), pp. 83–94.

[25] Sims-Williams, *Religion and Literature*, p. 59.

[26] A group of twenty-three graves, accompanied by a ploughed-out barrow burial, was found here within an Iron Age or Romano-British enclosure. A minimal quantity of grave goods (one iron buckle and two knives) was recovered at this site. See S. C. Stanford, *The Archaeology of the Welsh Marches* (London, 1980), pp. xv, 68 and 178–9.

[27] See Meaney, *Gazetteer*, 'Gloucestershire', pp. 90–3, 'Warwickshire', pp. 257–63 and addenda p. 217, 'Worcestershire', pp. 280–1. A number of burial sites have come to light since the publication of Meaney's work. In Gloucestershire a large cemetery was excavated in Lechlade parish in 1985. Over two hundred inhumations were excavated, as well as thirty-two cremations. A large quantity of typical Anglo-Saxon grave goods was recovered. Also in Gloucestershire, further burials have been identified in the parishes of Bourton-on-the-Water and Kemble, and unaccompanied, undated (but probably pre-tenth-century) inhumations were discovered during building works at the Royal Oak public house, South Cerney, in 1997 and again in 1999. I am grateful to Laura Butler of the Gloucester County Council Sites and Monuments Register for providing me with reports of these excavations. See also W. J. Ford, 'Some Settlement Patterns in the Central Region of the Warwickshire Avon', in *English Medieval Settlement*, ed. Peter H. Sawyer (London, 1976), pp. 143–63; Gelling, *West Midlands*, pp. 30–48.

[28] Geake, 'The Archaeology of the Pagan Period', p. 85.

[29] Geake, 'The Archaeology of the Pagan Period', p. 91.

[30] Sims-Williams, *Religion and Literature*, pp. 71–2.

these regions *immediately* abandoned their traditional mortuary customs.[31] This strongly suggests that there were few if any 'Anglian settlers', and that the Wreocensæte and the Magonsæte remained Christian and British in their cultural orientation until after the general abandonment of furnished burial in England, in the late seventh century or beyond.

The interface of Briton and Anglo-Saxon in the kingship of the Hwicce is rather more complex. In the Cotswolds and the Avon valley there are many sixth-century furnished burials, but none from the seventh century.[32] Both Stephen Bassett and Patrick Sims-Williams argue that Anglo-Saxon immigrants were converted to Christianity by local British Christians and adopted British burial practices.[33] However, if we accept this model we are faced with the difficulty of Bede's emphatic statement that the Britons never attempted to convert the English:

> Qui inter alia inenarrabilium scelerum facta, quae historicus eorum Gildas flebili sermone describit, et hoc addebant, ut numquam genti Saxonum siue Anglorum, secum Brittaniam incolenti, uerbum fidei praedicando committerent.[34]

Sims-Williams gets around this difficulty by choosing to interpret 'Britons' as 'Welsh', i.e. natives of what in later centuries was to become known as Wales,[35] but this is an unwarranted identification at this early date, and we must seek other models.

It could, of course, be that Bede was making this assertion for rhetorical effect, given his strongly anti-British stance and the likelihood that his statement was generally true, whatever the detailed picture. It might, however, be better to approach the problem from a slightly different direction. Both Bassett and Sims-Williams take an essentially migrationist line when addressing this issue: there are burials furnished with typically Anglo-Saxon artefacts here, *ergo* these are the remains of Anglian immigrants,[36] but it is possible that there never were any such immigrants. The accompanied burials may be those of local Christian elites who had temporarily adopted some elements of Anglian culture, in particular

---

[31] *Contra* Bassett, 'Church and Diocese', p. 16. More recently Bassett has suggested that changes in funerary customs in the western midlands may owe more to acculturation than to migration; Bassett, 'How the West was Won', pp. 113–14.

[32] A possible exception being the large cemetery at Lechlade referred to in note 27 above. A group of seventh-century burials were identified here but Lechlade is located on the borders of Gloucestershire and Oxfordshire, and thus is likely to have been at best on the periphery of the kingdom of the Hwicce. The groups using this cemetery may have been West Saxon.

[33] Bassett, 'Church and Diocese', pp. 13–19; Sims-Williams, *Religion and Literature*, pp. 75–9.

[34] 'To other unspeakable crimes, which Gildas their own historian describes in doleful words, was added this crime, that they never preached the faith to the Saxons or Angles who inhabited Britain with them.' *HE*, I, 22.

[35] Sims-Williams, *Religion and Literature*, p. 78.

[36] Though see also Bassett's views on the possibility of an explanation based on acculturation; Bassett, 'How the West was Won', pp. 113–14.

dress and funerary practice.[37] If this is the case the Britons did *not* convert the Anglo-Saxons here. Of course, this explanation is highly speculative, but it does reconcile the archaeological evidence with Bede's testimony.

Whichever model we prefer we are still faced with the probability that furnished burial was not practised among the Hwicce in the seventh century. This is all the more striking when we consider that in the same period regional variations in Anglo-Saxon funerary customs were declining, and we begin to see a more 'pan-English' practice.[38] In the kingdom of the Hwicce we appear to be seeing a society with mixed cultural references, yet one in which British culture was dominant in the seventh century.

Finally, some evidence suggestive of a British ecclesiastical structure in the western midlands is provided by a number of later churches. The earliest Anglo-Saxon church in Gloucester, St Mary-de-Lode, occupies the site and shares the alignment of an earlier Romano-British building. A number of east–west aligned graves are associated with the latter, which may have been a British church.[39] Two east–west aligned burials found beneath the one-time refectory of Worcester Cathedral may be British, but the dating evidence is not precise enough for us to say conclusively.[40] Stephen Bassett has argued that there are topographical grounds for supposing continuity of use from sub-Roman times at a number of church sites in the western midlands.[41] Looking at the relationship between the eleventh-century parishes of St Helens, Worcester and Worcester Cathedral, Bassett argues that the distribution suggests that the former originally had responsibility for the whole area, and that the cathedral's parish was later carved out of it.[42] Similar arguments are made for St Mary-de-Lode (Gloucester),[43] St Michael's (Lichfield)[44] and St Andrew's (Wroxeter).[45]

There is then a fair body of material, both literary and archaeological, suggesting that during the first half of the seventh century the social structure in large areas of the western midlands, areas which were ultimately to become English in cultural identity, incorporated a British Church. Individually the disparate pieces of evidence are not particularly compelling and are open to alternative interpretations.[46] But their volume and variety are difficult to disre-

---

[37] N. J. Higham, personal communication, 7 November 2000.
[38] Geake, 'The Archaeology of the Pagan Period', p. 94.
[39] Richard M. Bryant, 'St Mary de Lode, Gloucester', *Bulletin of the Council for British Archaeology Churches Commission* 13 (1980), 15–18; Bassett, 'Church and Diocese', p. 27.
[40] C^{14} dates for these burials are; Grave 1, 1414 BP = 536, +/– 107 = 429–643; Grave 2, 1395 BP = 585, +/– 102 = 483–687; P. A. Barker, A. L. Cubberly, Elizabeth Crowfoot and C. A. Ralegh Radford, 'Two Burials under the Refectory of Worcester Cathedral', *Medieval Archaeology* 18 (1974), 146–51, at p. 146. For sceptical comment see Bassett, 'Church and Diocese', p. 27.
[41] Bassett, 'Church and Diocese', pp. 19–39.
[42] Bassett, 'Church and Diocese', pp. 20–6.
[43] Bassett, 'Church and Diocese', pp. 26–9.
[44] Bassett, 'Church and Diocese', pp. 29–35. On Lichfield see below, pp. 99–100.
[45] Bassett, 'Church and Diocese', pp. 35–9.
[46] As Bassett acknowledges, 'Church and Diocese', p. 19.

gard.[47] The model which best fits the varied evidence is that among the peoples of the western midlands – the Wreocensæte, the Magonsæte and the Hwicce – a British ecclesiastical structure was operative continuously from sub-Roman times until the diocesan reforms instigated by Archbishop Theodore in the late seventh century. It seems hard to account for this without also accepting that the elites of these groups were British in their ethnic and cultural affiliation.

We shall now turn our attention to the 'core zone'. The early Mercian kingdom was based on the mid-Trent valley, and in broad terms probably included most of Staffordshire, northern Warwickshire, southern Derbyshire, parts of Leicestershire and possibly southern Nottinghamshire.[48] There are many furnished burial sites in this region, and the practice of accompanied burial continued here into the late seventh century.[49] Thus Bede's picture of the Mercians as a non-Christian, Anglo-Saxon people in the first half of the seventh century is supported by the surviving cemetery evidence.

It could be suggested that place-names also appear to support Bede's characterization of the Mercians as a purely English group. 'Pagan' Anglo-Saxon place-names are a potential guide to the interface between British and Anglo-Saxon areas of cultural dominance. Such place-names fall into two categories: god-type names, which incorporate the name of an Anglo-Saxon deity, such as Wednesbury (the fortress of Woden) in Staffordshire, and *hearg* or *weoh* type names, which are thought to be indicative of a shrine or cult centre.[50] There are several 'pagan' place-names in the Mercian heartland – Weeford, Wednesbury and Wednesfield, all in Staffordshire – and a number on the periphery of the kingdom of the Hwicce – Tyesmere, Tysoe and Thunresfield. There are none in the core area of the Hwicce, nor any in the territories of the Wreocensæte or the Magonsæte. It appears then that if Anglo-Saxon traditional religion was ever practised by the Magonsæte, the Wreocensæte and most of the Hwicce, it was so short-lived as to leave no trace on the nomenclature of the landscape.[51] In the 'core zone' of early Mercia, by contrast, English cult practice made a significant mark.

The material discussed above must, however, be considered in conjunction

---

[47] Bassett, 'Church and Diocese', p. 19.
[48] There is not the scope here to give the arguments behind this characterization. For a full discussion see Tyler, 'Kingship and Conversion', pp. 45–9 and the references given there.
[49] See Meaney, *Gazetteer*, 'Derbyshire', pp. 72–80, 'Leicestershire', pp. 144–50, 'Nottinghamshire', pp. 186–97, 'Staffordshire', pp. 220–3, 'Warwickshire', p. 217 and pp. 257–63.
[50] On 'pagan' place-names see, *inter alia*, Frank M. Stenton, 'The Historical Bearing of Place-Name Studies: Anglo-Saxon Heathenism', *Transactions of the Royal Historical Society*, 4th series 23 (1941), 1–24; reprinted in D. M. Stenton, *Preparatory to Anglo-Saxon England: The Collected Papers of Frank Merry Stenton* (Oxford, 1970), pp. 281–97; Audrey Meaney, 'Woden in England: A Reconsideration of the Evidence', *Folklore* 77 (1966), 105–15; David Wilson, 'A Note on *Hearg* and *Weoh* as Place-name Elements Representing Different Types of Pagan Anglo-Saxon Worship Sites', *ASSAH* 4 (1985), 180–3; Margaret Gelling, *Signposts to the Past: Place-names and the History of England*, 2nd edn (Chichester, 1988), pp. 158–61.
[51] This is the explanation favoured by Margaret Gelling, *Signposts to the Past*, p. 159.

with other place-names. There are several place-names in the western midlands with *eccles-* prefixes. *Eccles-* place-names are generally thought to indicate British church sites, places which were recognizable as churches when their English names were formed.[52] The *eccles* element derives ultimately from the Latin *ecclesia*, via Old Welsh *egles* and Old English *ecles*.[53] Place-names of the *eccles* type in England are concentrated in the North West and the western midlands. Both simplex names, such as Eccles, west of Manchester, and *eccles*-plus-a-suffix forms are known, though only the latter survive in the area under consideration here; these are Eccleston (south of Chester), Eccleshall (south-west of Stone, Staffs.), two Exhalls (one near Alcaster and the other north of Coventry, both Warw.) and possibly Eccleswall (south-east of Ross, Hereford.).[54]

The question of whether or not these names indicate that a church was still functioning on the site when the place acquired its Anglo-Saxon name is a difficult one to answer. Given Stephen's comments regarding the appropriation of the lands of British clerics, it seems likely that this was the case in the North.[55] Della Hooke argues that Eccleshall, Staffordshire, at the time it gained its English name was the centre of a multiple-estate,[56] and a similar suggestion has been made by Margaret Gelling regarding both of the Warwickshire Exhalls. The *-hall* suffix may here indicate part of an administrative unit,[57] suggesting that when the name developed the church was still an operating concern, not merely ruined buildings.

There is also some reason to think that in the mid-seventh century there may have been a British church active at Wall, near Lichfield. The old Welsh poem *Marwnad Cynddylan* refers to a raid in this area and mentions 'book-clutching monks'.[58] The date of this poem is not beyond dispute, but it is possible that it is of seventh-century origin.[59] Nicholas Brooks has suggested that the ecclesiastic

---

[52] On *eccles* place-names see in the first instance, Jackson, *LHEB*, p. 227; Kenneth Cameron, 'Eccles in English Place-names', in *Christianity in Britain 300–700*, ed. Maurice W. Barley and Richard P. C. Hanson (Leicester, 1968), pp. 87–92; Gelling, *Signposts to the Past*, pp. 96–9. See also Hooke, *Kingdom of the Hwicce*, p. 76; Sims-Williams, *Religion and Literature*, p. 80.

[53] Jackson, *LHEB*, p. 412; Cameron, 'Eccles in English Place-names', p. 87.

[54] The *-wall* suffix, originally Old English *wæll* (spring), is found only in this example. It has been suggested that this may indicate that the *eccles* prefix derives from a personal name: Gelling, *Signposts to the Past*, p. 97.

[55] Stephen, *Vita Wilfridi*, in *The Life of Bishop Wilfrid by Eddius Stephanus*, ed. and trans. B. Colgrave (Cambridge, 1927), p. 17.

[56] Hooke, *The Kingdom of the Hwicce*, p. 76.

[57] Gelling, *Signposts to the Past*, p. 97.

[58] Jennifer Rowland, 'A study of the Saga of Englynion' (University College of Wales, Aberystwyth PhD thesis, 1982), pp. 306–7; Jennifer Rowland, *Early Welsh Saga Poetry. A Study and Edition of the Englynion* (Cambridge, 1990), pp. 174–9, line 57.

[59] The earliest extant copy of *Marwnad Cynddylan* is of mid-seventeenth-century date; National Library of Wales MS 4973, folios 108a–109b. For editions and translations of these texts see Rowland, 'Saga of Englynion' and *Early Welsh Saga Poetry*. Rowland herself suggests an early date for the poem, 'Saga of Englynion', p. 303 and pp. 321–62, *passim* and *Early Welsh Saga Poetry*, pp. 122–3, 125, 131–6. Also giving at least cautious credence to this material are Finberg, 'Mercians and Welsh', p. 80; Jim Gould, 'Letocetum,

community here may have been Irish, installed by Penda's brother Eowa and Oswald, king of the Northumbrians,[60] but the possibility remains that there was an indigenous church here. Such a possibility may explain Stephen's remark that Lichfield, given to Bishop Wilfrid by Wulfhere, king of the Mercians, was a place suitable for a bishopric.[61]

The situation in the Mercian kingdom is thus very interesting. This area has 'pagan' place-names and burials, which fit Bede's characterization of Penda's Mercians as a non-Christian, English group but we also see *eccles* place-names at Eccleshall and Exhall, and a possible church site at Lichfield. It could be that the situation implied by one set of evidence succeeded that suggested by the other. If this is correct, however, 'original Mercia' is somewhat atypical of England as a whole. There are two simplex *eccles* place-names in Norfolk, and one in Kent, but nowhere do we see quite so much variety as we do in 'original Mercia'. Alternatively, it is possible that both sets of cultural references were operative concurrently. If this were the case then we must accept the existence of high-status Christians in seventh-century Mercia, as it is difficult to account for the presence of an ecclesiastical structure here if we do not also accept the existence of Christians among the local elite. In order to function medieval churches needed lands, servants and trained clerics, none of which could be provided by purely low-status Christians. If this hypothesis is correct it follows that the Mercian kingship at this time was rather more diverse in its social makeup than Bede suggests, including 'British Christians' as well as 'Anglo-Saxon pagans'.

Conclusions

This essay has posited a model of Penda's Mercian hegemony as a political system consisting of a number of zones. At the core was the kingdom of the Mercians. Around this core was an inner zone of closely dependent polities. At the periphery were largely autonomous peoples whose kings acknowledged the superior authority of the Mercian ruler. Each of these zones encompassed ethnically British groups. The outer zone included the unambiguously British kingdoms of Wales. The 'inner zone' embraced the Wreocensæte, the Magonsæte and the Hwicce, groups generally thought of as Anglo-Saxon but who appear to have been largely British in their cultural orientation in the middle of the seventh century. Even in the core area we have seen that there is reason to believe there was a significant British element among the elite.

There were also Anglo-Saxon elements in each of the zones. Clearly there was a non-Christian, ethnically-English elite community in the early Mercian kingdom. The inner zone of dependent polities included the Middle Angles, and

---

Christianity and Lichfield (Staffs.)', *Transactions of the South Staffordshire Archaeological and Historical Society* 14 (1972/3), 30–1; Brooks, 'The Formation of the Mercian Kingdom', pp. 168–9. More pessimistically, David Dumville places the poem no earlier than the ninth century, 'Sub-Roman Britain: History and Legend', *History* 62 (1977), 173–92, at p. 186.

[60] Brooks, 'Formation of the Mercian Kingdom', pp. 168–9.
[61] Stephen, *Vita Wilfridi*, 15.

the East Angles on occasion formed part of the outer zone. Penda's Mercian hegemony was therefore ethnically pluralist at every level. I do not suggest that Mercia was unique, or even unusual, among the Anglo-Saxon kingdoms in this respect. The other contributions to this volume make it clear that socio-political polarization between Britons and Anglo-Saxons in sub-Roman and early-medieval Britain was much less clear-cut than once assumed.

In later ages the Mercians appear to have been less ambiguous in their 'Englishness'. In the eighth century Æthelbald referred to himself in one charter as 'Rex non solum Marcensium sed et omnium provinciarum quæ generale nomine Sutangli dicuntur'[62] and Offa used the title *Rex Anglorum* on at least one occasion.[63] Similarly in the late ninth century King Alfred's biographer Asser stated that Offa had built a wall between the Britons and the Mercians.[64] This hardening of attitudes may have been caused in part by ideas about ethnicity propagated by Christian Anglo-Saxon authors like Bede.[65] In the Mercian hegemony of the mid-seventh century, however, non-ethnic forms of group identity seem to have been more important than ethnic divergence. Despite their heterogeneous nature it can be suggested that the elites of this system had a cohesive solidarity, a consciousness of group identity based on shared elite status and outlook, common aims and enemies, and shared economic and patronage networks. This group identity, I suggest, was more significant to them than differing ethnic identities.[66] In Penda's hegemony we see a situationally determined, primary group identity focused on the Mercian kingship. As a non-Christian Penda may have been better able to accommodate ethnic diversity than were his sons and later Mercian kings, who were more directly exposed to biblical and Roman ideas about ethnicity. This model is necessarily speculative, given the paucity of evidence, but if Penda had his origins in such a society, it could help explain his success and his ability to create an overkingship which embraced both British and English kings and elites, to the benefit of both groups.

---

[62] 'King not only of the Mercians but of all the provinces known by the general name Southern English'; Walter de Gray Birch, *Cartularium Saxonicum*, 3 vols. (London, 1885–93), I, 154.

[63] Birch, *Cartularium Saxonicum*, I, 213.

[64] Asser, *De Rebus Gestis Ælfredi*, in *Asser's Life of King Alfred*, ed. W. H. Stevenson (Oxford, 1904), cap. 14.

[65] Patrick Wormald, 'Bede, the *Bretwaldas* and the Origins of *Gens Anglorum*', in *Ideal and Reality in Frankish and Anglo-Saxon Society – Studies presented to J. M. Wallace-Hadrill*, ed. Patrick Wormald, Donald Bullough and Roger Collins (Oxford, 1983), pp. 99–129, *passim*.

[66] There is a huge literature on ethnicity and group identity. For useful introductions to more recent anthropological visions see Azril Bacal, *Ethnicity in the Social Sciences: A View and Review of the Literature on Ethnicity* (Coventry, 1991) and the various essays in *Ethnicity: Anthropological Constructions*, ed. Marcus Banks (London and New York, 1996). On medieval studies and ethnicity see Walter Pohl, 'Conceptions of Ethnicity in Early Medieval Studies', in *Debating the Middle Ages – Issues and Readings*, ed. Lester K. Little and Barbara H. Rosenwein (Malden, MA, and Oxford, 1998), pp. 15–24, at p. 15. This article was first published in *Archaeologica Polona* 29 (1991), 39–49.

9

Britons in Early Wessex: The Evidence of the Law Code of Ine

MARTIN GRIMMER*

ONE of the 'facts' about the modern study of Anglo-British relations is the extent to which the historian, generally speaking, is afforded a very circumscribed array of references with which to work, and the more so for the early Anglo-Saxon period. Certainly, a reasonable corpus of material survives which can be accessed to inform an understanding of how Anglo-Saxons and Britons may have interacted with one another, but the issue has to be approached by examining often peripheral and sometimes incidental references in a range of texts written for a variety of different purposes. And when attention is focussed specifically on the investigation of putative Britons living within Anglo-Saxon kingdoms, the selection from which to choose narrows quite substantially. It is in this context that the Law Code of Ine, king of Wessex *c*.688–726,[1] deserves particular attention as it provides a rare glimpse of Britons living within an Anglo-Saxon kingdom around the turn of the eighth century. It also reveals a different view of relations between Britons and West Saxons to the unremittingly bellicose narrative enumerated in the *Anglo-Saxon Chronicle*.[2] My aim in this paper is, therefore, to discuss Ine's Code and what it implies for relations between Britons and Saxons in early Wessex.

The Law Code of Ine was promulgated between *c*.688 and *c*.693.[3] It is the

---

* An earlier version of this paper appeared as 'Britons and Saxons in pre-Viking Wessex: Reflections on the Law Code of King Ine', *Parergon* 19.1 (2002), 1–17.

[1] *Anglo-Saxon Chronicle* s.aa. 688, 726 E, 728 A. All references to the *Anglo-Saxon Chronicle* (henceforth *ASC*) will be cited by year from *The Anglo-Saxon Chronicles*, new edition trans. and ed. Michael Swanton (London, 2000).

[2] The *ASC* presents a clear picture that relations between Saxons and Britons were antagonistic; virtually the only type of interaction mentioned for the early Anglo-Saxon period is warfare. See the discussion in Patrick Sims-Williams, 'The Settlement of England in Bede and the Chronicle', *ASE* 12 (1983), 1–41, and Barbara Yorke, 'Fact or Fiction? The Written Evidence for the Fifth and Sixth Centuries', *ASSAH* 6 (1993), 45–50.

[3] In the prologue to his Code, Ine says that he had been consulting with 'my bishop Earconwald', who died on 30 April in 693. Ine also speaks of his father Coenred as still being alive, which would indicate a date early in his reign – although the laws may have been extended and built upon throughout his kingship. See Patrick Wormald, *The Making of English Law: King Alfred to the Twelfth Century*, I, *Legislation and its Limits* (Oxford, 1999), p. 103. All references to Ine's laws will be cited by number from *English Historical Documents*

earliest West Saxon law code to survive and has done so only as an appendix to the Laws of Alfred,[4] both of which are contained at the earliest in a manuscript dated c.930.[5] What is significant about Ine's Code with regard to the question of Anglo-British relations is that it is the only surviving early Anglo-Saxon law code which includes explicit provision for Britons, granting them legal status.[6] If it is assumed that laws can be defined as 'written statements of observed and enforceable social norms',[7] then in codifying these social norms, Ine expected that there would be situations in his kingdom involving Britons that could be met with by legal process.[8] His Code thus unveils a West Saxon society which

---

c. 500–1042, ed. Dorothy Whitelock, English Historical Documents 1 (London, 1955), no. 32, pp. 364–72 (henceforth *EHD*). All references to Alfred's laws will be cited by number from *EHD*, no. 33, at pp. 407–16. An edition of the Old English text of Ine's laws, and of Alfred's, may be found in *The Laws of the Earliest English Kings*, ed. and trans. F. L. Attenborough (Cambridge, 1922), at pp. 36–60 and pp. 62–92 respectively.

[4] For the sake of brevity I will leave aside the matter of whether Ine's laws, being appended to Alfred's, were revised or supplemented or abridged in the late ninth century. It is the case that some of Alfred's laws contradict those of Ine, which would indicate that Alfred did not tamper with the text as it had descended to him. For example, fines for theft: Ine 43, 60 shillings, compared to Alfred 9.2, 120 shillings. There are also differences in the sums levied in fighting before an ealdorman (Ine 6.2; Alfred 15 and 38), or felling another's trees (Ine 43.1; Alfred 12), or differences in the actual circumstances surrounding fighting in the king's hall (Ine 6; Alfred 7–7.1). See Wormald, *Making of English Law*, pp. 103, 278.

[5] See Louis M. Alexander, 'The Legal Status of the Native Britons in Late Seventh-Century Wessex as Reflected by the Law Code of Ine', *Haskins Society Journal* 7 (1995), 31–8, at p. 31; and Wormald, *Making of English Law*, pp. 163–263. Ine's laws and those of Alfred survive at the earliest in Corpus Christi College Cambridge MS 173 ff. 32r–52v ('E' also known as the 'Parker Manuscript'), which was compiled from c.930, though not all its contents were written at the same time. Later manuscripts include Corpus Christi College Cambridge MS 383 ff. 13–42 ('B') of c.1100–25 and the *Textus Roffensis* ff. 9r–31v of c.1123–4. There is also a fragment of Ine from the prologue to Ine 23 in British Library, Burney MS 277 f. 42 dating from c.1060–70. A further manuscript, British Library, Cotton MS Otho B.xi of c.1000–15, was partly destroyed in the Cottonian fire of 1731, but a copy was fortunately made by Laurence Nowell in 1562, and subsequently glossed, and is contained in British Library, Additional MS 43703 (the so-called 'Nowell Transcript'). Ine's and Alfred's codes are the only ones surviving for Anglo-Saxon Wessex.

[6] There is only one other instance of a *wergild* structure for Britons (*wealas*) being included in an Anglo-Saxon text: the early eleventh-century re-statement of *Norðleoda laga* by Archbishop Wulfstan II of York. *Norðleoda laga* is contained at the earliest in Corpus Christi College Cambridge MS 201 ('D') of the mid-eleventh century. For an edition, see *Die Gesetze der Angelsachsen*, ed. F. Liebermann, 3 vols. (Halle, 1903–16), I, pp. 458–61, or Margaret L. Faull, 'The Semantic Development of Old English *Wealh*', *Leeds Studies in English* 8 (1975), 20–44, at p. 25, where the relevant laws are reproduced. The text was discussed by Patrick Wormald in his paper 'Legislating for 11th Century Northerners', delivered at the Britons in Anglo-Saxon England Conference, Manchester Centre for Anglo-Saxon Studies, 14–16 April 2004.

[7] Patrick Wormald, 'Laws', in *The Blackwell Encyclopaedia of Anglo-Saxon England*, ed. Michael Lapidge, John Blair, Simon Keynes and Donald Scragg (Oxford, 1999), p. 279. Wormald also refers to early Anglo-Saxon laws as '"Germanic" in so far as [they are] predicated on the mechanisms of feud'.

[8] Alexander, 'Legal Status of the Native Britons', p. 32.

had Britons living within it, but in an inferior social position to their West Saxon counterparts, as will be shown.⁹

There are eight laws that relate specifically to Britons: five regarding free persons, and three regarding slaves.¹⁰ The Britons are described using variations of Old English *wealh* (plural *wealas*) or *wyliscmon*. In origin this was a word for a 'foreigner', used more specifically of Romance speakers, but which came to mean 'Briton', and by the tenth century could also be used to denote a 'slave'.¹¹ It can be reasonably deduced that 'Briton' is the correct interpretation in this context as the Code makes use of other terms for foreigner and slave: *elðeodigan* and *ðeow*, respectively. And *wealh* could not yet stand alone to mean slave but had to be qualified by *ðeow*, i.e. *ðeowwealh*.¹² The laws pertaining to free Britons are essentially about the setting of their *wergild*: the sum payable to the next of kin of a slain person in order to buy off a feud.¹³ This was, of course, one of the two basic rights of a free person which afforded them protection in Germanic society; the other was being considered 'oathworthy', a right also extended to Ine's British subjects.¹⁴

The *wergild* for a Briton ranged from a maximum of 600 shillings down to a minimum of 60 shillings, such that: a Briton with five hides of land had a *wergild* of 600 shillings; a Briton who was a horse-rider (*horswealh*) for the king, 200 shillings; one with one hide of land, 120 shillings; a tax/tribute-payer

---

[9] In his chapter on the writings of Aldhelm, Bede mentions Britons being subject to the West Saxons in the final quarter of the seventh century (*HE*, V, 18).

[10] Free Britons: Ine 23.3, 24.2, 32, 33, 46.1. British slaves: Ine 54.2, 74, 74.1.

[11] Debby Banham, 'Anglo-Saxon Attitudes: In Search of the Origins of English Racism', *European Review of History* 1 (1994), 143–56, at p. 150; Rosamund Faith, *The English Peasantry and the Growth of Lordship* (London, 1997), p. 60; Faull, 'Semantic Development of *Wealh*', pp. 34–7; David Pelteret, 'Slave Raiding and Slave Trading in Early England', *ASE* 9 (1981), 99–114, at p. 107. Paul Barnwell, 'Britons and Warriors in post-Roman South-East England', *ASSAH* 12 (2003), 1–8, at pp. 3–4, has recently argued that *wealh* may also have come to describe someone who was not subject to military service, and has drawn parallels with Continental uses of terms such as *barbarus*, Frank, Goth and Roman which may have had social as well as ethnic meanings. While this argument has some merit, since ethnicity and social function may have overlapped in the fifth and sixth centuries, by the time of Ine's Code and subsequently, *wealas* was clearly used *ethnically* in Anglo-Saxon sources, for example the *ASC*. Barnwell's hypothesis that the 'racial connotation' of *wealas* died away (p. 4) is questionable. Indeed, it is from *wealas* that the country name Wales derives.

[12] For example, Ine 23 and 74. On this point see Faull, 'Semantic Development of *Wealh*', pp. 20, 26. Faull maintained that *wealh* in Ine 23.3 meant both 'Briton' and 'slave', though this interpretation is questionable; see Pelteret, 'Slave Raiding and Slave Trading', p. 107, and Whitelock, *EHD*, p. 367. *Wealh* is also recorded as a personal name element in all of the four main Old English dialects (Faull, 'Semantic Development of *Wealh*', p. 31). In this regard the use of the element in the name Cenwalh (*ASC* 658) appears to pre-date Ine's Code. For what it is worth, *wealh* may also be observed in *Beowulf* (line 612) in the person of Hrothgar's Queen Wealhþeow. In this case it is uncertain exactly what meaning should be ascribed to *wealh*; she is unlikely to have been a British slave herself.

[13] Carole Hough, 'Wergild', *The Blackwell Encyclopaedia of Anglo-Saxon England*, ed. Michael Lapidge *et al.*, p. 469.

[14] Alexander, 'Legal Status of the Native Britons', p. 32; Patrick Wormald, 'Oaths', *The Blackwell Encyclopaedia of Anglo-Saxon England*, ed. Michael Lapidge *et al.*, p. 338.

Table 9.1: *Comparative Wergilds of Saxons and Britons in Ine's Law Code*

Saxons	Wergild (shillings)	Britons
Geneat (of the king's household)	1200	
Unspecified (*gesið*-born?)	600	Owner of five hides
Not of noble birth (*ceorl?*)	200	*Horswealh* (in the king's service)
	120	Owner of one hide; *gafolgelda*
	100	Son of a *gafolgelda*
	80	Owner of one-half hide
	60	Owner of no land

(*gafolgelda*), also 120 shillings; the son of a tax/tribute-payer, 100 shillings; a Briton with half a hide, 80 shillings, and a Briton with no land, 60 shillings (see Table 9.1).[15] The *wergild* for a Saxon, on the other hand, was not so explicitly stated. Their identity, though defined in some instances by the terms *Englisc* or *Engliscmon*,[16] is principally assumed when none other is specified. Nevertheless, Saxons appear to be granted a *wergild* ranging from 1200 down to 200 shillings. A member of the king's household (a *geneat*) had a *wergild* of 1200 shillings.[17] Elsewhere a 200-shilling *wergild* is used to establish the amount of compensation due for a man killed by a raiding party with the instruction that the same formula be applied 'in the case of the nobler born'.[18] This can be taken to mean that a 200-shilling man was not of the nobility and was therefore probably a *ceorl* (the lowest rank of the law-worthy). A further law sets out compensations for 200-, 600- and 1200-shilling men, from which it might be deduced that a 600-shilling man was of a class higher than *ceorl*, perhaps of the *gesið* class.[19]

It is possible then to determine that there was a disparity between the value placed on the life of a Briton and that of a Saxon in Ine's Code. A Briton who was a horse-rider in the service of the king – a position which could reasonably

---

[15] Ine 23.3, 24.2, 32, 33. Ine 23.3 also states that a Briton must pay twelve shillings to avoid a flogging.

[16] Ine 24, 46.1, 54.2, 74. The use of the term *Englisc* in the law code of a Saxon king is somewhat curious. Bryan Ward-Perkins, 'Why did the Anglo-Saxons not become more British?', *EHR* 115 (2000), 513–33, at p. 524, suggests that it might be possible the term was introduced in a later version of the text when the concept of 'Englishness' may have had more currency, perhaps in the ninth or tenth century.

[17] Ine 19. According to W. G. Runciman, 'Accelerating Social Mobility: the Case of Anglo-Saxon England', *Past & Present* 104 (1984), 3–30, at pp. 5, 19, in the seventh century, a *geneat* was a person of quite high rank.

[18] Ine 34–34.1.

[19] Ine 70. *Gesiðcund* seems to have meant the same class that was referred to in the earlier Kentish laws as *eorlcund* (Runciman, 'Accelerating Social Mobility', 23). It may have been derived from an original meaning denoting a member of a king's *comitatus* (Whitelock, *EHD*, p. 362). The 200–600–1200 differentiation can be seen more explicitly in the laws of Alfred, where it is made clear that 1200- and 600-men are definitely not of the *ceorl* class (for example, Alfred 10, 18.1, 18.2, 18.3, 26, 27, 28, 39.2, 40).

be regarded as one of status[20] – only attracted a *wergild* equivalent of a Saxon *ceorl*, namely, 200 shillings. While Britons could own land, they are not included in the top-most layer of society: 600 shillings is the highest *wergild* mentioned, in comparison with 1200 shillings for a Saxon. Further, their status seems to have been tied more to land ownership than to birthright. The *wergild* of Britons was essentially stratified according to how many hides of land they owned, at a rate of approximately 120 shillings per hide. A Saxon *ceorl* seems to have been protected at 200 shillings with no particular specification for land-ownership, though it should be allowed that the 600- and 1200-men may have been differentiated in this way.[21]

British slaves were also less valued than their Saxon counterparts. An oath of twelve hides was required to compel the public whipping of a British slave; however, a Saxon slave could only be whipped with a 34-hide oath (the original reading might have been twenty-four hides).[22] In general, though Britons were oath-worthy, their word held less value than that of a Saxon. The accusation of cattle-theft, for example, could be denied by an oath to the value of sixty hides if the accuser was British, but a Saxon accuser could only be denied by an oath of 120 hides.[23]

One can, therefore, conceptualise the society described in Ine's Code as being arranged in what Thomas Charles-Edwards refers to as a 'parallel hierarchy', with the Saxons in the more favourable position.[24] The sense of ethnic superiority on the part of the Saxons is not unusual in the context of some Germanic law codes from the Continent. The Frankish *Lex Salica*, for example, distinguished Gallo-Romans from Franks, recording for them a half-*wergild* and a reduced oath-value.[25] But what is unique about Ine's Code is the relatively late

---

[20] A king's horse-rider is usually thought to have been a noble (Faull, 'Semantic Development of *Wealh*', 29), though not so elevated as a king's *horsðegn* (*ASC* 897 A [= 896]). The horse-rider of Ine's Code might be compared to the 'messenger' (*laadrincmannan*) of Æthelberht of Kent's early seventh-century Code (Æthelberht 7, *EHD*, no. 29, pp. 357–9).

[21] Hector Munro Chadwick, *Studies on Anglo-Saxon Institutions* (Cambridge, 1905), at pp. 93–8, argued that the difference between a 600- and a 1200-man was that the latter owned land. In this sense, the distinction being made in Ine's Code may have been between the landless young warrior employed in the king's service (the 600-man) and the veteran who had settled down with land and family (the 1200-man). Such a conceptualisation is echoed in the *geogoð* (youth) versus *duguð* (veteran) distinction drawn in *Beowulf* (e.g. lines 160, 621). I would like to express my thanks to the late Patrick Wormald for drawing these references to my attention.

[22] Ine 54.2. Whitelock (*EHD*, p. 370) suggests that the original reading might have been a 24-hide oath for a Saxon slave – double the oath for a Briton – rather than a 34-hide oath. This would be consistent with their comparative *wergild* structure. John Moreland, 'Ethnicity, Power and the English', in *Social Identity in Early Medieval Britain*, ed. William O. Frazer and Andrew Tyrrell (London, 2000), pp. 23–51, at p. 45, notes that slaves in Burgundian law codes had no ethnicity, as compared to the upper ranks of society. But they clearly do in Ine's Code.

[23] Ine 46–46.1.

[24] Thomas Charles-Edwards, 'Anglo-Saxon Kinship Revisited', *Anglo-Saxons from the Migration Period to the Eighth Century: An Ethnographic Perspective*, ed. John Hines (Woodbridge, 1997), pp. 171–210, at pp. 199, 209.

[25] The clause which most clearly distinguishes Franks and Romans is *Lex Salica* Title XLI,

date at which this differentiation occurs.²⁶ In this context what stands out as most remarkable about Ine's Code is that Britons were legislated for at all. The fact of their inclusion in the Code obviously implies a large enough population of Britons in Wessex to require protection under the law. It has been argued that in doing so Ine was attempting to placate British interests and that he was in a political position that required him to do so.²⁷ The *Anglo-Saxon Chronicle* certainly provides evidence that during his reign, Ine was engaged against Kent, against Mercia, against the South Saxons, and against Geraint of Dumnonia, as well as having to deal with internal disputes within Wessex itself.²⁸ Thus, it is possible to construct a scenario whereby it was prudent for Ine to refrain from antagonising his British subjects and so decrease the likelihood of having to deal with rebellion at an otherwise inopportune time.²⁹

One of the difficulties with this argument, however, is that the Britons were not afforded equal status with their Saxon counterparts; thus, there is a limit to how much they might have been 'appeased' by such an arrangement. The fact that Britons had a *wergild* implies the king's protection, and that at least in theory they could pursue accusations against Saxons.³⁰ But they needed twice the oath-help of a Saxon to proceed with any accusation, and their lives were compensated at a lower value. It is unlikely that the Britons would have simply accepted Ine's promulgation with naïve gratitude; there would still have existed the potential for discontent. It could be equally likely that what Ine's Code represents was not an attempt to placate British interests as such, but rather to set a framework for settling disputes between Saxons and Britons who had kin and lords within Wessex capable of waging vendettas and disturbing the peace, making it essential for him to include them in the Code. Indeed, Ine's laws differ from the

---

though other instances include Title XIV.1–3, Title XXXII.3–4, and Title XLII.1–4. See *The Laws of the Salian Franks*, ed. and trans. Katherine Fischer Drew (Philadelphia, 1991), pp. 79, 95, 104–7. On the status of Franks and Romans in the *Lex Salica*, see Barnwell, 'Britons and Warriors', p. 3; Faull, 'Semantic Development of *Wealh*', p. 21; Wormald, *Making of English Law*, p. 42.

[26] Barbara Yorke, 'Settlement, Anglo-Saxon', *The Blackwell Encyclopaedia of Anglo-Saxon England*, ed. Michael Lapidge *et al.*, pp. 415–16. The end of the seventh century is a time when there was increasing uniformity within Anglo-Saxon England, perhaps due to the influence of Christian culture. Material culture, for example, becomes more similar; Anglian, Saxon and Jutish variations in clothing (especially female) disappear.

[27] For example, Alexander, 'Legal Status of the Native Britons', pp. 36–7; L. F. Rushbrook-Williams, 'The Status of the Welsh in the Laws of Ine', *EHR* 30 (1915), 271–7, at pp. 273, 276–7.

[28] According to the *ASC*, in 694 the inhabitants of Kent 'came to terms with Ine and granted him 30,000 [pounds]'. Before Ine Cædwalla had ravaged Kent in 686 and 687. In 715, Ine fought Ceolred of Mercia at Woden's Barrow in Wiltshire, and in 725 he fought against the South Saxons, killing Ealdberht, an *ætheling* he had previously expelled from Wessex. There may have been other internal conflicts in Wessex, for in 721 Ine killed the *ætheling* Cynewulf. In addition to his military campaigns against other Anglo-Saxon kingdoms, Ine fought with Geraint, 'king of the Britons (*Wealas*)' of Dumnonia (i.e. Cornwall and Devon), in 710.

[29] Alexander, 'Legal Status of the Native Britons', p. 37.

[30] Yorke, *Wessex*, p. 72.

earlier Kentish codes in reflecting a more aggressive stance on enforcement and payment of fines against the social order, and as Patrick Wormald argues, incorporating the king more prominently in the vocabulary of atonement.[31]

This, of course, begs the question of who were the Britons for whom the laws in Ine's Code were enacted? In particular, were they descendants of Romano-Britons living in the long-conquered eastern region of Wessex (roughly Hampshire, Wiltshire and parts of Dorset)?[32] Or, given that there appears to have been a period of westward expansion in the seventh century, up to and including the reign of Ine, ultimately encompassing Dorset, Somerset and parts of Devon,[33] were the laws enacted for British farmers and landowners whose land had been progressively incorporated into Wessex through this process?[34]

In order to answer this question, it is first necessary to speculate on a number of matters implied by the Code. To begin with, it must be assumed that there existed some mechanism, some 'British' feature or features, that allowed for Britons to be recognised as such. One of the central conclusions that can be drawn from Ine's Code regarding relations between West Saxons and Britons is that complete assimilation had not yet occurred between the two groups, such that a distinction could still be made in terms of ethnicity. There must have been some sense of British identity as distinct from Saxon identity: it would have been nonsensical to talk in terms of differentiating Britons from Saxons in the Code if it were practically impossible to do so. And indeed, it would have been important, especially for a Saxon as a person of higher status than a Briton, to be able to *be* differentiated given the differences in *wergild*. In such a situation identity and ethnicity become matters of some significance. Further, the use of the term *wealh* – with its implication of foreignness – does provide some sense of British and Saxon identities being in binary opposition,[35] and it is significant that the only instances in which the term *Englisc* is used in the Code are whenever the context involves

---

[31] Wormald, 'Laws', p. 279; *idem, Making of English Law*, p. 105.

[32] The distribution of Saxon material culture, reflected for example in grave goods, can be taken to indicate Saxon control of the eastern shires of Wessex by the end of the sixth century. See Bruce Eagles, 'Anglo-Saxon Presence and Culture in Wiltshire AD c.450–c.675', *Roman Wiltshire and After: Papers in Honour of Ken Annable*, ed. Peter Ellis (Devizes, 2001), pp. 199–233; Yorke, *Wessex*, pp. 12–13. The argument that the Britons in the code were descended from the original Romano-British inhabitants has been promoted by Leslie Alcock, *Arthur's Britain: History and Archaeology AD 367–634* (Harmondsworth, 1971), p. 312, and Faull, 'Semantic Development of *Wealh*', p. 23, and is implied by Alexander, 'Legal Status of the Native Britons', p. 36.

[33] The evidence of charters indicates that there was a period of westward expansion which is first documented during the reign of Centwine (676–685). See Malmesbury: S1170/BCS71, pp. 94–7, and Glastonbury: S236/BCS61, pp. 11–15; S237/BCS62, pp. 15–17. In reference to charters BCS = W. de G. Birch, *Cartularium Saxonicum*, 3 vols. (London, 1885–93), with page numbers from Heather Edwards, *The Charters of the Early West Saxon Kingdom* (Oxford, 1988).

[34] This possibility was implied by J. N. L Myres, *The English Settlements* (Oxford, 1937), pp. 447–8.

[35] Walter Pohl, 'Ethnic Names and Identities in the British Isles: a Comparative Perspective', *Anglo-Saxons from the Migration Period to the Eighth Century*, ed. John Hines, pp. 7–40, at p. 34.

a contrast with the Britons.[36] It is, therefore, reasonable to assume that Ine's Code reflects a society that was segmented, or at least able to be segmented, in terms of ethnicity.

How then would a Briton have been identified? Style of Christianity is a possibility; Britons conceivably may have continued to eschew Roman practice. However, this is unlikely to have been the case within Wessex, especially the eastern half, by the time of Ine's reign. The Synod of Hertford, which sought to extend the decisions taken at Whitby to the rest of the Anglo-Saxon kingdoms, had been held some twenty years earlier in 672.[37] It was about this time that the West Saxon cleric Aldhelm wrote to Geraint of Dumnonia, exhorting him to instruct his bishops to follow Roman practice.[38] It is very doubtful that non-orthodoxy would have been tolerated within Wessex by the end of the seventh century.

There are other cultural characteristics which may have operated as potential identifiers, such as dress, social custom, diet, mode of housing and style of agriculture. However, a more enduring mechanism would have been language and oral culture. Language can operate as one of the most definitive markers of ethnic identity,[39] as well as acting as a means of maintaining and reinforcing that identity.[40] Bede, of course, differentiated the peoples of Britain according to the language they spoke: English, British, Irish and Pictish.[41] And in the story of the Northumbrian thegn Imma who, when captured by Mercians, attempted to pass himself off as a peasant but was found out by his mode of speech, Bede also provides grounds for allowing that a person's status could be determined by how he or she spoke.[42] While I am not suggesting that Imma's status was necessarily revealed by the *language* he used, as opposed to his vocabulary or grammar or

---

[36] Thomas Charles-Edwards, 'Language and Society among the Insular Celts 400–1000', *The Celtic World*, ed. Miranda J. Green (London, 1995), pp. 703–36, at p. 733. However, see note 16 above regarding the use of the term *Englisc*.

[37] *HE*, IV, 5.

[38] Aldhelm, *Epist.* IV, *Aldhelm: The Prose Works*, ed. Michael Lapidge and Michael Herren (Cambridge, 1979), at pp. 155–60.

[39] John Hines, 'The Becoming of the English: Identity, Material Culture and Language', *ASSAH* 7 (1994), 49–59, at p. 51; Maryon McDonald, 'Celtic Ethnic Kinship and the Problem of being English', *Current Anthropology* 27 (1986), 333–47, at pp. 339–40; James Milroy and Lesley Milroy, 'Social Network and Patterns of Language Change', in *Migrations and Invasions in Archaeological Explanation*, ed. John Chapman and Helena Hamerow (Oxford, 1997), pp. 73–81, at p. 73; Patrick Sims-Williams, 'Celtomania and Celtoscepticism', *Cambrian Medieval Celtic Studies* 36 (1998), 1–35, at pp. 28–9; Ward-Perkins, 'Why did the Anglo-Saxons not become more British?', p. 524, and references cited therein.

[40] Charles-Edwards, 'Language and Society', p. 733; Della Hooke, 'The Anglo-Saxons in England in the Seventh and Eighth Centuries: Aspects of Location in Space', *Anglo-Saxons from the Migration Period to the Eighth Century*, ed. John Hines, pp. 65–99, at p. 68.

[41] *HE*, I,1. Bede also includes Latin as the unifying language of them all. In the Topographical Preface of the *ASC* E, British (*Brittisc*) is distinguished from Welsh (*Wilsc*), perhaps referring to Cornish versus Welsh. When the *ASC* began to be compiled, these two languages would have been distinguishable. In the Topographical Preface Latin is referred to as 'Book Language'.

[42] *HE*, IV, 22. Charles-Edwards, 'Language and Society', p. 732.

phonology, the point to be made is that it was possible to use mode of speech to differentiate amongst people in Anglo-Saxon England.[43]

In order to accept the first proposition canvassed that the Britons towards whom Ine's Code was directed were those descended from the Romano-British inhabitants in eastern Wessex, it must be assumed that the language of the Britons survived and continued to be a valid marker of identity from the Invasion Period through to the end of the seventh century. It must also be assumed that to be a numerically significant proportion of the population, the Britons must to some extent have remained differentiated from the Saxons so that they could pass on their language and oral culture in such a way that their identity was not extinguished by assimilation. Further, it has to be assumed that this policy of separation, which had continued in some form for up to 200 years, fell out of practice at some point after Ine's reign so that assimilation then began to occur, and the language of the Britons, as well as their cultural distinctiveness, disappeared.[44]

It would be more reasonable to opt for the second proposition: that the Britons for whom the laws in Ine's Code were enacted were principally those living in West Saxon territory that was acquired in the second half of the seventh century. Westward expansion could certainly have meant an increase in the number of British subjects within Wessex, necessitating their inclusion within the Code. There would also have been less time for assimilation to occur, such that the language of the Britons could still have been spoken, and any other distinctive cultural conventions still practised. To quote Susan Reynolds:

> Apartheid is hard enough to maintain even when physical differences are obvious, political control is firm, and records of births, deaths, and marriages are kept.[45]

In other words, given the often inevitable pressure to assimilate by the dominant culture, the incorporation of British subjects into Wessex via expansion in the seventh century would make it more probable that Britons could still have been readily distinguished from Saxons.[46] This is not to say that the laws for

---

[43] For a recent discussion of the Imma episode within an ethnographic context, see Moreland, 'Ethnicity, Power and the English', p. 48.

[44] This latter point might be qualified to allow that language-borrowing from British to Old English was also impeded by the perceived lower status of the former. Thus, the limited influence of British may not have been solely due to its rapid demise within Wessex and the other Anglo-Saxon kingdoms but rather its perceived inferiority in Saxon eyes. In addition, I do not mean to say that assimilation began only after Ine's reign. See Charles-Edwards, 'Language and Society', pp. 730–1.

[45] Susan Reynolds, 'What do we mean by "Anglo-Saxon" and "Anglo-Saxons"?', *Journal of British Studies* 24 (1985), 395–414, at pp. 402–3.

[46] It is instructive here to note that a similar circumstance may account for the other instance of a *wergild* structure for Britons in the early eleventh-century *Norðleoda laga*. Immediately prior to the time of Wulfstan, the British province of Cumbria (or Cumberland) suffered invasion and annexation by English kings, for example, Edmund (*ASC* 945) and Æthelred II (*ASC* 1000 E). Such an eventuality no doubt resulted in the very problem that Ine had faced in seventh-century Wessex: of Britons newly living under Anglo-Saxon control. I would like to thank Patrick Wormald for alerting me to this explanation.

Britons in the Code only applied to western Wessex; there would be no reason to suppose that this was the case. Rather, I would argue that the *impetus* for the specific laws came from there being an increasing number of identifiable Britons in the west of the kingdom.

There is, of course, some question over the value of Germanic law codes and the extent to which they provide an accurate mirror of the society that produced them. It was important in the years following the decline of the Western Empire for so-called barbarian kings to ape Roman legal precedent and to promulgate something that *looked like* a written law code, irrespective of its actual judicial value.[47] Thus, a Germanic law code might tell more about the image which the barbarian kings and their advisers wished to project of themselves and their people rather than actual 'on the ground' conditions.[48] That said, Patrick Wormald has explained that such a symbolic purpose was characteristic of only certain early Germanic codes, for example, the Frankish, Lombardic and Alamannic laws.[49] Others, such as the Visigothic and Burgundian, seem rather to display real law-making in response to individual circumstances and conditions.[50] In addition, the former group of laws did eventually evolve to become more like the latter, incorporating measures designed to deal with newly occurring situations of real import to the peoples being legislated for.[51] Roger Collins has also argued that Germanic codes had practical value and similarly notes instances of Visigothic, Ostrogothic and Burgundian codes which show examples of 'case law' and of laws adapted to specific fifth- or sixth-century social realities, thus indicating that law-making was an active exercise in these societies.[52]

Ine's Code certainly appears to conform to this pattern. Even though the laws appear as a single text, they seem more like a series of pronouncements, each developed to accommodate an eventuality that needed legislative attention.[53] Indeed, a large number of laws give the impression that Ine was responding to particular cases as they were presented to him by petitioners, such as those

---

[47] Patrick Wormald, '*Lex scripta* and *verbum regis*: Legislation and Germanic Kingship from Euric to Cnut', in *Early Medieval Kingship*, ed. P. Sawyer and I. N. Wood (Leeds, 1977), pp. 105–38, at pp. 115, 135.

[48] Wormald, '*Lex scripta* and *verbum regis*', p. 136. On this point, see also Robin Chapman Stacey, 'Law and Order in the *very* Old West: England and Ireland in the Early Middle Ages', *Crossed Paths: Methodological Approaches to the Celtic Aspect of the European Middle Ages*, ed. Benjamin T. Hudson and Vickie Ziegler (Lanham, MD, 1991), pp. 39–60, at pp. 40–1.

[49] Patrick Wormald, '*Inter cetera bona ... genti suae*: Law-making and Peace-keeping in the Earliest English Kingdoms', *Settimane di Studio del Centro Italiano di Studi Sull'alto Medioevo* 42 (1995), 963–96, at p. 968.

[50] Wormald, '*Inter cetera bona ... genti suae*', pp. 967–8.

[51] Wormald, '*Inter cetera bona ... genti suae*', pp. 968, 980–1. See also J. M. Wallace-Hadrill, *The Barbarian West 400–1000* (Oxford, 1985), p. 73.

[52] Roger Collins, 'Law and Ethnicity in the Western Kingdoms in the Fifth and Sixth Centuries', in *Medieval Europeans: Studies in Ethnic Identity and National Perspectives in Medieval Europe*, ed. Alfred P. Smyth (Basingstoke, 1998), pp. 1–23, at pp. 2, 16–18.

[53] Wormald, '*Inter cetera bona ... genti suae*', pp. 981–2; *idem*, 'Laws', p. 279.

regarding a British slave killing a Saxon freeman.[54] Strictly speaking, this means that not all the laws in Ine's Code are necessarily his; there could conceivably have been an original core of enactments that was added to over years or decades by his successors.[55] Nevertheless, the conclusion of most significance here is that the Code does, more or less, represent conditions in Ine's time or in the time of his immediate successors.

What Ine's Code achieved was to ensure that the Saxons in Wessex, at least in a legal sense, were entrenched in the superior position. The Code reveals that complete integration between Saxons and Britons had not yet occurred in Wessex. But the fact that the Code did legislate for Britons as well as Saxons reveals one stage in the process of assimilation.[56] Irrespective of Ine's motivation in the matter, it was possible for Britons to own land; their inclusion in the Code gave them legal standing and shows that they were part of West Saxon society. This permits a broadening of the picture of West Saxon and British interaction from that gained in the *Anglo-Saxon Chronicle* and other sources to allow that relations were not exclusively antagonistic.

In addition, there does not appear to be anything in Ine's Code which explicitly prohibited assimilation, beyond the caveat that people of different social strata do not generally associate as equals. The laws tell us that Britons and Saxons co-existed in Wessex under the same authority.[57] The fact of their differentiation strongly suggests the circumstance of West Saxons living amongst Britons, or vice versa; otherwise there would have been no need for the enacted provisions.[58] In this regard, it has been argued, for example by Bryan Ward-Perkins, that the Code may have acted as a mechanism of social engineering which in fact *encouraged* assimilation.[59] It *was* a liability in Ine's Wessex to be identified as a Briton, given the inferior *wergild* and oath value. It may have been Ine's deliberate policy to enact laws which were designed to compel the Britons within his kingdom to abandon their separate identity and become Saxon.[60] Thus, a political and social imperative could have been embedded into his laws for the Britons.

Was it then a matter of choice on the part of the Britons who found themselves living within West Saxon territory to abandon their identity? The assumption in some of the recent literature concerning the ethnogenesis of Anglo-Saxon identity

---

[54] Ine 74–74.1 sets out the legal procedure to be followed when a British slave kills a Saxon free-person. Another example is Ine 67, a complex statement regarding procedures for the enlargement of a ploughed landholding. On this point, see Wormald, 'Laws', p. 279; and *idem*, *Making of English Law*, p. 104, who states that Ine's Code is 'much the least organised post-Roman legal statement' and thus difficult to conceptualise as being pre-planned in its extant form.

[55] Wormald, *Making of English Law*, p. 105.

[56] Yorke, *Wessex*, p. 72.

[57] Heinrich Härke, 'Early Anglo-Saxon Social Structure', *Anglo-Saxons from the Migration Period to the Eighth Century*, ed. John Hines, pp. 125–70, at p. 149.

[58] Charles-Edwards, 'Anglo-Saxon Kinship Revisited', p. 199.

[59] Ward-Perkins, 'Why did the Anglo-Saxons not become more British?', pp. 523–4. See also Banham, 'Anglo-Saxon Attitudes', p. 149.

[60] Charles-Edwards, 'Language and Society', p. 733; Wormald, *Making of English Law*, p. 106.

in the earlier sub-Roman period is that a substantial number of the native Britons who came into contact with the newcomers *voluntarily* gave up their British identity to become *Englisc*.⁶¹ Although not infinitely malleable nor entirely arbitrary, ethnic identity does indeed have an element of personal choice.⁶² However, the ethnographic processes that produced the Anglo-Saxon polities of the sub-Roman period were not necessarily the same as those which marked the assimilation of Britons into the expanding Anglo-Saxon kingdoms of later centuries. Anglo-Saxon expansion in the seventh and eighth centuries was by people and over people already led by kings and thus already with an emergent identity; and this would have been increasingly the case the further we progress through the Anglo-Saxon period. The clear implication here is that the new Anglo-Saxon ruler over British territory, irrespective of whether he was a more distant overlord or a direct king, was less a *primus inter pares*, less a raised war leader than (say) a tyrant.⁶³ His rulership was something that was externally imposed rather than something that emerged from within.

During the period when Ine's laws were promulgated, therefore, being West Saxon, whatever that meant, was something that was increasingly likely to be imposed rather than embraced.⁶⁴ There were doubtless Britons who decided to make their way within the new social order – for example, the 600-shilling men – but they would have had little choice as to who their new masters were. In addition, the supposition that Britons in Wessex would have voluntarily relinquished their identity for the purposes of upward social mobility can only be taken so far; the abandonment of British identity may have been a matter of attempting to make the best of a poor situation.⁶⁵ In this sense successive generations of

---

61 Charles-Edwards, 'Language and Society', pp. 729–35; Paul Garwood, 'Social Transformation and Relations of Power in Britain in the Late Fourth to Sixth Centuries A.D.', *Scottish Archaeological Review* 6 (1989), 90–106; Margaret Gelling, 'Why aren't we Speaking Welsh?', *ASSAH* 6 (1993), 51–6; Helena Hamerow, 'Migration Theory and the Anglo-Saxon "Identity Crisis"', in *Migrations and Invasions in Archaeological Explanation*, ed. John Chapman and Helena Hamerow, pp. 33–44; Higham, *RBAS*, pp. 198, 224, 236; Hooke, 'Anglo-Saxons in England in the Seventh and Eighth Centuries', pp. 65–99; Harald Kleinschmidt, 'Beyond Conventionality: Recent Work on the Germanic Migration to the British Isles', *Studi Medievali*, 3rd series 36 (1995), 975–1010; Moreland, 'Ethnicity, Power and the English', pp. 23–51; Christopher Scull, 'Approaches to Material Culture and Social Dynamics of the Migration Period in Eastern England', in *Europe between Late Antiquity and the Middle Ages: Recent Archaeological and Historical Research in Western Europe and Southern Europe*, ed. John Bintliff and Helena Hamerow (Oxford, 1995), pp. 71–83.

62 Patrick J. Geary, 'Ethnic Identity as a Situational Construct in the Early Middle Ages', *Mitteilungen der anthropologischen Gesellschaft in Wien* 113 (1983), 15–26, at pp. 21–5; Hines, 'The Becoming of the English', p. 49; McDonald, 'Celtic Ethnic Kinship', p. 333; Sims-Williams, 'Celtomania and Celtoscepticism', p. 26; Ward-Perkins, 'Why did the Anglo-Saxons not become more British?', p. 523.

63 Alex Woolf, 'Community, Identity and Kingship in Early England', in *Social Identity in Early Medieval Britain*, ed. William O. Frazer and Andrew Tyrrell, pp. 91–109, at p. 108.

64 David N. Dumville, cited in Giorgio Ausenda, 'Current Issues and Future Directions', in *Anglo-Saxons from the Migration Period to the Eighth Century*, ed. John Hines, pp. 411–50, at p. 420.

65 Moreland, 'Ethnicity, Power and the English', pp. 46–51.

Britons in Wessex can be envisaged as losing their 'Britishness', or indeed their more specific, native regional identity. But the assimilation of Britons and the loss of their ethnic identity was not inevitable within the borders of early Wessex. Ethnicity, first of all, is not always easy to forsake successfully,[66] and second, is something which emerges out of social interaction.[67] A change in identity, therefore, cannot simply have been a matter of Britons 'giving up' their identity but must have required the complicity and active participation of a whole social system, in this case West Saxons as well as Britons.

It could even be argued that the loss of identity amongst Ine's Britons became an imperative along the frontier. It is here that any differences between Britons and West Saxons would have stood out, where the contrast between the peoples would have been most pronounced. And indeed, within a newly established frontier, a West Saxon identity, or a sense of 'Englishness', would have been more tenuous and most under threat.[68] West Saxon kings who expanded their rule over British territory would have been faced with the problem of a multi-lingual and multi-cultural population, with divergent traditions and possibly divergent loyalties. Newly conquered Britons undoubtedly had more in common, at least initially, with their former compatriots across the frontier than with their new king. West Saxon rulers may not have been willing to tolerate such a situation indefinitely without working these Britons into the new social order and, in essence, making them West Saxon subjects. Thus, the 'otherness' of the Britons may have been emphasised through the Laws of Ine, in order to manufacture a more unified West Saxon society. Through a process of social categorisation and consequent social disadvantage, the identity of the Britons was engulfed by the overall dominance of West Saxon political, economic and social culture so that by the time King Alfred promulgated his Code, there was no apparent differentiation made between Britons and Saxons.[69]

---

[66] Hines' point, 'The Becoming of the English', p. 50, is well made that, 'Although theoretically exchangeable, it may in practical terms be impossible for an individual to successfully divest himself of one identity and to adopt another.'

[67] Hines, 'The Becoming of the English', p. 49.

[68] Nicholas Higham, 'The Anglo-Saxon/British Interface: History and Ideology', in *The Celtic Roots of English*, ed. Markku Filppula, Juhani Klemola and Heli Pitkanen (Joensuu, 2002), pp. 29–46, at p. 43.

[69] In his will, Alfred talked of two properties he owned in *Wealcynne*. Simon Keynes and Michael Lapidge, *Alfred the Great: Asser's 'Life of King Alfred' and other Contemporary Sources* (Harmondsworth, 1983), p. 175, translate this term explicitly as Cornwall, and not as meaning amongst Britons within Wessex proper.

10

Apartheid and Economics in Anglo-Saxon England

ALEX WOOLF

WHEN considering and discussing the fate of the Britons within Anglo-Saxon England, we invariably seem to find ourselves forced to choose between two hypotheses. The first of these, and perhaps currently the less fashionable, is that a 'mass migration' of Germanic peoples committed genocide against the inhabitants of the Insular territories they conquered, creating a situation in which all subsequent generations of Anglo-Saxons were descended entirely, or almost entirely, from fifth-century immigrants. The second, the 'elite emulation model', perhaps most clearly articulated in our editor's 1992 monograph *Rome, Britain and the Anglo-Saxons*, holds that incoming Germans supplied only an aristocratic elite who farmed large estates tilled by native Britons, who gradually aped their lords and became culturally indistinguishable from them over time.[1] Whilst the elite emulation model has become widely accepted amongst British archaeologists, who have, perhaps, become used to the concept of the diffusion of trends in material culture without recourse to models requiring large-scale population movement, it has proved less easy for historians and linguists to accept. This has largely been due to the perceived problem created by the Anglo-Saxon language: Old English seems far too close in both structure and form to its nearest Continental Germanic neighbours and to lack any substantive evidence of influence from either a Celtic or Romance substratum underlying it, which one would expect had large numbers of Britons switched language on passing acquaintance with their landlords then reinforced their competence only by practising amongst themselves. Archaeologists have tended to be dismissive of this evidence, Richard Hodges even describing language as an insoluble 'conundrum'.[2] To some extent this disciplinary divide is the result of natural selection. As youngsters beginning to show an interest in the past, most of us did not clearly distinguish between Archaeology and History, but at university, or shortly before, when we were forced to make the choice between the two, it was only natural that those of us who were more attracted to and had a greater affinity for material culture went down one route and those whose fascination lay with words down another. For this reason archaeologists and historians are likely to place different values upon linguistic evidence.

---

[1] Higham, *RBAS*.
[2] Hodges, *ASA*, pp. 65–8.

Of course one of the problems with the debate concerning the fate of the Britons is the presumption that a single model might apply across the whole country. England took longer to conquer than any of the Continental provinces taken over by the Germans in Late Antiquity. Even if we exclude the anomalous case of Cornwall, a frontier approximating to the enduring medieval and modern frontier between England and Wales was probably only reached in the 680s or thereabouts, while southern Dorset and much of Devon were probably conquered at about the same time. Thus, a period of more than 250 years was required to conquer England. In the early part of this conquest, the conflict was between pagans on the one side and Christians on the other and between Germanic speakers and Romance speakers,[3] whilst in the west the later Anglo-Saxon conquerors were already Christian and the natives probably speaking British Celtic at the time of conquest and may well have lost much of the veneer of *romanitas*.[4] These varying conditions will have almost certainly affected the nature of culture contact and interaction.

In a recent contribution to the debate concerning the 'elite emulation' model, Bryan Ward-Perkins intelligently rephrased the central question and asked not, 'What happened to the Britons in Anglo-Saxon England?' but rather 'Why did the Anglo-Saxons not become more British?'[5] This is indeed a better way of asking the question for it highlights the fundamental difference between Britain's experiences of fifth- and sixth-century Germanic invasions and those of its Continental neighbours. In most of Gaul, political leadership, an ethnonym and most male personal names were adopted from, or maintained by, the conquering Franks, but otherwise most of the cultural practices of the Early Middle Ages, including language, religion, a monetary economy and at least some degree of urban survival, were inherited from native Gallo-Roman society. *Mutatis mutandi*, the same could be said for Visigothic Spain and Langobard Italy. Into the Central Middle Ages the people of these regions came to think of themselves as Franks, Goths and Langobards, but in reality they all shared a late Roman culture inherited from the Empire. In Spain the abandonment of a distinct, Arian form of Christianity by the Gothic ruling elite in the 580s is probably representative of the decline of ethnic segregation in the kingdom as a whole.[6] In contrast Britain shares its post-Roman experience only with apparently marginal areas such as the Rhineland, Flanders and Bavaria.

To some extent we can think of early medieval linguistic replacement in terms

---

[3]   See Peter Schrijver, this volume.

[4]   Alex Woolf, 'The Britons: From Romans to Barbarians', in *Regna and Gentes: The Relationship between Late Antique and Early Medieval Peoples and Kingdoms in the Transformation of the Roman World*, ed. H.-W. Goetz, J. Jarnut and W. Pohl, with S. Kaschke (Leiden, 2003), pp. 345–80.

[5]   Bryan Ward-Perkins, 'Why did the Anglo-Saxons not become more British?', *EHR* 115 (2000), 513–33.

[6]   For the conversion of the Goths under King Reccared see Isidore of Seville's *History of the Kings of the Goths* § 52 ff. Text in *Las Historias de los Godos, Vandalos, y Suevos de Isidoro de Sevilla: estudio, edición crítica y traducción*, ed. C. Rodríguez Alonso (Leon, 1975) and English translation in *Conquerors and Chroniclers of Early Medieval Spain*, ed. K. Baxter Wolf (Liverpool, 1990).

of upward and downward trends; that is to say the linguistic identity either moves up or down the social scale. In Anglo-Norman England and Ireland, Kievan Rus, Visigothic Spain, Langobardic Italy, much of Frankish Gaul and western Britain (where British Celtic replaced Latin in the course of Late Antiquity), replacement was upwards, the incoming rulers, or in western Britain the Romanised elite, being acculturated linguistically by the natives. In Anglo-Saxon England, Bavaria, Flanders, Alba (in northern Britain), the territories conquered by the Slavs in the Balkans and British-occupied western Armorica, replacement was downwards, the language and identity of the conquerors becoming, eventually, that of the general population.[7] In both scenarios the process appears to have been drawn out rather than rapid.

The key to this rather crude binary opposition would seem to lie in socio-economic structures. The relatively flat, early Anglo-Saxon society, as indicated by the lack of clear hierarchy in settlement morphology before the seventh century (and then only a clear distinction between royal sites and others) is in stark contrast to the situation in Merovingian Gaul, where the kings seem to have taken over the imperial estates, complete with tenants, slaves and administrators, and to have continued to receive tax revenues from the *civitates*.[8] Whether or not the armed followers of the Frankish, Gothic and Langobard kings were given landed estates themselves[9] or direct access to fiscal revenues,[10] they were scattered relatively thinly across their territories, and the kings relied for their political hegemony not upon their corporate ethnic integrity but upon the continuity of rulership from the imperial regime which they represented.[11] The soldiers of the Frankish and Gothic kings differed little in their role within society from the soldiers of the last emperors. In Langobardic Italy similar conditions seem to have prevailed, although here continuity of authority may have lain, for the most part, with the *duces* rather than with the king.[12] By and large, late Roman society continued intact or gradually transformed itself as it did in south-east Wales.[13]

Interestingly, the portion of Gaul which became Germanic in speech and culture in Late Antiquity was that portion which the Franks won from the Romans in the first half of the fifth century. This is an obscure period terminated by the defeat of the Frankish leader Clodio near Arras by Aëtius and Majorian, probably

---

[7] The situation in the Rhineland appears to have been more complex and to have resolved itself over a much longer time period.
[8] Ian N. Wood, *The Merovingian Kingdoms, 450–751* (London, 1994), pp. 64–6.
[9] Edward James, *The Franks* (Oxford, 1988), pp. 108–16.
[10] Walter Goffart, *Barbarians and Romans, AD 418–584: The Techniques of Accommodation* (Princeton, 1980).
[11] Herwig Wolfram, 'The Shaping of the Early Medieval Kingdom', *Viator* 1 (1970), 1–20. P. Amory, *People and Identity in Ostrogothic Italy* (Cambridge, 1997).
[12] Chris Wickham, *Early Medieval Italy: Central Power and Local Society, 400–1000* (London, 1981).
[13] Wendy Davies, 'Land and Power in Early Medieval Wales', *Past & Present* 81 (1978), 3–23; Woolf, 'The Britons' and Chris Wickham, 'The Other Transition: From the Ancient World to Feudalism', *Past & Present* 103 (1984), 3–36.

in 448.[14] Despite this defeat, however, and the halting of their advance, the Franks remained in possession of much of the territory between the Rhine and the Somme. It is not known for certain whether Clodio was, in his day, the sole king of the Salian Franks (as this northern, maritime branch of the nation were called), but between his time and the rise of Clovis (Chlodovech) in the years around 500, each of the *civitates* within the Frankish occupied territory seems to have had its own king, a situation paralleling that in Germanic Britain. These events in fifth-century Flanders may well be the most appropriate comparison for events in eastern England in the same period. The Franks remained pagan and do not seem to have attempted, or been able, to use the imperial administrative system, and they lacked political unity. This is the world of the *Pactus legis Salicae*, the most purely Germanic of the Continental barbarian law-codes.[15] When Childeric and his son Clovis, successively kings of the Franks occupying the *civitas* of Tournai, rose to prominence they did so operating as agents and eventually rulers of what survived of the Roman government in Armorica beyond the Somme. Clovis only turned back to Belgica to extinguish the other Frankish rulers at the end of a long career as a sub-Roman general and ruler.[16] The pattern seems clear. Those territories occupied by the Franks up to the defeat of Clodio ultimately became Frankish in character, with Germanic language and Germanic paganism superseding native tongues and cults, while those territories which Clovis added to his *imperium* retained their native, Gallo-Roman characters.

Unfortunately for the purposes of comparative research, the largest part of the Continent to switch to Germanic speech in our period, Bavaria, is particularly poorly documented. Wolfram has termed the Bavarians the 'foundlings of the *Völkerwanderung*', for they appear already settled in the old province of Raetia in the mid-sixth century, with no hint of whence they came.[17] Their failure to adopt inhumation as a regular funerary practice has prevented archaeological analysis from shedding any light on their origins. They do not seem, however, to have possessed a centralised kingship, and the Agilolfing dynasty which provided their *duces* seems to have achieved its pre-eminent position through clientage to the Frankish kings.[18] We may see here a parallel to the situation amongst the early Anglo-Saxons, particularly if we allow Wood's suggestion that Kentish predominance in late sixth-century Britain owed something to Frankish patronage.[19]

To the west of the Bavarians dwelt the Alamanni, whose myriad kinglets crowd the pages of Ammianus Marcellinus and Gregory of Tours. They had seized

---

[14] Wood, *Merovingian Kingdoms*, pp. 36–8. This campaign occurred between the third consulate of Aëtius (446) and his death (452), and it may have been this restoration of Roman fortunes on the Channel coast that prompted the 'Groans of the Britons' reported by Gildas, *De Excidio Britanniae*: *Gildas: The Ruin of Britain*, ed. Michael Winterbottom (Chichester, 1978), chap. 20.

[15] For an edition and translation see Katherine Fisher Drew, *The Laws of the Salian Franks* (Philadelphia, 1991), and for a discussion see Wood, *Merovingian Kingdoms*, pp. 108–13.

[16] James, *The Franks*, pp. 64–90 and Wood, *Merovingian Kingdoms*, pp. 36–50.

[17] Herwig Wolfram, *A History of the Goths* (London, 1988), p. 319.

[18] Wood, *Merovingian Kingdoms*, p. 117.

[19] Ian N. Wood, *The Merovingian North Sea* (Alingsås, 1983) *passim*.

the *Agri decumates*, the region between the Danube and the Rhine, in 260.[20] In an account of the full Alamannic nation on a war-footing in 357, Ammianus describes an army comprising seventeen kings and 35,000 warriors.[21] Some of these warriors are said to be mercenaries or allies from other tribes, which may suggest, if the figures are in the slightest bit trustworthy (and they are more likely to be exaggerated than under-estimated), that the average kingdom was capable of raising less than 1,500 warriors. Hummer argues that the leader of 'the *gens* in arms' was a temporary leader who rose up in times of crisis or through success as a leader of raiding expeditions.[22] In the long term this region (essentially modern Baden-Württemberg) emerged as a thoroughly Germanic-speaking country to which Christianity had to be reintroduced. Once again we see linguistic replacement coinciding with a failure to adopt Roman governmental structures. The containment of the Alamanni within their own territory after the 260s, and of the Franks in theirs after the defeat of 448, may also have hindered the development of a strong dynastic kingship, for no one dynasty was able to provide a constant supply of booty and glory to their followers.[23]

In Bavaria, Flanders and Britain, Germanic conquest was probably preceded by a break-down of Roman imperial control. In the *Agri decumates* that were to become Alammania, Romanization may never have fully taken root. As important as this, however, may have been the failure of temporary *Heerkönige* to establish dynasties, or at least traditions of centralised kingship, as Childeric and Clovis did for the Franks and as Alaric and Athaulf did for the Visigoths.[24] But assessing which of these two factors was more important may be something of a chicken-and-egg dilemma. To some extent the success of the Gothic and Frankish kingships was dependent upon access to revenues, through tribute or plunder, that were independent of the relatively simple dues and services which tribesmen paid and performed for their kings. This in turn was linked to the existence of tenurial structures and a monetary economy which could only be maintained within a highly stratified society.

The relationship between linguistic replacement, on the one hand, and centralised kingship and complex tenurial patterns, on the other, as outlined above, is one of correlation rather than of cause and effect. It can be tested at the other end of the chronological sequence with reference to the linguistic history of Cornwall. The West Saxons appear to have established a western frontier broadly similar

---

[20] Heiko Steuer, 'The Hierarchy of the Alamannic Settlements in the former *limes* region of south-western Germany to AD 500', *Journal of European Archaeology* 2.1 (1994), 82–96. Hans Hummer, 'The Fluidity of Barbarian Identity: the Ethnogenesis of the Alemanni and Suebi, AD 200–500', *Early Medieval Europe* 7 (1998), 1–27.
[21] Hummer, 'Fluidity of Barbarian Identity', p. 8.
[22] Hummer, 'Fluidity of Barbarian Identity', p. 9.
[23] The history of the *Agri decumates* in antiquity is closely paralleled by that of Dacia which was seized by the Terving Goths. The subsequent history of Dacia, however, does not lend itself to comparison in the present case. See Wolfram, *History of the Goths*, pp. 57–64.
[24] Cf. Wolfram, 'Early Medieval Kingdom', pp. 7–8.

to the modern western border of Devon by the end of Ine's reign (688–726).[25] Expansion into Cornwall proper may have begun in Ecgbert's reign (802–39), but the Cornish certainly had their own king as late as 875, under which year the *Annales Cambriae* record the drowning of Dungarth *rex Cerniu*.[26] Some measure of independence may even have been maintained into the tenth century. This is one possible reading of William of Malmesbury's account of Æthelstan's expulsion of the British minority from Exeter and the setting of the frontier of their province at the Tamar, as he had set that of the 'North Welsh' at the Wye.[27] William at no point, however, explicitly mentions a Cornish king.

We can thus discern two distinct periods of English conquest: one, encompassing the greater part of Devon and all that lay to its east, concluded by about 730, and the other encompassing Cornwall and perhaps a few districts in west Devon, taking place after 850. The areas conquered in the first phase seem to have become fully anglicised within the Anglo-Saxon period whilst in Cornwall English remained a minority language, largely confined to the upper echelons and townspeople into the sixteenth or, perhaps, seventeenth centuries. This suggests, at a very conservative estimate, that the predominance of Cornish survived the English conquest for 600 years (i.e. 950–1550), the language itself surviving for a further 200 years after that. If language death had occurred at the same rate in East Anglia, for example, we might have expected British or Insular Romance to be still relatively healthy in the area around Norwich in the time of Cnut; this was clearly not the case.

The key to this problem may lie in the transformation of the nature of English society as a whole over time. What happened between 750 and 950 was a tremendous change in tenurial practice and in the hierarchy of social and economic relations within Anglo-Saxon society. This transformation has been reviewed by David Pelteret.[28] As can be seen from the archaeological evidence, a settlement hierarchy indicative of differential access to resources had begun to develop amongst the Anglo-Saxons in the seventh century. At first, however, the high status settlements seem to have been relatively few in number and to have been for the most part royal residences, the centres of redistributive chiefdoms rather than proprietorial estates. Although the term 'estate centre' is often used for such *villae regales*,[29] one should be careful to distinguish clearly between the use of the term 'estate' to denote two quite different phenomena. On the one hand, it has been used to describe the tenurially diverse territory exploited through

---

[25] Herbert P .R. Finberg, 'Sherborne, Glastonbury and the Expansion of Wessex', *Transactions of the Royal Historical Society* 5 (1953), 101–24, M. Todd, *The South-West to AD 1000* (London, 1987), pp. 267–75.

[26] *Annales Cambriae, AD 684–954: Texts A–C in Parallel*, ed. David N. Dumville (Cambridge, 2002).

[27] William of Malmesbury, *Gesta Regum Anglorum*, ed. Roger A. B. Mynors, Rodney M. Thomson and Michael Winterbottom (Oxford, 1998), II, 134.6.

[28] David Pelteret, *Slavery in Early Medieval England* (Woodbridge, 1995), pp. 24–37.

[29] E.g. Martin Welch, 'Rural Settlement Patterns in the Early and Middle Anglo-Saxon Period', *Landscape History* 7 (1985), 13–25 at p. 16.

extensive lordship, identified by Jones as a 'multiple estate'[30] but perhaps best thought of as a 'shire',[31] and essentially the same as Steven Bassett's supposed 'embryonic kingdoms'.[32] On the other hand it is used for an alienable, divisible property of the sort with which we are familiar from late Roman land-law and the Domesday Survey of eleventh-century England.

Within the 'shire' the ordinary land-holders (*ceorlas*) probably inherited, divided and exchanged their allodial holdings with very little interference from the king.[33] There may have been tenants on lands immediately attached to the shire's *caput* and perhaps even on other large holdings, but the shire itself was not an 'estate' of this sort. Such 'manorial' estates probably began to proliferate after the establishment of the Church, when the kings were placed in a position in which they had to provide economic support for the new institution. The development of alienable 'book-land', granted by charter and able to be passed on as a discrete block of territory not subject to partition at inheritance, may have had a role in encouraging their growth,[34] though not all such estates need have been held by book.[35] The key period for the study of the growth of the manor appears to be the ninth and tenth centuries, a period for which we are lamentably short of settlement archaeology. If we were to base our judgement upon sites excavated, and published, to date, we should be obliged to confine ourselves to two East Midlands sites, Goltho and Raunds.[36] Both these sites seem to have experienced the development of two features which would come to typify manorial estates in southern and midland England: the nucleated village and the lordly residence.[37] Whilst the initial reports date this change to the mid-ninth to early tenth centuries, Martin Welch (pers. comm.) tells me that at both sites the sequences may

---

[30] Classically in 'Multiple Estates and Early Settlement', in *Medieval Settlement: Continuity and Change*, ed. Peter H. Sawyer (London, 1976), pp. 15–40, but see also Wendy Davies, *Wales in the Early Middle Ages* (Leicester, 1982), pp. 43–7 and Nicky Gregson, 'The Multiple Estate Model: some critical questions', *Journal of Historical Geography* 11 (1985), 339–51 for important critiques.

[31] Geoffrey W. S. Barrow, *The Kingdom of the Scots* (Edinburgh, 2003), pp. 7–56.

[32] 'In Search of the Origins of Anglo-Saxon Kingdoms', in *The Origins of Anglo-Saxon Kingdoms*, ed. Steven Bassett (Leicester, 1989), pp. 3–27 at p. 19. For a critique of Bassett's view that such units were indeed 'embryonic kingdoms' see Alex Woolf, 'Community, Identity and Kingship in Early England', in *Social Identity in Early Medieval Britain*, ed. W. O. Frazer and A. Tyrrell (Leicester, 2000), pp. 91–110.

[33] Patrick Wormald, *Bede and the Conversion of England: The Charter Evidence* (Jarrow, 1984), pp. 21–2. The use of the term 'shire' here, and in Professor Barrow's work (see n. 31), does not of course refer to the tenth-century shires of the Midlands and the South which became the pre-1974 English counties.

[34] Wormald, *Bede and the Conversion of England*, pp. 22–4.

[35] I am grateful to Patrick Wormald for discussing this with me.

[36] Guy Beresford, *Goltho: the Development of an Early Medieval Manor, c.850–1150* (London, 1987). Raunds is not, so far as I am aware, fully published but the relevant aspects of the site are reported in *South Midlands Archaeology* 18 (1988) 50–1, and 19 (1989) 34–5.

[37] For a textual description of relations on just such a manor see the *Rectitudines singularum personarum*, in *Die Gesetze der Angelsachsen*, ed. Felix Liebermann (Aalen, 1960) I, 444–53.

be consistently slightly later than the published work would lead one to believe. This would mean that we are looking at the mid-tenth century for the significant developments. Pelteret, rightly in my view, links the growth of the manor (with its more specialised and intensive lordship, geared towards surplus production rather than the cementing of social relations) to the growth of towns and a rural market which could now supply needs that in previous centuries would have been catered for within the more varied and extensive landscape of the 'shire'.[38] This picture is reinforced by the massive increase in charter material and wills from the late ninth and tenth centuries.[39] As a rough indication of this, we might note that in Sawyer's hand-list of *Anglo-Saxon Charters*, 357 royal diplomas are listed from the 295 years between 604 and 899, while 806 are listed from the 167 years between 899 and 1066.[40] John Blair concurs, suggesting that a 'concomitant of this tighter definition and exploitation was that much of the land was administered in smaller units: the "classic manor", containing one or two village communities rather than many, became normal in the two centuries after 850'.[41]

One is tempted to connect the Cornish question (outlined above) with this development of the manor and to suggest that it is this socio-economic development which brings an end to, or slows down, linguistic replacement in medieval Britain; the border between Cornwall and Wessex, in effect, marks the point which Anglo-Saxon political expansion had reached before the full development of the manorial economy. West of here, and the same applies for the border of the same period to the north of the Bristol Channel, linguistic change did not follow on rapidly after conquest, and when it did come, slowly and grudgingly, the shift-speakers maintained their own sense of non-Englishness. Indeed, in the first centuries of 'post-manorial conquest', it seems to have been as likely that the new aristocracy would switch to the language of the people, as the Normans did in Ireland, Wales and England and as the Varangians seem to have done in Russia, as the other way around. In the latter case the parallel is exceedingly close to what happened in England between, say, 650 and 950, with royal tribute-collecting regions being carved up and distributed amongst the ruler's retainers.[42] This does not of course mean that no features of the classic Domesday manorial economy had developed prior to the mid-eighth century,[43] but simply that the manorial mechanism of exploitation had not become the dominant form and had not begun to drive the development of society to the extent which it later would. Before the Viking Age there may have been islands of manorialism but these were surrounded by a sea of kin- and client-based social relations.

---

[38] Pelteret, *Slavery*, p. 37.
[39] Pelteret, *Slavery*, p. 36.
[40] Peter H. Sawyer, *Anglo-Saxon Charters: an Annotated List and Bibliography* (London, 1968).
[41] John Blair, *Anglo-Saxon Oxfordshire* (Stroud, 1994), 132.
[42] Jerome Blum, *Lord and Peasant in Russia: From the Ninth to the Nineteenth Century* (Princeton, 1971), pp. 40–2.
[43] See Trevor H. Aston, 'The Origins of the Manor in England', *Transactions of the Royal Historical Society*, 5th series 8 (1958), 59–83 and Anthony R. Bridbury, *The English Economy: From Bede to the Reformation* (Woodbridge, 1992), pp. 56–85.

Such a view is entirely at odds with the vision of Anglo-Saxon society presented by Higham in 1992 in which he argued that the archaeologically visible Anglo-Saxons made up only a small, aristocratic proportion of the population supported by an agrarian labour force, both free and unfree, made up of Britons.[44] He went on to argue that:

> the bulk of the Anglo-Saxon community could have been recruited internally from Britons, some of whom were able to take advantage of the transitional period to slough off the role of unfree peasant, while others continued to occupy the lower and less privileged strata in the social hierarchy.[45]

Higham was aware that the linguistic evidence posed a major problem to this model, particularly noting that even words associated with low status activities and experience were Germanic. Like many archaeologists and historians, Higham focused on lexicon (words), but the story is the same with regard to morpho-syntactical features.

By analogy with other studies of large-scale language shift, we ought to expect morpho-syntactical structure to be the most favourable field in which to identify indigenous substrate interference in English. Here the most significant work appears to have been that of Walther Preussler who identified a number of features which he claimed indicated such interference.[46] Most significantly he argued that the periphrastic use of the verb 'do' and the progressive tense in English have their origins in Celtic interference but neither of these points has been accepted in their entirety. The origin of the periphrastic use of 'do' in the period of pre-Viking Age Anglo-British contact has not been widely accepted,[47] although this position has been championed recently by Poussa.[48] The problems with the Preusler/Poussa position fall into two categories: firstly, there are alternative explanations for the origin of the periphrastic use of 'do' in English, which do not require a substrate explanation and secondly, this particular phenomenon is only visible in texts from the late thirteenth century onwards, when it is initially confined to verse and is very rare.[49] It becomes common only in the modern period, and then it is largely confined to western dialects of English. This last point is, perhaps, the more significant objection, since if we could not establish that an alternative method of generation had occurred, we could at least ask why there was no evidence of this form in Old English or early Middle English texts. Poussa argues that it had remained a low register form in the pre-Norman period,

---

[44] Higham, *RBAS*, pp. 183–8.
[45] Higham, *RBAS*, 189. Later in his text Higham suggests that 'the mass of unfree population was probably indigenous. In important respects, this society was one which practised apartheid': 193. It might be argued, however, that a slave society is not the same thing as one which practised apartheid.
[46] Walter Preussler, 'Keltischer Einfluss im Englischen', *Revue des Langues Vivantes* 22 (1956), 322–50.
[47] David Denison, *English Historical Syntax* (Harlow, 1993), pp. 255–91.
[48] Patricia Poussa, 'A Contact-universals Origin for Periphrastic *Do*, with Special Consideration of OE-Celtic Contact', in *Papers from the 5th International Conference on English Historical Linguistics*, ed. Sylvia Adamson *et al.* (Amsterdam, 1990), pp. 407–34.
[49] Denison, *English Historical Syntax*, pp. 255–91.

and this is possible, but it is also possible that, even if it is of Celtic origin, it is the result of late medieval language shift in south-east Wales and Cornwall and of immigration from Celtic-speaking parts of Britain into England in the later Middle Ages.[50] Poussa has also argued that the use of the words 'as' and 'what' as relativizers (e.g. 'That is the dog as bit me' and 'He is the man what done me wrong') in some modern English dialects is the result of 'Celtic' substrate interference, but the same problems of very late attestation occur here.[51] I must stress that it is the lateness of attestation rather than the Celtic origin of these features which is the main obstacle to accepting them as evidence for events in Late Antiquity.

It is often said that the progressive aspect found in Middle and Modern English (i.e. 'While I was walking' rather than the simple past 'While I walked') derives from external influence, and this was Preussler's other main example of Celtic substrate interference. Gerhard Nickel, however, demonstrated that the Old English progressive was internally generated.[52] The possibility that at least some aspects of the Middle and Modern English progressive was generated by contact with outside languages, including perhaps Celtic, was considered by Mossé, though he stressed that this was a modern phenomenon.[53] A more recent champion of the substrate hypothesis for the progressive tenses has appeared in Braaten, but his defence of the position has not met with widespread acceptance.[54] The idea that Modern English might be influenced by Celtic>English shift dialects should not surprise us when we consider the kind of figures for immigration from Ireland and Wales in the last two centuries, marshalled by Ewen.[55] We should therefore be wary when it seems that significant evidence for syntactical features which *may possibly* reflect Celtic usage are not clearly evident before the period when large-scale immigration from countries in which Celtic languages were still spoken and in which local Englishes undeniably contained Celtic interference. It should be stressed that caution here is urged on chronological not linguistic grounds.

Recently Peter Schrijver has produced an interesting phonological study

---

[50] Chris Hall, *Periphrastic Do: History and Hypothesis* (Ann Arbor, 1983). I am grateful to Dr Hall for discussing this topic with me and confirming that he still holds the views expressed in his thesis.

[51] Patricia Poussa, 'Origins of the non-Standard Relativizers WHAT and AS in English', in *Language Contact in the British Isles*, ed. Per Sture Ureland and George Broderick (Tübingen, 1988), pp. 295–316.

[52] Gerhard Nickel, *Die Expanded Form im Altenglischen: Vorkomme, Funktion und Herkunft der Umschreibung 'beon/wesan' +Partizip präsens* (Neumünster, 1966). For an English discussion see B. Mitchell, *Old English Syntax* (Oxford, 1985) §§ 682–701.

[53] Fernand Mossé, *Histoire de la forme périphrastique 'être + participe présent' en germanique, II, moyen-anglais et anglais moderne* (Paris, 1938).

[54] Bjørn Braaten, 'Notes on the Continuous Tenses in English', *Norsk Tidskrift for Sprogvidenskap* 21 (1967), 167–80. His views are dismissed by Denison, *English Syntax*, pp. 370–412.

[55] Cecil L'Estrange Ewen, *The British Race – Germanic or Celtic?* (Paignton, 1945).

which has some bearing on these issues.⁵⁶ Schrijver's basic premise is that Old English and Coastal Dutch (OCstDu.) share a number of phonological innovations with each other and with British Celtic, which mark them out from the other Germanic languages as a whole and even from other Ingvaeonic dialects such as Old Saxon. His study focuses on the vowel systems of these languages and comprises a survey of the fate of each of the Proto-Germanic (PGm.) vowels within North-Sea Germanic (NSGm). His conclusion is as follows:

> The earliest of the common developments of the NSGm. languages (OE, OFris., OCstDu.) show the hallmarks of being adaptions of the PGm. system to the system of British Celtic or a closely related Celtic dialect on the Continent around the fifth to ninth centuries A.D. The presence of a British Celtic substratum or a substratum closely cognate to it, in early Medieval Britain, along the Dutch coasts and in Frisia would account for the observed phenomena. The most specific phenomenon that receives an explanation is the difference between Kentish, CstDu. and OFris. on the one hand and the other OE dialects on the other in the treatment of rounded front vowels, which appears to follow an isogloss separating West British [i.e proto-Welsh] from South-West British [i.e. proto-Cornish and Breton].⁵⁷

Central to Schrijver's interpretation is that the region in which Old Coastal Dutch and Old Frisian came to be spoken in the Early Middle Ages had previously been occupied by peoples speaking a dialect of Celtic close to British. He justified this assumption on the basis of an admittedly historical, rather than linguistic, argument that suggested plausibly that Belgic Celtic may well have been closer to British than to the normative reconstructions of Gaulish produced on the basis of data largely drawn from central and southern France.⁵⁸ One detail of this argument worth noting is his suggestion that the ancient *Frisii* were in fact Celtic speakers rather than Germanic speakers (he cites Seebold in support of this hypothesis).⁵⁹ Schrijver's observation that the OCstDu. vowel system was especially close to that of Kentish and South-West British would seem to further justify his suggestion of the existence of a distinct 'Belgic Celtic' influencing the dialects of northern Gaul and south-eastern Britain. It is also significant to note that few if any of these 'British' features appear in Old Saxon. Had they done so one might have argued that Germanic speakers could have brought them to Britain, but this seems, if his analysis is to be trusted, to be unlikely. It is also worth noting that, unlike the scholars putting forward the other tentative examples of substrate interference discussed above, Schrijver has placed a great deal of emphasis on chronological development within the Middle Ages.

Indeed, this is potentially the most difficult part of his argument with which to come to terms. Schrijver is not claiming simply that certain phonological

---

⁵⁶ Peter Schrijver, 'The Celtic Contribution to the Development of the North Sea Germanic Vowel System, with Special Reference to Coastal Dutch', *NOWELE* 35 (1999), 3–47.
⁵⁷ Schrijver, 'Celtic Contribution', p. 33.
⁵⁸ Schrijver, 'Celtic Contribution', pp. 9–11.
⁵⁹ Elmar Seebold, 'Wer waren die Friesen? – sprachlich gesehen', in *Friesische Studien* II, ed. Volkert Faltings, Alastair Walker and Ommo Wilts (Odense, 1995), pp. 1–17.

features present in fifth- and sixth-century British influenced the pronunciation of Germanic in shift dialects but that certain sequences of phonological development continued in tandem in both North Sea Germanic and British Celtic over a sustained period of time. If I have understood Schrijver's proposals correctly this is most likely to have occurred if there were fairly sustained bilingualism amongst a significant proportion of the population. This said, my impression is that linguists do not currently feel secure in identifying what factors govern processual phonological shift in languages. Nevertheless, Schrijver's phonological observations deserve serious consideration.

Hildegard Tristram's contribution to the debate is more wide-ranging and holistic.[60] She argues that British interference has been understudied due to prejudicial pre-assumptions inherited by successive generations of historians going back to Bede. She also believes that British did not survive, in the 'English' zone, for more than six generations after the Anglo-Saxon conquest, although she does not give her reasons for believing this.[61] She recognises, however, that if rapid and widespread language shift took place, we should expect to find 'significant typological changes in morphosyntax', and indeed claims that these can be found. Her linguistic study is divided into two main sections: firstly, an analysis of converging morphosyntax in English and Welsh (mostly using late medieval and modern examples),[62] and secondly, a legitimation of using such late evidence for inferring historical processes in Late Antiquity.[63]

Tristram admits that the examples of similarities between English and Welsh she identifies may not be exhaustive and have not themselves been exhaustively analysed. Most of them are only visible in the later medieval period or later, and one or two of them, at first sight, do not seem exclusive enough to bear the burden she suggests might be put on them. Others may, however, and a great deal depends upon whether her arguments for accepting 'latency' can be held to be generally sound. Before going on to discuss these arguments, it should be noted that Tristram is to a large degree interested in 'Present Day English' (her preferred term) and for her purposes it is not so important when English 'became a Celtic language' as whether it is or is not one now. Thus, for her purposes both latency, that is the failure of linguistic interference to show up in the record until long after its appearance in the spoken language, and continued contact are valid mechanisms for introducing Celticisms into English. For our purposes in contrast it must be stressed that interference subsequent to *c*.800 is largely irrelevant.

The argument for latency depends upon a literary norm covering up real innovation and variation within the spoken language. No one could argue with this position in principle and similar situations certainly occur elsewhere. Old Irish remained a standard for 300 years (*c*.600–900) and Classical Irish for 500 (*c*.1200–1700), and at the end of each period quite radical innovative features

---

[60] Hildegard Tristram, *How Celtic is Standard English?* (Petersburg, 1999), and her contribution to this volume.
[61] Tristram, *How Celtic*, p. 16.
[62] Tristram, *How Celtic*, pp. 19–27.
[63] Tristram, *How Celtic*, pp. 27–30.

emerged suggesting that they had been developing for some time. This is precisely what did happen to English during the century or so when French became the normal literary language in England. Most famously, of course, we have the sudden emergence of written Romance from under the wings of literary Latin in the ninth century, after nearly a millennium of divergent development.

In the case of English, however, we are faced with the problem that the development of a standard, early West-Saxon, literary form almost certainly dates to the decades around AD 700, after, presumably, nearly 300 years of shift of British-born individuals into English-speaking communities. So why did no, or at most only an extremely small number of, 'Celticisms' make it into standard Old English despite the fact that regional dialects are discernible?[64] For much of that time, even amongst the Germanic-speaking groups, there was no cohesive sense of shared English identity and significant dialect variation.[65] This may only have preceded writing by about a century.

The key to understanding Anglo-British relations in the crucial early centuries of Anglo-Saxon England is the law code promulgated by Ine, king of the West Saxons, at some point between 688 and 694.[66] Ine 24.2 states that a Welshman who owned five hides of land had a *wergeld* of 600 shillings. 23.3 states that a Welsh taxpayer (*gafolgelda*), or owner of a single hide of land, has a *wergeld* of 120 shillings and that his son has one of 100 shillings. This compares unfavourably with the equivalent English ranks which have *wergelds* of 1200 and 200 shillings respectively.[67] The property qualification of five hides is that which was required to qualify as a member of the nobility, and one of the most significant pieces of information we are given here is that there were Welsh nobles within Ine's *imperium*. Although the Welsh noble's *wergeld* is only half that of the English nobleman's it is, nevertheless, three times as high as that of the English *ceorl*. This should immediately alert us to the fact that we are not looking at a society in which the Britons are uniformly regarded as lower status than the Anglo-Saxons. It should also be pointed out that any society which strictly regulates on the basis of ethnic affiliation is unlikely to be one in the process of transforming its ethnic identity en masse. If firm legal distinctions existed between Britons and Anglo-Saxons, individuals and communities will not have slipped

---

[64] Alistair Campbell, *Old English Grammar* (Oxford, 1959), §§ 6–22, 4–11.
[65] John Hines, 'The Becoming of the English: Identity, Material Culture and Language in Early Anglo-Saxon England', *Anglo-Saxon Studies in Archaeology and History* 7 (1994), 49–60.
[66] The code was printed by Liebermann, *Gesetze*, and again, with modern English translation, in *The Laws of the Earliest English Kings*, ed. Frederick L. Attenborough (Cambridge, 1922 and Felinfach, 2000) and has been described by Patrick Wormald in *The Making of English Law* (Oxford, 1999), pp. 103–6. The code is discussed thoroughly by Martin Grimmer in this volume.
[67] It should be noted that a similarly low *wergeld* for Britons is recorded in surviving manuscripts of the eleventh-century Northumbrian code text known as *Norðleoda Laga*. This clause, however, 7, is one of a group of clauses, 6–8, which list *wergelds* in southern denomination *scillingas* rather than the Northumbrian *þrymsas*. Since the first of these clauses, 6, is explicitly a citation of Mercian law, otherwise unrecorded, we should perhaps view the other *scillingas* clauses, including that dealing with Britons, in the same light.

from one identity to another with ease. Indeed, there are strong economic incentives to preserve this segregation when viewed from an English perspective.

It is important to note that the presence of a Welsh nobility within Wessex implies the existence of British-dominated districts within West Saxon jurisdiction, though whether large *regiones* or smaller, more strictly local territories it is impossible to tell, and, indeed, conditions presumably changed over time. Since both Welsh and English law practised the subdivision of allodial lands between agnates,[68] it is unlikely that Welsh nobles would have lived isolated amongst the Anglo-Saxon population rather than surrounded by kinsmen of a similar status, and the Welsh tax-payers are also most likely to have been their clients. Taken in its context of tenurial practice and clientage, it is almost certainly the case that Ine's law code is *not* presenting an image of late seventh-century Wessex as a heterodox, multiethnic state but as a patchwork of separate *regiones*, some at least of which were dominated by Britons, held together by the overall supremacy of an English redistributive chieftaincy. It may be that it was one of the predominantly British *regiones* whose dead were commemorated by the inscribed stones now located at Lady St Mary Church in Wareham.[69] This said, the imbalance in *wergelds* between the two groups may hold within it the very key to the disappearance of the Britons. The *wergeld* provided the basic honour price for an individual and represented the compensation that would be paid to his kin on his death. Other legal compensations, for injury to self or property, however defined, were computed as a proportion of one's *wergeld*. The long term effects of Britons being valued at about half the *wergeld* of their English counterparts was that, in the normal course of things, large amounts of property would gradually pass from the British community to the English. If, for example, a hypothetical English and British nobleman each owning five hides of land got into a series of disputes with one another and were dealt with fairly by the courts, sometimes giving judgement in favour of the one and sometimes of the other, then all compensations paid by the Briton to the Englishman would be twice the value of those paid to him by his opponent. The end result would be that the property and finally the land would pass to the Englishman.

By giving the Britons protection under the law and by preserving their basic civil rights – indeed, by giving them access to the courts, the Anglo-Saxons were able to reduce the risk of wholesale and persistent resistance which a policy of naked aggression would inevitably have aroused. The likelihood would be that in the short term the system would protect most individual Britons and that the erosion of their economic base would generally be so gradual as to be barely perceived on the basis of individual experience. It is interesting to note that *Lex Salica*, the Frankish law code drawn up in precisely those territories where the Frankish language, religion and cultural identity replaced Gallo-Roman, utilised

---

[68] Thomas M. Charles-Edwards, 'Kinship, Status and the Origins of the Hide', *Past & Present* 56 (1972), 5–35.
[69] David A. Hinton, 'The Inscribed Stones in Lady St. Mary Church, Wareham', *Proceedings of the Dorset Natural History and Archaeological Society* 114 (1992), 260.

a precisely similar mechanism of apartheid.[70] In the long run individual British households would, one by one, become bankrupt and break down, with children being sold into slavery or sent to live with relatives as prospect-less hangers-on. The apartheid of the law codes would also doubtless be compounded by the partial patronage of redistributive chiefdoms. Whilst Britons might be *gafolgeldas*, it is unlikely that many of them were the beneficiaries of royal largesse. In comparison to English districts, British areas would be regions of high production and low consumption, tribute and disproportionate legal costs flowing out and few gifts flowing in. The lack of opportunities for young British males to become retainers of chieftains would, perhaps, have encouraged them to leave for British-controlled kingdoms or led to increasing poverty as inherited farms became subdivided between co-heirs. In this long drawn-out process of economic decline, many individual Britons may have found themselves drifting into Anglo-Saxon households, as slaves, hangers-on, brides and so forth, but they would have come into these communities as one among many. Their ability to impact on the cultural or linguistic identity of the community would have been minimal, and such households would have become ethnic sausage machines, recycling stray biological material in such a way that it would not carry its ethnicity with it into the next generation. Cumulatively, however, the biological contribution of this steady trickle of Britons into English households will have been enormous over several generations. Such a model allows us to escape the problems of both the genocide and the elite emulation models and complies with all the constraints left us by the evidence, archaeological, linguistic and textual.

---

[70] Katherine Fisher Drew, *Laws*, and discussion by Wormald, *Making*, pp. 105–6.

11

Welsh Territories and Welsh Identities in Late Anglo-Saxon England

C. P. LEWIS

RECENT work on late Anglo-Saxon England has paid only fitful attention to the kingdom's undoubted cultural and linguistic diversity. That must be a matter of regret given the potential of such an approach for the exploration of English attitudes to 'Others' in the shaping of Englishness and the formation of the Anglo-Saxon state.[1] There has, of course, been some excellent discussion of the continuing Scandinavian character of the Danelaw,[2] and some interest in French and Lotharingian incomers,[3] and in the Britons of Cornwall and Cumbria.[4] However, little has been written lately on the Welsh of the western border shires. This paper uses some underexploited evidence, in Domesday Book and from territorial names, to show how Welsh-speaking inhabitants of late Anglo-Saxon England were organized and hence, indirectly, to probe the degree of their assimilation, English attitudes towards them (at least at an 'official' level) and perhaps even their own cultural identity.

---

[1] Strikingly demonstrated in works such as Katharine Scarfe Beckett, 'Old English References to the Saracens', in *Essays on Anglo-Saxon and Related Themes in Memory of Lynne Grundy*, ed. Jane Roberts and Janet Nelson (London, 2000), pp. 483–509; Brian McFadden, 'The Social Context of Narrative Disruption in *The Letter of Alexander to Aristotle*', *ASE* 30 (2001), 91–114. I am grateful to Dr David Parsons (Institute for Name-Studies, University of Nottingham) for his invaluable comments on an earlier version of this paper.

[2] Recent work includes D. M. Hadley, 'Viking and Native: Re-thinking Identity in the Danelaw', *Early Medieval Europe* 11 (2002), 45–70; Matthew Townend, *Language and History in Viking Age England: Linguistic Relations between Speakers of Old Norse and Old English* (Turnhout, 2002); and several of the papers in *Vikings and the Danelaw*, ed. James Graham-Campbell, Richard Hall, Judith Jesch and David N. Parsons (Oxford, 2001).

[3] C. P. Lewis, 'The French in England before the Norman Conquest', *Anglo-Norman Studies* 17 (1994), 123–44; Simon Keynes, 'Giso, Bishop of Wells (1061–88)', *Anglo-Norman Studies* 19 (1996), 203–71.

[4] Karen Jankulak, *The Medieval Cult of St Petroc* (Woodbridge, 2000); Charles Phythian-Adams, *Land of the Cumbrians: A Study in British Provincial Origins, A.D. 400–1120* (Aldershot, 1996).

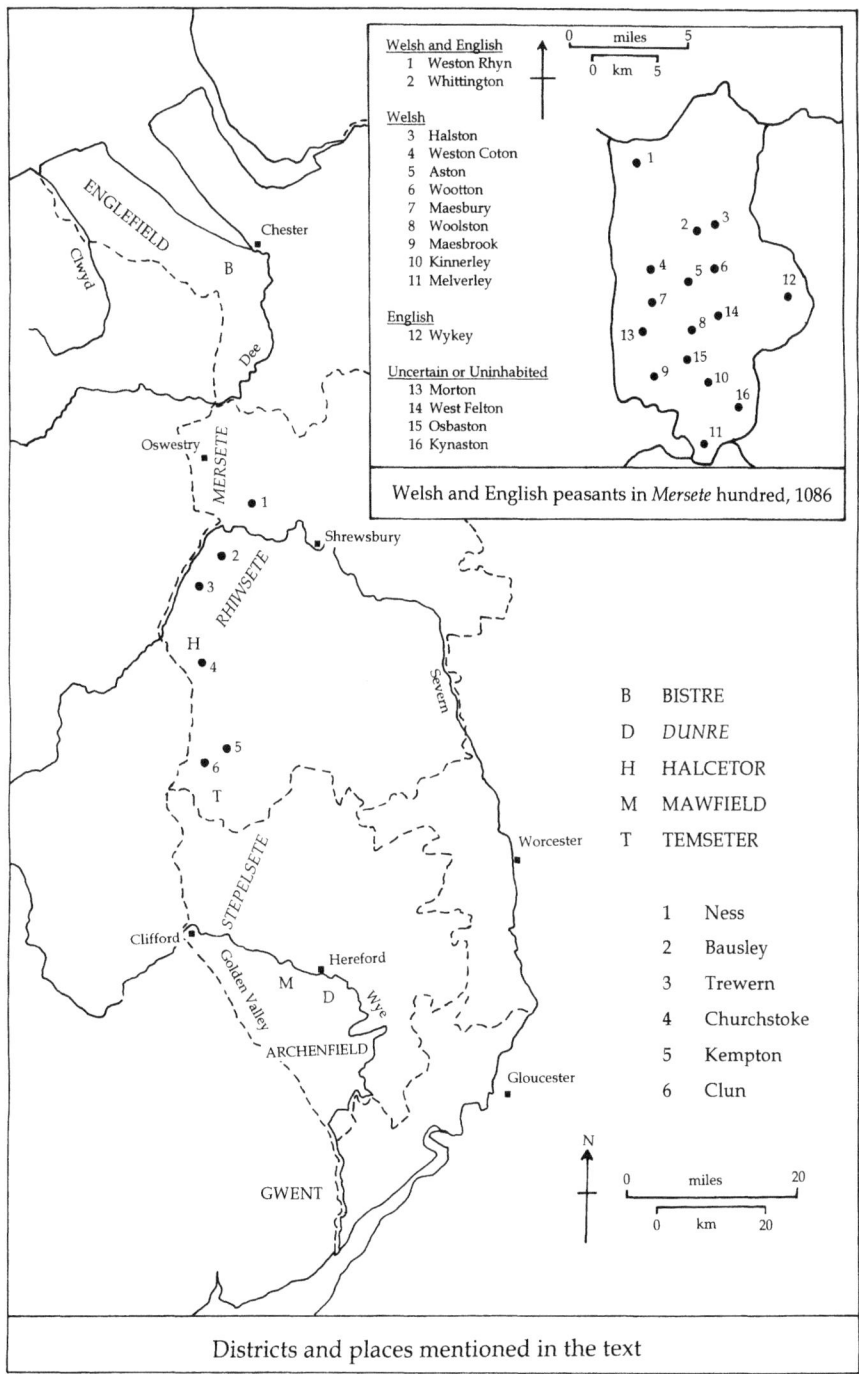

11.1 The Welsh borders in the late Anglo-Saxon period

Welshmen in Domesday Book

Domesday Book in 1086 enumerated peasants denoted *Walenses* or *Waleis* at several manors along the border. They lived in places which were assessed in hides, had named pre-Conquest owners and belonged to English hundreds and shires, in other words places which had been fully part of Anglo-Saxon England. An example is the Shropshire manor of Melverley near Oswestry. It lay in *Mersete* hundred, paid tax on one hide and was owned before 1066 (TRE) by an Eadric who was almost certainly the Eadric the wild who rebelled against the Normans. The only peasants recorded at Melverley in 1086 were two Welshmen who had one ploughteam between them and paid their Norman lord thirty-two pence in rent.[5] It seems fair to assume that Melverley was equally Welsh before 1066.

The western boundary of the Anglo-Saxon state from the Dee to the Severn was defined in 1066 by the limits of land which, like Melverley, was hidated, held by named lords, incorporated into shires and assigned to hundreds. Beyond the boundary were some districts recently acquired by the English or whose people enjoyed special privileges, either of which signalled the absence of full incorporation into England. For example, a holding at Clifford, on the river Wye at the limit of Anglo-Saxon territory, had an unambiguously English place-name and belonged TRE to a lord with an English name, Bruning, but it was neither hidated nor assigned to any hundred.[6] Similarly at the northern end of the marches, in the mountains and valleys west of Offa's Dyke, Edwin, earl of Mercia TRE, held the district of Englefield and the manor of Bistre, both recently taken from the defeated Welsh king Gruffudd ap Llywelyn; although the two territories were notionally assigned to a Cheshire hundred, they were not divided into hides.[7]

Domesday Book gives fuller pre-Conquest information about the Welsh territory of Archenfield, which was annexed to Herefordshire but not actually part of it and not assimilated into the English administrative system even in 1086. Although the Domesday description of Archenfield was written up in the folios for Herefordshire, the county heading distinguished between it and Herefordshire proper.[8] In 1066 the chief manor of Archenfield belonged to King Edward, and he and Earl Harold had one other manor each, but the rest was in the hands of Welsh lords, and its men had privileges which set them apart from their English neighbours. Archenfield generally was not hidated nor in any hundred, but significantly the king's central manor of 'Westwood' was rated at six hides and formed the only component of Wormelow hundred in 1066.[9] The manor was an outpost

---

[5] Great Domesday Book [henceforth GDB] 255r1 Melevrlei. To allow consultation of any edition of Domesday Book, references take this form, r or v standing for recto or verso and 1 or 2 for the column, followed when appropriate by the place-name.
[6] GDB 183r2 Cliford.
[7] GDB 269r1–2; C. P. Lewis, 'An Introduction to the Cheshire Domesday', in *The Cheshire Domesday*, ed. A. Williams and R. W. H. Erskine (London, 1991), pp. 1–25, at pp. 21–3.
[8] GDB 179r2; 181r1.
[9] GDB 181r1–2 Westuode, Westeude.

of the English local administrative system in the heart of a Welsh territory and may have been organized as such as recently as the early 1060s.[10]

On the eve of the Norman Conquest, Archenfield and Englefield and the Welshmen who lived there were thus under English control without being entirely part of the English state, if 'the state' is defined by its highly uniform system of local government. Their configuration as territories suggests some of the ways in which the apparatus of government was able to accommodate communities of Welshmen along the border without trying to make them Englishmen or their territories fully English. The men of Archenfield had collective duties and privileges in relation to the king of the English, notably their own law and an honourable place in the vanguard of English armies campaigning in Wales. The priests of three royal churches there said masses for King Edward, and other local notables might be summoned to attend the shire court of Hereford or the new hundred court of Wormelow. Such favourable arrangements suggest that the English were prepared to recognize and accommodate the cultural difference of the men of Archenfield even while bringing them under English rule. Anglicization was very limited in 1066, though the creation of a hundred court of Wormelow and the beginnings of assessment in hides may have been intended as an interim stage towards fuller integration with English administrative norms.

Elsewhere in the borders other Welshmen lived less ambiguously within the framework of shires, hundreds and hides which articulated the late Anglo-Saxon state and were therefore subject to the usual processes of law, taxation and other obligations. They can be seen most clearly along the western boundary of Shropshire, where in 1086 Welshmen were living on eighteen manors, as individuals or in small groups.[11] In eight of those manors the Welsh were the only inhabitants. Elsewhere they were counted separately from the villans, bordars, slaves and others, all of whom were presumably English. Some of the groups of Welshmen had their own ploughteams distinct from those held by the villans and bordars. Others paid collective rents to their Norman lords. In both cases the implication is that they conducted their farming operations separately from the English peasants even when they were tenants of the same manor.

The Welshmen's ploughteams did not number more than one or two except at Maesbury, the head manor of *Mersete* hundred, where ten Welshmen and a priest had eight ploughs. Maesbury, however, consisted of a central manor and five unnamed berewicks, so that probably even there the Welsh lived in smaller groups with no more than two teams each. The landscape was thus one of individual Welsh farms, or at most a hamlet of two or three homesteads. The rents which the Welsh paid were modest, typically five shillings by an individual or ten shillings

---

[10] C. P. Lewis, 'An Introduction to the Herefordshire Domesday', in *The Herefordshire Domesday*, ed. A. Williams and R. W. H. Erskine (London, 1988), pp. 1–22, at pp. 8–12.

[11] GDB 253v1 Alretone [Trewern], Meresberie [Maesbury*], Wititone [Whittington*]; 253v2 Nessham [Ness]; 254v2 Halstune [Halston*], Westone [Weston Rhyn*], Meresbroc [Maesbrook*], Tibetune [unidentified*]; 255r1 Melevrlei [Melverley*], Westune [Weston Coton*], Udetone [Wootton*], Osulvestune [Woolston*]; 255v1 Beleslei [Bausley]; 256r2 Estone [Aston*]; 258r1 Chenpitune [Kempton]; 258r2 Clune [Clun]; 259r2 Chenardelei [Kinnerley*]; 259v1 Cirestoc [Churchstoke]. Those marked * were in *Mersete* hundred.

by a group of twelve, figures in line with the values of nearby manors inhabited by English peasants. The Shropshire Welsh, in other words, were peasant farmers resembling their English neighbours in wealth and social standing.

At the local level Welshmen thus did not live with and among the English peasantry in 1086 but separately, and presumably the same was true before the Conquest. Even where they were tenants of the same manor they had their own ploughteams and so probably their own fields. Even when incorporated into English manors, subject to English hundred courts and taxed by the English state, the Welsh of the border districts lived as distinct communities apart from the English in the mid-eleventh century.

Mersete hundred

One part of the English marches was especially full of Welshmen in 1086, *Mersete* hundred just east of Offa's Dyke in north-west Shropshire, a district which later formed the marcher lordship of Oswestry. The core manors of Maesbury and Whittington have been claimed as a specifically Welsh territory in 1086:

> this Domesday description merely conceals a *maenor* [the characteristically north Welsh form of territorial organization] at a late stage of development.[12]

It is certainly true that Norman reorganization of *Mersete* hundred was only just getting under way in 1086. The castle at Oswestry was then new enough to be known simply as 'the Earthwork' (*Luvre*, that is *l'oeuvre*), and the Norman sheriff Reynold de Bailleul's estate centre was still at the pre-Conquest hundredal capital of Maesbury.[13] Closer scrutiny of the hundred's territorial organization, however, shows something other than a Welsh *maenor*.

Mersete hundred included nineteen manors comprising twenty-one named places.[14] All the place-names were English, including the six which have not been identified.[15] As many as fifteen had as their generic second element *tun* ('settlement' or 'township'), a proportion unusual in most parts of England but paralleled in other border areas, including Englefield and the Golden Valley of Herefordshire.[16] It may suggest that the place-names had been coined fairly

---

[12] G. R. J. Jones, 'The Pattern of Settlement on the Welsh Border', *Agricultural History Review* 8 (1960), 66–81, at p. 79.

[13] GDB 253v1 Meresberie.

[14] Asterisked references in n. 11 above; GDB 254v2 Mortune & Aitone [Morton and unidentified]; 255r1 Feltone [West Felton], Sbernestune & Chimerestun [Osbaston and Kynaston]; 257v2 Wiche [Wykey]; 259v2 Haustune & Burtone [both unidentified], Newetone [unidentified], Wlferesforde [unidentified].

[15] B. G. Charles, 'The Welsh, their Language and Place-Names in Archenfield and Oswestry', in *Angles and Britons: O'Donnell Lectures* (Cardiff, 1963), pp. 85–110, at pp. 100–7; Margaret Gelling with H. D. G. Foxall, *The Place-Names of Shropshire, Part One: The Major Names of Shropshire*, English Place-Name Society 62/63 (1990); the six 'lost' names and Halston await a future volume in the series.

[16] C. P. Lewis, 'English and Norman Government and Lordship in the Welsh Borders, 1039–1087' (D.Phil. thesis, Oxford University, 1985), pp. 154–8; Hywel Wyn Owen, 'Old

recently. Nearly all the descriptive first elements of the names were drawn from just two types: dithematic Old English personal names (Cyneheard, Cyneweard, Osbeorn, Oswulf and Wulfhere) and the simplest topographical identifiers (east, west, field, wood, marsh, island, nook and fortification or manor-house). The topographical names might represent relatively recent translations of Welsh place-names, while the personal names were perhaps those of the first English owners of the manors concerned, not more than a few generations before 1066.

The named manorial centres were not the only places in *Mersete* hundred in 1066. Domesday Book also counted twenty-seven and a half unnamed berewicks, many of which must have been at the places which emerged in later records as townships. Except in the far west of the lordship of Oswestry (an area not for certain part of England in 1066), the later township names were every bit as English as the manorial names recorded in Domesday, and broadly speaking they were formed as names from the same range of elements and in similar ways.[17] In other words, so far as can be judged, the Welsh of *Mersete* hundred at the time of the Norman Conquest were living on manors and at places with English names.

Their pre-Conquest lords also had English names. Besides King Edward and Earl Edwin, they included Eadric the wild and a Siward who was almost certainly the other leading pre-Conquest Shropshire magnate, like Eadric a distant kinsman of King Edward.[18] The lesser thegns of the hundred had common English names: Ælfgar, Ælfnoth, Ælfwig, Dunning, Leofnoth, Wulfgeat and Wulfric, besides one of ultimately Scandinavian origin, Turgot (from Þorgautr). Although it is impossible to know anything for certain about their ancestry, it seems likely that they were Englishmen through and through.

The English-named and English-owned manors of *Mersete* hundred were full of Welsh peasant tenants in 1086. Six of the nineteen had only Welshmen as inhabitants, and another six had Welshmen alongside others. Four manors were waste and untenanted, leaving only three populated manors without Welshmen, one of which was occupied by 'men' whose status and ethnicity were not stated. Another was the manor of 'Newton', where there were two villans and two bordars: the place-name might be taken to indicate a recent settlement of incoming English peasants.

The Welsh formed a majority of the free population of *Mersete* in 1086: fifty-eight households (allowing ten for the vague 'some Welshmen' at Whittington),[19] as against thirty-two headed by English villans and bordars. There were also seven unspecified 'men', the priest at Maesbury, some French newcomers and a

---

English Place-Name Elements in Domesday Flintshire', in *Names, Places and People: An Onomastic Miscellany in Memory of John McNeal Dodgson*, ed. Alexander R. Rumble and A. D. Mills (Stamford, 1997), pp. 269–78.

[17] Township names from *Victoria County History Shropshire* II (London, 1973), 223–9, parishes of (West) Felton, Kinnerley, Knockin, Llansilin, Llanyblodwel, Llanymynech, Melverley, Oswestry, Ruyton in the Eleven Towns, St Martin's, Selattyn and Whittington. Most of the township names await full documentation and discussion in *PN Shropshire*.

[18] Lewis, 'English and Norman Government and Lordship', pp. 82–4, 105–6, 112–13.

[19] They paid 20s. rent and may have numbered as few as four if they owed as much as the Welshman at Maesbrook, or as many as twenty if as little as those at Weston Cotton.

servile population of twenty-eight oxmen. The distribution of Welsh and English inhabitants differed greatly. English peasants were concentrated on only four manors, which also housed over half the oxmen. Two thirds of the English were tenants of just one manor, the large royal estate of Whittington. By contrast Welshmen were found almost everywhere in the hundred in 1086.

Late Anglo-Saxon *Mersete* thus had an English superstructure of lords, manors and place-names overlying a largely Welsh substructure of peasants and farms. Only a few places in the hundred were occupied by English peasants. The relationship of Whittington to the rest of the hundred was not much different from that of King Edward's manor of 'Westwood' to Archenfield. It was an English bridgehead in Welsh territory, though at a more advanced stage of development. Archenfield may have been embarking in the mid 1060s on processes of economic penetration and territorial development which *Mersete* hundred had gone through a few decades or a few generations earlier.

There was also a striking pattern in the tax assessment of manors in *Mersete* hundred which served to distinguish Welsh lands from English. As throughout Shropshire, Domesday Book gives figures for both hides and ploughlands, the latter likely to represent an estimate of real arable capacity, the former an artificial rating. All eight manors whose only free inhabitants were Welsh and all four uninhabited places (as well as one with a mixed population) were taxed on hidages set at fixed and regular ratios to ploughlands, either 1:2 (nine cases) or 1:3 (four cases). The other three mixed manors and two with only English peasants had irregular ratios and were all taxed more heavily in relation to their arable, in excess of one hide to each two ploughlands. The most favourable tax regime in the hundred was at 'Newton', with a ratio of 1:4; its English peasants were perhaps given a low hidation because they were relatively recent settlers. Otherwise all the Welsh manors in *Mersete* were taxed more leniently than ones inhabited by English or mixed populations. The arrangements look contrived to favour the Welsh.

Mersete hundred can thus be characterized as inhabited largely by Welsh free peasants answering to English lords; it had Welsh-run farms organized in manors with English place-names; and it was under normal English shire and hundred administration but with tax-breaks for the Welsh. The embryonic marcher lordship of 1086 and its Anglo-Saxon precursor were not a lightly disguised Welsh *maenor* undergoing organic change. Rather there had been transformations, some of them radical, under quite recent English political, administrative and manorial control. The Welsh were nonetheless left largely in occupation of their land and were not degraded in status; in fact they enjoyed privileges and safeguards. They had been incorporated into the English state but were recognized as *Walenses* distinct from the English peasantry; they had been brought into the shire and hundred system but were concentrated within a single hundred where they were the dominant group; and they were taxed beneficially in comparison with their English neighbours. Welsh cultural identity within England was thus preserved and quite probably with deliberation and purpose.

Territorial names in *feld*

Anglo-Saxon attitudes towards the Welsh within England can be further explored by considering the English names given to Welsh-occupied territories which incorporated the words *feld* and *sæte*.

Two district names ending in *feld* were recorded in Domesday Book: Archenfield and Englefield. Archenfield is the less problematic. It had been coined as an English name by 914, when the *Anglo-Saxon Chronicle* described how a Viking fleet captured its bishop (later ransomed by Edward the Elder) and then raided towards Archenfield before being beaten off by an English army.[20] The passage occurs in the West Saxon continuation of the Alfredian *Chronicle*, suggesting that the name was current at the West Saxon court, unsurprisingly if Edward the Elder exercised some kind of protectorate. Archenfield was hence a name at least sanctioned in government circles and perhaps coined there. It consisted of the Welsh name of the district, Ergyng, with Old English *feld* added.[21]

Englefield has been regarded as a more difficult name. Superficially it seems to mean 'the *feld* of the English' and to be formed in the same way as the place-name Englefield (Berks.), 'the *feld* of the Angles', and others such as Conderton (Worcs.), 'the *tun* of the Kentishmen'.[22] In those cases the names signalled a difference between the perceived 'ethnicity' of the people in the named locality and the inhabitants of the wider region: the Angles of the Berkshire Englefield were different from the Saxons of the immediate neighbourhood, and the Kentishmen of Conderton different from the Mercians around Worcester. The names worked as ethnic identifiers whether they were coined self-referentially or by the majority community.

Englefield in north Wales, however, does not work like that as a name.[23] The Domesday place-names there were a mixture of English names and Welsh names, neither set showing any apparent influence from the other language. It seems likely that there were separate communities of Welsh and English speakers in the territory in 1066. The area seems to have been under English control from the 790s until perhaps the 1010s, then in Welsh hands until 1063 or 1064.[24] Judging from the distribution of place-names, English settlement was confined to the narrow coastal strip from the Dee estuary round to the marshy land at the mouth of the river Clwyd, and to the hillsides immediately behind the coast. The name Englefield, however, applied not just to those English-settled lands but to the whole territory, including the mountainous interior and the lower Clwyd valley, both of which had exclusively Welsh place-names in 1086.

---

[20] *Anglo-Saxon Chronicle* 918 ABC, 915 D (= 914): *Two of the Saxon Chronicles Parallel*, ed. Charles Plummer (Oxford, 1892–9) I, 98–9.
[21] Bruce Coplestone-Crow, *Herefordshire Place-Names*, BAR, BS 214 (Oxford, 1989), p. 2.
[22] *The Cambridge Dictionary of English Place-Names*, ed. Victor Watts (Cambridge, 2004), pp. 154, 216, and sources and other examples cited there.
[23] Contrary to Ellis Davies, *Flintshire Place-Names* (Cardiff, 1959), p. 53.
[24] Henrietta Quinnell and Marion R. Blockley, *Excavations at Rhuddlan, Clwyd, 1969–73: Mesolithic to Medieval*, Council for British Archaeology Research Report 95 (York, 1994), pp. 7–8.

The origin of the name Englefield thus has to be sought elsewhere, in an English adaptation of the territory's Welsh name, Tegeingl. The name Tegeingl had evolved from the British tribal name of the *Deceangli*, securely recorded on first-century lead pigs and in a corrupt form by Tacitus.[25] The Welsh form was not recorded until the twelfth century, in a poem enumerating the districts of Wales[26] and in the Welsh chronicles,[27] but it must have been the established name of the area when the English first encountered it. The processes by which 'Tegeingl' was Anglicized as 'Englefield' are perhaps illuminated by Gerald of Wales in the course of recounting a laboured joke which he alleged illustrated the witticisms of the Welsh. The joke hinged on the coincidence that Tegeingl was also the name of a woman who had slept with each of two princes, Dafydd ab Owain Gwynedd and his brother, who ruled the territory of Tegeingl in turn. Its punchline was a supposed saying from the time that Dafydd succeeded his brother as prince: 'I don't think Dafydd should have Tegeingl. His brother's had her already.'[28] At first sight Gerald's shaping of the story seems to be directed against the Welsh (dirty-minded, not funny), but it also acts in a more sophisticated way to score points off the English too. *Teg* was the Welsh for 'beautiful', and *Teg-engel* might be (deliberately) mistaken by a quick-witted Anglo-Welsh bilingual, such as Gerald, as meaning 'the beautiful English(woman)'. Read like that, Gerald's unfunny joke may have concealed a clever dig at the English: by ruling successively over the province of Tegeingl the two princely brothers had taken turns with a beautiful Englishwoman.[29] When English speakers first reached north-east Wales, they may well have heard the Welsh name of the territory as Gerald later would, as *teg eingl*, and understood its proper name to be *Eingl*, particularly appropriate (if misunderstood as a homophone) when they settled in part of it. By a roundabout route it is therefore possible to argue that the name Englefield was constructed on the same principle as the name Archenfield: an existing Welsh district name suffixed with *feld*.

Feld in territorial names was not used in quite the same way as in place-names, though it lay within the same semantic range of 'country' or 'tract of land'. Margaret Gelling has shown that in settlement names (and there are some 250 major names of the type) *feld* normally meant 'open country' in distinction to wooded or marshy or hill country.[30] The 'open country' referred to in place-names such as Huddersfield was restricted in area and topographically uniform. In contrast, Archenfield and Englefield were the names of large territories which

---

[25] A. L. F. Rivet and Colin Smith, *The Place-Names of Roman Britain* (London, 1979), p. 331; Davies, *Flintshire Place-Names*, pp. 160–1.
[26] J. Vendryes, 'Le poème du Livre Noir sur Hywel ap Gronw', *Etudes Celtiques* 4 (1948), 275–300, at pp. 281, 288.
[27] *Brut y Tywysogyon, or The Chronicle of the Princes: Red Book of Hergest Version*, ed. and trans. Thomas Jones (Cardiff, 1955), pp. 144–5, 148–9.
[28] Gerald of Wales, *Descriptio Kambriae*, in *Works*, ed. J. S. Brewer, James F. Dimock and George F. Warner, 8 vols., RS 21 (1861–91) VI, 153–227, at pp. 190–1.
[29] Walter Map would have told the same joke better.
[30] Margaret Gelling, *Place-Names in the Landscape* (London, 1984), pp. 235–45; Margaret Gelling and Ann Cole, *The Landscape of Place-Names* (Stamford, 2000), pp. 269–78.

included a mixture of marshland, mountain and woods as well as open country. *Feld*, it can be suggested, had a specialized use when the English wished to coin Anglicized versions of Welsh district-names.

That being so, it would be worth revisiting at greater length than is possible here some of the other place-names of western England which end in *feld*, to look for further examples which might incorporate a Welsh or British district name. Makerfield springs to mind, that intriguing and as yet unexplained district name in south Lancashire. It would also be worth reconsidering names where *feld* is preceded by what has hitherto been regarded as an otherwise unrecorded personal-name, such as the Maccel said to have given his name to Macclesfield (Ches.), or where the first element is definitely a British word, as at Lichfield (Staffs.), or where it is unexplained, as with Morville (Salop.).[31] All three names applied to extensive territories as well as individual settlements within them.[32]

Elsewhere in the Welsh borders there were a few other districts whose names ended in *feld*. Mawfield in Herefordshire (a name transferred by the eleventh century to an individual manor) was the English name for a small district immediately north of Archenfield, a name formed by adding *feld* to the Welsh name *Mael Lochu* or *Malochu*. The Welsh version of the name occurs in the Book of Llandaff as *Mais* [i.e. *Maes*] *Mael Lochou* and in Latin as [*in*] *Campo Malochu*, both *maes* and *campus* being equivalent to Old English *feld*.[33]

Finally we can return to *Mersete* hundred in north-west Shropshire and to Bede's name for the place where Oswald, Christian king of the Northumbrians, fell in battle against Penda, the pagan Mercian king, in 642, 'which in the language of the English is called *Maserfelth*'.[34] It is impossible to be sure in any formal sense that *Maserfelth* was Oswestry.[35] Bede himself may not have known where it was. At the end of the twelfth century, Gerald of Wales was arguably aware of local traditions putting Oswald's death at Oswestry, though that does not make them true historically. There is no formal etymological connection between *Maserfelth* and the names of *Mersete* and Maesbury, since *Mersete* and Maesbury (*Meresberie* in 1086) both contained as first element Old English (*ge-*)*mære*, 'boundary', and *Maserfelth* did not.[36] The first part of *Maserfelth* could well be an obscure Welsh district name (perhaps garbled by Bede), afterwards misconstrued (or reconstructed) by the English as their own word (*ge-*)*mære*. But in any case, for present purposes it can be deemed probable

---

[31] Current interpretations in *Cambridge Dictionary*, ed. Watts, pp. 372, 392, 393, 423.
[32] Evident even in GDB 263v2 Maclesfeld; 247r1 Lecefelle; 253r2 Membrefelde.
[33] Coplestone-Crow, *Herefordshire Place-Names*, pp. 14–16.
[34] *HE*, 242–3.
[35] Cautiously for the identification: Clare Stancliffe, 'Where Was Oswald Killed?', in *Oswald: Northumbrian King to European Saint*, ed. Clare Stancliffe and Eric Cambridge (Stamford, 1995), pp. 84–96; cautiously against: N. J. Higham, *The Convert Kings: Power and Religious Affiliation in Early Anglo-Saxon England* (Manchester, 1997), p. 270; strongly against: Margaret Gelling, *PN Shropshire* I, 230–1.
[36] O. S. Anderson, *The English Hundred Names*, 3 vols. (Lund, 1934–9), I, 155; *PN Shropshire* I, 192–3; *Cambridge Dictionary*, ed. Watts, pp. 392–3.

that *Maserfelth* was another territorial name in *feld*, with an unexplained first element which might conceivably be its earlier Welsh name.

Bede does not say whether *Maserfelth* was under English control in the 640s, but it seems likely, given that it was the location of a battle between the rulers of two English kingdoms. Nor does he say directly whether the people of *Maserfelth* were English or Welsh, though one of the miracles which he reports involved a Welshman taking away a bagful of the earth sanctified by Oswald's blood.[37] It seems reasonable to suppose that *Maserfelth* was a Welsh territory controlled by an Anglo-Saxon king.

The Anglo-Saxons thus seem to have coined a small number of territorial names in *feld* for Welsh districts under English control. Significantly there is no evidence that they had similar names for districts deep in Wales. Anglicization of the names was something more than just renaming, acting also as a form of cultural appropriation, a process implicit whenever other people's place-names are deliberately distorted. At one level the English were making Welsh territorial names pronounceable in their own language and intelligible as onomastic items. More fundamentally they were also repositioning in an English-speaking world the names of Welsh districts which they now ruled. The new names worked by what seems a minimal intervention in the existing Welsh name, one which simultaneously preserved its integrity but also made it accessible to the English. For the future it guaranteed continuing transformation, since the further evolution of the name would now be as an English onomastic item. If *Maserfelth* is an example of the type, those processes had been going on since Bede's time and may well have resonances for much earlier phases of British assimilation in Anglo-Saxon England than have been the focus of this paper.

Bede may himself hint at such a cultural appropriation of Welsh territory in his story of the Welshman and the bag of earth from *Maserfelth*. That evening the Welshman hung his bag from a wall post inside the house where he dined, and the post alone survived a fire because of the holy power of Oswald's blood. Oswald's was a very English cult,[38] but Bede took pains to show that it was observed at its place of origin by a Welshman, and quite probably one living under English rule.

Territorial names in *sæte*

The other territorial naming element for discussion here is *sæte*, meaning 'dwellers, people of a district', widely used in Anglo-Saxon England in a variety of contexts. Some of the *sæte* districts existed at an early date and were named from extensive ranges of hills, like the *Pecsæte* ('Peak dwellers') and *Cilternsæte*

---

[37] *HE*, 244–5.
[38] Clare Stancliffe, 'Oswald, "Most Holy and Most Victorious King of the Northumbrians"', in *Oswald*, ed. Stancliffe and Cambridge, pp. 33–83; Alan Thacker, '*Membra Disjecta*: The Division of the Body and the Diffusion of the Cult', in *Oswald*, ed. Stancliffe and Cambridge, pp. 97–127.

('Chiltern dwellers') listed in the Tribal Hidage. Others, also early, indicated the people of territories attached to particular central places, like the *Sumorsæte* of Somerton (Somerset), the *Dornsæte* of Dorchester (Dorset) and possibly the *Wreocensæte* if they were named from Wroxeter (Salop.) rather than the Wrekin.[39] Smaller districts were named in an analogous way from rivers, the Warwickshire Arrow giving rise to the *Arosæte* of the Tribal Hidage and the Kentish Stour to the hundred-name *Estursete*.[40] Although the *sæte* names coined early are sometimes regarded as 'tribal', in reality they were territorial, drawing attention not to group identity through supposed common descent but rather to the common occupation of a tract of land. The word was also used late in the Anglo-Saxon period in Old English charter boundary clauses to refer to the people of parish- or township-sized territories, in elliptical phrases which dropped the generic second element from a place-name X in order to coin a new proper name which meant 'the people of X'.[41]

The Welsh borders had a particular concentration of *sæte* names of a further, perhaps distinct type, referring to medium-sized territories: three Domesday hundreds (*Mersete* and *Rhiwsete* in Shropshire and *Stepelsete* in Herefordshire), two other small districts, Halcetor or Alcester (from *Halhsæte*) and Temseter or Tempsiter (from *Temesæte*), and the *Dunsæte* and *Wentsæte* who are named in the legal text known as the 'Ordinance concerning the *Dunsæte*'. Margaret Gelling has suggested that they all belonged to a system created by Offa in the late eighth century to maintain the newly defined Welsh frontier by assigning specified sections of his great earthwork to different groups of 'dwellers' along its length.[42] Such an early date is unpersuasive. Three of the territories were hundreds, and throughout western Mercia an articulated system of hundreds, and thus the need to name them, dated only from the mid-tenth century.[43] It seems preferable to look for the origins of the marcher *sæte* names in the late Anglo-Saxon period rather than Offa's time.

It is clear that the 'Ordinance concerning the *Dunsæte*' used the name *Wentsæte* for the men of Gwent, Anglicizing the Welsh territorial name by adding *sæte* in a naming process similar to that argued above for names in *feld*. Most of the other marcher *sæte* names were coined from geographical features rather than territories or central places. The *Temesæte* were certainly named from the little

---

[39] David Dumville, 'The Tribal Hidage: An Introduction to its Texts and their History', in *The Origins of Anglo-Saxon Kingdoms*, ed. Steven Bassett (London, 1989), pp. 225–30; *Cambridge Dictionary*, ed. Watts, pp. 134, 192, 464, 559, 704–5.
[40] Eilert Ekwall, *English River-Names* (Oxford, 1928), pp. 16–17, 378–9.
[41] G. H. Wheeler, 'The Method of Formation of Old English Place-Names in "-hæme", "-sætna", "-tuningas"', *Modern Language Review* 11 (1916), 218–19.
[42] Margaret Gelling, 'The Early History of Western Mercia', in *Origins of Anglo-Saxon Kingdoms*, ed. Bassett, pp. 184–201, at pp. 199–201.
[43] F. M. Stenton, *Anglo-Saxon England*, 3rd edn (Oxford, 1971), pp. 298–9; Ann Williams, *Kingship and Government in Pre-Conquest England, c. 500–1066* (London, 1999), pp. 88–9.

river Teme in south-west Shropshire.[44] The *Rhiwsæte* were named from the Rew, a prominent ridge dominating the hamlet of Alberbury, chief manor of *Rhiwsete* hundred.[45] The *Stepelsæte* of Herefordshire were named from a *stepel*, a place-naming term meaning 'a steep place' used elsewhere in the borders.[46] Very likely it was the proper name of some particular hill, but as the hundred was full of steep places, it is not possible to identify which one was meant. The *Halhsæte* were named from a *halh*, in its sense of 'river-meadows' and referring to the flat Camlad valley downstream from Churchstoke (Montgomeryshire). Arguably the *Dunsæte* were named from the *dun* (the Old English word for a particular shape of hill) which also gave rise to the Domesday name *Dunre* for a hundred and manor (later Dinedor) across the Wye from Hereford.[47]

There is one further feature common to most of the *sæte* territories along the border, namely their Welshness. The *Wentsæte* of Gwent were certainly Welshmen. So, contrary to what has sometimes been said, were the *Dunsæte* of the Ordinance. Halcetor became the name of a small marcher lordship which had English place-names but Welsh inhabitants (so, like *Mersete* hundred). Temseter was the name of part of the Welshry of the marcher lordship of Clun.[48] Only *Rhiwsete* hundred in Shropshire and *Stepelsete* in Herefordshire were not Welsh when first recorded, but no detailed research has been done on their early history and it is not possible to say at present when they were Anglicized. All the *sæte* names could have been coined in the later Anglo-Saxon period as English names for territorial groupings of Welshmen newly brought within the orbit of English kings, whether by treaty (as seems clear in the case of the *Dunsæte* and the *Wentsæte*) or conquest.

Conclusion

The historiography of the territories discussed here has been dominated by work intended to uncover their authentic underlying Welshness. They have been regarded, on the whole, as little Waleses within England rather than as transitional marcher territories, a bias which itself reflects a mid-twentieth-century phase of the long contest over their linguistic and cultural identity. More interesting is to consider them as multicultural societies and as districts with plural identities, bicultural before 1066, tricultural afterwards. The sources allow only fleeting glimpses of how the English, and more particularly the English state, configured them in the mid-eleventh century. Next to nothing can be deduced about how local English lords or neighbouring English communities regarded these English Welshmen, and still less about their own senses of identity. They also raise intriguing questions about the stages of historical development which

---

[44] Ekwall, *English River-Names*, pp. 398–400.
[45] *VCH Shropshire* VIII (London, 1968), 178, 183.
[46] *PN Shropshire* I, 278–80.
[47] C. P. Lewis, 'The Name and Location of the *Dunsæte*' (in preparation).
[48] R. W. Eyton, *Antiquities of Shropshire*, 12 vols. (London, 1854–60) XI, 233–4.

led to what can be observed on the eve of the Norman Conquest, and about possible parallels between the place in the late Old English state of these Britons and their territories and the position of earlier Britons and earlier British territories within Anglo-Saxon England.

12

Some Welshmen in Domesday Book and Beyond: Aspects of Anglo-Welsh Relations in the Eleventh Century

DAVID E. THORNTON

WHEREAS the importance for the study of eleventh-century English history of William the Conqueror's great land survey known, since the twelfth century, as 'Domesday Book' hardly needs stating, its value as a source for the history of Wales during the same period is perhaps less self-evident.[1] True, Welsh historians from Sir John Lloyd onwards have drawn on the survey for their historical reconstructions, but most of these studies have tended to 'sample' Domesday Book in order to supplement information drawn from their other – main – primary sources. While there are notable exceptions to this rule, a thorough analysis of Wales and Welshmen in Domesday Book *per se* remains to be undertaken.[2] My purpose in the present paper is to make a contribution towards redressing this historiographical deficiency,[3] by offering a prosopographical analysis of the Welsh individuals who occur in Domesday Book and especially those who occur before the Norman Conquest – that is, *tempore regis Edwardi*, or TRE as it is usually indicated in the text itself. The starting point is the data presented in Table 12.1 below: that is, a total of seventy-nine entries

---

[1] In this paper I shall cite Domesday Book from Farley's edition, which employs the folios of the original manuscripts: *Domesday Book seu Liber Censualis Willelmi Primi Regis Angliae*, ed. Abraham Farley, 2 vols. (London, 1783), *hereafter* DB. Farley's text is most readily available in the so-called 'Phillimore' edition and translation, which also uses a more specific means of locating entries: *Domesday Book. A Survey of the Counties of England*, gen. ed. John Morris, 35 vols. in 40 (Chichester, 1975–86). Pending a full scholarly response by historians to David Roffe's reassessment of the position and date of Domesday Book in his *Domesday: The Inquest and the Book* (Oxford, 2000), I shall follow here the more traditional interpretation of the relationship between William I and Great and Little Domesday Books.

[2] A volume of articles on Welsh history and Domesday Book by various specialists in the field is currently under proposal: *Domesday Book and Wales: Anglo-Saxons, Anglo-Normans and the Welsh in the Eleventh Century*, ed. David E. Thornton (forthcoming). For a cartographic depiction of Wales according to Domesday Book, see Illus. 12.1 below.

[3] A companion piece, provisionally entitled 'More Welshmen in Domesday Book and Beyond: The Welsh and the Norman Conquest', is expected to appear in *Domesday Book and Wales*, ed. Thornton.

from Domesday Book (both TRE and for 1086) which may be considered in some way to refer to Welshmen. The criteria for compiling this list are onomastic and geographical, though as might be expected neither is straightforward and both require some preliminary comment.

There are three main categories of Welsh personal names in Domesday Book.[4] Firstly come those which, judging from the Domesday form, would appear to be linguistically or etymologically Brittonic: these are explained more clearly in Table 12.2 below. Obviously, the Welsh were not the only 'Britons' to occur in Domesday Book, so it is necessary to weed out any occurrences of Cornish or Breton personal names – though one would expect the former to be limited mostly to the West Country and the latter to occur mostly in 1086. Secondly, Table 12.2 lists a number of strange or 'corrupt' onomastic forms which, given their geographical location, may represent Welsh names. In addition to commonly attested forms such as *Grifin* for Gruffudd and *Mariadoc* for Maredudd, there are other names which require some degree of correction, such as *Elmui* for Old Welsh (OW) *Elinui* where a Domesday scribe has apparently confused his minims, or *Saisi* for OW *Saissil*, now Seisyll.[5] More difficult forms include *Costelin* and *Taldus*, both names of TRE tenants in Archenfield where genuine Welsh names are attested,[6] or the Gloucester Domesday name *Ouus*, which is usually taken to represent a form of Welsh *Owain*, though it could perhaps be a corruption of *Nouis*, now Nowy.[7] Similar problems of interpretation arise for the forms *Genut, Genust* and *Gethne*, which probably all refer to the same TRE tenant in Shropshire.[8] Such erroneous and strange forms should be understood in the context of the development of the Domesday manuscripts themselves. Scholars no longer regard the main scribe of Greater Domesday Book, which concerns us here, as an Anglo-Norman who 'Normanized' Old English names but rather as a native Englishman whose aim was to Latinize the orthography of personal and place-names, while also occasionally 'correcting' some extreme instances of 'Normanized' name forms.[9] Before him, however, was a less clearly

---

[4] For the study of Domesday anthroponomy, Olof von Feilitzen, *The Pre-Conquest Personal Names of Domesday Book* (Uppsala, 1937) remains a useful, if dated, starting point. See also, K. S. B. Keats-Rohan and David E. Thornton, *Domesday Names. An Index of Latin Personal and Place Names in Domesday Book* (Woodbridge, 1997), and K. S. B Keats-Rohan, *Domesday People. A Prosopography of Persons occurring in English Documents, 1066–1166. 1: Domesday Book* (Woodbridge, 1999).

[5] For *Elmui* see Wendy Davies, *The Llandaff Charters* (Aberystwyth, 1979), p. 162; A. G. Williams, 'Norman Lordship in South-East Wales during the Reign of William I', *Welsh History Review* 16 (1992–3), 445–66, at p. 450. For *Saisi* von Feilitzen, *The Pre-Conquest Personal Names*, p. 351; note also the form *Aisil*.

[6] On which, see below, p. 163.

[7] Williams, 'Norman Lordship in South-East Wales', p. 463.

[8] von Feilitzen, *The Pre-Conquest Personal Names*, pp. 259–60.

[9] Alexander R. Rumble, 'The Palaeography of the Domesday Manuscripts', in *Domesday Book. A Reassessment*, ed. Peter Sawyer (London, 1985), pp. 28–49, at pp. 45–9; *idem*, 'The Domesday Manuscripts: Scribes and Scriptoria', in *Domesday Studies. Papers Read at the Novocentenary Conference of the Royal Historical Society and the Institute of British Geographers, Winchester, 1986*, ed. J. C. Holt (Woodbridge, 1987), pp. 79–99, at p. 84; Cecily Clark, 'Domesday Book – A Great Red-Herring: Thoughts on Some Late Eleventh-

Table 12.1: Welshmen in Domesday Book

DB Form	ID	Farley	County	Date	Place
Aisil (?)		259c	Salop	1066	Brockton (Wrockwardine)
Aisil (?)		257a	Salop	1066	Brockton (Wrockwardine)
Aluric Mapesone		176c	Worcs	1066	Droitwich (Clent)
Beluard de Caruen (?)		162b	Glouc	1086	W:
Berdic joculator regis	Berddig Gwent	162a	Glouc	1086	W:
Blein	Bleddyn ap Cynfyn	181a	Heref	1066+	(narrative: Archenfield)
Bleio (prepositus)		162a	Glouc	1086	W:
Cadiand (*Cadian*)	Cadien Ddu	181a	Heref	1066	Kilpeck (Archenfield)
Caraduech regem	Caradog ap Gruffudd	162a	Glouc	1086–	W: (narrative)
Chenesis (?)		162a	Glouc	1086	W:
Costelin (?)	(Custennin ap Cadien)	181a	Heref	1066	Birch (Archenfield)
Eduinus	(Edwin of Tegeingl)	268d	Chesh	1066–86	W: Coleshill (Atiscross)
Eduinus (?)	(Edwin of Tegeingl)	268d	Chesh	1066	W: Castretone (Atiscross)
Eduinus (?)	(Edwin of Tegeingl)	268d	Chesh	1066	W: Aston (Atiscross)
Eduinus (?)	(Edwin of Tegeingl) (?)	267a	Chesh	1066	W: Hope (Exestan)
Eli		264c	Chesh	1066–86	Crewe Hall (Broxton)
Elmui (prepositus)	Elynwy ab Idnerth	162a	Glouc	1086	W:
filius Wasuuic	Gwasfwyth, son of	162a	Glouc	1086	W:
Genust (?)		258c	Salop	1066	Holdgate (Patton)
Genut (?)		258c	Salop	1066	Uffington (Wrockwardine)
Gethne (?)		258c	Salop	1066	Bosle (Alnothstree)
Godric Mappesone		181a	Heref	1086	Goodrich (Archenfield)
Grifin		246d	Staff	1066	Biddulph (Pirehill)
Grifin		267b	Chesh	1066	Newton (Northwich)
Grifin	(Gruffudd ap Maredudd)	184d	Heref	1086	Kings Pyon (Stretford N)
Grifin	(Gruffudd ap Maredudd)[1]	180c	Heref	1086	*Le Oake*[2] (Leominster)
Grifin	Gruffudd ap Maredudd	179b	Heref	1086	(list)

Name		Folio	County	Date	Place
Grifin (filius Mariadoc regis)	Gruffudd ap Maredudd	187a	Heref	1086	Kenchester (Staple)
Grifin [puer]	(Gruffudd ap Maredudd)[1]	180c	Heref	1086	*Le Oake* (Leominster)
Grifin filii Mariadoc	Gruffudd ap Maredudd	187c	Heref	1086	(heading)
Grifin puer	(Gruffudd ap Maredudd)[1]	180c	Heref	1086	*Le Oake* (Leominster)
Grifin regis	(Gruffudd ap Llywelyn)	162a	Glouc	1066+	W:
Grifin rex	Gruffudd ap Llywelyn	181a	Heref	1066–	(narrative: Archenfield)
Grifin, Aldgid uxor	Gruffudd ap Llywelyn	238d	Warw	1066	Binley (Stoneleigh)
Grifin, rex	(Gruffudd ap Llywelyn)	269b	Chesh	1086–	W: Bistre (Atiscross)
Grifini	Gruffudd ap Maredudd	183d	Heref	1086	Lye (Hazeltree)
Grifino, regi; Grifin	Gruffudd ap Llywelyn	263a	Chesh	1066–	W: land beyond river Dee
Grifinus	Gruffudd ap Maredudd	187a	Heref	1086	Kenchester (Staple)
Grifinus filius Mariadoc	Gruffudd ap Maredudd	187c	Heref	1086	*Mateurdin* (Elsdon)
Grifinus filius Mariadoc	Gruffudd ap Maredudd	187c	Heref	1086	Bunshill (Staple)
Grifinus filius Mariadoc	Gruffudd ap Maredudd	187c	Heref	1086	Mansell Lacy (Staple)
Grifinus filius Mariadoc	Gruffudd ap Maredudd	187c	Heref	1086	Mansell Lacy (Staple)
Grifinus filius Mariadoc	Gruffudd ap Maredudd	187c	Heref	1086	Stoke Bliss (Plegelgate)
Grifinus filius Mariadoc	Gruffudd ap Maredudd	187c	Heref	1086	Lye (Hazeltree)
Grifinus filius Mariadoc	Gruffudd ap Maredudd	187c	Heref	1086	*Curdeslege* (Elsdon)
Idhel (prepositus)	Ithel ap Tewdws	162a	Glouc	1086	W:
Iwardus (?)		259d	Salop	1086	Newetone (Merset)
Madoc	(Madog ab Bleddyn)	259d	Salop	1086	*Halston* and *Burtone* (Merset)
Madoc		187c	Heref	1086	Ashperton (Radlow)
Madoch		170d	Glouc	1066–86	Rudford (Botloe)
Madoch		179b	Heref	1086	(list)
Marcud	Marchudd ap Cynan	269a	Chesh	1086	W: Axton and Gellilyfdy (Atiscross)
Mariadoc regi	Maredudd ab Owain	187a	Heref	1066+	Kenchester (Staple)
Mariadoc regi	Maredudd ab Owain	187c	Heref	1066+	*Mateurdin* (Elsdon)
Mariadoc regi	Maredudd ab Owain	187c	Heref	1066+	Lye (Hazeltree)
Mereuin (?) teinus com' Odonis		184c	Heref	1066	Mathon (Worcs)
Mereuuin (?)		181a	Heref	1066	Baysham (Archenfield)

Name	Identification	Folio	County	Year	Location
Morganau		167c	Glouc	1066	English Bicknor (Westbury)
Noui (*Nouis*)		181a	Heref	1066–86	*Penebecdoc* (Archenfield)
Ouen (*Owein*)	Owain ab Edwin	187c	Heref	1066	Lye (Hazeltree)
Ouuin		265c	Chesh	1066	Basford (Nantwich)
Ouuine (?)		276b	Derby	1066	Bradwell (High Peak)
Ouuinus		265d	Chesh	1066	Austerton (Nantwich)
Ouuinus (?)		105b	Essex	1086	Colchester
Ouus prepositus regis		162a	Glouc	1086	W:
Rees	Rhys Sais	267c	Chesh	1066	W: Erbistock (Exestan)
Reuer (?)		186c	Heref	1066	Litley (Cutsthorn)
Reuer (?)		186b	Heref	1066	Bullinghope (Dinedor)
Riset de Wales	Rhys ap Tewdwr	179b	Heref	1086	W: (payment)
Ruillio (?)		183d	Heref	1066	Birley (Stretford)
Saisi		186d	Heref	1066	Lyde (Cutsthorn)
Saissil		186d	Heref	1066	Staunton on Arrow (Staple)
Taldus (?)	(Tewdws ap Marchci)	181a	Heref	1066	Goodrich (Archenfield)
Tuder quidam Walensis	Tudur ap Rhys Sais	253c	Salop	1086	W: (one district of Welsh land)
Wasuuic prepositus	Gwasfwyth	162a	Glouc	1086	W:
Werestan (?)[3]		181a	Heref	1086	(Harewood): Archenfield
Wonni (?)		184a	Heref	1066	Maund (Thornlaw)

1 This identification is strengthened by the fact that a later, marginal note in the 'Herefordshire Domesday' names the holder of this manor as William de Biez, who was also to hold some of Gruffudd ap Maredudd's other lands.
2 Coplestone-Crow has identified *Alac* with 'Le Oake' in Knoakes Court: *Herefordshire Place-Names*, p. 125.
3 This is evidently OE Wærstān, but is included here because of its Archenfield location and because the name was borrowed into Welsh as *Gwerystan*.

understood process of oral and written transmission by the agency of men of various ethnic and linguistic backgrounds, which has resulted in an extant text containing up to forty different types of mistakes when representing onomastic data.[10] Much of the discussion of these issues has inevitably focussed on the fate of English and Continental names at the hands of the main Domesday scribe and his predecessors; for present purposes it should be stated that the fate of the rarer and less familiar Celtic names in Domesday Book was no doubt even more problematic.

Thirdly, it is also necessary to mention a number of uncertain or ambiguous personal names: these include, on the one hand, linguistically English names which had been borrowed by the Welsh before or by the eleventh century; and, on the other hand, Domesday forms which may be understood to derive from either Welsh or English names. The most common English onomastic borrowing into Welsh in this period was probably Edwin (OE *Eadwine*), which is attested as early as the ninth century.[11] Other possible such 'loan names' to be found in Welsh sources include Welsh *Elystan* (from OE Æthelstān), *Gwerystan* (OE Wærstān), *Edryd* (OE Eadred) and *Uchdryd* (OE Uhtræd),[12] though all of these occur less frequently in Welsh sources than Edwin. Such names may therefore be considered socio-linguistically Welsh, despite their Insular Germanic origin, and so it is not impossible that such apparently English forms in Domesday Book may in fact conceal a Welshman. Here it should be emphasized that the etymology of a personal name need not necessarily be indicative of the ethnicity or descent of its bearer.[13] In addition there are a number of Domesday name forms which are open to either English or Welsh interpretation: for example, the form *Mereuuin* (in Archenfield) and maybe *Mereuin* (Worcs.) could reflect OE Merewine (like

---

Century Orthographies', in *England in the Eleventh Century. Proceedings of the 1990 Harlaxton Symposium*, ed. Carola Hicks, Harlaxton Medieval Studies 2 (Stamford, 1992), pp. 317–31, repr. in *Words, Names, and History. Selected Writings of Cecily Clark*, ed. Peter Jackson (Cambridge and Rochester, NY, 1995), pp. 156–67, at p. 159.

[10] J. McN. Dodgson, 'Domesday Book: Place-Names and Personal Names', in *Domesday Studies*, ed. Holt, pp. 121–37; and *idem*, 'Some Domesday Personal Names, Mainly Post-Conquest', *Nomina* 9 (1985), 41–51.

[11] David E. Thornton, 'Predatory Nomenclaure and Dynastic Expansion in Early Medieval Wales', *Medieval Prosopography* 20 (1999), 1–22, at p. 13; David N. Dumville, 'The Historical Value of the *Historia Brittonum*', *Arthurian Literature* 6 (1986), 1–26, at p. 25.

[12] For example, see *Early Welsh Genealogical Tracts*, ed. P. C. Bartum (Cardiff, 1966), pp. 185, 187, 193; C. A. Ralegh Radford and W. J. Hemp, 'The Cross-Slab at Llanrhaiadr-ym-Mochnant', *Archaeologia Cambrensis* 106 (1957), 109–16.

[13] For example, on the ethnic ambiguity of Scandinavian personal names in Anglo-Saxon England, see Cecily Clark, 'English Personal Names ca. 650–1300: Some Prosopographical Bearings', *Medieval Prosopography* 8/1 (1987), 31–60, at pp. 31–60; C. P. Lewis, 'Joining the Dots: A Methodology for Identifying the English in Domesday Book', in *Family Trees and the Roots of Politics. The Prosopography of Britain and France from the Tenth to the Twelfth Century*, ed. K. S. B. Keats-Rohan (Woodbridge, 1997), pp. 69–87, at pp. 77–9; Dawn Hadley, '"Cockles amongst the Wheat": The Scandinavian Settlement of England', in *Social Identity in Early Medieval Britain*, ed. William O. Frazer and Andrew Tyrrell (London, 2000), pp. 111–35, at pp. 127–8.

similar forms in Cambs., Surrey and Yorks.)[14] but, as they occur on the Welsh border, could equally reflect OW *Mermin*, later *Meruin*, now Merfyn. Similarly, the Derbyshire form *Ouuine* and Essex *Ouuinus* probably reflect the rare OE name *Ōwine*, not Welsh *Owain*, but what about similar forms in the Welsh March?

Clearly then, personal names alone are not always sufficient to determine Welshness in Domesday Book, and to some extent the geographical location of the relevant tenant must also be taken into account. The basic principle here is that someone who held land in Wales *may* have been Welsh himself. The main problem is how to define Wales: should we use the current administrative boundaries or attempt to define Wales according to the rather more fluid criteria of the eleventh century or even of Domesday Book itself.[15] The latter approach would omit much of the present-day Welsh counties of Flintshire and Wrexham, which were parts of the Cheshire hundreds of Atiscross and Exestan in 1086. Gloucestershire Domesday includes an introductory section before the main list of tenants-in-chief which specifically refers to a series of manors and other lands in modern Monmouthshire as *in Wales sunt*. There is a far higher proportion of Welsh personal names among the tenants of these lands than among those in Atiscross and Exestan. In contrast, in the Domesday description of Archenfield, which was roughly equivalent to the old Welsh kingdom of Ergyng but possibly under English rule for as long as Atiscross and Exestan, and still part of Herefordshire today,[16] there are a significant number of TRE tenants with etymologically Welsh names; and Domesday Book refers more than once to *Walenses* and contains a separate description of the *consuetudines* of the Welshmen in Archenfield. In the light of these brief comments, I shall attempt to be as inclusive as possible when defining Wales as a criterion for Welshness.

Accordingly, Table 12.1 lists Domesday tenants who may be defined as Welshmen because they bore a linguistically Welsh personal name and held land in Wales or on the English side of the Welsh border; or, who held land in Wales – maximally defined – but bore an English name known to have been borrowed by the Welsh; or, thirdly, who held land in Wales and bore a corrupt or ambiguous name form in Domesday Book which could be interpreted as Welsh. Obviously, this is a rather simplified pattern and assumes that Welsh and English were mutually exclusive groups, instead of accounting for the possibility of inter-marriage and mixed demography along either side of the shifting border: for instance, if an English name, like Edwin, could be borne by someone who considered himself

---

[14] DB, I, ff. 35c, 194c, 322d. Note also instances in Warwickshire: *ibid.*, ff. 240b, 244a.
[15] On the problem of defining Wales, and especially its eastern boundaries, in the eleventh and twelfth centuries, see R. R. Davies, *Conquest, Coexistence, and Change: Wales 1063–1415* (Oxford, 1987), pp. 3–7; also more briefly, *idem*, 'The Peoples of Britain and Ireland 1100–1400: II. Names, Boundaries and Regnal Solidarities', *Transactions of the Royal Historical Society*, 6th series 5 (1995), 1–20, at pp. 17–18; and most recently, Huw Pryce, 'British or Welsh? National Identity in Twelfth-Century Wales', *EHR* 116 (2001), 775–801, at pp. 776–7.
[16] Margaret Gelling, *The West Midlands in the Early Middle Ages* (Leicester, 1992), pp. 114–18; Bruce Coplestone-Crow, *Herefordshire Place-Names*, BAR, BS 214 (Oxford, 1989), pp. 2–5.

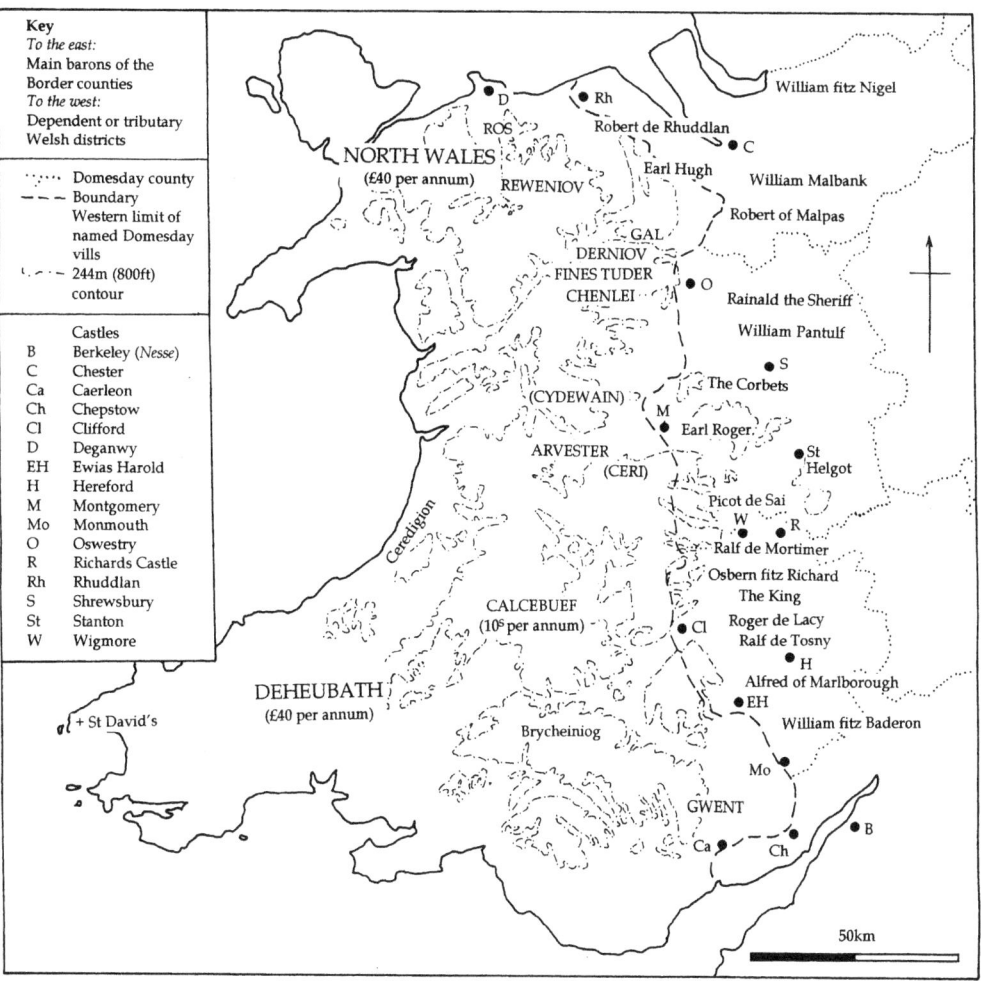

12.1 Domesday Wales (based on H. C. Darby, 'Domesday: 1086–1836–1986', National Library of Wales Journal 25/1 (1987–8), 1–17, fig. 8 at p. 15

Welsh, it is not impossible – though less likely – for an Anglo-Saxon in the 'March' to bear a Welsh name.

Table 12.1 contains 79 so-called 'Welsh' entries, of which most (73) refer to property- or land-holding, and the remaining 6 may be loosely described as 'narrative'.[17] As might be expected, the vast majority of these Welsh entries (74) occur in the Domesday accounts of the four English border-counties of Cheshire, Shrewsbury, Herefordshire and Gloucestershire, with one entry apiece for other

[17] 'Narrative' here includes references such as that to the devastation caused by kings Gruffudd ap Llywelyn and Bleddyn ap Cynfyn in Archenfield before 1066: DB, I, f. 181a.

Table 12.2: Welsh (and possible Welsh) Names in Domesday Book

DB Form	OW Form(s)	Mod Welsh Form	Notes
Aisil		Seisyll (?)	OE Æthelsige (?)[1]
Berdic	Berdic	Berddig	
Blein	Bledgint	Bleddyn	
Bleio	Bledgint (?)	Bleddyn (?)	
Cadiand	Catgen	Cadien	
Caraduech	Caratauc	Caradog	
Chenesis			OE Cynesige (?)
Costelin	Custennhinn	Custennin (?)	
Eli	Eli	Eli	but cf OE Eli (?)
Elmui	Elinui	Elynwy	
Genust			Cwnws (?)
Genut			Cwnws (?)
Gethne			
Grifin(us)	Gripuid, Grifud	Gruffudd	
Idhel	Iudhail	Ithel	
Iwardus			ON Ivarr (?); cf Staffs. DB *Iuuar*
Madoc	Matauc, Madoc	Madog	
Madoch	Matauc, Madoc	Madog	
Marcud	Marchiud	Marchudd	
Mariadoc	Margetiut, Margetud	Maredudd	
Mereuin	Meruin (?)	Merfyn (?)	OE Merewine (?)
Mereuuin	Meruin (?)	Merfyn (?)	OE Merewine (?)
Morganau	Morcenou	Morgeneu	
Noui	Nougoy, Nougui	Nowy	
Ouen	Ouein	Owain	
Ouuin	Ouein	Owain	
Ouuine		Owain (?)	OE Ōwine (?)
Ouuinus	Ouein	Owain	OE Ōwine (?)
Ouus		Owain (?)	OW Noui, Nouis (?)
Rees	Ris	Rhys	
Reuer[2]			
Riset[3]	Ris	Rhys	
Ruillic[4]	Riguallaun Riuguallaun	Rhiwallon (?)	
Saisi	Seissil, Seisill	Seisyll	
Saissil	Seissil, Seisill	Seisyll	
Taldus	Teudus	Tewdws	
Tuder	Teudebur, Teudur	Tudur, Tewdwr	
Wasuuic	Guasfuith	Gwasfwyth	
Wonni			OE Wunnig (?)

[1] von Feilitzen, *The Pre-Conquest Personal Names*, p. 142.
[2] von Feilitzen suggested that this name was based on Welsh *rhew*, 'frost, ice': *The Pre-Conquest Personal Names*, p. 348. I assume some kind of error is at play here, though the name does occur twice in Domesday Book with the same form.
[3] This strange form has been explained as containing the OF diminutive suffix *-et*: *Domesday Book: 17 Herefordshire*, ed. and trans. Thorn, n. A10. But cf. the form *Risen* in Orderic Vitalis.
[4] von Feilitzen thought that this is an OW name: *The Pre-Conquest Personal Names*, p. 350. My own derivation above assumes the miscopying of a form like *Riullio*.

Midlands counties: Warwickshire, Worcestershire and Staffordshire. In addition I have also included one entry from Domesday Essex and one from Derbyshire, though both of these are onomastically 'ambiguous'. Of this total of 79 entries, 50% (=39) occur in the Herefordshire survey alone, but it should be emphasized that about half of these Herefordshire entries are accounted for as part of the holding of the 1086 Welsh tenant-in-chief Gruffudd ap Maredudd, and the description of Archenfield covers a significant part of the remainder. Next we have 13 'Welsh' entries in Cheshire, 14 in Gloucestershire and lastly, Shropshire, with 8 entries.

About half of the 79 Welsh entries (again, 39) refer to pre-Conquest individuals, though 4 of these still held land in 1086. However, maybe as many as 17 of these 39 pre-Conquest entries are what I have referred to above as ambiguous or uncertain, which accounts for almost 75% of all the uncertain entries in the whole table. In terms of individual counties, the Herefordshire and Gloucestershire Domesday surveys contain more 1086 than TRE entries, again, partly due to the holding of Gruffudd ap Maredudd and also the 'Monmouthshire section' in Gloucestershire. On the other hand, Cheshire and Shropshire name more pre-Conquest than 1086 tenants who may have been Welsh, though for Shropshire all the 1066 Welsh entries are 'ambiguous'. Lastly, it is worth pointing out that only 22 (that is, just over a quarter) of these so-called Welsh entries in Domesday Book refer to landholding or narrative activity in what is *now* Wales, mostly Flintshire in Cheshire, and Monmouthshire in Gloucestershire, with the remainder relating to England. To this could be added the nine 'Welsh' entries relating to Archenfield.

Of course, these 79 Welsh entries in Table 12.1 need not all refer to different men: for example, the tenant-in-chief Gruffudd ap Maredudd occurs 9 times with reference to his Herefordshire holding (no. 31) and may occur up to 7 more times in the same county.[18] In fact, I would estimate that Table 12.1 perhaps accounts for about 40 or more different Welshmen. About half of these are attested uniquely in Domesday Book, but others may be found in other sources relating to eleventh-century Wales. I have indicated possible identifications in the second field of Table 12.1 called *ID*: here, identifications which are given in parentheses are less certain than those unbracketed. Accordingly, from the 79 entries I have made 32 fairly certain identifications plus an additional 13 less certain, currently totalling 45; these identifications account for 20 different individuals. The process of identification is initially an onomastic one. The Welshmen in Domesday Book, and especially the pre-Conquest ones, like their Anglo-Saxon counterparts are only recorded using a single forename. For the post-Conquest Welsh entries, we have a little more help, such as the 'bynames' *de Wales* and *Walensis*; 1 nickname (*puer*), 1 Welsh patronym in Latin (*filius Mariadoc*), plus 2 instances of the English patronym (or maybe surname?) *Mapesone*.[19]

In order to illustrate some of the general points outlined above and to indicate

---

[18] See below, pp. 157–60.
[19] The name *Mapesone* has been included as it probably contains the OW word *map*, later *ap*, meaning 'son'.

the value of Domesday Book as a source for Welsh history, the remainder of this paper will comprise three case studies, drawing where possible upon material 'beyond' the Domesday survey. The first case study is from the Cheshire lands held of Earl Hugh by Reginald Balliol: 'Isdem Rainaldus tenet ERPESTOCH. Rees tenuit sicut liber homo'.[20] The manor of *Erpestock* in Exestan hundred has been identified with Erbistock in the Welsh cantref of Maelor Gymraeg, later Bromfield (now the unitary authority of Wrexham). The form *Rees* suggests the modern Welsh personal name Rhys, OW *Ris*.[21]

This particular *Rees* has been identified by various scholars with Rhys Sais, that is, Rhys the Englishman.[22] Rhys Sais ab Ednyfed occurs as ancestor of various Maelor families in later genealogies, which would place him in the right region, though he was also claimed as ancestor by Flintshire and Shropshire families.[23] Furthermore, the vernacular chronicles refer to the killing of Gwrgeneu ap Seisyll by 'the sons of Rhys Sais' in the year 1081; this date would certainly allow their father to have lived around 1066.[24] In addition the 'Second Extent of Bromfield and Yale' (1391) refers to the progeny of one *Rees* holding lands in various parts of Bromfield as 'coparceners' of the earl of Surrey, and some have accordingly identified their ancestor with our Domesday namesake.[25] This accumulation of onomastic, geographical and chronological material would mean that it is at least

---

[20] 'The same Reginald holds Erbistock. Rhys held it as a free man': DB, I, f. 267c.

[21] von Feilitzen, *The Pre-Conquest Personal Names*, p. 348.

[22] A. N. Palmer and Edward Owen, *A History of the Ancient Tenures of Land in North Wales and the Marches* (Wrexham, 1885; rev. edn, Frome, 1910), p, 147; A. N. Palmer, 'Notes on the Early History of Bangor is y Coed', *Y Cymmrodor* 10 (1889), 12–28, at pp. 24–6; T. P. Ellis, *The First Extent of Bromfield and Yale, 1315*, Cymmrodorion Record Series 11 (London, 1924), p. 14; For a slightly more cautious approach, see P. C. Bartrum, 'Hen Lwythau Gwynedd a'r Mars', *National Library of Wales Journal* 12/3 (1962), 201–35, at p. 228; also, G. R. J. Jones, 'The Tribal System in Wales: A Re-assessment in the Light of Settlement Studies', *Welsh History Review* 1/2 (1961), 111–32, at p. 129. More recently, see Frederick Suppe, 'Roger of Powys, Henry II's Anglo-Welsh Middleman, and his Lineage', *Welsh History Review* 21/1 (2002), 1–23; and *idem*, 'Who Was Rhys Sais? Some Comments on Anglo-Welsh Relations before 1066', *Haskins Society Journal* 7 (1995), 63–73.

[23] P. C. Bartrum, 'Hen Lwythau Gwynedd a'r Mars', *National Library of Wales Journal* 12/3 (1962), 201–35: §§ 2(d), 12(a); Lewys Dwnn, *Heraldic Visitations of Wales and Part of the Marches*, ed. S. R. Meyrick, 2 vols. (Llandovery, 1846), I.324, II.295, 307, 313, 325, 327, 349, 357, 360, 362; 'Llyfr Silin yn Cynnwys Achau Amryw Deuluoedd yn Ngwynedd, Powys, etc.', *Archaeologia Cambrensis*, 5th series 5 (1888), 42–56, 105–21, 331–44, at p. 342, and 6 (1889), 148–63, 233–49, 327–42, at pp. 148–9, 151, 159, 241. Aberystwyth, National Library of Wales, Peniarth 127, p. 108, Pen. 128, p. 69, Pen. 129, p. 44, Pen. 130, p. 98, Llanstephan 157, p. 25, and Llanwrin 1, p. 90; BL, Harley 4181, ff. 146–9, 156–60.

[24] *Brut y Tywysogyon or The Chronicle of the Princes. Peniarth MS. 20 Version*, trans. Thomas Jones (Cardiff, 1952), p. 17; *Brut y Tywysogyon or The Chronicle of the Princes. Red Book of Hergest Version*, ed. and trans. Jones (Cardiff, 1973), pp. 30–1; *Brenhinedd y Saesson or The Kings of the Saxons. BM Cotton MS. Cleopatra B.v and The Black Book of Basingwerk NLW MS. 7006*, ed. and trans. Jones (Cardiff, 1971), pp. 80–1.

[25] This Second Extent is as yet unpublished; the relevant passage is cited in R. R. Davies, *Lordship and Society in the March of Wales 1282–1400* (Oxford, 1978), p. 359, see also pp. 361–2. Compare also the comments on the lineage of Elidir ap Rhys, including the suggestion that it originated in Trefydd Bychain, by Ellis, *First Extent*, pp. 15, 58–60, 126–30; and G. R. J. Jones, 'Rural Settlement: Wales', *Advancement of Science* 15 (1959), 338–42.

not impossible that the Domesday *Rees* was the same man as Rhys Sais. What light the Welsh material casts on the single Domesday reference is rather more problematic, however.

Firstly, it should be stated that the reliability and authenticity of the Welsh annalistic and genealogical references to Rhys Sais are not wholly certain. The attribution of the killing of Gwrgeneu ap Seisyll to Rhys's sons only occurs in the three vernacular chronicles, and the event itself only occurs, without mention of Rhys's sons, in one of the two relevant Latin chronicles – that being the one most closely related to the three Welsh-language texts. Therefore, it is by no means clear whether this killing was recorded contemporaneously in the original annals kept at St David's, or whether it is one of many additions made at the end of the thirteenth century. More significantly, the earliest genealogies to mention Rhys Sais may derive from a tract of the fifteenth century but are preserved in later manuscripts. Of course, that in itself need not pose a big problem, but full analysis of the genealogical schemes relating to Rhys suggests that previous historians have been too ready to accept the relevant pedigrees at face value; in particular, the alleged descent of Roger de Powis (henchman of Henry II in Shropshire and the Welsh border) from Tudur son of Rhys Sais should probably be rejected.[26] The relevant pedigrees appear to have formed part of a wider genealogical scheme to link Roger and other Anglo-Normans of the March – notably *Gwilym Befyr*, that is William Peverell,[27] and *Ffwc ap Gwaring*, Fulk FitzWarin – to an 'appropriate' Welsh ancestor, and thereby to provide the later gentry families with an interesting and mixed ancestry. The Welsh and Anglo-Norman versions of Roger's genealogy have been set out separately as Illus. 12.2. All that this may really tell us is that by the late Middle Ages the figure of Rhys Sais was regarded as having been relatively significant along the Welsh-Shropshire border region in the eleventh century. Any conclusions regarding his descendants and, for that matter, his own ancestry as described in the surviving pedigrees should perhaps be treated as dubious, to say the least.

Where does this leave poor Rhys? In terms of his own genealogical origins, the genealogies – if they are to be trusted at all – do not connect him with any existing Welsh royal lineages but rather trace his descent from Tudur Trefor who is a purely genealogical figure, regarded as ancestor of at least one other Maelor family. The main point to emphasize is that in the Welsh material Rhys is the first member of his family to appear in the sources and was probably of relatively obscure (and possibly local) origins. That he achieved some significance is no doubt reflected in his later genealogical importance as an apical ancestor and in the late fourteenth-century reference to 'the progeny of Rhys' in Maelor

---

[26] For an alternative origin for Roger, see K. S. B. Keats-Rohan, *Domesday Descendants: A Prosopography of Persons occurring in English Documents 1066–1166. II : Pipe Rolls to Cartae Baronum* (Woodbridge, 2002), pp. 648–9, citing F. M. Stenton, *The First Century of English Feudalism, 1066–1166* (Oxford, 1929), pp. 281–2.

[27] The 'surname' given in the genealogical manuscripts may be a play on the Welsh word *pefr* (lenited *befr*), 'radiant, beautiful'.

12.2: Genealogies of Rhys Sais and Roger de Powis

A. According to the Welsh genealogical manuscripts

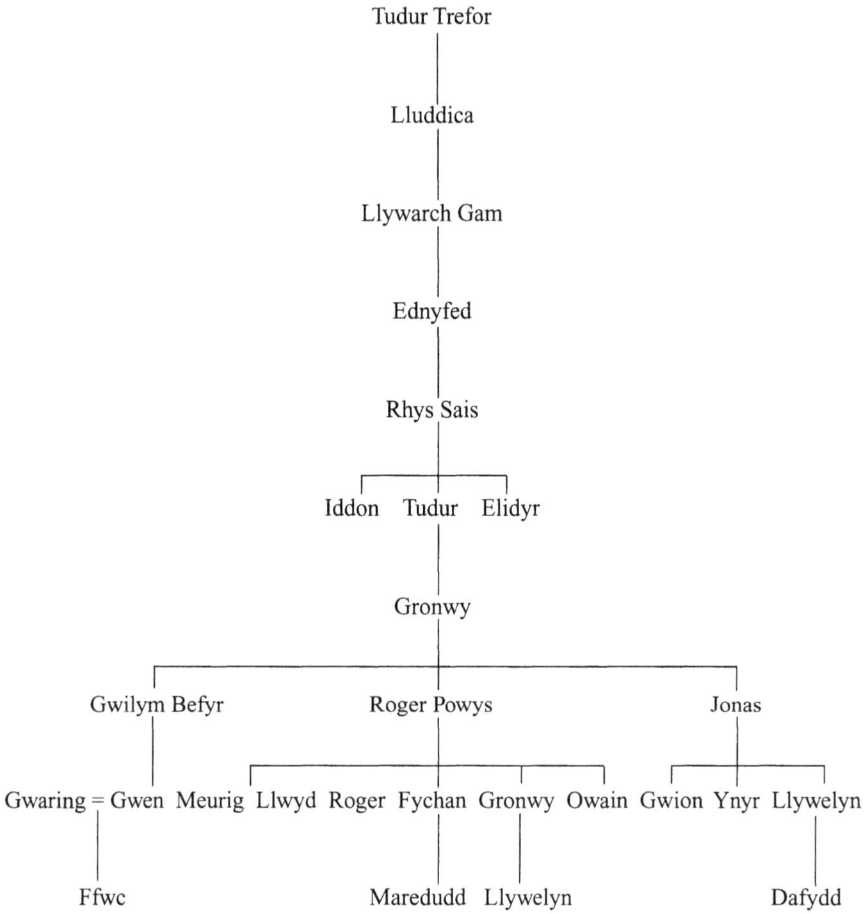

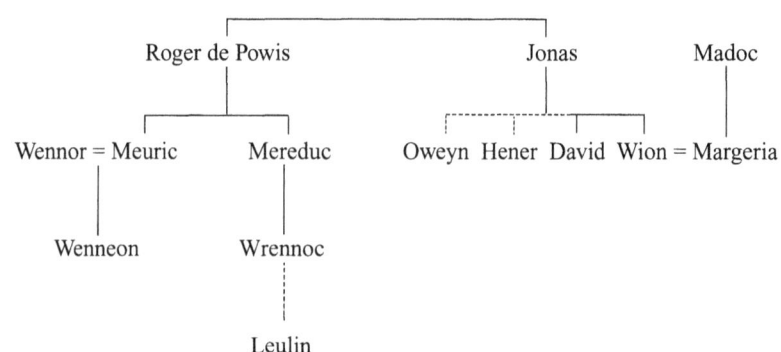

B. Reconstructed from Anglo-Norman Documents

Gymraeg.[28] His sons appear to have aspired to some sort of political influence – if the Welsh vernacular chronicles for 1081 are to be trusted – and one of them, Tudur ap Rhys, has indeed been identified with *Tuder quidam Walensis* named in Shropshire Domesday as holding *unum finem terrae Walensis*, for four pounds and five shillings (*solidi*), in 1086 from Roger of Montgomery, earl of Shrewsbury.[29] Lastly, Rhys's nickname *Sais*, 'the Englishman', whether a contemporary usage or a later invention, clearly indicates some strong connection with England or things English. The sixteenth-century Welsh antiquary Humphrey Llwyd explained Rhys's nickname thus: 'for so they used to name all suche as had served in England and coulde speake the Englyshe tonge'.[30] The fact that Rhys Sais, if correctly identified with the Domesday *Rees*, occurs as a tenant in Domesday Book could be taken as confirmation of this English connection.

The second case study is based on the following entry in the Herefordshire lands of the Welsh tenant-in-chief *Grifin filius Mariadoc*, Gruffudd ap Maredudd:[31]

> Isdem Grifinus tenet LEGE. Ouen et Elmer tenuerunt pro .ii. maneriis et wasti erant. … Comes Willelmus dedit Mariadoc regi … Rex Willelmus condonauit geldum regi Mariadoc et postea filio eius.

The *Lege* which *Ouen* and *Elmer* (OE Ælfmær) held as two manors has been identified as Lye in Hazeltree hundred. The form *Ouen* may suggest the name Owen, which is *Owain* in Modern Welsh,[32] though it should be recalled that similar forms elsewhere in England have been regarded as reflecting the OE name Ōwine.[33]

Gruffudd ap Maredudd held various lands in Herefordshire in addition to his own holding.[34] Domesday Book states that 'Earl William' (that is, William Fitz-Osbern, earl of Hereford, who died in 1071) had given the two Lye manors to 'king Maredudd' and that William the Conqueror had granted the tax to Maredudd and afterwards to his son Gruffudd. Now, Gruffudd and his father Maredudd

---

[28] The 'descendants' of Rhys are also attested as three *gwelyau* ('kinship/descent groups', lit. 'beds') – Gwely Ionas, Gwely Cuhelyn and Gwely Owain – in neighbouring Maelor Saesneg during the fifteenth century: see *36th Report of the Deputy Keeper of the Public Records* (London, 1875), Appendix II, no. 1, p. 435; *37th Report* (1876), Appendix II, no. 1, pp. 335–9; *39th Report* (1878), Appendix II, no. 1, pp. 139–40. I am grateful to the late Prof. Rees Davies for directing my attention to these references. See also *The History of Flintshire, Vol. I. From the Earliest Times to the Act of Union*, ed. C. R. Williams (Denbigh, 1961), p. 98.

[29] DB, I, f. 253c.

[30] *Humphrey Llwyd. Cronica Walliae*, ed. Ieuan M. Williams (Cardiff, 2002), p. 123; note also Melville Richards, 'Gwyr, Gwragedd a Gwehelyth', *Transactions of the Honourable Society of Cymmrodorion* (1965), 27–45, at p. 41; and Suppe, 'Who Was Rhys Sais?', pp. 64–5.

[31] 'The same Gruffudd holds Lye. Owain and Ælfmær held it as two manors and they were waste. Earl William gave [them] to king Maredudd … King William remitted the "geld" to king Maredudd and afterwards to his son': DB, I, f. 187c.

[32] von Feilitzen, *The Pre-Conquest Personal Names*, pp. 342–3; Raymond Perry, *Anglo-Saxon Herefordshire 410 AD – 1086 AD* (Gloucester, 2002), p. 140.

[33] See above, p. 148 Table 12.1.

[34] DB, I, ff. 180c, 183d, 184d, 187a, c.

are relatively well-known as representatives of one branch of the ruling line of Deheubarth in south Wales.[35] Maredudd had ruled briefly during the period 1069–72, but in 1086 the kingdom was in the hands of Rhys ap Tewdwr who was a member of a (until that time) lesser dynastic segment. Gruffudd ap Maredudd made an unsuccessful attempt to oust Rhys in 1091 and was killed in battle. The kingdom was subsequently monopolized by the descendants of Rhys and we hear no more of Gruffudd's branch. The genealogy of Deheubarth for this period is reconstructed as Illus. 12.3 below, with those named in Domesday Book indicated in **bold**.

This dynastic segment is *not* described in the surviving Welsh genealogical sources, perhaps in part because they were politically unsuccessful in the long run, and in part because it may have been in the interests of their erstwhile rivals – the line of Rhys ap Tewdwr – to exclude them. Whatever the case, the diagram must be reconstructed from annalistic references. What is interesting is that *sub anno* 1069 the chronicles refer to Maredudd as 'Maredudd ab Owain ab Edwin', that is, listing three generations, instead of the far more usual two (forename plus patronym). As far as I am aware, this is the only notice of Maredudd's father, Owain son of Edwin, in a Welsh source. He may have been a younger brother of 'the sons of Edwin', Maredudd and Hywel, who had ruled Deheubarth in the 1030s and early 1040s. The occurrence of the personal name Owain here is obviously compelling, and it is tempting to identify this Owain ab Edwin, who probably flourished in the mid-eleventh century and was grandfather of Gruffudd ap Maredudd, with the TRE Domesday tenant *Ouen* who was a predecessor of Gruffudd in Lye.

The Herefordshire connections of this Welsh family can be traced further back and would support this hypothetical Domesday identification. A document from the reign of Cnut (S 1462) describes a legal dispute between an 'Edwin son of Einion' and his English mother regarding lands in Wellington and (unidentified) *Crydesleah* in Herefordshire.[36] The second place may be the same as the unidentified *Curdeslege*, which was one of Gruffudd ap Maredudd's Herefordshire lands. The coincidence of the place-names, and also of the 'Welsh' personal name Edwin in both cases, surely strengthens the case for this reconstruction. Lastly, it should be added that an Edwin ab Einion had launched an unsuccessful bid for the kingship of Deheubarth against his uncle Maredudd ab Owain in 992, significantly enough using Anglo-Saxon support.

Various considerations, therefore, combine to make it at least not impossible that the *Ouen* who held one of the manors of Lye in 1066 was Owain ab Edwin, grandfather of his tenurial successor Gruffudd ap Maredudd. The lack of addi-

[35] K. L. Maund, *Ireland, Wales, and England in the Eleventh Century* (Woodbridge, 1991), pp. 22–38.

[36] S 1462. I have touched upon this material elsewhere: David E. Thornton, 'Maredudd ab Owain (d. 999): The Most Famous King of the Welsh', *Welsh History Review* 18/4 (1997), 567–91, at pp. 584–5. See also H. R. Loyn, *The Governance of Anglo-Saxon England 500–1087* (London, 1984), pp. 139–40; Coplestone-Crow, *Herefordshire Place-Names*, p. 45; and Perry, *Anglo-Saxon Herefordshire*, pp. 122–4. I am grateful to the late Patrick Wormald for discussing this document with me on more than one occasion.

12.3: The Family of Owain ab Edwin

(Individuals named in Domesday Book are in **bold**; kings of Deheubarth indicated by *k*)

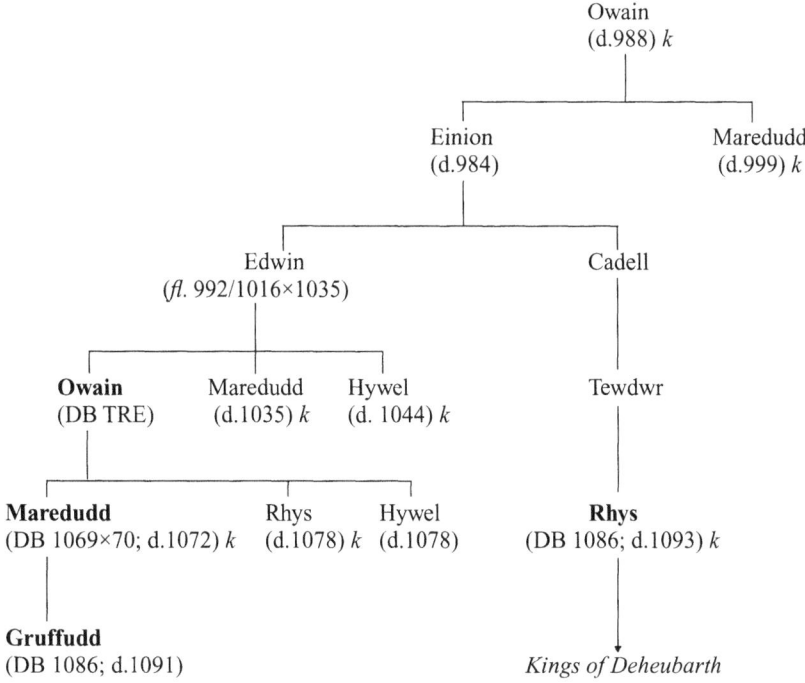

tional information about the Domesday *Ouen* means it is obviously difficult to be completely certain about this identification, but the case is certainly compelling. What broader conclusions may we draw from this accumulation of data? Firstly, it should be noted again that for the family of Owain, we are entirely dependent upon chronicle sources, and this contrasts with the case of Rhys Sais, for whom the later genealogies are more forthcoming. This fact may stand in Owain's favour, though there are a few chronological problems in the reconstruction presented here. In addition it is worth pointing out that if the reconstruction holds, then the family's property connections with Herefordshire evidently ante-dated William FitzOsbern's three grants to king Maredudd mentioned in Domesday Book *circa* 1069–70. Indeed, our Owain provides the link in this chain between the situation after 1066 as recorded in Domesday Book and that described four or five decades earlier in S 1462. Owain is the only member of the family who is *not* mentioned in the Welsh annals in his own right, and indeed, the fact that the chroniclers felt it necessary to include three generations when naming his son is perhaps symptomatic of Owain's relative obscurity. This obscurity is perhaps understandable. There is clearly a gap between the reign of Owain's brother Hywel, who died in 1044, and that of his son Maredudd, beginning in 1069, during which time South Wales including Deheubarth appears to have been dominated firstly by the dynasty of Rhydderch ab Iestyn, perhaps originating in neighbouring Morgannwg, and then, more significantly, by the powerful North Welsh king Gruffudd ap Llywelyn. During this period, we might postulate, Owain's own dynastic branch represented perhaps by Owain himself bided its time, possibly in England, just as Edwin ab Einion had done earlier and Gruffudd ap Maredudd was to do later on. On the other hand, the Welsh chronicles are notably silent about the kingdom of Deheubarth during the years between the death of Gruffudd ap Llywelyn in 1063 and the appearance of Maredudd ab Owain in 1069, which, of course, is precisely the time in which we know that Owain was alive, assuming he was indeed the TRE *Ouen* of Domesday Book.

We have here, therefore, a dynastic segment which played a not insignificant, yet clearly fluctuating, role in the politics of South Wales for a large part of the eleventh century. Furthermore, during times of political exclusion, members of the family appear to have found refuge across the border in Herefordshire, where they had claims to property, perhaps ultimately deriving from a marriage alliance with Anglo-Saxon landowners in the late tenth century. It is possible that when individual members of this family attempted to establish themselves in Deheubarth, they relied in part on English support.

The third and final case study will focus on the section in the Domesday survey for Herefordshire entitled *Hæ villæ vel terræ subscriptæ sitæ sunt in fine Arcenefelde*, which occurs towards the end of the king's holding (variant readings in brackets have been supplied from the later 'Herefordshire Domesday Book'):[37]

> Willelmus filius Normanni tenet CHIPEETE. Cadiand [*Cadian*] tenuit TRE ... Isdem Willelmus tenet BAISSAN et Walterus de eo. Mereuuin [*Merewin*] tenuit de rege E. ... Rogerus de Laci tenet MAINAVRE. [*Birches*, marg. 'Heref DB'] Costelin tenuit TRE. Nunc filius eius tenet de Rogero ... Isdem Rogerus tenet PENEBECDOC [*Penebrecdoc*, 'Heref. DB', *Penebredoc*, marg.] et Noui [*Nouis*] de eo. Isdem tenuit TRE ... Godric Mappesone tenet HVLLA. [*Castellum Goderich*, marg. 'Heref DB'] Taldus tenuit TRE ...

Here we find a nice series of Welsh, and some 'possibly Welsh', personal names: *Cadiand*, *Noui*, as well as the more problematic forms *Costelin*, *Mereuuin* and *Taldus*. All these men were TRE tenants, though *Noui* still held *Penebecdoc* in 1086,[38] and Costelin's anonymous son is also said to hold Birch from Roger de

---

[37] 'William FitzNorman holds Kilpeck. Cadien held it in the time of king Edward ... Roger de Lacy holds Birch. Custennin held it in the time of King Edward ... The same Roger holds *Penebecdoc* et Nowy [holds] from him. He [Nowy] also held in the time of king Edward ... Godric *Mappesone* holds Castle Goodrich [Howle Hill?]. Tewdws held it in the time of king Edward': DB, I, f. 181a; *Herefordshire Domesday, circa 1160–1170. Reproduced by Collotype from Facsimile Photographs of Balliol College MS. 350*, ed. Vivian Hunter Galbraith and James Tait, Pipe Roll Society new series 25 (London, 1950 for 1947–8), p. 19.

[38] The Domesday place-name *Penebecdoc* is unidentified, though may have been in Llanwarne parish: Richard Coates and Andrew Breeze, *Celtic Voices, English Places. Studies of the Celtic Impact on Place-Names in England* (Stamford, 2000), p. 310. Furthermore, Andrew Breeze has suggested to me that the various Domesday forms may reflect *Pen y*

Lacy in that year (*nunc*).³⁹ An interpretation of at least three of these five tenants is based upon an informative yet little studied document in the Book of Llandaff entitled *De terra Ercycg*.⁴⁰ This text begins with a list of churches in Ergyng (Archenfield) and then describes a series of consecrations of, and ordinations to, those churches by bishop Herewald for the period 1056–87. (For places in Archenfield mentioned in Domesday Book and *Liber Landavensis*, see Illus. 12.4 below.)

The first of the Domesday tenants in Archenfield is *Cadiand*, who is said to have held Kilpeck in the time of king Edward. The forms *Cadiand* and *Cadian* may reflect the Welsh name Cadien, which was usually *Catgen* in OW.⁴¹ Now, interestingly enough, the Llandaff document on Ergyng has the following entry for Kilpeck:⁴²

Tempore Uuillelmi, [Hergualdus episcopus] consecrauit Cilpedec et Morcenoui in presbiterum ordinauit, et mortuo illo filium suum Enniaun ordinauit, tempore Catgen Du et Ris filii Moridic.

The occurrence here of the relatively rare name Cadien in association with Kilpeck may be significant, and it is possible that this Cadien Ddu ('Cadien the Black') should be identified with his Domesday namesake.⁴³ The name *Catgen* occurs twice more in this document, for the consecration of the churches at 'Llanbedr' (now Peterstow) and Llanwarne:⁴⁴

Tempore Haraldi regis, [Hergualdus episcopus] consecrauit Lannpetir sub herede Cidrich filii Gunncu, et Catgen et filiis eius Gunna et Eutut, et filiis eius Merchiaun et Custennhin. ... Tempore Uuillelmi, [Hergualdus episcopus]

Beddeg ('Head of the Snare, Snare Head'), in which case it may have been near the modern farm of Poolspringe in Llanwarne (*springe* translating unattested Welsh **peddeg*, 'snare', from Latin *pedica*); see also Andrew Breeze, 'Kilpeck, near Hereford, and Latin *Pedica* "Snare"', *Nomina* 35 (2002), 151–2.

³⁹ For this section, the remaining TRE holders were King Edward himself and Earl Harold, who need not concern us directly here.

⁴⁰ *The Text of the Book of Llan Dâv reproduced from the Gwysaney Manuscript*, ed. J. Gwenogvryn Evans and John Rhys (Oxford, 1893), pp. 275–8. This interesting document has received little attention from historians; for some brief comments, see John Reuben Davies, *The Book of Llandaf and the Norman Church in Wales* (Woodbridge, 2003), esp. pp. 26, 84–5.

⁴¹ von Feilitzen, *The Pre-Conquest Personal Names*, p. 213

⁴² 'In the time of [King] William, [Bishop Herewald] consecrated Kilpeck, and ordained Morgeneu as priest, and after his death he ordained his son Einion, in the time of Cadien Ddu and Rhys ap Moriddig': *The Text of the Book of Llan Dâv*, ed. Evans and Rhys, p. 276.

⁴³ *Domesday Book: 17, Herefordshire*, ed. and trans. Frank and Caroline Thorn (Chichester, 1983), n. 1.53.

⁴⁴ 'In the time of king Harold, [bishop Herewald] consecrated Peterstow under the heir [or possessor] Cydrich ap Gwnncu, and Cadien et his sons Gwnna and Eudud, and his sons Meirchion and Custennin. ... In the time of [King] William, [Bishop Herewald] consecrated Llanwarne, and ordained as priest *Audi ab Achess* and Gwlged ab Asser and afterwards Semion under the heirs Custennin ap Cadien, [and] Ieuan ab Ecgni ab Asser ab Assennan': *The Text of the Book of Llan Dâv*, ed. Evans and Rhys, pp. 276–7.

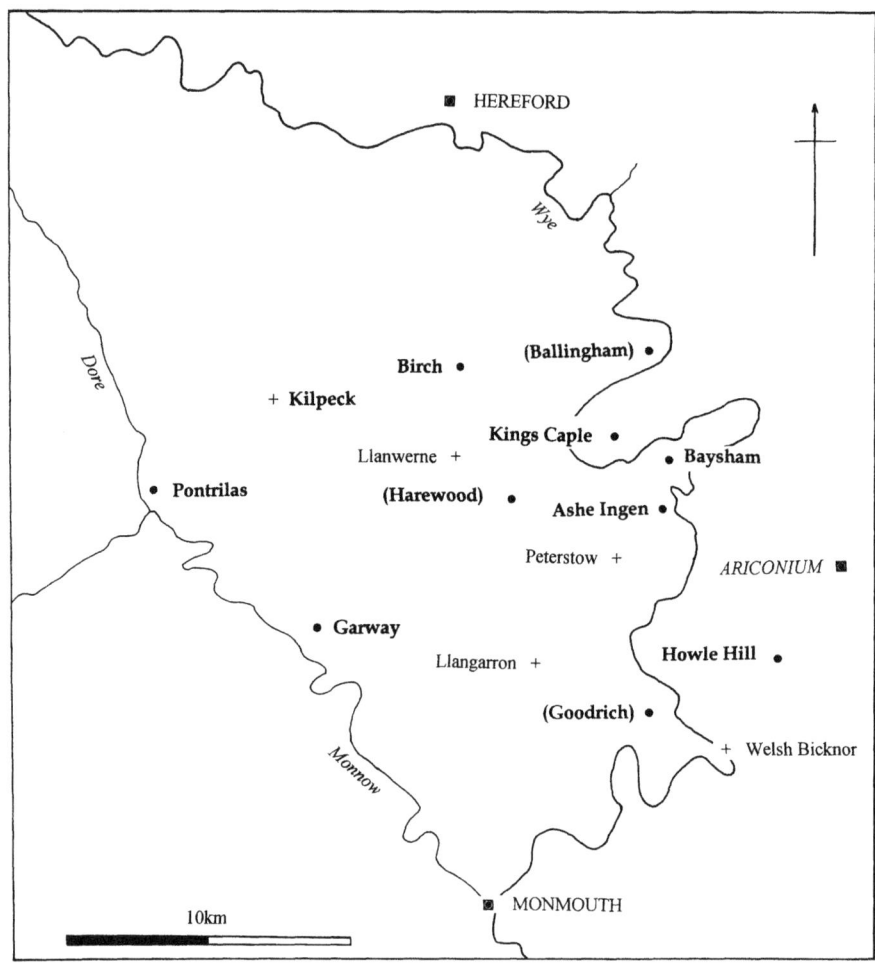

12.4 Domesday Archenfield: place-names in bold occur in Domesday Book [Penebecdoc unlocated]; names in (brackets) are identified in the 'Herefordshire Domesday' (Oxford, Balliol College, MS 350, ff. 11r–v); +indicates churches mentioned in Liber Landavensis, pp. 275–8

consecrauit Lannguern et in presbiterum ordinauit Audi filium Achess et Gulcet filium Asser et postea Semion sub heredibus Custennhinn filio Catgen, [et] Iouan filio Hecgni filii Asser filii Assennan.

It is not apparent whether these other Cadiens were the same as Cadien Ddu of Kilpeck, though it is certainly possible. Furthermore, the occurrence in both of these entries of the personal name Custennin, the Welsh form of Constantine, may be relevant here; the name of the Domesday tenant *Costelin* (who held Birch)[45] could well be a corrupt form of OW *Custennhinn*, but whether or not this was the same man as Custennin ap Cadien of the Ergyng document is more difficult to determine.[46] This possible onomastic correction led me to examine the Ergyng document further. There are three occurrences of the name Tewdws (OW *Teudus*), two of which at least must refer to the same layman, Tewdws ap Marchi (or *Marchci*).[47] The relevant churches include Llangarron and again perhaps Llanwarne, plus 'Llangustennin Garth Benni' (now Welsh Bicknor). Llangarron and Welsh Bicknor are very close to Goodrich, which was held TRE by *Taldus* according to the Herefordshire Domesday.[48] Once again, therefore, it is possible that *Taldus* is a corruption of the Welsh name Tewdws.[49] If so, then the Domesday tenant *may* have been Tewdws ap Marchi of the Book of Llandaff.

Further work needs to be done on this Ergyng document in the Book of Llandaff. However, what we seem to have in this text is a rather nice depiction of a proprietary church in mid-eleventh-century Archenfield. Domesday Book adds another dimension in showing that, as well as being the *heredes* – which I take to mean 'possessors', not simply 'heirs' – of these churches, some of the laymen were landholders in their own right, which we might expect. A detailed study of both documents together would prove to be both interesting and fruitful.[50]

A number of broad conclusions can be drawn about Welshmen in Domesday Book from the general comments made above and the three case studies. Firstly, it should be clear that there are two types of Welshmen in Domesday Book: those who can be identified in other documents, and those who cannot. As I have stated above, Table 12.1 contains 20 individuals who occur in *other* sources, and therefore as many as 25 others who do not. Furthermore, of the 20 identifications offered here, about a third occur *only* in the Book of Llandaff. Thus, Domesday

---

[45] John Freeman, 'Some Place-Names of Archenfield and the Golden Valley recorded in the Balliol Herefordshire Domesday', *Nomina* 10 (1986), 61–77, at p. 66.

[46] I wonder whether we have a case here of the Norman tendency to interchange/assimilate nasals (in *Custennin*) and liquids (in *Costelin*): Dodgson, 'Domesday Book', p. 125. Von Feilitzen, however, thought that *Costelin* was related to Continental Germanic *Costila*: *The Pre-Conquest Personal Names*, p. 219.

[47] *The Text of the Book of Llan Dâv*, ed. Evans and Rhys, pp. 276–7.

[48] The Domesday place-name *Hulla* has alternatively been identified with Howle Hill and Huntsham Hill. For a discussion, see Coplestone-Crow, *Herefordshire Place-Names*, pp. 91–3.

[49] von Feilitzen was unsure what to make of this name-form: *The Pre-Conquest Personal Names*, p. 382. The offending letter is again 'l', as with *Costelin*.

[50] I intend to examine this material in more detail in a paper provisionally entitled 'Archenfield in Domesday Book and *Liber Landavensis*', in *Domesday Book and Wales*, ed. Thornton (forthcoming).

Book provides a unique record of a relatively significant number of Welshmen for the period 1066–86. This in itself should be reason enough to want to investigate these individuals further.

Many of the Welshmen who can be identified in sources other than Domesday Book were politically important – such as Gruffudd ap Llywelyn, Bleddyn ap Cynfyn, Rhys ap Tewdwr and others – or were regarded, at least retrospectively, as having been genealogically important – such as Rhys Sais, Rhys ap Tewdwr and also others like Edwin of Tegeingl and Marchudd ap Cynan in Table 12.1. In most of these cases, however, their own political and/or genealogical origins are obscure and in some instances simply fabricated in the later genealogies. In addition, many of these Welshmen had political, family or 'onomastic' links with England: for example, the dynasty of Bleddyn ap Cynfyn claimed descent in the later manuscripts from one Gwerystan ap Gwaithfoed; or, Edwin of Tegeingl named one of his sons Uchdryd, and Marchudd ap Cynan had a son called Edryd. As stressed above these personal names could represent borrowings, yet this pattern is worthy of note. Furthermore, Domesday Book adds to this, by providing evidence of tenurial ties between England and these Welshmen before and after 1066. Thus, the admittedly 'Anglocentric' Domesday Book may provide a key for determining, to some extent, the origins of certain players in the eleventh-century Welsh political scene. Historians of medieval Wales, for a time, regarded the first half of the eleventh century especially as a period of dynastic instability, characterized by frequent usurpation of royal power, though more recent scholarship has challenged this idea.[51] Domesday Book reveals the extent of direct English territorial influence in parts of Wales, and I wonder if we can regard at least some of the alleged eleventh-century Welsh usurpers, whether they be total 'unknowns' or members of minor/disaffected dynastic branches, as owing their initial rise to prominence to their Anglo-Saxon or Anglo-Norman overlords.

---

[51] For example, see John Edward Lloyd, *A History of Wales from the Earliest Times to the Edwardian Conquest*, 2 vols. (3rd edn, London, 1939), I.346; Wendy Davies, *Wales in the Early Middle Ages* (Leicester, 1982), p. 112; K. L. Maund, *Ireland, Wales, and England in the Eleventh Century*, pp. 7–10, 207–9.

13

What Britons Spoke around 400 AD

PETER SCHRIJVER

Introduction

THIS article is about the contribution of historical linguistics to a reconstruction of the linguistic landscape that the Anglo-Saxons found on their arrival in Britain and to the way in which this linguistic landscape may have influenced the language of the newcomers. The bare bones are well known. British Celtic was spoken, both in the northern and western 'Highland Zone' and in the heavily Romanised, eastern 'Lowland Zone'. Latin was spoken, too, especially in the Lowland Zone, although to what extent remains unclear. It has often been suggested that Latinity was probably very much a question of social status and profession: the Roman military, which came from various parts of the Empire, as well as those frequently dealing with it and with the structures of Roman power must have been fluent speakers of Latin. City-dwellers and estate owners were probably more exposed to Latin than people dwelling in the countryside and working the land. With allowance being made for local and social differentiation, it is plausibly assumed that Latin-Celtic bilingualism must have been widespread.

I propose to refine this picture in two ways. First, by arguing that, in the Lowland Zone, at least, Latin was the predominant language; and second, by presenting a case for distinguishing Lowland British Celtic from Highland British Celtic around 400 AD and for regarding the former as a Latinised variety of British Celtic with stronger connections with varieties of Celtic spoken in northern Gaul than with Highland British Celtic (it is the latter that produced the medieval languages Welsh, Cornish and Breton; the former has no offspring).

The method I adopt here is based on a combination of language reconstruction (in the case of spoken Highland British, spoken British Latin and the language spoken by the Anglo-Saxon settlers, for which written sources of the period are absent) and the study of language contact. Languages in contact tend to influence one another in ways that can be modelled successfully.[1] Linguistic changes in British Highland Celtic and Lowland Celtic betray the influence of late-spoken Latin, but the way in which Latin influenced the one is different from the way

---

[1] Sarah Thomason and Thomas Kaufman, *Language Contact, Creolization and Genetic Linguistics* (Berkeley and Los Angeles, 1988); Uriel Weinreich, *Languages in Contact* (The Hague, 1968).

in which it influenced the other. This linguistic difference throws light on the different histories of Celtic speakers in the Lowland and Highland zone during the Roman period.

Latin Influence on Highland British Celtic

When considering the sound changes which occurred over the millennia separating Proto-Indo-European from Middle Welsh, Cornish and Breton, the observer is struck by the fact that sound changes are not equally distributed through time. Rather, long periods almost completely without sound change are interrupted by relatively brief bursts of rapid change. The first such cluster is connected with a handful of sound changes which define the Italo-Celtic branch of Indo-European. The second small cluster defines the separation of Celtic during the first half of the first millennium BC. During the period of Roman rule over a large part of the Celtic-speaking territory, a third cluster of innovation spread across Spain, Gaul and Britain but never reached Ireland.[2]

By far the largest cluster of sound changes, which resulted in a complete overhaul of the phoneme inventory, stress system and syllable structure of British Celtic, has been dated between the fifth and seventh centuries AD by Jackson,[3] largely confirmed by Sims-Williams.[4] It is this cluster that is of greatest interest to students of Roman and early post-Roman Britain. Closer inspection reveals that almost all sound developments occurring in this period have close contemporary counterparts in early Romance, especially in the early Romance of Gaul. Highland British Celtic sound changes with such counterparts can be represented briefly as follows:[5]

1. vowel system: replacement of phonemic length by qualitative oppositions (details differ);
2. stress shift to penultimate syllable, which became final;
3. loss of final nasals except in monosyllables (e.g. Breton *(h)en* 'him' < *em*, French *rien* < *rem*)
4. voicing of postvocalic *$\ast p$, $\ast t$, $\ast k$* to *$\ast b$, $\ast d$, $\ast g$*
5. consonant groups: *$\ast \chi t$* > *$\ast jt$*; *$\ast gR$* > *$\ast \gamma R$* > *jR*; *$\ast dR$* > *$\ast \delta R$* > *jR*; *$\ast kn$* > *$\ast gn$* > *$\ast jn$*; loss of opposition between *$\ast isC$-* and *$\ast sC$-*; *$\ast ns$* > *$\ast s$* (early in Latin; phonotactic adaptation to Latin in British Celtic)
6. apocope and syncope (details differ).

---

[2] Peter Schrijver, *Studies in British Celtic Historical Phonology* (Amsterdam, 1995), pp. 463–5; Peter Schrijver, 'The Rise and Fall of British Latin: Evidence from English and Brittonic', in *The Celtic Roots of English*, ed. M. Filppula, J. Klemola and H. Pitkänen (Joensuu, 2002), pp. 90–1.
[3] Kenneth H. Jackson, *Language and History in Early Britain* (Edinburgh, 1953).
[4] Patrick Sims-Williams, *The Celtic Inscriptions of Britain: Phonology and Chronology, c. 400–1200* (Oxford, 2003).
[5] For a full discussion see Schrijver, 'The Rise and Fall of British Latin'.

In the same period similar morphosyntactic changes affect Highland British Celtic and Romance:

7. loss of case system via reduced case system (Romance: two-case system)
8. loss of neuter gender
9. development of pluperfect (early in Latin; morphosyntactic adaptation to Latin in British Celtic)

These similar developments are so numerous and change the phonology of both languages in such a radical but similar way that they are most unlikely to represent independent developments. They must therefore be connected. The question arises whether British Celtic or early Romance or the contact zone between the two is responsible for the convergences. In Romance, these developments not only occur in contact zones with Celtic but also far outside, such as in Romanian, Sardic and southern Italian. It is most likely that what we are observing is a Latinisation of British Celtic rather than a Celticisation of Romance. It is also clear that this Latinisation affected Southwest-British, the predecessor of Cornish and Breton, more than it affected West-British, the predecessor of Welsh. Typical Cornish and Breton developments with Romance counterparts are the following:

10. loss of aspiration in voiceless stops *p, t, k*
11. development of (rounded) front vowels (as in Gallo-Romance) where Welsh has central vowels instead
12. *er > *ar in native words (*tigerno- 'lord' > OBreton *Tiern, Tiarn*)
13. *ng > *ηη > ñ (> *j) (*mong- 'mane' > Breton *moueñ, moueng, moueñk*)

Contact linguistics is capable of presenting a finer-grained picture of what went on in the British Highland Zone during and shortly after the Roman period. Highland British Celtic almost completely stopped adopting Latin loanwords during the period of its phonetic and morphosyntactic Latinisation, whereas before it had adopted many hundreds of them. We know this because almost all Latin loanwords passed through the British Celtic (and not the Romance) versions of the sound changes presented above, which implies that they must have been borrowed into British Celtic before those sound changes occurred.[6] Contact linguistics suggests what happened: Highland British Celtic borrowed masses of Latin loanwords during the Empire as Latin was at that time a prestige language, and prestige languages generally donate words. By contrast, after the collapse of Roman power in Britain in the early fifth century AD, Latin was no longer a high-prestige language. What has been called the Latinisation of Highland British Celtic phonology and morphosyntax is in fact typical of language shift: speakers of Latin shifted to speaking British Celtic but in doing so maintained features of the sound system and morphosyntax of Latin. Thus, they import a Latin 'accent' into Highland British Celtic; this accent managed to spread throughout Highland British Celtic. One might think that it spread because a Latinate pronunciation of British Celtic might have been considered prestigious and was therefore imitated

---

[6] See Schrijver, 'The Rise and Fall of British Latin', pp. 100–1 for more details.

by the native British Celts. That is most unlikely, however, as such high-prestige speakers would be expected to have donated Latin loanwords, but as we saw earlier, hardly any Latin loanwords entered Highland British Celtic after the early fifth century. An alternative explanation, which does not face any such objection, is that speakers of Latinate British Celtic indeed carried little prestige but were so numerous that they swamped the native British Celts in the Highland Zone. The picture that emerges in this way is one of masses of speakers of Latin arriving in the Highland Zone by the fifth century and rapidly, but not tracelessly, assimilating to their British Celtic environment. Where else could they have come from except from the Lowland Zone, where the collapse of Roman power and the incursions of the Anglo-Saxons left large numbers of people destitute who had previously been dependent on Roman society and its economy? If one accepts this conclusion, one must accept another: that the British Lowland Zone was largely Latin-speaking and that, as in the rest of the Western Roman Empire, the native language had all but died out. In this respect Roman Britain was no different from any other part of Roman Europe, where native languages disappeared except in marginal, relatively inaccessible areas such the Pyrenees (Basque), the Balkans (Albanian) and, in our case, the British Highlands (Welsh, Cornish and Breton). Indeed, the kind of British Latin that can be reconstructed on the basis of its influence on Highland British Celtic and that is to be dated right after the collapse of Roman rule in Britain was of the exact same type as underlies French.

Latin Influence of Lowland British Celtic

In the previous section I have argued that Welsh, Cornish and Breton descend from a variety of British Celtic that underwent lexical influence from Latin during the period of Roman rule and was subject to phonetic-phonological and morphosyntactical influence from (late-spoken) Latin right after the collapse of Roman rule in Britain.

There is one reason to assume that Lowland British Celtic was different from Highland British Celtic during the period of Roman rule. That reason is to be found in one of the two Celtic inscriptions from Roman Britain that have been found to date. I am referring to the so-called 'Bath pendant', a brief, coarse inscription on a small, round pewter disk found in Roman Bath (No. 18 of Tomlin's edition).[7] It may be, however, a lid of a seal box or a small jar rather than a pendant, as Henry Hurst (Cambridge) has kindly suggested to me. The text reads *adixoui deuina deueda andagin uindiorix cuamiinai* (alternative readings for *deuina* and *deueda* are *deiana* and *deieda*, respectively). I have interpreted this as, 'I have dedicated to the divine Deveda (Matrimony?) a bath ? (or ointment?). Vindiorix for the sake of Cuamijna (Darling)'.[8] What is of particular interest for the present

---

[7] R. S. O. Tomlin, 'The Curse Tablets', *The Temple of Sulis Minerva at Bath, Volume 2: The Finds from the Sacred Spring,* ed. B. Cunliffe (Oxford, 1988), pp. 59–277.

[8] Peter Schrijver, 'Early Celtic Diphthongization and the Celtic-Latin Interface', *New*

issue is the presence of the newly arisen diphthongs *ou* and *ua* in *adixoui* and *cuamiinai*, respectively.

Adixoui is probably a first-person singular verb in *-ou-i* < *-ū-mi*, which, apart from the diphthong, has an exact parallel in the forms *Ieg-umi* = *Ieg-ui* 'I ?proclaim' on the Châteaubleau tile, which was found during excavations in Châteaubleau, east of Paris, in 1997.[9] Châteaubleau lacks the diphthongisation of *ū to *ou* in this particular case but shows it regularly in word-final position, in the first-person singular verb forms *gniIou, siaxsiou, cluiou*, all with *-ou* from Proto-Celtic *-ū. Similarly, line 4 of the inscribed gold plate from Baudecet (Gembloux, near Namen, south-east Belgium) contains *in panou*, which most likely is the preposition *in* 'in' followed by a dative singular of an *o*-stem: *pan-ou* < *pan(n)-ū* < Proto-Celtic *-ūi*.[10]

Cuamiinai shows a diphthong *ua*, which defies a straightforward interpretation, either as Latin or as Celtic. A similarly remarkable diphthong is found on the Châteaubleau tile in the word *muana* (or *Nuana*??). If we derive both from an earlier long *ō (which is the regular reflex of Proto-Celtic *oi in British Celtic), straightforward Celtic interpretations arise: of *cuamiinai* as an *ā*-stem dative singular **koimignāi* 'darling' (cf. Old Irish *cóem* 'dear'), and of *muana* as a neuter nominative-accusative plural **moinā* 'treasures, valuables' (cf. Old Irish *moín* 'valuable').

Hence there is evidence that old long *ū and the long *ō which resulted from *oi were diphthongised to *ou* and *ua*, respectively, in the language of the inscriptions from Bath, Châteaubleau and Baudecet. The important point is that the inscription from Bath agrees with late northern Gaulish (of which Châteaubleau and Baudecet are virtually our only testimonies) but differs from the geographically much-closer Highland British Celtic, which shows no evidence of ever having undergone these diphthongisations. I suggest that diphthongisation marks a difference between Lowland and Highland British Celtic, on the one hand, and an agreement between Lowland British Celtic and northern Gaulish, on the other. It is easy to see the hand of the late-spoken Latin of northern Gaul in this: that dialect diphthongised Romance long-closed *ō to *ou* (> Old French *eu*) and long-open *ō to *uo* (> Old French *ue*). Apparently fluent bilingual speakers introduced the northern Gallo-Romance diphthongisation into their Celtic idiom.[11] Hence we may conclude that the influence of Latin on varieties of northern Gaulish and Lowland British Celtic had already become so strong during the period of Roman rule that phonetic features from late spoken Latin had begun to permeate the Celtic spoken in the area. The situation was quite different in Highland British Celtic, however, as we saw earlier, because there Latin phonetic influence did not begin

---

Approaches to Celtic Place-names in Ptolemy's Geography, ed. Javier de Hoz, Eugenio Luján and Patrick Sims-Williams (Oxford, 2005), pp. 55–67, with detailed discussion.

[9] See the edition and commentaries in *Études Celtiques* 34 (1998–2000), 57–142; the tile probably dates from around 200.

[10] Schrijver, 'Early Celtic Diphthongisation'.

[11] For a more detailed treatment, see Peter Schrijver, 'Der Tod des Festlandkeltischen und die Geburt des Französischen, Niederländischen und Hochdeutschen', in *Sprachtod und Sprachgeburt*, ed. P. A. Mumm and P. Schrijver (Bremen, 2004), pp.1–20.

to enter until after the collapse of Roman power. While Latin phonetic influence on Highland British Celtic is probably to be explained as the linguistic assimilation of large numbers of low-prestige speakers of late Latin, Latin phonetic influence on Lowland British Celtic and northern Gaulish is unlikely to have a similar historical background, as it occurred during the period when Roman power in the west was relatively intact and Latin-Celtic bilingualism tended to result in Latin monolingualism. The Latin phonetic influence on Celtic as seen in Bath, Baudecet and Châteaubleau was probably a symptom of Celtic language death as a Latin 'accent' gradually destroyed the phonetic and phonological structure of Celtic. This view of things ties in well with the conclusion above, where it was argued that a large proportion of the population in the British Lowland Zone spoke Latin rather than British Celtic by about 400 AD.

The argument concerning the difference between Lowland and Highland British Celtic hinges on two assumptions: first, that the Lowland Celtic diphthongisation that I have assumed to have occurred is real, which depends on the interpretation of admittedly problematic inscriptions; and second, that the Bath lid (or pendant) was produced in or around Bath by a local speaker. It is difficult to exclude completely the possibility that the Bath pendant belonged to a visitor from Gaul, which would of course defuse its relevance for the Celtic of Roman Britain. Leaving aside diphthongisation, however, the Bath pendant does pass two tests of Britishness: *iCi* > *eCi* in *deuina* (from *divina*) and *andagin* and *egi* > *agi* in *andagin* (if from *and-nagīnā < *ande-negīnā < *ande-nigīnā 'bath (oil)', cf. Middle Welsh *ennein(t)* 'bath, unguent'). But it is only fair to point out that as long as we do not know whether northern Gaulish went through those same developments, the two tests provide no more than arguments from silence. It has been argued that the *defixiones* found at Bath were probably written or at least commissioned by local people rather than by visitors from abroad; the fact that they concern petty thefts of small amounts of cash or relatively cheap objects suggests as much, and so does the preponderance of names of persons who were not Roman citizens. The Bath texts are not connected with the Roman army, whose members could have come from all over the Empire, but with the town of Bath and its inhabitants.[12] Although not a curse tablet, the lid (or pendant), being made of a cheap alloy of tin with a small amount of bronze and carrying a coarse inscription, looks like a local product as well. Hence the weight of the evidence, however small, argues for local manufacture commissioned by a Briton.

Conclusion and Outlook

The linguistic picture painted in this article suggests that Anglo-Saxon settlers met predominantly, if not exclusively, speakers of late-spoken Latin when they arrived in the British Lowland Zone. The further north and west they came, the higher will have been the proportion of Celtic speakers they met. The picture is not fine-grained enough to either exclude or demonstrate the possibility of

---

[12] Tomlin, 'The Curse Tablets', p. 74.

local pockets of Celtic speakers in the Lowland Zone. Nevertheless, as far as language contact is concerned, Old English, with its more important centres in the Lowland Zone, is unlikely to have undergone much in the way of Celtic substratum influence, and that is indeed the situation we find. I have attempted to show that British Celtic influence on the earliest Old English vowel system was probably introduced into Old English via the medium of a variety of late-spoken Latin that was more or less identical with the Romance variety underlying Old French.[13] In other words there is a British Celtic substratum underlying a northwestern Romance substratum underlying Old English, at least in the Lowland Zone.

A consequence of what I have argued is that the terms British Celtic and British Latin have a geographic rather than a linguistic meaning. Highland British Celtic is different from Lowland British Celtic, and the latter was, as far as can be observed, identical with northern Gaulish. Spoken British Latin was to all intents and purposes identical with the type of Romance underlying Old French. It is well-known that the spread (or non-spread) of linguistic features mirrors history. Viewed in this way the most important border of modern Britain over many centuries of its history has been not the English Channel but the one that runs right through it, from northeast to southwest.

---

[13] Schrijver, 'The Rise and Fall of British Latin', pp. 102–8.

14

Invisible Britons: The View from Linguistics[1]

RICHARD COATES

Introduction

IT has long been believed that the Britons of what became England were effectively exterminated – whether killed, driven out and/or culturally effaced by enslavement – by the incoming Anglo-Saxons; the basis for this belief was essentially derived from the documentary record. Over recent years, a competing view has arisen on the basis of a more critical assessment of the historical record as English foundation-mythmaking: that the Britons did not wholly disappear in any of these ways but that many 'became English' by taking on English practices, including the English language. This paper shows that the new view is not tenable in the light of what generally happens to languages involved in contact situations and that, at least in the English heartland, the observed patterns of lexical and onomastic borrowing suggest that the traditional view is more likely to be correct.

The Angles, Saxons and other peoples did not enter an empty landscape when they hauled their ships up on British beaches in the fifth century with the intention, for the first time, of carrying out more than a simple raid. The land was occupied by people speaking a Celtic language ancestral to Welsh and Cornish; scholars call it *British* during the Roman period and *Brittonic* after a large number of important changes affected it around the years 450–600 CE. There is little direct evidence that Latin was a flourishing *spoken* language anywhere in what would later become England, though it was of course the language of epigraphy and of writing in general. However, it is important to note Schrijver's opinion that the Brittonic languages as we know them are, in essence, deeply Latinized British

---

[1] For a full catalogue of literature before 1988 dealing with the Celtic impact on English place-names, see appendix 1 to Richard Coates, 'The Significances of Celtic Place-Names in England', in *The Celtic Roots of English* (henceforth *CRE*), ed. Markku Filppula, Juhani Klemola and Heli Pitkänen (Joensuu, 2002), pp. 47–85. For work published after 1987, see the relevant articles in Coates, *Toponymic Topics* (Brighton, 1988), the main text of Coates, 'Significances', and the forthcoming companion piece to this paper, 'Invisible Britons: The View from Toponomastics'. I am extremely grateful for comments on a draft of this paper or its content by Nick Higham and Max W. Wheeler, and for the generosity of comment by Larry Trask when seriously ill.

Celtic and that south-eastern Britain was at the crucial period Latin-speaking; the consequences of this are returned to below.[2]

The problem is to understand relations between the incomers and Britons in the settlement period. Traditional accounts focus on the expulsion, extermination and enslavement of Britons to explain the lack of Brittonic place-names in England, especially in the south-east, and the marked lack of Brittonic lexical borrowings into English. This view seems reasonable, and an uncritical assessment of the evidence transmitted from and about these times encourages it. Recently, a revisionist account has gained in popularity:[3] that the Britons were not entirely silenced but continued to form a majority of the population. Hard evidence might be: archaeological evidence of continuing Brittonic funerary customs, DNA evidence from burials, evidence for the continuation of farming practices and of other customs (e.g. religious ones), and linguistic evidence from inscriptions and from borrowings of place-names and vocabulary.

The strongest reason for thinking the Angles and Saxons did not take over in the conventional sense seems to be the fundamentally logistic idea that they just could not have done it: either there could not have been enough immigrants, or they could not or would not have displaced practically all the Britons even with sufficient manpower. Whilst archaeological evidence may eventually show much Brittonic survival, it is not available yet; Barbara Yorke affirms Brittonic numerical dominance for Wessex, despite the fact that 'so far there has been little archaeological evidence to support the contention'.[4] DNA analysis of skeletal material has been patchy, and we await a fuller representative survey of burial sites, but some recent research is broadly, and strikingly, consistent with the traditional view.[5] The possible continuation of religious practices in Wessex is interestingly set out by Yorke,[6] and there is an arguable case for agricultural continuity. But in this paper I argue that the linguistic evidence favours the traditional view, at least for the south and east, considering not merely place-name and vocabulary borrowing in this area but comparing the linguistic consequences of other conquests by military aristocracies and the settlers who possibly followed them. I argue that there is no reason to believe large-scale survival of an indigenous

---

[2] Jackson, *LHEB*, *passim*; Peter Schrijver, *Studies in British Celtic Historical Phonology*, Leiden Studies in Indo-European 5 (Amsterdam, 1995); Schrijver, 'The Rise and Fall of British Latin: Evidence from English and Brittonic', in *CRE*, pp. 87–110; Schrijver, this volume. The evidence of the place-names *Werlamacæstir* (i.e. *Verulamium*, St Albans) and *Binchester* also suggests Latin transmission.

[3] Nicholas Higham, *The English Conquest: Gildas and Britain in the Fifth Century* (Manchester, 1994); Higham, 'The Anglo-Saxon/British Interface: History and Ideology', in *CRE*, pp. 29–46; Keith Matthews, 'What's in a Name? Britons, Angles, Ethnicity and Material Culture from the Fourth to the Seventh Centuries,' *The Heroic Age* 4, web-site www.mun.ca/mst/heroicage/issues/4/Matthews.html (2000); Bryan Ward-Perkins, 'Why did the Anglo-Saxons not Become more British?', *EHR* 115 (2000), 513–33.

[4] Barbara Yorke, *Wessex in the Early Middle Ages* (London and Leicester, 1995), p. 69.

[5] Michael E. Weale, Deborah A. Weiss, Rolf F. Jager, Neil Bradman and Mark G. Thomas, 'Y Chromosome Evidence for Anglo-Saxon Mass Migration', *Molecular Biological Evolution* 19.7 (2002), 1008–21.

[6] Yorke, *Wessex*, pp. 155–65, 177–81.

population could so radically fail to leave linguistic traces. I have made this case in relation to place-names elsewhere,[7] and will concentrate on vocabulary here.

The Linguistic Literature on Contact

There is a literature in linguistics which deals with the effects of language contact. Lexical (vocabulary) borrowing is a prerequisite for any other type of borrowing, for example of grammatical forms and constructions and of features of pronunciation,[8] and lexical borrowing (specifically of 'content' words) testifies to contact of the lowest intensity, where all conversation is essentially 'about' concrete situations and physical or conceptual necessities.[9] Borrowing will not take place at all without the prospect of 'projected gain' for the borrower,[10] and, equally, borrowing will be avoided in situations where the unconscious use of borrowed material will result in stigma for the borrower. Borrowing must be risk-free in situations where something more than need-driven communication is at stake. Vocabulary will not be borrowed where it would cover part of the denotational range of existing vocabulary, because of the way expertise and knowledge are distributed between the speakers of the two languages;[11] prior expertise will discourage borrowing. April McMahon suggests that a basic level of contact typically results in the borrowing of place-names and terms denoting landscape, together with others contributing local colour, essentially, those terms which have no equivalent in the borrowing language because its speakers have never encountered the topography or cultural expertises in question before.[12] This results in a demonstrable gain in the expressive power of the borrower's language and cannot produce the stigma of using inappropriate new vocabulary.

Contact-induced language change at any linguistic level amounts to reducing the difference between the codes of a speaker's repertoire.[13] Borrowing the sorts of item mentioned, the least theoretically difficult, makes them available to both codes, though their use in the borrowing language may at first be felt to be quotative ('spoken in inverted commas'), marked and exotic (and therefore

---

[7] Coates, in *CRE*; Coates, 'Invisible Britons: The View from Toponomastics' (forthcoming).
[8] Edith Moravcsik, 'Language Contact', in *Universals of Human Language*, ed. Joseph Greenberg, Charles A. Ferguson and Edith Moravcsik, vol. I (Stanford, 1978), pp. 93–123, at p. 110; R. L. Trask, *Historical Linguisitics* (London, 1996), p. 314.
[9] *Language Contact, Creolization and Genetic Linguistics*, ed. Sarah Grey Thomason and Terrence Kaufman (Berkeley, 1988), p. 74.
[10] Werner Winter, 'Areal Linguistics: Some General Considerations', in *Current Trends in Linguistics 11: Diachronic, Areal and Typological Linguistics*, ed. Thomas A. Sebeok (The Hague, 1973), pp. 135–48, at p. 138; April M. S. McMahon, *Understanding Language Change.* (Cambridge, 1994), p. 201.
[11] William Croft, *Explaining Language Change: An Evolutionary Approach* (London, 2000), p. 205.
[12] McMahon, pp. 203–4.
[13] Lars Johanson, 'Contact-Induced Change in a Code-Copying Framework', in *Language Change: The Interplay of Internal, External and Extra-linguistic Factors*, ed. Mari C. Jones and Edith Esch (Berlin and New York, 2002), pp. 285–313.

risk-free and not stigma-producing) until the concepts they denote become an accepted part of the discourse of users of the borrowing language. In talking about *borrowing*, rather than the preferable *copying*, we must accept that what is borrowed is not linguistically identical with its source, and that use of this term may lead to 'misleading metaphorics'.[14]

Borrowing involving Brittonic and Old English: general and comparative comments
One might think that the amount of borrowing is related to the amount and nature of the conversational interaction between the invaders and the invaded. What, if anything, the Britons and the English said to each other during these earliest contacts has become controversial. The Britons certainly communicated some of their place-names to the newcomers. In recent work it has been argued that there are more such place-name traces than has generally been recognized, though, frankly, not a huge amount more.[15]

There is an apparent paradox in the fact that the Angles and Saxons seem

---

[14] Johansson, p. 288.
[15] See the papers in Richard Coates and Andrew Breeze, with a contribution by David Horovitz, *Celtic Voices, English Places* (Stamford, 2000; hereafter *CVEP*), and subsequent papers by the same authors. The Britons may also have given some of their personal names to the English. If so, that would indicate that the Britons were a sufficiently positive 'outside influence' in English society for the English to imitate their naming practices and therefore for Clark's First Law of Applied Anthroponymics to apply (for which see Cecily Clark, 'Clark's First Three Laws of Applied Anthroponymics', *Nomina* 3 (1979), 13–19, reprinted in *Words, Names and History. Selected Writings of Cecily Clark*, ed. Peter Jackson (Cambridge, 1995), pp. 77–83). This 'law' states: 'In any homogeneous community, naming-behaviour will remain constant, except when disturbed by outside influence.' The Third Law adds a rider about the strength of such influences. Unfortunately, we cannot tell whether a Brittonic name in an Anglo-Saxon source is actually the name of a Briton or a Saxon even where it is ostensibly that of a Saxon, as in the case of *Cerdic* or *Cædmon* (see Coates, 'On Some Controversy surrounding *Gewissæ/Gewissei, Cerdic* and *Ceawlin*', *Nomina* 13 (1989/90), 1–11, vs. David N. Parsons, 'British *Caratīcos, Old English *Cerdic*', *Cambrian Medieval Celtic Studies* 33 (1997), 1–8; Clark, 'Onomastics', in *The Cambridge History of the English Language*, ed. Richard M. Hogg, vol. I: *The Beginnings to 1066* (Cambridge, 1992), pp. 452–89, at p. 463). But Clark plausibly suggests that Brittonic names may have been chosen for the fruits of early dynastic marriages between Brittonic and English royals. It is safest to assume that Brittonic names in such texts as the Durham *Liber vitae* (in *The Oldest English Texts*, ed. Henry Sweet, Early English Text Society, old series 83 (London, 1885), pp. 153–65) belong to Britons. Also, we cannot reliably identify Brittonic names in the form in which they were used by the English. Mats Redin's 'Studies on Uncompounded Personal Names in Old English' (PhD dissertation, Uppsala, 1919), contains material that might serve as a starting-point for identifying such names in use in the Anglo-Saxon period. But he observes of one of the most plausible candidates, *Tuda* (p. 71), that 'it will be safest to assume that Tuda is a short form of ... Celtic compounds [in **Touto-*, RC], perhaps coined by the Anglo-Saxons', and that leaves us unsure what the available anthroponymic material tells us about ethnicity and therefore about what was actually adopted from the Britons. Clark does not address the question of which otherwise obscure English short-names might be of Brittonic ancestry. Given these difficulties, no conclusions will be drawn here from personal-name evidence.

content to have taken some place-names from the Britons and yet took practically no Brittonic vocabulary in the earliest centuries of settlement. There was virtually no early lexical traffic in the other direction either,[16] and all we have for sure is the talismanic word *cyulis* '(Saxon long)ships' in Gildas's *De excidio Britanniae*[17] which is actually just a mention, not a use – Gildas glosses it in the running Latin of his text – and therefore not a certain borrowing. This all appears to suggest little contact in which meanings were exchanged. The borrowing of vocabulary presupposes purposeful human interaction and is therefore a secure sign that that has happened. When European powers set up colonies and imperial administrations, English and the other languages received a considerable amount of vocabulary, notwithstanding how technologically (un)developed their dominions were.

At one end of the scale is the legacy of imperial rule in India: the Hobson-Jobson vocabulary, with sources in many different languages;[18] at the other is the estimated 200 words (from a wide range of indigenous languages and of wildly differing text-frequency) in Australian English from the various Aboriginal languages.[19] Many of the expressions found in Indian English are also found in the general standard language of the high imperial period, and not just in the discourse of expatriates or local adopters of English; they belong to a wide range of semantic fields (*sahib, raj, raja, rani, nawab/nabob, brahmin, khidmutgar, ayah, (punkah-)wallah, nautch(-girl), dhobi, mahout, pundit@, sadhu, swami, yogi, pariah@, thug@, sari@, dhoti, pyjama(s)@, cashmere@, khaki@, sati/ suttee, ghat, nirvana, karma@, yoga@, swastika@, mongoose@, cheetah@, gaur, jairou, nilgau, bandicoot, jungle@, bhang, char(@)* 'tea', *chota peg* 'whisky and soda', *betel, ghee, curry@, korma, chapati, dal, naan, rupee, pice, chit@, pukka(@), cushy@, dekko(@)* 'look', *sitar@, tabla, polo@, gymkhana@, durbar, bungalow@, Blighty*). Words marked with @ are exceptionally well-embedded (by my subjective judgement) in the modern standard language even back home in Britain, and those marked (@) were formerly. Those due to native Australian languages are more obviously concentrated in those semantic fields identified by McMahon, namely (1) native flora and particularly fauna (*mulga, budgerigar, dingo, koala, wombat, wallaby, kangaroo, barramundi*) and (2) aspects and objects of Aboriginal culture (*corroboree, boomerang, didgeridoo*). The English took over Indian toponymy practically entire because they took on the pre-existing nucleated settlement pattern of India practically entire, and Australian and Amerindian languages had a proportionally smaller but still very significant impact on place-naming, as a glance at maps of these areas reveals.

[16] T. E. Parry-Williams, *The English Element in Welsh: A Study of English Loan-Words in Welsh* (London, 1923), ch. 2.
[17] *Gildas: The Ruin of Britain and Other Documents*, ed. and trans. M. Winterbottom (Chichester, 1978), pp. 87–142, §23.
[18] Represented in the 1000 pages of William Crooke, 3rd edn of Henry Yule and A. C. Burnell, *Hobson-Jobson: A Glossary of Colloquial Anglo-Indian Words* [etc.] (London, 1903).
[19] Hiroyuki Yokose, 'Aboriginal Words in Australian English'. Web-site www.kasei.ac.jp/ library/kiyou/2001/13.yokose.pdf. (Bears page numbers 169–80; place of publication unknown, dated 2001.)

No one, to my knowledge, has demonstrated conclusively that Brittonic had an impact on Old English (OE) grammar. In the longer term, the Celtic languages have certainly had deeper effects, it has been argued, on the development of both dialect and the standard language,[20] and there may be significance in the similarity of the typological shifts undergone by both languages.[21] Most provocatively, Klemola draws attention speculatively to the West Wiltshire heartland of DO-support in declarative sentences and compares the toponymic evidence for the survival of a late variety of Brittonic in the same area investigated by this author.[22] But since it is hard to be sure of causal connections between Brittonic and English grammatical phenomena because of the time-depth and the silence of the record at key periods, my discussion of the literature will focus on lexical borrowing, which has undoubtedly happened, even if on a restricted scale.

Borrowed words and place-name elements
Brittonic place-name elements and general lexis will be treated as a single class for the purposes of analysis. The tally of lexical borrowings into OE is in Baugh and Cable's words 'almost negligible'.[23] The canonical list is brief; Förster recognized 15,[24] of which only 4 are still generally accepted:

binn 'manger'
brocc 'badger'
cumb 'valley', but found only in place-names until its descendant Welsh *cwm* was re-borrowed late in the second millennium
luh 'sea; pool'

There is a native English word covering part of the denotational range of what we now call a valley, namely *denu*. Gelling and Cole have shown convincingly that a *cumb* had a different profile from a *denu*.[25] Surely *denu* could be applied in the continental landscape (cf. Middle Low German *dene* 'valley'), but there was a sort of feature in Britain which seemed inadequately described by this term; so the word *cumb* was borrowed for a feature with a bowl-shaped end to contrast

---

[20] For England itself see especially the papers by David L. White ('Explaining the innovations of Middle English: what, where and why?') and Juhani Klemola ('Periphrastic DO: dialectal distribution and origins') in *CRE*, pp. 153–74, 199–210; and also Hildegard L. C. Tristram, *How Celtic is Standard English?* (St Petersburg, 1999).
[21] Hildegard L. C. Tristram, 'Attrition of Inflections in English and Welsh', in *CRE*, pp. 111–49.
[22] Coates, in *CVEP*, pp. 112–16, and in *CRE*.
[23] Albert C. Baugh and Thomas Cable, *A History of the English Language*, 5th edn (London, 2002), p. 76.
[24] Max Förster, 'Keltisches Wortgut im Englischen: eine sprachliche Untersuchung', in *Texte und Forschungen zur englischen Kulturgeschichte. Festgabe für Felix Liebermann*, ed. M. Förster and K. Wildhagen (Halle an der Saale, 1921), pp. 119–242. (Also published separately.)
[25] Margaret Gelling, *Place-names in the Landscape* (London, 1984), pp. 88–94, 97–9; Margaret Gelling and Ann Cole, *The Landscape of Place-Names* (Stamford, 2000), pp. 103–9, 113–22.

with a long, narrow, relatively steep-sided *denu*. We get an echo here of the kind of place-name-element borrowing found in other situations where unfamiliar topography, geology and ecology presented themselves to English speakers, and which resulted in the borrowing (with different degrees of discourse frequency) of such terms as *mesa, kopje, volcano, pingo, arroyo, bayou, wadi, corrie (coire), karst, tundra* and *taiga*.

Förster's canon of borrowed words had not quite been published when Ekwall proposed the Brittonic origin of *torr* 'outcrop, peak'.[26] This suggestion found general favour (including that of Förster himself); this borrowing may also have been encouraged by the absence of comparable features near continental, North Sea coasts. He also suggested *funta*, a Brittonic mediation of Latin *fontana*, and this is also universally accepted. First attested after the Old English period, *coble* '(ferry-)boat' can probably be added, possibly because this inland-waterway form of transport was of a different construction from the Saxon boat, for example wickerwork as opposed to planking. There has been a recent argument that Old/MiddleWelsh *genou* 'mouth' was borrowed early, principally (but not only) as a place-name element.[27] It has long been thought that *crag* 'rock' is a further possibility (endorsed by Förster), though aspects of the phonology of this word are obscure (cf. and ctrst. Middle Welsh *creig*). Förster's original work was discussed further by Ekwall and Pokorny,[28] and Förster added another supposed borrowing from Irish to his list (*stor*) which has now been convincingly shown to be Brittonic.[29]

Ten items from Förster's original list have been questioned and/or rejected by later scholarship, as referenced here:

assa 'ass' (cf. *assen* 'she-ass'), more likely from Irish, for morphological reasons, as Förster himself suggested

bannuc 'bit',[30] might also be claimed as Goidelic on the basis of the modern (re)borrowing in the sense 'flat oatcake')[31]

becca 'fork, 'Gabelaxt" (questioned by Brunner; see note 30)

bratt 'cloak', now believed more likely to be from Irish[32]

---

[26] Eilert Ekwall, 'Zu zwei keltischen Lehnwörtern im Altenglischen: (1) Ae. *funta* "Quelle"; (2) Ae. *torr*, ne. *tor* "a high rock, a pile of rocks; ... a hill"', *Englische Studien* 54 (1920), 102–10.

[27] Andrew Breeze, 'Welsh *geneu* "mouth, jaws" and the Middle English *Seinte Margaret*', *Notes and Queries* 238 (1993), 13–14; David Horovitz and Richard Coates, 'Gnosall, Staffordshire, and the Middle English Word <genow>', in *CVEP*, pp.184–92.

[28] Eilert Ekwall, review of Förster, 'Keltisches Wortgut ...', *Beiblatt zur Anglia* 33 (1922), 73–82; Julius Pokorny, review of Förster, 'Keltisches Wortgut ...' (in 'Erschienene Schriften'), *Zeitschrift für celtische Philologie* 14 (1923), 298–9.

[29] Max Förster, 'Altenglisch *stor*, ein altirisches Lehnwort', *Englische Studien* 70 (1936), 49–54; Andrew Breeze, 'A Brittonic Etymology for Old English *stor* "incense"', *Anglia* 116 (1998), 227–30.

[30] Questioned by Karl Brunner, *Die englische Sprache: ihre geschichtliche Entwicklung* (Tübingen, 1960), p. 27.

[31] *Oxford English Dictionary*, 2nd edn.

[32] Andrew Breeze, 'Irish *brat* "cloak, cloth": English *brat* "child"', *Zeitschrift für celtische Philologie* 47 (1995), 89–92.

carr 'rock'[33]
dunn 'dun' (colour-term)[34]
gafeluc 'spear'[35]
hogg 'hog'[36]
mattuc 'mattock' (questioned by Brunner; see note 30)
toroc 'bung' (whose status as a word of English has even been questioned, though I have recently argued that it is an English word meaning 'throat' but not of Brittonic origin)[37]

Of the nine accepted words, some six are topographical terms or have quasi-topographical applications, one a term for an animal known also in the continental homeland, one a Christian cultural term and one general.

The state of scholarship on these items in the 1930s was usefully reviewed by Serjeantson.[38] Kastovsky's conservative survey acknowledges twelve true Brittonic borrowings *binn*, *bannoc*, *gafeluc*, *dunn*, *broc*, *assen*, and, from the glosses to the Lindisfarne gospels, *bratt*, *carr* and *luh* 'pool', as well as the toponymic elements *torr* and *cumb*, plus *funta*.[39] He observes that

> the Celts have left remarkably little behind in English, a phenomenon that has not really been explained satisfactorily. True, the surviving Celts were a conquered race, but their culture must have been more developed than that of the German invaders due to the 400 years of Romanisation, and from that point of view more loans would not have been completely unlikely ... contrary to all expectations, [Celtic] has not really left its mark on the English language[.][40]

But recent archaeological work suggests that at the end of the Romano-British (RB) period there was not much to pass on materially, if a band across central southern England from the eastern boundary of Oxfordshire to Essex were typical.[41] Over a wider landscape, Wacher notes a patchy decline in RB culture

---

[33] For discussion see David N. Parsons and Tania Styles, *The Vocabulary of English Place-Names*, fasc. II, *brace-cæster* (Nottingham, 2000), pp. 143–4.
[34] The counter argument is based on H. Weyhe, 'Beiträge zur westgermanischen Grammatik', *Beiträge zur Geschichte der deutschen Sprache und Litteratur* 30 (1905), 55–111, at 56–9.
[35] See now Andrew Breeze, 'Celtic Etymologies for Old English *cursung* "curse", *gafeluc* "javelin" [etc.]', *Notes and Queries* 238 (1993), 287–97, and further comment below.
[36] Richard Coates, 'Phonology and the Lexicon: A Case Study of Early English Forms in -gg-', *Indogermanische Forschungen* 87 (1982), 195–222.
[37] Richard Coates, in as yet unpublished work on the Lincolnshire place-name *Torksey*.
[38] Mary S. Serjeantson, *A History of Foreign Words in English* (London, 1935), pp. 55–60.
[39] Other Brittonic-mediated Latin loans might have been mentioned: see Margaret Gelling, *Signposts to the Past*, 3rd edn (Chichester, 1997), ch. 3.
[40] Dieter Kastovsky, 'Semantics and Vocabulary', in *The Cambridge History of the English Language*, vol. I: *The Beginnings to 1066*, ed. Richard M. Hogg (Cambridge, 1992), pp. 290–408, at pp. 319–20.
[41] John T. Baker, 'The Transition from Romano-British to Anglo-Saxon Culture in the Chilterns and Essex Region' (PhD dissertation, University of Birmingham, 2001), *passim*.

after the late fourth century and refers to its eventual 'almost complete eclipse'.[42] If there is no distinctive material culture, there is no lexis to offer to incomers except landscape terms, including place-names. It does not follow that the material culture of the invaders must have been technologically superior. However, Kastovsky's assessment that British culture 'must have been more developed' appears unsound, and possibly dependent on the glories of Celtic-derived Christian sculpture and book-creation, new during the Anglo-Saxon era rather than present at the dawn of it.

Andrew Breeze has suggested that some words of OE, most of which have not survived into Modern English, may expand the list somewhat. The possibilities he has identified include: *trem* 'pace' and *trum* 'strong',[43] *wered* 'sweet drink',[44] *stor* 'incense' or better 'medicinal wax',[45] and *dēor* 'brave';[46] see the fuller list of claims and the wider discussion in Breeze's paper at the Mekrijärvi conference.[47] He has also returned to an earlier view that one of the controversial ones, *gafeluc* 'javelin', is after all ultimately Celtic but shows that it is actually Goidelic, and must have entered English via Old Norse.[48] Borrowed early non-Brittonic Celtic material is equally sparse. One might adduce a few possibilities from the period of continental contact: *ambeht* 'servant, official', *dūn* 'hill(fort)', *īsern* 'iron', *rīce* 'realm'; some early words authoritatively considered of Irish origin, in some cases possibly mediated by Brittonic: *ancor(a)* 'hermit', *assa* 'ass', *bannoc* 'bit', *bratt* 'cloak; child [acc. Breeze]', *clucge* 'bell', *drŷ* 'magician', *stær* 'history', and probably even *Christ* (on the basis of the long vowel, a Celtic phenomenon: OW *Crist*, OIr *Críst*); and also a single-figure list of other words attributable to the influence of Irish missionary Christianity, of which only two remain in use in Modern English, *curse*[49] and *cross* (like *gafeluc*, via Old Norse), and some added by Breeze in recent work: *Beltancu* 'Beltaine cow, 'heriot'[50] and *deorc* 'bloody(-red)'.[51] But even taking all these into account the total impact of Celtic on OE in the era of colonization, expansion and consolidation is extremely small, and that of Brittonic only a part of it.

In addition to the generics *cumb* and *torr*, some words were borrowed for

---

[42] John Wacher, *The Towns of Roman Britain*, 2nd edn (London, 1998), pp. 297–9; Wacher, *Roman Britain*, new edn (Stroud, 1995), p. 409.

[43] Andrew Breeze (1) '*Beowulf* and *The Battle of Maldon*: *trem* "pace" and Welsh *tremyn* "journey",' (2) 'Old English *trum* "strong", *truma* "host": Welsh *trwm* "heavy"', *Notes and Queries* 238 (1993), 9–10, 16–19.

[44] Andrew Breeze, '*Wered* "sweet drink" at *Beowulf* 496: Welsh *gwirod* "liquor, drink"', *Notes and Queries* 238 (1993), 433–4.

[45] Breeze; see note 29.

[46] Andrew Breeze, 'A Celtic Etymology for Old English *dēor* "brave"', in *Alfred the Wise: Old English Studies Presented to Janet Bately on her Sixty-Fifth Birthday*, ed. Jane Roberts and Janet Nelson, with Malcolm Godden (Cambridge, 1997), pp. 1–4.

[47] Andrew Breeze, 'Seven Types of Celtic Loanword', in *CRE*, pp. 175–81.

[48] Andrew Breeze, 'Celtic Etymologies for Old English *cursung* "curse", *gafeluc* "javelin" [etc.]', *Notes and Queries* 238 (1993), 287–97.

[49] According to J. R. R. Tolkien; see Breeze, as note 48.

[50] Andrew Breeze, 'Irish *brat* "cloak, cloth"', 89–92.

[51] Andrew Breeze, '*Deorc* "bloody" in *The Dream of the Rood*: Old Irish *derg* "red, bloody"', *Éigse* 28 (1994/5), 165–8.

which there is no evidence outside place-names. The English seem to have taken some monomorphemic Brittonic words for landscape features to be proper names, possibly many times over, in such a way that no new lexical item of the relevant form entered English. Into this category fall *genou* and (pre-modern) *crag*, already mentioned, and the following: **cēd* 'wood', found in wood-names in forms like *cheet* and *chet*; **cors* 'reeds, bog', in names in south-western counties; **crūg* 'barrow', found countrywide in barrow-names in forms like *crook*, *crick*, *creek*, *creech*, these names collectively deserving further study because of their difficult historical phonology; **eglēs* 'church', regularly found as *Eccles*; **lux* 'lake', in some Northumbrian local coastal names [possibly lexicalized] and in *Lutton* (Lincolnshire, Holland); **penn* 'head, top, end' (confusable with certain OE words); **poll/*pull* 'pool' (phonological uncertainties, unclear connection with modern *pool* with which it may sometimes have become identified); and **ros* 'moor', widespread though with a regional phonological complication concerning the length of the vowel in borrowed names. Significantly, none of these is ever found as the generic in an early, two-element, English place-name, though *luh* may have been so used in Northumberland if the suggestive evidence of some modern coastal names is allowed, whilst some are used as single-element names (*Creech*, *Crick*, *Eccles*, *Penn*, *Ross*, *Roos*). That reinforces the view gained from the minimal lexical borrowing: Brittonic was not much understood by the incomers, and most items that were borrowed were understood as making reference but not as denoting by virtue of their lexical content. That is, they performed the task of naming but rarely attained lexical status. This is illustrated perfectly by the fate of Brittonic **aβon* 'river', which has given English no lexical item but appears as the proper name of, not a word for, six rivers in England. If these had become true English words, there is no reason why they should not, like *cumb* and *torr*, have served as generics like their English translation-equivalents.

Parallels for near-zero lexical borrowing and sparse onomastic borrowing?
We need to explain, then, the fact that the Britons transmitted to the English a small number of place-names and an extremely small number of lexical items. Are there any other historical situations where a military aristocracy, whether or not strengthened by later settlers, maintained a language which owed so little to its substrate? What we need to find parallels for is as follows:

- A new language arrives borne by military conquest, followed by mass immigration (though in the case of England this assumption has been vigorously questioned recently: the major reason for the conference from which this volume stemmed)
- The indigenes have a material culture technologically no more advanced than that of the newcomers[52]
- The indigenous language gives practically no vocabulary to the newcomers and only a rather small number of place-names and personal names
- The indigenous population can be seen documentarily only in scattered

---

[52] Compare the material presented in Baker's PhD dissertation, *passim*.

(relict) polities (cf. small kingdoms recorded by Bede such as Cornwall, Deira and Elmet) and by their concentrated onomastic traces in such areas as north-west Wiltshire and the Pennine Wales,[53] Cornwall and Wales (including Marcher counties) where their language persisted, and perhaps south Lancashire and parts of the Lake District
- DNA evidence is equivocal but may suggest survival of the indigenous population over at least some of the conquered/resettled area (as has recently been claimed for England by Brian Sykes and others)
- Some, perhaps many, indigenes were enslaved

Possible parallel case no. 1: Basque and Latin
Larry Trask observed that the Romanization of the Basque Country offers some striking parallels to the case of English, though the securest evidence for early Basque comes from Aquitania, i.e. north of the Pyrenees, and it is uncertain how most of the modern Basque provinces of Spain came to be populated by Basques.

<> *The indigenes have a material culture technologically no more advanced than that of the newcomers*
There is no evidence for Basque cities (or even settlements of significance), coinage, writing, roads, political entities beyond tribes, armies, substantial seafaring or a legal system. This echoes the archaeologically-verified collapse of Romano-British material culture and the historically-verified collapse of its central administration in the fourth and fifth centuries.

<> *The indigenous language gives practically no lexis to the newcomer*
There appears to be not a single Basque word in Latin. The total Basque lexical contribution to Romance before about 1900 probably does not reach a dozen words, except in the dialects of Álava and the Rioja (excluding Basque words used in Romance only by native speakers of Basque, i.e. a clear bilingual phenomenon). Possibly ancient words of Castilian of supposedly Basque origin are discussed in depth by Trask.[54] He concludes that only about seven of the claims are even remotely plausible. None approaches certainty. This low number closely parallels the number of reasonably secure, early English borrowings from Brittonic. Professor Trask commented in correspondence (10/03/2004) that if Basque had died out like its neighbours between 400 and 600 CE, there would be little hard evidence for its former existence.[55]

---

[53] Richard Coates, 'Invisible Britons: The View from Toponomastics,' in *Language Contact in the Place-Names of Britain and Ireland*, ed. Paul Cavill (Nottingham, forthcoming). The 'Pennine Wales' is an area with an unusual concentration of Celtic names near the village of Wales (Yorkshire West Riding).
[54] R. L. Trask, *The History of Basque* (London, 1997), pp. 415–21.
[55] See also Trask, *History of Basque*, pp. 9–12.

<> The indigenous language gives the newcomers only a rather small number of personal names and place-names
There is no evidence for Basque or Basque-mediated personal names in use among non-Basques before well into the Middle Ages, and even then there were not many. There are very few toponyms in the Basque Country used by the Romans which can be shown to have existed before the Roman settlement, and some of these are non-Basque. Documentation is patchy, but there were apparently few Basque settlements. However, the modern toponymy is quite substantially Basque. Brittonic toponymy in England is much less conspicuous than Basque toponymy in the Basque Country.

<> The indigenous population can be seen documentarily only in scattered (relict) polities
The Basques in the Roman period can be seen only as a collection of tribal names, and we have no evidence for which tribes spoke Basque. Most of the personal names recorded from the region are non-Basque. We only know the Basques were there at all because they were there later, and because some Aquitanian personal and divine names can be readily interpreted as Basque. By contrast there are ample references in Old English sources to Britons, their activities, their ethnicity, and the social and legal status that derive from it.

<> DNA evidence is equivocal but may suggest survival of the indigenous population over at least some of the conquered/resettled area
Genetic evidence is not even equivocal: the Basques are in certain respects definitely very distinct from their neighbours.[56] By contrast the most that has been claimed for Britons in England is that their descendants represent one genetic strain, even if a very important one.

<> Some, perhaps many, indigenes were enslaved
Professor Trask knew of no evidence for a single Basque slave, but it seems unlikely that the Basques escaped this Roman practice. We know that the English enslaved Britons, and the word *w(e)alh* notoriously means both 'Briton' and 'slave'.[57]

However, practically all the evidence for the existence of Basque or its ancestor in Roman times comes from the Romanised area north of the Pyrenees. The Romans built a fort at Lapurdum, modern Bayonne. So Romanisation of a size-

---

[56] See Luigi Luca Cavalli-Sforza, A. Piazza, P. Menozzi and J. L. Mountain, 'Reconstruction of Human Evolution: Bringing Together Genetic, Archaeological, and Linguistic Data', *Proceedings of the National Academy of Sciences* 85 (1988), 6002–6, and Cavalli-Sforza, *Genes, Peoples and Languages* (London, 2000), pp. 21–2, on the high incidence of the negative allele of the RH gene among the Basques.

[57] See the extensive discussion of this topic by Kenneth Cameron, 'The Meaning and Significance of Old English *walh* in English Place-Names', *Journal of the English Place-Name Society* 12 (1979/80), 1–53 (with appendices by Malcolm Todd and John Insley). It is of course possible that some such names contain *Walh* as a personal name.

able Basque-speaking area is assured, as far north as the Garonne, to judge by epigraphic anthroponymic evidence, and the opportunity for lexical borrowing from the ancestor of Basque must have existed here if nowhere else. Gorrochategui argues that the available evidence favours 'shallow latinization' in the Pyrenees and western Aquitania in the Roman period: the adoption of Latin anthroponymy but no other cultural activities such as writing full, Latin funerary epigraphs.[58] The Romans administered what is now the southern Basque Country but nominally; Roman settlement is highly unlikely to have occurred even though military units were raised there. It is very difficult to establish that the local language was Basque in Roman times; the evidence consists of three brief inscriptions and the fact that the Romans' name for the inhabitants of most of the territory was *Vascones*, later applied universally by Romance-speakers to the Basques.

The most important lesson from this material is that the imposition of a military aristocracy may have near-zero substratal effects but only where the conquerors' presence is slight and no appreciable co-settlement occurs. The Indian case, and even the Australian one, reminds us that deeper interaction will lead to measurable linguistic effects. The Basque case is not a model for what happened in England.

Possible parallel case no. 2: Norse and Gaelic
More briefly, the pattern involving Brittonic and English may also appear consistent with what happened with Norse-Gaelic contacts in Scotland. Regrettably, as with the Basque Country, the sequence of historical events there is not known for sure, but in the Western Isles, at least, Gaelic probably replaced Scandinavian;[59] whether this was a reintroduction, i.e. whether Gaelic was also substratal to Norse, is not clear. The number of Scandinavian borrowings in Gaelic probably does not exceed fifty,[60] with a possible few more in island dialects,[61] though this is a much larger tally than that of borrowings from Brittonic into English. Topographical terms, especially as applied in place-names, constitute the bulk of them, as with: *òb* 'bay', *cleit* 'rock', *sgeir* 'skerry', *acarsaid* 'anchorage', *gil* 'narrow valley', *geàrraidh* 'home pasture', and seabird-names such as *sgarbh* 'cormorant', *làmhaidh* 'guillemot', and *mall* 'gull' on St Kilda. A few more enter place-names but not the lexicon: Scand. *nes* 'headland', *fjal-* 'fell', and *bólstað-* 'farm'.

---

[58] Joaquín Gorrochategui, 'The Basque Language and its Neighbours in Antiquity', in *Towards a History of the Basque Language*, ed. José Ignacio Hualde, Joseba A. Lakarra and R. L. Trask (Amsterdam and Philadelphia, 1995), pp. 31–63, at p. 49.

[59] W. F. H. Nicolaisen, *Scottish Place-Names*, 1st edn (London, 1976), p. 138, quoting an anonymous source, ?Magne Oftedal.

[60] Magne Oftedal, 'On the Frequency of Norse Loanwords in Scottish Gaelic', *Scottish Gaelic Studies* 9 (1961), 116–27; Kenneth H. Jackson, 'The Celtic Languages during the Viking Period', in *Proceedings of the International Congress of Celtic Studies*, ed. B. Ó Cuív (Dublin, 1962), pp. 3–11.

[61] See e.g. Richard Coates, 'Notes on the Past of the Gaelic Dialect of St Kilda', *Cognitive Science Research Paper* 081 (University of Sussex, Brighton, 1988).

Discussion

Both the Norse and the Brittonic cases appear consistent with withdrawal of speakers of the previously dominant language, rather than cultural assimilation of numerically dominant classes by the incomers. 'Withdrawal' can be achieved in a number of ways: murder ('ethnic cleansing'), enslavement (whence zero cultural impact), flight, exile, negotiated withdrawal. But eastern England and the Scandinavian kingdom of the Hebrides show the lexical and onomastic (non-) evidence that the incomers moved into a landscape from which a major withdrawal had taken place. This older view need not be rejected in favour of the survival of a substantial local population having the option of cultural assimilation,[62] especially given the solid historical evidence for flight across the Channel (in the existence of the Bretons), massacre of local Britons, the evidence of non-assimilation and the use of the word *wealh*, primordially 'Briton', to mean 'slave'.[63] Ward-Perkins is aware of the tension between his essentially Highamist viewpoint and the invisibility of the Britons when he says that 'what needs to be explained is why ... the necessary cultural changes all occurred in one direction: in favour of the conquerors'. Given his assumptions, we cannot have an answer.[64]

Professor Higham argues that a political élite governing a large underclass may be sufficient to account for the facts as presented. But evidence presented above suggests any political ascendancy which is more than nominal absorbs

[62] Higham, *RBAS*, pp. 209–36; I follow Yorke, *Wessex in the Early Middle Ages*, p. 48.
[63] The direct evidence for withdrawal from parts of England includes: the alleged facts that the Britons 'forsook Kent' (*Anglo-Saxon Chronicle*, edn *ad libitum*, MS A, annal 457); the Welsh 'fled from the English like/ as from fire' (A, 473); the English slew all the inhabitants of Pevensey (A, 491); slaughter of countless Welsh at Chester including 200 priests (A, 607), fulfilling a prophecy of Augustine. Even allowing for rhetorical overstatement, the general picture is pretty clear. The alternative is that this is merely a conventionalized land-taking myth. In corroboration from the Brittonic side, Gildas notes deaths, enslavements and flight to mountains, forests, coasts and overseas. (It should be recognized, as Nick Higham has emphasized to me, that the independence of the Welsh and English testimonies may be questioned, since the compilers of the *Chronicle* knew Gildas indirectly, through Bede.) There are Brittonic missions to Brittany after 500, suggesting attempts to consolidate the faith, and there are Brittonic hosts on the continent according to Jordanes, writing in 551 (both these facts being interpretable as self-perceived Roman citizens going to the aid of other Roman citizens). Jackson, on the basis of the evidence of continental writers, hypothesizes two peaks of emigration to Brittany, the first from 450 to 550, and the second after 577. General considerations pointing in the same direction are the fact that flight is a constant after battle, and that raiding may be aimed at damaging agriculture, giving another incentive for flight, namely from famine; any famine must have been exacerbated by the world-wide climatic downturn of 535–545 (whatever the ultimate origin of that may have been: possibly volcanic activity in the Far East, according to David Keys, *Catastrophe! An Investigation into the Origins of the Modern World* (London,1999)).
[64] Ward-Perkins, 'Why Did the Anglo-Saxons', at 526 (see footnote 3). Whilst I have spoken of the 'vacated' east as the main domain of early Germanization, I should note that the case of Dorchester-on-Thames, with sub-Roman and English archaeology overlapping, is a special one (Yorke, *Wessex*, p. 30; archaeological references in Richard Coates, 'The Pre-English Name of Dorchester-on-Thames,' *Studia Celtica* 40 (2006), 51–62).

local vocabulary at least, if not, in the fullness of time, the entire vernacular. Western Romance has a significant Celtic substrate.[65] Local Castilian borrows richly from Basque.[66] Hiberno-English has a 'huge regional lexicon' with many borrowings from Irish.[67] Contact in differing degrees may have consequences ranging all the way from vocabulary adoption to full language-shift. Language-shift *by* an élite is perfectly possible. French yielded before Middle English in England, and Clovis's descendants spoke Gallo-Roman, not Frankish. *I know of no case where a political ascendancy has imposed its own language without significant impact from the language of the conquered.*

Entwistle noted the fairly substantial amount of Celtic vocabulary in Iberian Romance even though it 'betray[s] a culture below that of the invaders';[68] so where there are practically no borrowings at all, the conclusion to be drawn is obvious: there was practically no culture to betray, i.e. there were practically no speakers in a position to betray it, whatever its material level. The Brittonic-English situation we are contemplating bears comparison with the English advance into sparsely-populated Australia where murder and displacement of the Aboriginal population were normal. There numbers of place-names are adopted and a vocabulary for unfamiliar flora and fauna; the European flora and fauna of Britain would have been largely familiar to the English, and therefore such borrowing from Brittonic is predictably small. But one does not have to believe in blood- or gene-given ethnicity to question the proposition that many Britons voluntarily became English (and were allowed the opportunity to do it), because, if they did, so little linguistic material came with them. Where they had the opportunity, as the pace of westward conquest relented, we unsurprisingly find signs of greater Brittonic impact, especially in the retention of more place-names, though only in Cornwall does lexical borrowing become really important.[69] It is relevant that some of the defunct borrowings claimed for Middle English (ME) in Breeze's studies[70] appear to have a West Midland incidence; they appear for instance in *Ancrene Wisse* and its associated texts in Tolkien's 'AB language' (possibly written in or near Herefordshire), in the lyrics in MS Harley 2253 (copied at Ludlow), and in other texts which appear to have spent some period of their textual history in Mercia.[71] But this apparent geographical effect may be an artefact of Dr Breeze's as yet incomplete coverage of ME texts (as he observes in correspondence, 02/04/2004), and it is true that he finds good evidence for borrowings in texts that appear to originate elsewhere, such as *Beowulf*.[72] Moreover, evidence for significant numbers of lexical survivals in the modern dialects of the Marcher counties is lacking. Leeds,

---

[65] Pierre-Yves Lambert, *La langue gauloise* (Paris, 1997), pp. 185–204.
[66] Mikel Zárate, *Influencias del vascuence en la Lengua castellana* (Bilbao, 1976).
[67] David Crystal, *Cambridge Encyclopedia of the English Language* (Cambridge, 1995), p. 338.
[68] William Entwistle, *The Spanish Language* (London, 1936), p. 41.
[69] Martyn Wakelin, *Language and History in Cornwall* (Leicester, 1975), ch. 7.
[70] See e.g. *CRE*, p. 177.
[71] See especially his comments in 'Exodus, Elene and The Rune Poem: *milpæð* "army road, highway"', *Notes and Queries* 236 (1991), 436–8, at 438.
[72] Cf. footnotes 43 and 44.

for example, claims that 'the number of words of Welsh derivation in general use is small and confined almost entirely to the western and north-western areas [of Herefordshire]'.[73]

Where discussion turns on the survival of Brittonic in England,[74] it does not engage with any traces in local English dialect. It was Jackson's view that

> the natives learned Anglo-Saxon thoroughly and accurately, so accurately that they had to mangle their own names to suit the new language rather than the new language to suit their own sound-system ... [i]t is impossible to point to any feature about Anglo-Saxon phonology which can be shown conclusively to be a modification due to the alien linguistic habits of the Britons ... they must have learned the new phonology very completely.[75]

He compares the 'few Gaulish words in Romance',[76] but Lambert actually identifies forty-odd Gaulish borrowings into Latin and 116 into French or Provençal (counting only the secure ones in Lambert's survey),[77] and this is a far greater tally than that of supposed Brittonic survivals in English. Jackson's scenario depends on the integration of individual Britons into the English-speaking community and the disappearance of any Brittonic communities that might sustain the ancestral language. This cannot easily be squared with 'genetic' Britons forming a massive element of the population of England.

I believe therefore that Wordsworth was essentially correct as far as the east was concerned when he wrote in the poem 'Monastery of Old Bangor':

> ... Mark! how all things swerve
> From their known course, or vanish like a dream;
> Another language spreads from coast to coast,
> Only perchance some melancholy Stream
> And some indignant Hills odd names preserve,
> When laws, and creeds, and people all are lost![78]

Several papers, both those given at the Mekrijärvi conference in 2001[79] and those recently published elsewhere, have argued for early Brittonic impact on English at levels other than the lexicon: phonology (Schrijver and Laker, both Mekrijärvi) and grammar,[80] even if some of the impact remained submerged

---

[73] Winifred Leeds, *Herefordshire Speech: the South-West Midland Dialect as Spoken in Herefordshire and its Environs* (privately published, 1972), p. 1; and cf. B. G. Charles, 'The Welsh, their Language and Place-Names in Archenfield and Oswestry', in *Angles and Britons* (six O'Donnell Lectures), ed. Henry Lewis (Cardiff, 1963), pp. 85–110.

[74] E.g. W. H. Stevenson, *Asser's Life of King Alfred* (Oxford, 1904; new edn by Dorothy M. Whitelock, 1959), pp. 248–50, for Dorset; Jackson, *LHEB*, pp. 234–43, for the whole of England.

[75] *LHEB*, p. 242.

[76] *LHEB*, p. 243.

[77] Lambert, pp. 186–203.

[78] William Wordsworth, *Ecclesiastical Sonnets*, no. XII (1821/2).

[79] Proceedings published as *CRE*, see footnote 1.

[80] Juhani Klemola, 'The Origins of the Northern Subject Rule: A Case of Early Contact?' in

till the Middle English period (White, Mekrijärvi).[81] Significantly, many of the phenomena discussed relate to areas other than my proposed 'vacated' southeast (Klemola; Laker; White[82]); White is quite explicit about the resistance of south-eastern English to innovations he believes to originate through contact with Celtic.

Conclusion

The evidence for Brittonic impact on English vocabulary is minimal. The most sociolinguistically persuasive account of this is that after initial contact in which little more was achieved than the transmission of certain place-names and of words construed as names, the invisibility of the Britons was due to some or all of the following factors:

- the English didn't need to borrow topographical or toponymic vocabulary because their own sufficed
- the English didn't need to borrow vocabulary for flora and fauna because their own sufficed
- Brittonic social and cultural institutions were imperceptible (even the OE word *drý* 'druid' is an Irish borrowing)

The last point can only mean that in the initial contact period Brittonic culture was either indistinguishable from that of the English (which is scarcely credible) or literally invisible (because it wasn't there). If it had been there, even marginalized, borrowed vocabulary would have betrayed its presence. If a Brittonic population had redefined itself as English through being 'absorbed by degrees into the population of the English settlements',[83] and assuming that the English would have tolerated this, experience elsewhere suggests that this could not have happened without substantial lexical copying from the substrate language(s) as the newcomers' language was appropriated (as in India) and/or without structural and lexical transformation of the dominant language (as throughout the world, for example by pidginization and subsequent creolization, and by the relatively subtle, e.g. phonological, changes due to local substrate effects seen in e.g. Irish and other extraterritorial Englishes, South African Dutch (Afrikaans), Latin American Spanish and Portuguese, Southern Bantu as influenced by the Khoi-San languages, the Indo-Iranian languages in India). As we shall note, though, Brittonic underwent far more massive structural transformation than English did during the initial contact period.

The Celtic Englishes, vol. II, ed. Hildegard L. C. Tristram (Heidelberg, 2000), pp. 329–46; Tristram, *How Celtic* ... *?*, pp. 19–30.
[81] See note 20.
[82] Klemola, 'Northern Subject Rule'; Stephen Laker, 'An Explanation for the Changes *kw-, hw-* > χw- in the English dialects', in *CRE*, pp. 183–98; White, note 20.
[83] R. G. Collingwood and J. N. L. Myers, *Roman Britain and the English Settlements*, 2nd edn (Oxford, 1936), p. 318; cf. implicitly Yorke, *Wessex in the Early Middle Ages*, p. 69, and the work of Higham in this area in general, referred to esp. in footnote 3.

I therefore accept the traditional view that in parts of what became England there were few visible Britons and that this state might have been achieved by emigration, annihilation or enslavement, for each of which there is evidence in English sources, though much hinges on whether these sources are credible witnesses. The *Chronicle*'s accounts of flight by and extermination of the Britons are undermined, as Prof. Higham reminds me in correspondence (07/04/04), by Bede's declaration that Æthelfrith (i.e., as late as 600) ravaged the Britons more extensively than any other English ruler '… for no ruler or king had subjected more land to the English race or settled it, having first exterminated or conquered the natives'.[84] He uses the word *exterminare*, and what he meant depends on his Latinity. This word does not mean 'to exterminate' in the classical language but 'to drive off', as the etymology, involving the word for 'boundary', would suggest. A conquered native need not be a slave.

My reasons for accepting this are essentially sociolinguistic. One must allow the possibility of politically motivated exaggeration of the severity of what happened to the Britons, and also that some key sources were written (in their current form) over 300 years after the events they purport to describe. Could this have been enough time for a borrowed vocabulary to disappear along with the Britons' institutions and any English interest in recording them? The English may not have had the anthropological impulses which writers of the later second millennium had towards peoples with different customs and institutions. Even Bede is interested principally, and not dispassionately, in the Britons' Christianity, and does not care about their other customs.

Any conclusion is speculative, but maintaining that the coming of the English was essentially the displacement of one aristocracy by another, with minimal genetic impact on the general population, means we *must* provide an explanation for the paucity of lexical borrowing. The most basic level of lexical borrowing, presupposed by all other types of linguistic borrowing, involves taking significant terminology and words for distinctive flora and fauna. Lower technological advancement in the subjected people does not rule this out (witness the Celtic borrowings concerning horsemanship in Latin). Marginalization of the subjected people and their institutions is also not a necessary condition (witness the contribution of subjected peoples to later English vocabulary). Perhaps, however, the late appearance of the known texts may make marginalization sufficient for silence. Lack of interest in the customs of the 'Others' among early English writers may have contributed. But our explanation must also take into account that the Britons, in allegedly accepting English, left no imprint of their own, which gives us a major problem. They were an ethnically and therefore legally distinct(ive) group deep into the Anglo-Saxon period (as in the laws of Ine and even of Alfred),[85] which need not, but presumably does, imply they were still Brittonic-speaking. When did they give up Brittonic, and how, whilst remaining distinctive, did they fail to evolve a distinctive variety of English as they passed

---

[84] Bede, *HE*, I, 34.
[85] Frederick L. Attenborough, ed. and trans., *The Laws of the Earliest English Kings* (Cambridge, 1922), §23; Yorke, *Wessex in the Early Middle Ages*, pp. 72, 259–60, 285.

through the bilingual stage of language shift? How come, if they were a majority, our present language is not a heavily Brittonicized variety of Germanic? Not all the major pronunciation and grammar features which distinguish Old English (OE) from Continental Germanic can be explained as Celtic, even of the Latinized variety that Schrijver envisages. Palatalization of velar consonants before front vowels is shared with Frisian, not Welsh, though also with Latin, but breaking of vowels before certain consonant clusters is unparalleled in Welsh and in Latin. Conversely, Welsh innovations from 450 to 600, even if shared with Latin, reveal no similarity to those of English. The Welsh reduction of clusters of a nasal and a stop has no contemporary parallel in English, nor does postvocalic lenition of stops, and nor does the Welsh redistribution of vowel length according to syllable structure. There is a similarity between the phonetic effects of OE *i*-umlaut and Brittonic *i/j*-affection, but they differ strikingly in that the Brittonic change affects only short vowels, unlike *i*-umlaut, and Latin has nothing similar. Brittonic changes typologically in radical ways at the time it is meeting OE, and OE shares none of them: for instance, Brittonic becomes a verb-first language, loses its case-system and adopts quite rigid noun-adjective order in noun phrases. This could hardly differ more from early Old English. How did the supposedly majoritarian Welsh adopt English in such a Germanic form without formal instruction, without a substantial immersion programme for all speakers and without making it more like Welsh? These are the questions that must be answered by those who propose a massive contribution of Britons to the 'English' gene pool.

On the other hand, absence of Britons is a sufficient condition for the absence of Brittonic-coloured English!

Possible common ground between the pro- and anti-'annihilation' positions lies in enslavement, that is cultural annihilation, for in enslavement in its classical form the masters make no effort to communicate in the slaves' languages; the onus rests on the slaves themselves to adopt, or adapt, the masters'.[86] If slavery entails the breakup of communities, rapid mastery of the conquerors' language becomes necessary for individuals to form human relations of any sort; but if homogeneous slave communities might be retained, as is implied by the frequent place-name types *Walton* and *Walcot*,[87] that would act as a retardant to language-shift and lead to possible 'slave-coloured' varieties of English. Possibly the illiteracy of the crucial period (450–600) is another important factor in the invisibility of the Britons. In recent cases of colonial conquest, especially by Western powers, writers have been on hand to record native customs and terminology, which only became important in the light of later concerns (as for instance in Australia). If Whites had started writing about Australian Aboriginals only in 1970, much less would have been recoverable about their anthropology and languages – perhaps practically nothing – and certainly that would have been so if Whites had been as aggressive towards Aboriginal communities everywhere as

---

[86] See the extensive literature on pidgin-formation, e.g. Peter Mühlhäusler, *Pidgin and Creole Linguistics* (Oxford, 1986), ch. 4.
[87] Cameron, *Walh*, note 58.

they were in Tasmania.[88] If this imperfect analogy holds, the most likely reasons for the invisibility of the Britons appear to be enslavement and dispersal, on the one hand, and the lack of contemporary chronicling on the other. But the view from linguistics clearly suggests that fragmentation of communities – dispersal – is a key agent in rapid language-shift. There is still a tension to be resolved: we know that Britons were identifiable as such to lawmakers till at least 900, by which time there is no evidence at all for the continuation of even the most meagre linguistic impact on OE. But the crux of the matter is whether Brittonic communities survived or were dispersed.

We must finally focus clearly on Schrijver's view that the south and east of Britain must have been Latin-speaking at the time of the English arrival. Clearly, such a scenario would account for the lack of Brittonic impact on the earliest English. Schrijver's case is brilliantly argued and represents one of the most exciting new ideas for some years. That case also, however, requires a period during which the south-east was emptied, at least to some degree, under the pressure of invasion; either significant numbers of Latin-speaking Britons moved north and west, or numbers of significant Latin-speaking Britons did so, influencing the British spoken in that area. This Latinized British, or Brittonic, eventually flowed back into the south-east to influence Old English to a fairly small degree, either directly or indirectly via the impact which it had had on the local Latin. This is speculative but coherent, and his argument is in tune with the preconceptions of modern sociolinguistics, up to the point at which the south-east resumed the speaking of British, for which the rationale remains unclear to me if the indigenes had really been thoroughly Latinized. Further, I am not yet persuaded that the facts really indicate that West Germanic in Britain converged with British of any description, in the south and east, to become (West-Saxon) Old English; I have listed above those developments in OE which appear to be clearly unrelated to the contemporaneous changes in Brittonic; they should be set against Schrijver's tally of positives.[89] I also cannot easily reconcile the idea with toponymic and archaeological evidence for the late survival of Brittonic in an area not so far from the West-Saxon heartland, namely Wiltshire.[90] There is room for debate to continue, but it might be apposite at the close to bear in mind a seventeenth-century view of contemporary colonial experience:[91]

> ... where the accessions are but thin and sparing, and scattered among the natives of the country ... and are driven to conform themselves unto their customs for their very subsistence, safety and entertainment, it falls out that the very planters do soon degenerate in their habits, customs and religion; as a little wine poured into a great vessel of water loseth itself.

---

[88] And of course elsewhere: R. M. W. Dixon, *The Languages of Australia* (Cambridge, 1980), pp. 78–9.
[89] *CRE*, pp. 102–8.
[90] *CVEP*, pp. 112–16.
[91] Matthew Hale, *The primitive origination of mankind, considered and examined according to the light of nature* (London, 1677).

15

Why Don't the English Speak Welsh?[1]

HILDEGARD TRISTRAM

Introduction

ALONG with many eminent British linguists, such as Robert W. Burchfield[2] or David Crystal,[3] Richard Coates,[4] in a recent study on the Late British contribution to the making of English toponymy,[5] commented on the absence of ordinary lexis of Late British origin in the English lexicon by saying that:

> We shall need to confront the apparent paradox that whilst the Angles and the Saxons seem content to have taken some place-names from the Britons – not an enormous number, but not negligible either – they took practically no ordinary vocabulary.

Is this really a paradox? I would claim that comparison with other instances of historical *shift* situations should lead us to *expect* that English did not borrow much lexical material from Late British. I would also suggest that while English did not borrow much lexis, the language was indeed affected by grammatical[6]

---

[1] I gratefully acknowledge that I owe this question to Dr Heinrich Härke (Reading), who in turn had been asked the same question by a journalist of BBC Radio 4. I am also most thankful to Dr Gary German (Brest, France), Dr David L. White (Austin, TX) and Prof. Erich Poppe (Marburg) for commenting on earlier drafts of this paper and for generously sharing their observations with me. I also owe sincere thanks to Prof. Nick Higham's extremely helpful linguistic corrections. Needless to say that all errors and infelicities are entirely my own responsibility.

[2] Richard W. Burchfield, *The English Language* (Oxford, 1986), p. 4.

[3] David Crystal, *The Cambridge Encyclopedia of the English Language* (Cambridge, 2003), p. 6.

[4] Richard Coates, 'The Significance of Celtic Place-names in England', in *The Celtic Roots of English*, ed. Markku Filppula, Juhani Klemola and Heli Pitkänen, Studies in Language 37 (Joensuu, 2002), pp. 47–85, at p. 47; see also Coates in this volume. This echoes earlier statements made by Margaret Gelling, 'Why Aren't We Speaking Welsh?', *ASSAH* 6 (1993), 51–6, at p. 51, and Bryan Ward-Perkins, 'Why did the Anglo-Saxons not become more British?', *EHR* 115 (2000), 513–33, at p. 514.

[5] For the term 'Late British' see Karl Horst Schmidt, 'Late British', in *Britain 400–600: Language and History*, ed. Alfred Bammesberger and Alfred Wollmann (Heidelberg, 1990), pp. 121–48.

[6] For a comparison of the earliest Old English and earliest Old Welsh texts that have been preserved and where the latter show many features which later became characteristic of English as opposed to other Germanic languages, see Hildegard L. C. Tristram, 'Attrition

and phonological transfer from Late British before the impact of the Vikings and the Normans made itself felt, but that this only showed in *writing* in the Early Middle English period after the demise of Old English diglossia. It was the lack of earlier scholarly attention given to the different *types* of linguistic contact situations as well as to the complex processes of language acquisition, change, death and birth,[7] which prompted the question: 'Why did the Britons not contribute more loan words to English?' In the following paper, I am going to discuss a few recent linguistic approaches and explore what they may tell us about the *type* of linguistic situation which obtained in Britain during the period of the Anglo-Saxon takeover and before the advent of the Vikings. I will then concentrate on two salient *grammatical* characteristics of English which are likely to have been calqued[8] from Late British.[9]

Recent Linguistic Approaches

Contact linguistics

Contact linguistics investigates the types of interaction between languages in both forced and peaceful contact situations across the world and through time.[10] It seeks to establish an understanding of the divers processes of cross-linguistic interaction based on the contact between speakers of different languages and of the catalytic agency of bilingual speakers. Language contact and contact-induced language change means interaction between speakers because, from a socio-linguistic point of view, it is not the languages themselves that interact but people who communicate and adapt their linguistic usage to the exigencies of the contact situation in order to be able to satisfy their communication needs.[11]

Thomason and Kaufman (1988) have convincingly shown that a distinction needs to be drawn between different contact scenarios. *Borrowing* scenarios differ from *shift* scenarios. Borrowing presupposes language maintenance between the respective languages or dialects in contact. If two or more languages or

---

of Inflexions in English and Welsh', in *The Celtic Roots of English*, ed. Markku Filppula *et al.*, pp. 111–49, at pp. 127–53, 138–44.

[7] See for instance *Sprachtod und Sprachgeburt*, ed. Peter Schrijver, Münchner Forschungen zur historischen Sprachwissenschaft 2 (Bremen, 2004).

[8] Calques (from French *calque* 'trace') are loan translations where the components of words, phrases and grammatical structures are translated item by item from one to another language. Cf. David Crystal, *A Dictionary of Linguistics and Phonetics*, 5th edn (Maldon, MA, 2003), s.v. *calque*. Calques thus may not only be lexical but also grammatical, i.e. morphosyntactic.

[9] On phonological transfer see Schrijver in this volume.

[10] Uriel Weinreich, *Languages in Contact* (The Hague, 1953, repr. 1968); Sarah G. Thomason and Terrence Kaufman, *Language Contact: Creolization, and Genetic Linguistics* (Berkeley and Los Angeles, 1988); Sarah G. Thomason, *Language Contact: An Introduction* (Washington DC, 2001); Donald Winford, *An Introduction to Contact Linguistics* (Oxford, 2003).

[11] Cf. James Milroy, 'A Social Model for the Interpretation of Language Change,' in *History of Englishes: New Methods and Interpretations in Historical Linguistics*, ed. Matti Rissanen, Ossi Ihalainen, Terttu Nevalainen and Irma Taavaitsainen (Berlin, 1992), pp. 72–91.

dialects are maintained within one and the same society, and one of them carries more prestige than the other and consequently may be more widely used than the other, then linguists speak of 'diglossia'.[12] Most borrowing, however, takes place between the languages of adjacent population groups. Borrowing may, of course, also take place between the languages of non-adjacent peoples, such as, for instance, all European languages now borrow extensively from British and American English as the languages of globalizing economies.[13] Shift scenarios, on the other hand, involve the language death of source languages and restructuring of target languages.

These two contact scenarios (*borrowing* and *shift*) seem to be subject to different patterns of feature transfer between languages. The *borrowing* gradient depends on the intensity and length of contact as well as on the socio-economic structures involved. Nouns are commonly transferred first, then verbs and adjectives. Function words are only borrowed in cases of very intensive contact.[14]

The different types of *shift* scenarios depend on the social prestige of the people involved and the power relationships between the social groups; these determine the direction of the shift. In fifth- and sixth-century Britain, supposing an elite dominance situation, linguistic contact may have taken place between a relatively small military elite, i.e. the social group in power, and the subservient population. The members of the evolving elite were originally speakers of prestigious varieties of Germanic (Frisian, Saxon, Anglian, Jutish, Frankish),[15] while the bulk of the population is likely to have consisted of low prestige speakers of Late British and/or British Latin in the Lowlands and Late British in the Uplands.[16] These seem to have shifted to the evolving Old English dialects over quite some time (fifth to ninth century).[17] The shift pattern is likely to have been uneven and variously conditioned, with some areas, such as in the south-east, shifting much earlier than the north and south-west, with pockets in remoter areas preserving their British cultural and linguistic identity longer than elsewhere.[18] In all prob-

---

[12] Charles A. Ferguson, 'Diglossia', *Word* 15 (1959), 325–340; Joshua A. Fishman, 'Bilingualism with and without Diglossia, Diglossia with and without Bilingualism', *Journal of Social Issues* 23 (1979), 29–38.

[13] *A Dictionary of European Anglicisms*, ed. Manfred Görlach (Oxford, 2001); *An Annotated Bibliography of European Anglicisms*, ed. Manfred Görlach (Oxford, 2002); *English in Europe*, ed. Manfred Görlach (Oxford 2002).

[14] See Thomason and Kaufman, *Language Contact*, pp. 74–7 ('Borrowing Scale').

[15] Cf. Hans Frede Nielsen, *The Continental Backgrounds of English and its Insular Development until 1154* (Odense, 1998), pp. 77–9; Peter Trudgill, *New-Dialect Formation: The Inevitability of Colonial Englishes* (Edinburgh, 2004), p. 11.

[16] For British Latin in the island of Britain, see Peter Schrijver, *Studies in British Celtic Historical Phonology* (Amsterdam, 1995); 'The Rise and Fall of British Latin', in *The Celtic Roots of English*, ed. Markku Filppula *et al.*, pp. 87–110.

[17] Ward-Perkins, 'Why did the Anglo-Saxons', 258, suggested that the successful native resistance of local, militarised tribal societies to the invaders may perhaps account for the fact of the slow progress of Anglo-Saxonisation as opposed to the sweeping conquest of Gaul by the Franks.

[18] On the existence of the *Wal-* element in English place names, indicating the presence of identifiable 'others' in the Anglo-Saxon naming period, see J. R. R. Tolkien, 'English and

ability the *shift* process was one of adults and not of children, as children up to around seven years of age learn second languages as native children do,[19] i.e. with no transfers from the source languages.[20]

Strata linguistics
The study of strata linguistics began as early as the nineteenth century. In 1881–2, the Italian dialectologist Graciadio Ascoli (1829–1907)[21] suggested that the origin of the differences within and across the Romance languages[22] were due to the interaction between colonising speakers of (vulgar) Latin and speakers of what he termed *il sostratto* ('substrate' languages), such as Etruscan or the Celtic languages of Gallia Cisalpina and Gaulish in Gallia Transalpina.[23] The term *substrate* refers to the languages of the speakers colonised by the Romans, who had no prestige and power. The terms *superstrate* and *adstrate* were coined later;[24] *superstrate* denotes a prestige language forcibly imposed upon substrate speakers and *adstrate* denotes two (or more) prestige languages in collateral interaction with each other.

Welsh', in *Angles and Britons*, O'Donnell Lectures (Cardiff, 1963), pp. 1–41, at pp. 26ff.; Margaret L. Faull, 'The Semantic Development of Old English *wealh*', *Leeds Studies in English* 9 (1976), 20–44; Kenneth Cameron, 'The Meaning and Significance of Old English *walh* in English Place-names', *Journal of the English Place-Name Society* 12 (1979/80), 1–53; Michael Cichon, 'Indigenous "foreigners": Legal, Poetic and Historical Sources for Old English *wealh*' (paper given at the 12th International Congress of Celtic Studies, University of Wales, Aberystwyth, 26 August 2003, publication forthcoming). On the social structure of Anglo-Saxon England, see below, footnote 52.

[19] Jack Chambers, *Sociolinguistic Theory: Linguistic Variation and its Social Significance*, 2nd edn (Oxford, 2003), ch. 4.

[20] See below the section on psycholinguistics. I do not agree with Raymond Hickey, 'Early Contact and Parallels between English and Celtic', *Vienna English Working Papers* 4/2 (1995), 87–119, who suggests that the children of the Britons and the Anglo-Saxons played together and/or the Anglo-Saxons had Late-British-speaking nurses and that therefore the elite adopted linguistic features from Late British. Hickey cites parallel cases in the southern United States, where the language of superstratal whites is supposedly hard to distinguish from rural African-American Vernacular English, or in Finland, where superstratal Swedish-speaking Finns adopted prosodic features from Finnish. If child acquisition of Old English by speakers of Late British had obtained, it would be difficult to explain why the written Old English standard was kept remarkably free of Brittonicisms until the Norman Conquest.

[21] Graziado Isaia Ascoli, 'Die ethnologischen Gründe der sprachlichen Umgestaltungen', authorised translation of Ascoli's *Sprachwissenschaftliche Briefe* by Bruno Güterbock (Leipzig, 1887), pp. 13–45; first published in *Rivista di filologia e d'istruzione classica* 10 (1881–2); reprinted in *Substrate und Superstrate in den romanischen Sprachen*, ed. Reinhold Kontzi (Darmstadt, 1982), pp. 29–54.

[22] Cf. Walter von Wartburg, *Die Ausgliederung der romanischen Sprachräume* (Halle a.d.S., 1936).

[23] See also recently Salikoko S. Mufwene, 'Competition and Selection in Language Evolution', *Selection* 3 (2002), 45–56, at p. 53; 'Language Birth and Death', *Annual Review of Anthropology* 33 (2004), 201–222, at pp. 212ff.

[24] The term 'superstrate' was first used by Walter von Wartburg in 1932 and the term 'adstrate' in the same year by Marius Valkhoff; cf. Kontzi, *Substrate und Superstrate*, pp. 9–10.

When one language ('superstrate') is forcibly imposed upon the language of a subjected population ('substrate'), the sociolinguistic result, as mentioned before, may be that of 'diglossia'.[25] The 'high' language of the political elite (L_H), which symbolizes wealth, power and prestige, dominates the 'low' language (L_L) spoken by most of the population; indeed, the speakers of L_H may actively seek to suppress L_L. The outcome depends on the strategies of linguistic norm enforcement wielded by the respective political elite. Situations of diglossia may remain stable for short or long periods of time. This depends on the social barriers between the two groups of speakers. The type of social barrier will also determine the number of bilingual speakers of the respective languages. When the social barriers erode, diglossia leads to language *shift*, i.e. to the 'death' of one of the two languages. The shift process gives 'birth' to a modified form of the target language on account of inevitable, linguistic accommodation processes.[26]

There are two possible scenarios of linguistic shift, top down scenarios and bottom up scenarios, i.e. speakers of a substrate language (L_L) may shift to the language spoken by the superstrate speakers (L_H) or superstrate speakers (L_H) may shift to the language of the substrate language (L_L). Both scenarios are common. Which direction the shift takes depends on language-external factors, such as social structures and power conditions. In the following I leave aside the field of the sociology of language shift,[27] and confine myself to discussing some of its internal, i.e. linguistic aspects.

For the three basic types of strata contact (superstrate, substrate and adstrate), Theo Vennemann (1995) has proposed the following rules of thumb:[28]

(1) *Superstrate rule or lexical rule* (top down)
Superstrates exert influence on the *lexicon* of their substrates, especially in the areas of social contact but less so in the domains of morphosyntax and

---

[25] Cf. Ferguson, 'Diglossia' (footnote 12). Annette Sabban, 'Operationalising the Concept of Diglossia', in *The Celtic Englishes II*, ed. Hildegard L. C. Tristram (Heidelberg, 2000), pp. 18–39.

[26] Of the many publications on the topic of language death and birth, I only refer to three recent ones: Theo Vennemann, 'Sprachgeburt durch Sprachkontakt', in *Sprachtod und Sprachgeburt*, ed. Peter Schrijver and Peter-Arnold Mumm (Bremen, 2004), pp. 21–56; Peter Schrijver, 'Der Tod des Festlandkeltischen und die Geburt des Französischen, Niederländischen und Hochdeutschen', in *Sprachtod und Sprachgeburt*, ed. Peter Schrijver and Peter-Arnold Mumm, pp. 1–20; Salikoko Mufwene, 'Language Birth and Death' (see footnote 23 above).

[27] Cf. Joshua Fishman, *Readings in the Sociology of Language* (The Hague, 1968); *Advances in the Sociology of Language*, 2 vols. (The Hague, 1972); *The Sociolinguistics of Society* (Oxford, 1984).

[28] Theo Vennemann, 'Etymologische Beziehungen im Alten Europa', in *Der Ginkgo Baum*, Germanistisches Jahrbuch für Nordeuropa 13 (Helsinki, 1995); repr. in *Europa Vasconica – Europa Semitica*, ed. Patrizia Noel Aziz Hanna (Berlin, 2003), pp. 203–97.

phonology. Examples include Latin and British/Brittonic,[29] Anglo-Norman/ Angevin French and English,[30] and English and Welsh.[31]

(2a) *Substrate rule (morphosyntactic rule)* (bottom up)
Substrates exert influence on the morphosyntax and the phonology (prosody in particular) of their superstrates as well as on their idiomatic structure, and not (so much) on their lexicon. Examples include Gaulish and Latin,[32] Late British and English,[33] West Slavic and German,[34] Old Prussian (a Baltic language) and German,[35] and Latin or Greek and Arabic in the Middle East and North Africa.[36]

(2b) *Toponymic rule*
Substrates often determine the toponymy of their superstrates, while anthroponyms tend to behave like ordinary nouns, i.e. they do not influence their

[29] On the substantial influence of Latin on British/Brittonic, see Henry Jones, *Yr Elfen Ladin yn yr Iaith Gymraeg* (Cardiff, 1943), repr. 1980; Stefan Zimmer, 'Latin and Welsh', *Donum grammaticum. Studies in Latin and Celtic Linguistics in Honour of Hannah Rosén*, ed. Lea Sawicki and Donna Shalev (Leuven, 2002), pp. 395–406.

[30] The literature on this topic is legion and, because of the prestige of the French language as the language of Norman power and later of diplomacy and culture, the study of French loan words in English has attracted the special attention of scholars since the nineteenth century; see for instance Otto Jespersen, *Growth and Structure of the English Language* (Oxford, 1954; orig. pub. 1905), ch. V, pp. 85–113; repr. Oxford (with a foreword by Randolf Quirk, 1990), pp. 78–105; Fernand Mossé, 'On the Chronology of French Loan Words in English', *English Studies* 25 (1943), 33–40; Manfred Scheler, *Der englische Wortschatz* (Berlin, 1977), pp. 52–63; Xavier Dekeyser, 'Romance Loans in Middle English: a Re-assessment', in *Linguistics across Historical and Geographical Boundaries*, ed. Dieter Kastovsky and Aleksander Szwedek (Berlin, 1986), pp. 253–66; Thomason and Kaufman, *Language Contact*, pp. 306–15; David Burnley, '5. Lexis and Semantics', *The Cambridge History of the English Language*, ed. Richard M. Hogg, vol. VII, *1066–1476*, ed. Norman Blake (Cambridge, 1992), pp. 409–99 at pp. 423–32 (the influence of French); Julie Coleman, 'The Chronology of French and Latin Loan Words in English', *Transactions of the Philological Society* 93 (1995), 95–124.

[31] On the influence of English on Welsh, see for instance Thomas H. Parry-Williams, *The English Element in Welsh* (London, 1923), and 'English–Welsh Loan-Words', in *Angles and Britons*, ed. N. K. Chadwick, O'Donnell Lectures (Cardiff, 1963), pp. 42–59; Clive Grey, 'English Loanwords in Welsh: Some Aspects', (unpublished BA dissertation, Bangor, 1978). I am very grateful to Prof. Alan Thomas (Bangor) for pointing out this valuable study to me and to Clive Grey for allowing me to read a copy of it.

[32] Cf. Brigitte L. M. Bauer, 'Language Loss in Gaul: Socio-historical and Linguistic Factors in Language Conflict', *Southwest Journal of Linguistics* 15 (1996), 23–44; G. Woolf, *Becoming Roman: The Origins of Provincial Civilization in Gaul* (Cambridge, 1998).

[33] Due to widespread 'Anglo-Saxonism' not much research has been undertaken in this field until recently; see Gary German, 'Britons, Anglo-Saxons and Scholars: 19th Century Attitudes towards the Survival of Britons in Anglo-Saxon England', in *The Celtic Englishes II*, ed. Hildegard L. C. Tristram (Heidelberg, 2000), pp. 347–74.

[34] G. Bellmann, 'Slawisch/Deutsch', *Sprachgeschichte. Ein Handbuch zur Geschichte der deutschen Sprache und ihrer Erforschung*, ed. Werner Besch, O. Reichmann and S. Sonderegger, vol. 4 (Berlin, 2000), pp. 3229–59, at pp. 3230–5.

[35] G. Bellmann, 'Baltisch/Deutsch', *Sprachgeschichte. Ein Handbuch zur Geschichte der deutschen Sprache und ihrer Erforschung*, ed. Werner Besch *et al.*, pp. 3269–82, at p. 3272.

[36] Cf. R. H. Bulliet, *Conversion to Islam in the Medieval Period* (Cambridge, MA, 1979).

superstrates. Examples include 'native' place-names in Cornwall, Wales, Ireland, Scotland or North America.

(3) *Adstrate rule*
Adstrates exert influence on their adstrates on all levels but mostly on their lexicon. Examples include Old Norse and English in the Danelaw,[37] Vlaams/ Flemish and Walloon (in Belgium), and Finnish and Swedish (in Finland).

Since Late British served as a substrate to the nascent Old English dialects, we should therefore hardly expect any bottom up lexical transfer. What we should expect, however, is phonological and morpho-syntactic transfer, and this is exactly what we find in the early history of the English language. The domain of phonological transfer has been broached by Peter Schrijver.[38] I therefore limit myself to the field of morphosyntactic transfer. But before I discuss two of the more salient morphosyntactic transfer features ('calques') from Late British to English, I will very briefly point out three other recent, linguistic study fields which, beside contact and strata linguistics, are relevant to the understanding of how language shift works in general and how the shift from Late British to English may have worked in particular. These fields are creole studies, psycholinguistics and social psychology.

Creole studies
Within the English overseas colonies, from the beginning of the seventeenth to the twentieth centuries, large numbers of non-standard, English-speaking colonisers entered into contact with many different, ethno-linguistically heterogeneous populations.[39] As the different colonial economies varied, for example as trading colonies, exploitation/plantation colonies or settlement colonies,[40] so also did the complex, adaptive linguistic systems among the respective speakers, which arose as the outcome of linguistic contact.[41]

---

[37] John H. McWhorter, 'What happened to English?', *Diachronica* 19 (2002), 217–72; D. Gary Miller, 'The Morphosyntactic Legacy of the Scandinavian–English Contact', in *For the loue of Inglis lede*, ed. Marcin Krygier and Liliana Sikorska, Medieval English Mirror 1 (Frankfurt-am-Main, 2004), 9–39.

[38] Peter Schrijver, *Studies in British Celtic Historical Phonology* (Amsterdam and Atlanta, 1995); 'The Celtic Contribution to the Development of the North Sea Germanic Vowel System,' *NOWELE* 35 (1999), 3–47; 'The Rise and Fall of British Latin'; see also his contribution to this volume.

[39] *The Other Tongue: English across Cultures*, ed. B. Kachru (Urbana, IL, 1982); Klaus Hansen, Uwe Carls and Peter Lucko, *Die Differenzierung des Englischen in nationale Varianten* (Berlin, 1996); Tom McArthur, *The English Languages* (Cambridge, 1998).

[40] The same type of ecologies, of course, also obtained in the Portuguese, French and Dutch colonies.

[41] The publications in creole studies are legion. Suffice it to point out here Robert A. Hall Jr, *Pidgin and Creole Languages* (Ithaca, NY, 1966); *Pidginization and Creolization of Languages*, ed. Dell Hymes (Cambridge, 1971); Derek Bickerton, *Dynamics of a Creole System* (Cambridge, 1975); *Roots of Language* (Ann Arbor, MI, 1981); Robert B. LePage and Andrée Tabouret-Keller, *Acts of Identity: Creole-Based Approaches to Language and Ethnicity* (Cambridge, 1985); Peter Mühlhäusler, *Pidgin and Creole Linguistics* (Oxford, 1986: exp. and rev. ed., London, 1997); *Linguistic Ecology: Language Change and*

It has recently been shown that the processes underlying the birth of creoles and the speciation of genetically related languages are closely connected, if not the same.[42] Speakers invariably create and adapt languages according to their needs to adjust to changing socio-economic conditions. The adaptive processes depend on the respective linguistic input.[43] Speakers select those linguistic features from their contact languages which are salient and therefore serve their communication needs best.[44]

In the case of the contact situation between speakers of Late British and speakers of the Old English dialects, this may have been exactly what happened. The speakers of Late British shifted to the language of their conquerors and selected for transfer those features of their native language which were the most salient ones.[45]

Psycholinguistics

Contact linguistics, strata and creole studies explain *how* languages interact under specific contact conditions; they do not, however, explain the psychological aspects of the linguistic behaviour of the shifters. This falls into the domain of psycholinguistics.[46] Psycholinguistics deals with first language (L_1) and second language acquisition (L_2), bilingualism, code-switching, language shift and language loss.[47] Psycholinguistics also explores the age factor relevant

---

Linguistic Imperialism in the Pacific Region (London, 1996); John R. Rickford, *Dimensions of a Creole Continuum* (Stanford, CA, 1987); *Pidgins and Creoles – An Introduction*, ed. Jacques Arends, Pieter Muysken and Norval Smith (Amsterdam, 1995); Herman Wekker, *Creole Languages and Language Acquisition* (Berlin, 1996); Salikoko S. Mufwene, *The Ecology of Language Evolution* (Cambridge, 2001).

[42] Mufwene, *The Ecology*; 'Competition and Selection'.
[43] Cf. Susanne E. Carroll, *Input and Evidence: The Raw Material of Second Language Acquisition* (Amsterdam, 2000).
[44] On the impact of salience in dialect and language contact see Paul Kerswill and Anne Williams, '*Salience* as an Explanatory Factor in Language Change: Evidence from Dialect Levelling in Urban England', *Reading Working Papers in Linguistics* 4 (2000), 63–94.
[45] I am *not* arguing here that English is a creole on the basis of Late British *cum* the nascent Old English dialects prior to the advent of the Scandinavians. Nor would I subscribe to the views of Charles-James Bailey and Karl Maroldt ('The French Lineage of English', *Langues en contact* (Tübingen, 1977), pp. 21–53) nor to Patricia Poussa's view ('The Evolution of Early Standard English: the Creolization Hypothesis', *Studia Anglica Posnaniensa* 18 (1982), 69–85) that English has to be considered as a creole with French and Old Norse as input. There are, of course, broad and narrow definitions of what a 'creole' is; see for instance Bickerton's narrow view as opposed to Bailey and Marold's very broad view. In my understanding a 'creole' is a variety of a language where speakers of more than two languages in contact, with one of them a prestige language, form a new and independent communicative system by creatively restructuring the input features of the source languages. The restructuring process, however, is the same as in 'ordinary' 'bottom-up' or 'top-down' shift processes, only that the degree of congruence of the 'creole' with the input languages is much less pronounced.
[46] I gratefully acknowledge the help with this paragraph from my Potsdam colleagues Prof. Susanne E. Carroll and Dr Hartmut Burmeister. All errors and infelicities are, however, my own responsibility.
[47] From the host of publications in this field, I would like to single out Joshua A. Fishman, 'Bilingualism with and without Diglossia' (see footnote 12 above); Susan Gal, *Language*

for native-like acquisition of target languages. The proficiency of child and adult L_2 acquisition differs considerably. Adult L_2 learners are far less successful in their replication of target languages than children are: the younger the children, the better their proficiency.[48] Also of relevance is the distinction between 'naturalistic' or 'unmonitored' acquisition modes and acquisition by 'special monitoring', such as structured acquisition in the classroom.[49]

Psycholinguistics is a vast and fast developing field of research that I cannot go into in any detail here. I will only mention those basics, which may be relevant to our problem as to what happened when the speakers of Late British chose to speak the nascent Old English dialects.

There seems to be a two-stage, natural time course operating in unmonitored L_1 and 'bottom up' L_2 acquisition. The first stage is that of the acquisition of the lexicon, i.e. the vocabulary. The second stage is that of the acquisition of morphosyntax. The difference between L_1 and L_2 acquisition of morphosyntax lies in the observation that, especially among adult L_2 learners, speakers often remain restricted to a pidgin type version of L_2, i.e. they largely communicate with lexicon but without, or with only little, 'correct' morphosyntax.[50] This phenomenon is called 'fossilisation'. In spite of a long exposure to the target language, adult L_2 speakers commonly do not improve their proficiency in the grammatical replication of the target language. Thus, in the case of adult, 'bottom up' L_2 acquisition, the learners usually tend to acquire the L_2 lexicon consciously and deliberately, while the morphosyntax (and phonology) of the target language are acquired unconsciously and imperfectly. The imperfectly acquired and fossilised L_2 structures are then passed on by the learners to their children. In situations of slow language shift over a number of generations, the fossilisations may then become grammaticalised.[51]

Shift (New York, 1979); René Appel and Pieter Muysken, *Language Contact and Bilingualism* (London, 1987); Terence Odlin, *Language Transfer: Cross-linguistic Influence in Language Learning* (Cambridge, 1989); Don Kulick, *Language Shift and Cultural Reproduction* (Cambridge, 1992); *One Speaker: Two Languages. Cross-disciplinary Perspectives on Code-switching*, ed. Lesley Milroy and Pieter Muyskens (Cambridge, 1995); Suzanne Romaine, *Bilingualism* (Oxford, 1995); Josiane F. Hamers and Michel H. A. Blanc, *Bilinguality and Bilingualism* (Cambridge, 2000); Susanne E. Carroll, *Input and Evidence*, and 'Language Contact from a Developmental Perspective', in *The Celtic Englishes II*, ed. Hildegard L. C. Tristram (Heidelberg, 2000), pp. 9–17.

[48] Psycholinguists consider the proficiency of twelve-year-olds as already that of adult learners (personal communication, Susanne Carroll, Potsdam, 31/10/03).

[49] See for instance *Bilingualism across the Lifespan: Aspects of Acquistion, Maturity and Loss*, ed. Kenneth Hyltenstam and Loraine K. Obler (Cambridge, 1989); *Trends in Bilingual Acquisition*, ed. Jasone Cenoz and Fred Genesee (Amsterdam, 2001); Fred Genesee, Johanne Paradis and Martha B. Crago, *Dual Language Development and Disorders* (Baltimore and London, 2004).

[50] Cf. T. Givón, L. Yang and M. A. Gernsbacher, 'The Processing of Second Language Vocabulary: From Attended to Automated Word-recognition', *Institute of Cognitive & Decision Sciences, Technical Report* No. 90–4 (n.d.), 1–19, at p. 1. (I owe access to this publication to Dr Hartmut Burmeister, Potsdam.)

[51] A prime example in modern times of a slow shift over many generations occurred in Ireland between the seventeenth and the twentieth centuries. Here adult learners passed on their

In the case of our Britons acquiring the dialects of Old English, the first step thus seems to have been that of unstructured adult acquisition of the Old English target dialects as L_2. Perhaps, initially, there may have been only a small stable group of adult bilinguals who mediated between the speakers of Late British and the Old English dialects. Social segregation, as in Ireland before the end of the eighteenth century, may have generally kept the two population groups apart. As long as the social barrier lasted, this scenario will have meant for adult bilinguals a native-like acquisition of the lexicon but transfer on the level of phonology and morphosyntax because of their unconscious, imperfect replication of the target language. In the course of time, however, the number of bilinguals increased. This would eventually have led to child language acquisition. Children would have learned the imperfectly acquired L_2 from their parents as their L_1 and subsequently passed on their linguistic knowledge of the modified target language to their own children.

From the textual evidence we have, the social barriers between the free and land-holding elite of Anglo-Saxon society and their dependents were perhaps fairly stable until the advent of the Normans.[52] I would thus assume that the diglossia between Late British-derived Old English$_L$ and elite Old English$_H$, spoken by the comparatively small number of people forming the aristocracy, was very pronounced. Only the language of the elite, the high variety of Old English narrowly monitored and standardised, seems to have been codified in writing, and it was this version of the language which remained remarkably constant over many centuries. This written code continued to be adhered to until the effect of the Norman Conquest was increasingly felt in the twelfth century, when the spoken language of the erstwhile illiterate mass of the population – arguably of largely British extraction – made inroads into the written vernacular.[53]

---

fossilised L_2 phonology and morphosyntax to their children to the effect that present-day Irish English is easily recognisable by its pronunciation, prosody, grammar and phraseology, while lexical transfers from Irish are rather limited. Knowledge of lexical Irishisms is rapidly decreasing among the young generation, as a Potsdam study in the 1990s, on the recognition of Irishisms by Irish university students compared to over-sixty-year-old interviewees, has shown. For the early contact situation between Irish and English, see for instance Raymond Hickey, 'An Assessment of Language Contact in the Development of Irish English', *Linguistic Change under Contact Conditions*, ed. Jacek Fisiak (Berlin, 1995), pp. 109–30, at pp. 113ff., and 'Arguments for Creolisation in Irish English', in *Language History and Linguistic Modelling. A Festschrift for Jacek Fisiak*, ed. Raymond Hickey and Stanisław Puppel (Berlin, 1997), pp. 969–1038, at pp. 977–81.

[52] On the social structure of Anglo-Saxon England, see, for instance, Dorothy Whitelock, *The Beginnings of English Society*, Pelican History of England 2 (Harmondsworth, 1952), pp. 111ff.; Stenton, *ASE*, 3rd edn (Oxford, 1971), pp. 141–8; Heinrich Härke, 'Early Anglo-Saxon Social Structure', in *The Anglo-Saxons from the Migration Period to the Eighth Century*, ed. John Hines (Woodbridge, 1997), pp. 125–70 at pp. 141–8. On slavery in Anglo-Saxon England and the mixed ethnic origin of the unfree population, see David Pelteret, 'Slave Raiding and Slave Trading in Early England', *ASE* 9 (1981), 99–114, and *Slavery in Early Medieval England* (Woodbridge, 1995). See also footnote 18 above.

[53] Heinrich Härke, 'Kings and Warriors: Population and Landscape from Post-Roman to Norman Britain', in *The Peopling of Britain: the Shaping of a Human Landscape*, ed. Paul Slack and Ryk Ward, Linacre Lectures 1999 (Oxford, 2002), pp. 145–75; Hildegard L. C.

Social psychology: Speech accommodation theory

Why would substrate speakers want to acquire the language of their masters? What would their personal motivation be? The trivial answer is, of course, because of their desire to partake in the prestige, social advancement and economic success of the elite and above all because of their desire to gain access to the social benefits associated with prestige status. Bilingual speakers already have social advantages compared to monolingual substrate speakers.[54] The main incentive for superstrate, second language acquisition in diglossic societies therefore is utilitarian.

On the psychological level the basis for this utilitarian behaviour has been explained by the linguistic adaptability of individual speakers as well as groups of speakers. In order to communicate effectively, people unconsciously adapt their linguistic behaviour to that of their interlocutors. The mental attitude which fuels the desire to communicate successfully leads the speaker to adjust her/his speech to that of her/his interlocutor. Without speaker accommodation, linguistic interaction would not be possible, as we would all be idiosyncratic speakers of our own idiolects. The extent of adjustment depends on a large variety of psychological factors.[55] Speaker accommodation as a social technique operates in all communicative situations, including those of inter-language communication and L_2 acquisition.[56]

Tristram, 'Diglossia in Anglo-Saxon England, or What was spoken Old English like?', *Studia Anglica Posnaniensia* 40 (2004), 87–110.

[54] Cf. Pierre Bourdieu's theory of 'superlégitimation' of speakers who are able to make use of more than one language in the 'marché linguistique', when they have access to the 'symbolic capital' of the prestige language: Bourdieu, *Ce que parler veut dire: l'économie des échanges linguistiques* (Paris, 1982); *Language and Symbolic Power* (Oxford, 1991); *Langage et pouvoir symbolique* (Paris, 2001).

[55] Speech Accommodation Theory was developed in the 1960s and 70s by Howard Giles and his colleagues. See Giles and Robert N. St. Clair (1979), eds., *Language and Social Psychology* (Oxford, 1979); Giles and P. M. Smith, 'Accommodation Theory: Optimal Levels of Convergence', in *Language and Social Psychology*, ed. Giles and St. Clair (Oxford, 1979), pp. 45–65; Giles, 'Accommodation Theory: Some New Directions', in *Aspects of Linguistic Behaviour, Festschrift for R. B. LePage*, ed. M. V. S. de Silva, York Papers in Linguistics (York, 1980); R. L. Street and Howard Giles, 'Speech Accommodation Theory', in *Social Cognition and Communication*, ed. M. Roloff and C. R. Berger (Beverly Hills, CA, 1982), pp. 193–226; Giles, Nikolas Coupland and Justine Coupland, 'Accommodation Theory. Communication, Context, Consequences', in *Contexts of Accommodation, Developments in Applied Linguistics*, ed. Giles, Coupland and Coupland (Cambridge, 1991), pp. 1–68.

[56] Speech Accommodation Theory originally arose out of four different theories developed in social psychology, which have found wide acceptance: *similarity attraction theory* (people need approval from others to be able to successfully communicate among each other), *social exchange theory* (people minimize their social costs and maximize their social rewards in communicating with each other), *causal attribution theory* (people constantly attribute causes to their interlocutors' motives and intentions when communicating) and *intergroup distinctiveness theory* (people constantly compare themselves across social groups on valued social dimensions, concerning power, social prestige, possessions etc.). Cf. Leslie M. Beebe and Howard Giles, 'Speech Accommodation Theories: A Discussion in Terms of Second-Language Acquisition', *International Journal of the Sociology of Language* 46 (1984), 5–32; Leslie M. Beebe, 'Five Sociolinguistic Approaches to Second

Supposing that social behaviour did not change much in this respect over the past 1,500 years, the insights of modern social psychology may also have had some relevance to the motivations of speakers of Late British in their desire to adapt themselves linguistically and to communicate as effectively as possible with Anglo-Saxon speakers of higher status.

Transfer from Late British to the Anglo-Saxon Dialects

What was spoken Old English like, the language of the bulk of the population? Unfortunately, we know nothing about spoken Old English to the extent that it differed from the language as it was committed to writing, which was an instrument of power enforcement in the hands of a very few monastics belonging to the elite. In Old English literature we seldom hear about non-aristocratic people; they were given no voice.[57] The spoken language only became visible (literally) after the Norman Conquest, after William the Conqueror effectively replaced the Anglo-Saxon aristocracy by Norman-French speaking barons, clerics and their followers. Spoken Old English therefore only started to be admitted to the realm of writing at the beginning of the twelfth century: witness the so-called 'Continuations' of the *Peterborough Chronicle*.[58]

As pointed out before, elite written Old English was kept remarkably unchanged over the long period of Anglo-Saxon cultural and political dominance. The continued use of the Irish-derived insular script saw only minor adaptations of the graphemes (use of runic characters etc.). The limited spelling variations, e.g. West Saxon <y> for earlier <ie>, matched the rather unexciting dialect variations between early recorded Northumbrian and the later Mercian, Kentish, Northumbrian and West Saxon written dialects. These suggest that the Anglo-Saxon elite, as mentioned before, used the technology of writing for the purposes of the creation and maintenance of ethnic identity[59] and the affirmative unity of

---

Language Acquisition', in *Issues in Second Language Acquisition. Multiple Perspectives*, ed. Beebe (New York, 1988), pp. 43–77 at pp. 61–8.

[57] There are very few exceptions, such as the mention of the cowherd Cædmon in Bede's *HE* IV, 24, who bears a Brittonic name, and the swineherd (OE *swan*) in the entry of the *Anglo-Saxon Chronicle* (Parker MS) for AD 754 and 755, who revenged his master named Cumbra, another Brittonic name, by killing his murderer, the deposed king of the West Saxons, Sigebryht. For the complete text of this *Chronicle* entry, see *The Anglo-Saxon Chronicle: A Collaborative Edition*, vol. 4, *MS A*, ed. Janet Bately (Cambridge, 1986), *sub anno* 755.

[58] *The Peterborough Chronicle 1070–1154*, ed. Cecily Clark (Oxford, 1957, 2nd edn 1970); Tristram, 'Diglossia' (footnote 53 above), pp. 89ff. Interestingly, the earliest documents issued by William's administration were written in the OE standard, as Anglo-Norman had not been codified as yet.

[59] Witness for instance the evidence of the heroic epic *Beowulf*. Its singular copy is contained in the Nowell Codex (BL MS Cotton Vitellius A.xv), dated between the end of the tenth century (Neil R. Ker) and the earlier eleventh century (Kevin S. Kiernan). The historical distance between the sixth century in which the plot of *Beowulf* is set and the extant text in the manuscript directed at an elite audience is remarkable. The very uniformity of the use of the Old English language and even more so the transparency of the Old English names of

their culture.⁶⁰ The Benedictine Reform enforced the uniformity of the written standard across the entire area of England.⁶¹ When this standard was devalued under the Normans, the spoken language became more socially acceptable and eventually assumed the status of a written code. This was no unified interregional code but a localised and, in a number of cases, even personalised one.⁶² In a recent paper I suggested that early Middle English reflected spoken Old English, because the written divide between Old and Middle English was only apparent.⁶³ The real communicative divide came with the massive influx of French lexis, especially between the end of the thirteenth and the fifteenth centuries. French lexis estranged the language so much that sixteenth-century Renaissance scholars did not consider the earlier period to be 'English' but 'Saxon'⁶⁴ and led scholars

---

the characters in the poem show that the time depth of the story was deliberately telescoped into a uniform ethnic present. On the dating of *Beowulf* see Kevin S. Kiernan, *Beowulf and the Beowulf Manuscript* (New Brunswick, NJ, 1981); Colin Chase, *The Dating of Beowulf* (Toronto, 1997). On the elite character of the four poetic manuscripts and their political background in the tenth-century Benedictine Reform, see Gunhild Zimmermann, *The Four Old English Poetic Manuscripts. Texts, Contexts and Historical Background* (Heidelberg, 1995).

60 Cf. John Hines, 'The Becoming of the English: Identity, Material Culture and Language in Early Anglo-Saxon England', *Anglo-Saxon Studies in Archaeology and History* 7 (1994), 49–59; 'Britain after Rome: Between Monoculturalism and Multiculturalism', in *Cultural Identity and Archaeology: The Construction of European Communities*, ed. Paul Graves-Brown, Siân Jones and Clive Gamble (London, 1996), pp. 256–70; 'Welsh and English: Mutual Origins in Post-Roman Britain?', *Studia Celtica* 34 (2000), 812–84; 'Attitude Problems? The Old Saxon and Old English *Genesis* Poems', in *Language Structure and Variation*, ed. Magnus Ljung (Stockholm, 2000), pp. 69–90, esp. at p. 78; Walter Pohl, 'Conceptions of Ethnicity in Early Medieval Studies', *Archaeologia Polona* 29 (1991), 39–49; 'Ethnic Names and Identities in the British Isles: A Comparative Perspective', in *The Anglo-Saxons from the Migration Period to the Eighth Century*, ed. John Hines, pp. 7–40 (see footnote 52 above).

61 Lucia Kornexl, '*Concordes equali consuetudinis usu* – Monastische Normierungsbestrebungen und sprachliche Standardisierung in spätaltenglischer Zeit', in *Prozesse der Normbildung und Normveränderung im mittelalterlichen Europa*, ed. D. Ruhe and Karl-Heinz Spieß (Stuttgart, 2000), pp. 237–73; Mechthild Gretsch, 'Winchester Vocabulary and Standard Old English: the Vernacular in Late Anglo-Saxon England', The T. Northcote Toller Memorial Lecture 2000, *Bulletin of the John Rylands University Library of Manchester* 83 (Manchester, 2001), 41–87; 'In Search of Standard Old English', in *Bookmarks from the Past. Studies in English Language and Literature in Honour of Helmut Gneuss*, ed. Lucia Kornexl and U. Lenker (Frankfurt, 2003), pp. 33–67.

62 As for instance the twelfth-century *Ormulum*; cf. Robert Burchfield, 'The Language and Orthography of the *Ormulum* MS', *Transactions of the Philological Society* 54 (1956), 56–87; Manfred Markus, 'The Spelling Peculiarities of the *Ormulum* from an Interdisciplinary Point of View: a Reappraisal', in *Studies in Mediaeval English Literature and its Tradition: A Festschrift for Karl Heinz Göller*, ed. Uwe Böker, Manfred Markus and Rainer Schöwerling (Stuttgart, 1985), pp. 69–86; Stephen Morrison, 'Vernacular Literary Activity in Twelfth-Century England: Redressing the Balance', in *Culture politique des Plantagenêt (1154–1224)*, ed. M. Aurell (Poitiers, 2003), pp. 253–67; Meg Worley, 'Using the *Ormulum* to Redefine Vernacularity', in *The Vulgar Tongue: Medieval and Postmedieval Vernacularity*, ed. Fiona Somerset and Nicholas Watson (University Park, PA, 2003), pp. 19–30.

63 Tristram, 'Diglossia' (see footnote 53 above).

64 See Angelika Lutz, 'When did English begin?', in *Sounds, Words, Texts and Change*.

like Reinard W. Zandvoort to pose the question whether or not 'English' should be considered as a Germanic language.[65]

Grammatical features
In which areas of morphosyntax is substrate transfer from Late British to spoken Anglo-Saxon most likely to have occurred? In my 2002 paper given at Mekrijärvi, I suggested that, beside other features,[66] the attrition of nominal inflexions and consequently the rise of a fixed word order are the least ambiguous transfer features from Late British because these already showed in Old Welsh texts.[67] Another very likely transfer feature not linked to the attrition of noun inflexions concerns the syntax of the verbal nucleus of the verb phrase and, here in particular, the development of periphrastic constructions (periphrastic aspect, periphrastic DO).

The typological change of English from a predominantly synthetic language to a predominantly analytical language and the consequent loss of inflexions, have commonly been attributed to two causes, either to language contact between Old English and Old Norse or to the prosodic impact of the strong stress on the (first) stem syllable of a lexeme. Both hypotheses can be refuted on cross-linguistic evidence. Spoken Old Norse was as strongly inflected as written OE_H. Even if the Scandinavians had only communicated with the Anglo-Saxon elite, why should this contact involving two inflected languages have led to the attrition

---

Selected Papers from 11 ICEHL, Santiago de Compostela, 7–11 September 2000, ed. Teresa Fanego and Elena Seoane (Amsterdam, 2002), pp. 145–71.

[65] Reinard W. Zandvoort, 'Is English a Germanic Language?', in *Collected Papers II* (Groningen, 1955/1970), pp. 54–66.

[66] Morphosyntactic transfer features, which have been proposed as to their possible origin in Late British, are discussed by W. Preussler, 'Keltischer Einfluss im Englischen', *Revue des Langues Vivantes* 22 (1956), 322–50; David L. White, 'Brittonic Influence in English', unpublished undergraduate thesis (Austin, TX, 1987); 'Explaining the Innovations of Middle English', pp. 169 f.; 'On the Areal Pattern of "Brittonicity" in English and its Implications', in *The Celtic Englishes IV*, ed. Hildegard L. C. Tristram (Potsdam, 2006), pp. 306–35; Hildegard L. C. Tristram, *How Celtic is Standard English?* (Saint Petersburg, 1999); 'The Politics of Language: Links between Modern Welsh and English', in *'Of dyuersitie & chaunge of langage.' Essays Presented to Manfred Görlach on the Occasion of his 65th Birthday*, ed. Katja Lenz and Ruth Möhlig (Heidelberg, 2002), pp. 257–75, at p. 272.

[67] Tristram, 'Attrition' (see footnote 6 above). The following four criteria need to be met for the possible identification of morphosyntactic parallels between English and Welsh as transfer features: the *priority of attestation*, the *frequency of occurrence*, the *conformity with other syntactic structures in the source language* and the *degree of grammaticalisation* in the source language; see Hildegard L. C. Tristram, 'The Celtic Englishes – Zwei grammatische Beispiele zum Problem des Sprachkontaktes zwischen dem Englischen und den keltischen Sprachen', in *Akten des zweiten deutschen Keltologensymposiums (Bonn, 2.–4. April 1997)*, ed. Stefan Zimmer, Rolf Ködderitzsch and Arndt Wigger (Tübingen, 1999), pp. 254–76, at p. 274; Tristram, 'The Politics of Language', pp. 257–75, at p. 270; see Thomason and Kaufman, *Language Contact*, pp. 93 f. for a different catalogue of requirements as evidence for the assumption of contact-induced language change; see also Erich Poppe, 'Zu den "erweiterten Formen" des Englischen und der inselkeltischen Sprachen', *Sprachwissenschaft* 27 (2002), 249–81.

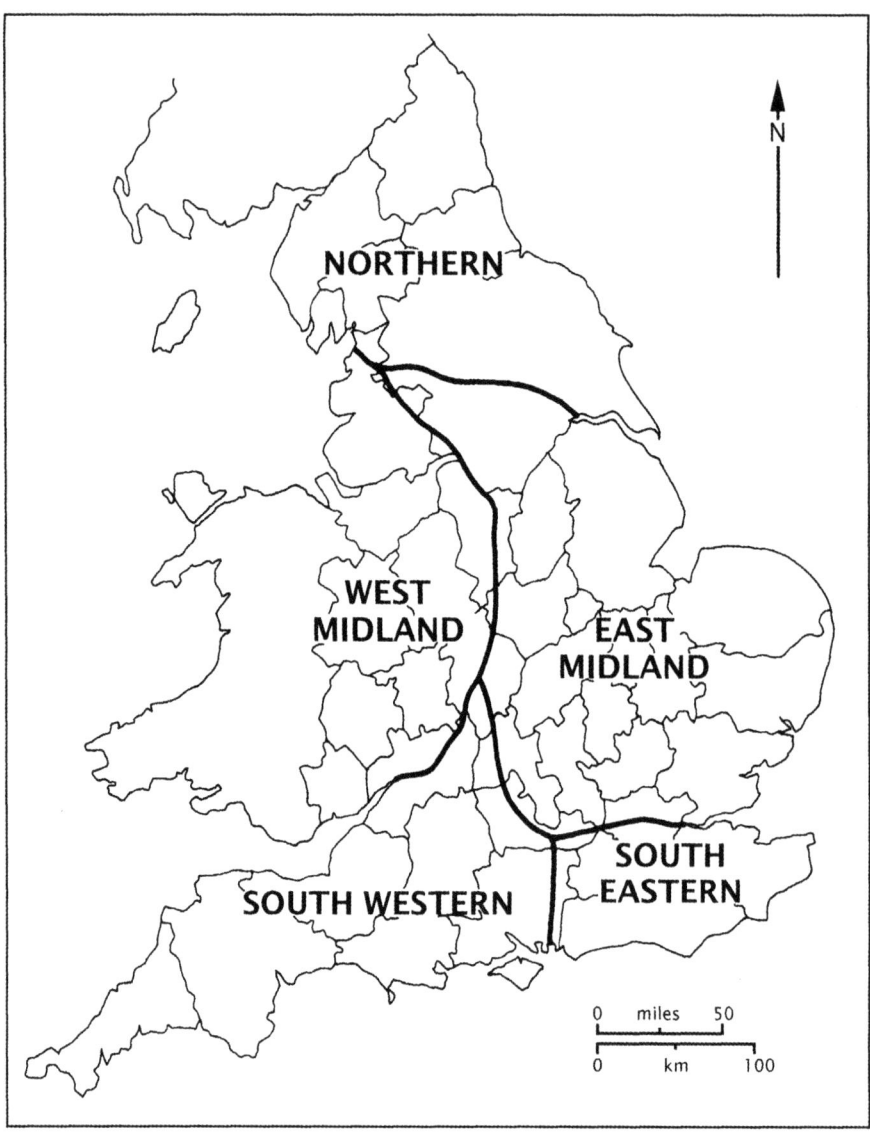

15.1 Map of English regional dialects, taken from Lilo Moessner and Ursula Schaefer, Proseminar Mittelenglisch (Darmstadt, 1974), p. 126; see also George L. Brook, English Dialects (London, 1963), p. 60.

of inflexions? This hypothesis is not empirically borne out by cross-linguistic evidence. German ethnic groups in Russia, for instance, who shifted to Russian in the twentieth century did not do away with the Russian inflexions. If the strong initial accent was responsible for the attrition of unstressed syllables, why did High German not lose its inflexions?

Another hypothesis that has been advanced to explain the loss of inflexions is to suppose that the languages of the western European seaboard took part in the common typological drift of the Indo-European languages in Europe from a predominantly synthetic character to a predominantly analytic character, with Vulgar Latin, Welsh and English leading the way.[68] But why should English seemingly have developed its analyticity only in the Middle English period?

The rise of periphrastic aspect (imperfective vs. perfective) and DO periphrasis have been variously explained as having been influenced by Latin or French participial constructions.[69] However, Latin, as the language of learning, and societal French were superstratal languages with respect to spoken English and as such are unlikely to have influenced the syntax of their substrate (see above, p. 196).

The most likely hypothesis for both the nominal attrition of inflexions and the verbal periphrases is that of transfer through 'bottom-up' shift from Late British to Old English dialects. This transfer arguably started during the first centuries of the Anglicization of Britain and showed in written form during the Middle English period. This hypothesis will be further explored in the following.

Two innovative areas

Compared to the written Old English standard, the Middle English dialect zones reveal two innovating areas on the level of morphosyntax, the northern dialect zone and the south- western dialect zone. Interestingly, the attrition of inflexion was first attested in the northern zone and verbal periphrases seem to have arisen in the south-western zone. David White has argued that attrition is due to the substratal contact of English with a substantial Late-British-speaking population as well as with later adstratal Old Norse, which reinforced the attrition already under way when the Scandinavians started to settle. White has also suggested that the rise of verbal periphrases derived from the contact of West Saxon with substratal Late British speakers. Wessex had relatively few contacts with the

---

[68] Cf. Uwe Hinrichs and Uwe Büttner, eds., *Die europäischen Sprachen auf dem Weg zum analytischen Sprachtyp* (Wiesbaden, 2004). Unfortunately, and perhaps rather tellingly, the discussion of the Celtic languages is not included in this book. On the hypothesis of the typological cycle of long term development from syntheticity to analyticity and back to syntheticity, see Carleton T. Hodge, 'The Linguistic Cycle', *Language Sciences* 13 (1970), 1–7. On drift see Edward Sapir, *Language* (New York, 1921), ch. VII 'Language as a Historical Product: Drift'; Theo Vennemann, 'An Explanation of Drift', in *Word Order and Word Order Change*, ed. Charles N. Li (Austin, TX, and London, 1975), pp. 269–305; Dieter Kastovsky, 'The "Invisible hand," Drifts, and Typological Shifts. Examples from English', in *A Companion to Linguistics. A Festschrift for Anders Ahlqvist on the occasion of his sixtieth birthday*, ed. Bernadette Smelik *et al.* (Münster, 2005), pp. 286–95.

[69] See for instance Tauno Mustanoja, *A Middle English Syntax. I: Parts of Speech* (Helsinki, 1960).

Scandinavians.[70] These innovations are significant, as they seem to have diffused from their respective focal centres over the centuries until they entered Standard English from the Tudor period onward. It is telling that these 'innovations' have close parallels in the Old Welsh and Middle Welsh texts.[71] It can be assumed quite independently that they originated in Late British.[72]

As I discussed the attrition of inflexions *in extenso* in my Mekrijärvi article,[73] I will not repeat myself here but concentrate instead on the rise of the south-western feature of verbal periphrasis.

Periphrastic aspect

The most salient south-western innovations occurred in the verb phrase (VP). Here the Late British-speaking learners of Old English seem to have modelled the syntax of the VP of their target language on analytic constructions of the Late British VP. These analytic constructions consisted of a form of the verb **BOT** + *yn* (construction marker) + **Verbal Noun** (VN)[74] in order to express the semantic category of aspect, here the imperfective aspect ('progressive') in the present tense. In the past tense, imperfective aspect was grammaticalised synthetically in Late British and Old Welsh by distinctive verbal inflexions. These marked the perfective aspect by *preterite* inflectional endings (also called 'aorist' in Welsh grammar books) and the imperfective aspect by *imperfect* inflectional endings,

---

[70] David L. White, 'Explaining the Innovations of Middle English: What, Where, and Why?', in *The Celtic Roots of English*, ed. Markku Filppula et al., pp. 153–74; 'Brittonic Influence in the Reductions of Middle English Nominal Morphology,' in *The Celtic Englishes III*, ed. Hildegard L. C. Tristram (Heidelberg, 2003), pp. 29–45; 'On the Areal Pattern of "Brittonicity" in English'.

[71] As a typical colonial substrate language, Brittonic under the Romans was not recorded. We have to resort to Old Welsh and Middle Welsh texts as the closest cognates to Late British for comparison with English. Cf. Patrick Sims-Williams, *The Celtic Inscriptions of Britain: Phonology and Chronology, c. 400–1200* (Oxford, 2003).

[72] There is a methodological problem to be considered here. Welsh is not the direct descendant of the Late British (and British Latin) spoken by the language shifters in the Lowland and Upland Zones. The Welsh language is a descendant of a peripheral variety of Late British. In dialect research it is common knowledge that peripheral dialects tend to be more conservative that dialects spoken in more focal centres. It therefore has to be assumed that central Late British was more advanced in its developmental stages from, among other features, syntheticity to analycity than the ancestor of Medieval and Modern Welsh. But since, unfortunately, we have no coherent records of central Late British, the closest we can get is Old Welsh and Middle Welsh. It may be assumed, however, that their broad developmental tendencies may have been similar to those varieties of Late British in the central areas.

[73] Hildegard L. C. Tristram, 'Attrition' (see footnote 6 above).

[74] Welsh **BOT** means 'be'. It is important to note that the Celtic languages do not have infinitives (INF) but verbal nouns (VN). Among the infinite verb forms of Indo-European languages, the grammatical category of the *verbal noun* needs to be formally distinguished from the *infinitive* and also from common nouns denoting actions (*action nouns*). The VN is inflected for all cases, and it governs a genitive attribute instead of an accusative object, as the INF of a transitive verb did in Old English and in other Germanic languages. On the morphosyntax of the VN in Welsh, see Stefan Schumacher, *The Historical Morphology of the Welsh Verbal Noun* (Maynooth, 2000). For the Celtic languages in general, see Jean Gagnepain, *La syntaxe du nom verbal dans les langues celtiques* (Paris, 1963).

much as in Classical French (*passé simple vs. imparfait*) or as in Spanish (*pretérito vs. imperfecto*), Italian (*passato remoto vs imperfetto*), the South Slavic languages, Albanian, Classical Greek and Modern Greek.[75] Learners of Old English are likely to have felt the need to express the distinction between perfectivity and imperfectivity in addition to the rather simple tense marking of their 'Germanic' Old English. They resorted to a calque of analytic constructions, such as in the present tense of Late British, the use of which, by overgeneralisation, came to be extended to mark imperfectivity in the past as well.[76] As Old English had no VN as a distinctive grammatical category that could be used for calquing Late British aspect marking,[77] the learners first seem to have resorted to the use of the OE present participle as the semantically closest infinite form. Such constructions occasionally surfaced in written OE_H, as shown for instance in the OE *Orosius*:[78]

swa hit **heofones tungul** on þæm tidun **cyþende wæron**[79]
*as **the stars of heaven were announcing** it in those times* (i.e. the birth of Alexander the Great)

hie þær mid micelre bliþnesse buton gemetgunge þæt win **drincende wæron**
*there **they were drinking** the wine with great joyfulness (and) without moderation*[80]

Dr Ilse Wischer analysed three sections of the Old English *Orosius* from the Helsinki Corpus comprising 8,660 words for the occurrence of periphrastic aspect forms. She found sixty-nine **BE + V-ende** constructions. This amounts to 8% of the verb forms used in these passages, quite an impressive result. Reading through the *Orosius* in Janet Bately's edition, I noticed that the use of the periphrastic aspect clusters in certain passages while it is virtually absent in passages of original prose, such as in the travel accounts by Ohthere and Wulfstan.[81] A

---

[75] Personal comment, Elton Prifti (Berlin, 05/07/04).
[76] A circumspect discussion of language contact as a necessary and sufficient condition for the use of imperfective aspect in Welsh and in English can be found in Ingo Mittendorf and Erich Poppe, 'Celtic Contacts of the English Progressive?', in *The Celtic Englishes II*, ed. Hildegard L. C. Tristram (Heidelberg, 2000), pp. 117–45; Erich Poppe 'Zu den "erweiterten Formen" des Englischen'.
[77] See Hildegard L. C. Tristram, 'Aspect in Contact', in *Anglistentag 1994 Graz*, ed. Wolfgang Riehle (Tübingen, 1995), pp. 269–94, at p. 282; 'The Politics of Language', p. 271 (see footnote 66 above).
[78] Janet Bately, ed., *The Old English Orosius,* Early English Text Society, supplementary series 6 (Oxford, 1980); Peter Kitson, 'The Dialect Position of the Old English Orosius', *Studia Anglica Posnaniensia* 30 (1996), 3–35; Ilse Wischer, 'Old English Prefixed Verbs and the Question of Aspect and Aktionsart', in *Anglistentag 2003*, ed. Christoph Bode, Sebastian Domsch and Hans Sauer (Trier, 2004), pp. 71–84.
[79] Bately, *The Old English Orosius*, p. 58, line 8.
[80] Bately, *The Old English Orosius*, p. 44, lines 29–30.
[81] Bately, *The Old English Orosius*, pp. 13–18.

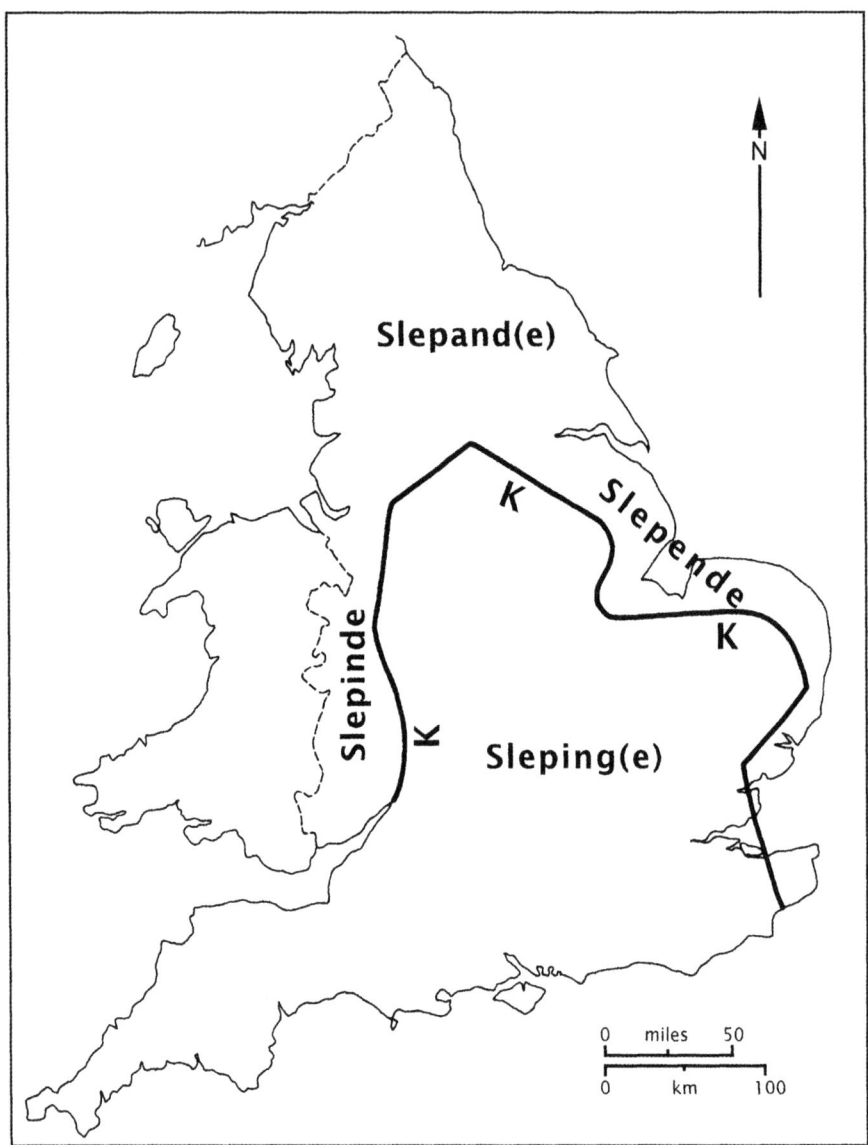

15.2 Map of the present participle in Middle English, taken from Fernand Mossé, Manuel de l'anglais du moyen âge, II, moyen anglais (Paris 1959), p. 114.

total analysis of the use of periphrastic aspect in the various manuscript copies of the *Orosius* is still a desideratum.[82]

While in written OE the present participle invariably occurred with the ending *-ende*, in Middle English texts the participle occurred with four different endings: *-ende*, *-and(e)*, *-inde*, and *-ing(e)*. These showed a curious geographical distribution. Eastern England and Kent preserved the OE *-ende* inflexion, the north had *-and(e)* (which was probably influenced by Old Norse), the West Midlands had *-inde*, while the entire south and the central Midlands had *-ing(e)*. The rise of the Middle English *-ing(e)* ending for the present participle and its possible derivation from OE action nouns ending in *-ung* and later *-ing*, e.g. *huntung* 'hunt' and *rǣding* 'reading', has been much discussed. Suffice it to say here that the entire south-west, i.e. the former kingdom of Wessex, forms a large part of the Middle English *-ing(e)* area and seems to have been a focal point in the development of *-ing(e)* as the ending of the present particle. It looks as if the endings of the two OE infinite verb forms, i.e. of the present participle and the action noun, or gerund, merged, the *-ing(e)* ending doing service for both functions, present participle and action noun. This may again be due to substratum influence, as Late British/Old Welsh had no present particle and the OE action noun was the closest analogue to the Late British/Old Welsh VN. It is therefore plausible that this merged form diffused into the central Midlands pushing conservative participle *-nd-* forms to the periphery.[83] As mentioned before the use of the analytic expression of imperfect aspect in the present tense of Late British and Old Welsh eventually extended in English to its use in the other tenses as well.[84]

Periphrastic DO

Another grammatical calque, which is characteristic of the South West of England and became grammaticalised in the standard language, is the use of periphrastic DO in the verb phrase.[85] Here it is interesting to note that Welsh GWNEUTHUR

---

[82] Kitson, 'The Dialect Position of the Old English Orosius', pp. 27 f., tentatively sees the language of the *Orosius* as a late-ninth-century approximation of the West Saxon dialect of the Bristol area.

[83] Tristram, 'Aspect in Contact', p. 282; White, 'Explaining the Innovations', pp. 161–4, takes the *-ing* forms to be gerunds used as predicate adjectives forming a progressive construction. It should also be mentioned that constructions like *be ahunting* etc. in Middle English texts, surviving in modern dialects are commonly derived from OE *be on huntunge*, which would be even closer to Welsh **BOT + yn + VN** constructions, as some scholars take the Welsh *yn* construction marker to be derived from a locative particle.

[84] A comparison of the expression and use of the imperfect aspect in Modern English and Welsh is given by Johannes Heinecke, 'The Temporal and Aspectual System of English and Welsh', in *The Celtic Englishes III*, ed. Hildegard L. C. Tristram (Heidelberg, 2003), pp. 85–110; cf. Heinecke, *Temporal Deixis in Welsh and Breton*, Anglistische Forschungen 272 (Heidelberg, 1999).

[85] Of the very extensive literature on the rise of DO constructions in English, special mention should be made of Patricia Poussa, 'A Contact Universal Origin of Periphrastic DO with Special Consideration of Old English – Celtic Contact', in *Papers From the 5th International Conference on English Historical Linguistics*, ed. Sylvia Adamson *et al.* (Amsterdam, 1990), pp. 407–34; Johan van der Auwera and Inge Genee, 'On the Convergence of Languages and Linguists', *English Language and Linguistics* 6 (2002), 283–307;

's/he does' in periphrastic constructions was extraordinarily common in Middle Welsh prose texts, much more common than in Middle English ones, especially in the form **VN + a** (construction marker) + **GWNEUTHUR**.[86] In fact it was so common that Welsh scholars have wondered whether its meaning may have been bleached and assumed the function of the simple verb construction. It is important to note that this type of periphrasis involving a verb meaning DO also occurred in Middle Cornish and in Middle Breton. In modern Breton this periphrasis is fully grammaticalised for focus marking.[87] Interestingly, Modern Welsh has not reached the same degrees of grammaticalisation of periphrastic DO constructions as Breton and English.

In the texts written in the insular languages during the High and the Late Middle Ages, the use of periphrastic DO was quite fluid and allowed a number of uses: contrastive emphasis, focus marking, causativity (as in French for instance), habituality, iterativity etc. Causativity, for instance, is in evidence in the following Middle English sentence:

> þi soule cnul ich wile **do ringe** (*The Fox and the Wolf*, 251)[88]
> *I will make the knell of your soul ring.*

Middle English texts experimented with the use of a variety of periphrastic, aspectual constructions, such as the inchoative use of **gin(ne) + INF** or **gin(ne) (for) to INF** :

> þe wolf **gon** sinke, þe vox arise (*The Fox and the Wolf*, 239)
> *The wolf began to sink, the fox to rise.*

The use of *will* (pres.) and *would* (past) was common to express habituality:

> þu draȝst men to fleses luste þat **willeþ** þine songes **luste** (*Mandeville's Travels*)
> *You entice people who commonly listen to your songs to the lust of the flesh*

Andrew Garrett, 'On the Origin of Auxiliary DO', *English Language and Linguistics* 2 (1998), pp. 283–330; David L. White, 'On the Origin of DO: Brittonic Influence Reconsidered', *English Language and Linguistics* (forthcoming).

[86] The Middle Welsh verb form **GWNEUTHUR** 'does', developed into Modern Welsh **GWNEUD** 'does'. To my knowledge the very few extant genuine Old Welsh texts unfortunately do not contain instances of periphrastic constructions of the type of **VN + a** (construction marker) + **GWNEUTHUR**. On the use of this construction in Middle Welsh, see Arwyn Watkins, 'Trefn yn y Frawddeg Gymraeg', *Studia Celtica* 12/13 (1977/78), 367–95; Proinsias Mac Cana, 'Further Notes on Constituent Order in Welsh', in *Studies in Brythonic Word Order*, ed. James Fife and Erich Poppe (Amsterdam, 1991), pp. 45–80; James Fife and Gareth King, 'Focus and the Welsh "Abnormal Sentence": a Cross-Linguistic Perspective', in *Studies in Brythonic Word Order*, pp. 81–153; Erich Poppe, 'Word order in Middle Welsh: the Case of Kedymdeithyas Amlyn ac Amic', *Bulletin of the Board of Celtic Studies* 40 (1993), 95–117; see also Hildegard L. C. Tristram; 'DO-Periphrasis in Contact?', in *Language in Time and Space. Festschrift für Wolfgang Viereck*, ed. Heinrich Ramisch and Kenneth Wynne (Stuttgart, 1997), pp. 401–17, at pp. 408f.

[87] Tristram, 'DO-Periphrasis in Contact?', pp. 409–11.

[88] The unique manuscript of *The Fox and the Wolf*, MS Digby 86, is dated to c.1271–83, while the text is considered to have been composed around 1250. The dialect is southern with traces of West Midlands forms.

Most of these aspectual experiments did not enter the English Standard, but many of them survived in the dialects. In the modern Standard periphrastic DO has two functions which are clearly distinguished by stress. Stressed DO expresses emphasis (i.e. marking by 'contrastive accent'), while unstressed DO means support of negation and question marking. Non-standard periphrastic DO expressing habituality is widely used in south-west England,[89] Ireland[90] and Newfoundland.[91]

Conclusion

I hope to have shown that morphosyntactic 'innovations' of Middle English which made it into the present day English Standard may have arisen as syntactic calques initiated by the large number of shifters from Late British to Old English. It is suggested that these shifters typologically changed the structure of English grammar from a predominantly synthetic, *cum* tense language to a predominantly analytic, *cum* aspect language.[92] Half a century ago the aforementioned grammarian Reinard W. Zandvoort raised the question whether or not English is a Germanic language at all.[93] As a Dutchman he compared English with Dutch and German (and some Scandinavian languages). He expected to find an East-West dialect continuum between these Germanic languages, but he found a gap, Dutch siding very strongly with German and English being typologically different from both. According to Zandvoort the difference is less pronounced on the phonological level than on the syntactic one. Zandvoort's discussion of the differing syntactic features is impressive and would certainly warrant a closer examination as to when and in which dialect area English started to diverge from the 'Germanic' patterns largely preserved in Dutch, German and the Scandinavian languages. As a synchronic linguist Zandvoort did not investigate the historical reasons for this divergence but confined himself to presenting the data 'for further consideration'.[94] For some of the most interesting features of the many referred to

---

[89] Cf. Ossi Ihalainen, 'Periphrastic "Do" in Affirmative Sentences in the Dialect of East Somerset', *Neuphilologische Mitteilungen* 67 (1976), 608–22, repr. revised and abbreviated in *Dialects of English: Studies in Grammatical Variation*, ed. Peter Trudgill and J. K. Chambers (London, 1991), pp. 148–60.

[90] Markku Filppula, *The Grammar of Irish English: Language in Hibernian Style* (London and New York, 1999), pp. 130–50.

[91] Sandra Clarke, 'On Establishing Historical Relationships between New and Old World Varieties: Habitual Aspect and Newfoundland Vernacular English', *Englishes Around the World*, ed. Edgar W. Schneider (Amsterdam, 1997), pp. 277–93; Graham Shorrocks, 'Celtic Influences on the English of Newfoundland and Labrador', in *The Celtic Englishes*, ed. Hildegard L. C. Tristram (Heidelberg, 1997), pp. 320–61, at p. 343.

[92] Cf. Graham Isaac, 'Perfectivity, Transitivity, Ergativity: the Grammar of Case in Welsh Non-finite Clauses', *Journal of Celtic Linguistics* 7 (1998), 39–61. Isaac claims that 'Welsh sentences ... are structurally dominated by the aspectual opposition of imperfective vs. perfective' (p. 39). English may be considered to be close to that.

[93] Zandvoort, 'Is English a Germanic Language?' (footnote 65 above).

[94] Zandvoort, 'Is English a Germanic Language?', p. 66.

by Zandvoort, I would suggest that we should consider Late British origins as the ultimate source, such as the attrition of the inflexions of the NP, fixed word order, periphrastic aspect and DO support, as argued above.

So, why then don't the English speak Welsh? My suggestion is that the English don't speak Welsh because the native Britons chose to give up their native varieties of Late British and shift to the emerging Old English dialects first in the British Lowland Zone and later in the Highland Zone over a period of some 300 years. In doing so they are likely to have Brittonised spoken Old English on the level of phonology and above all morphosyntax. By shifting they produced OE_L, i.e. vernacular Old English or what we eventually encounter as 'Middle English', which only surfaced in writing after the Norman Conquest. These shift-induced analyticising tendencies were reinforced by contact with adstratal Old Norse in the Danelaw areas, particularly in the north. The aspectual tendencies, however, arose in the south west, where Scandinavian influence was far less pronounced and substratal influence of Late British therefore likely to have been solely responsible for grammatical calques.

The psychological reasons for this hypothesised, massive language shift of the British population may be sought in a number of socio-economic and political incentives, among which the potent construction of a unifying ethnic identity of the Anglo-Saxon elite may have been the decisive one. From a linguistic point of view, it is perfectly plausible that, as the 'substrate rule' says, there was next to no lexical transfer. 'Bottom-up' shift scenarios prompt phonological and morphosyntactic transfer, as L_2 lexis is usually acquired consciously by adult learners, while phonology and morphosyntax are acquired unconsciously. The psychological motivation for such a 'bottom up' shift may then be sought in the speakers' desire to emulate the prestige language for the sake of approval and participation in the social benefits of elite Anglo-Saxon society.

16

Place-Names and the Saxon Conquest of Devon and Cornwall

O. J. PADEL

THE comparative absence of Brittonic place-names in most of England has long been a notable problem for anyone wishing to postulate large-scale survival of the native British population into the Anglo-Saxon period. In recent years these names have received useful attention,[1] but the overall picture nevertheless remains little changed from what it was fifty years ago.[2] Linguistically, too, the lack of British loan-words or other influences in English continues to be a powerful argument, despite unconvincing attempts to suggest syntactic and other borrowings. In recent years Margaret Gelling has given the question brief but valuable discussion;[3] here I shall demonstrate one aspect of the lack of Brittonic place-names, and discuss its implications and some possible models for interpreting it.

Cornwall is almost the only part of England where extensive Brittonic survival is not in question, since the language continued to flourish, in the western half of the county, down to the early modern period, and has left remains in the form of medieval literary works. As one crosses the county boundary from Devon, the place-names change noticeably. The situation can be illustrated by means of maps showing complementary images: first, the distribution of a habitative place-name element, Cornish *tre* 'farmstead, estate' (Illus. 16.1), which is so widespread that it almost serves to define Cornishness in place-names.[4] With about 1,200 examples in total, *tre* occurs almost throughout Cornwall, except on the upland moors for obvious reasons. It extends up to the county boundary on the river Tamar, in both the middle and the south. However, it is absent from two areas of Cornwall bordering on Devon, namely the whole of the northernmost end of the county and a region towards the south-east, around Hingston Down

---

[1] Especially Richard Coates and Andrew Breeze, *Celtic Voices, English Places: Studies of the Celtic Impact on Place-Names in England* (Stamford, 2000).
[2] Alan James, review of *Celtic Voices*, *Nomina* 27 (2004), 147–50.
[3] M. Gelling, 'Why aren't we Speaking Welsh?', *ASSAH* 6 (1993), 51–6.
[4] The maps which constitute Illus. 16.1–4 come from my chapter, 'Place-names', in *Historical Atlas of South-West England*, ed. R. Kain and W. Ravenhill (Exeter, 1999), pp. 88–94; for *tre* see also my *Cornish Place-Name Elements*, English Place-Name Society 56/57 (Nottingham, 1985), pp. 223–32 and map, p. 352.

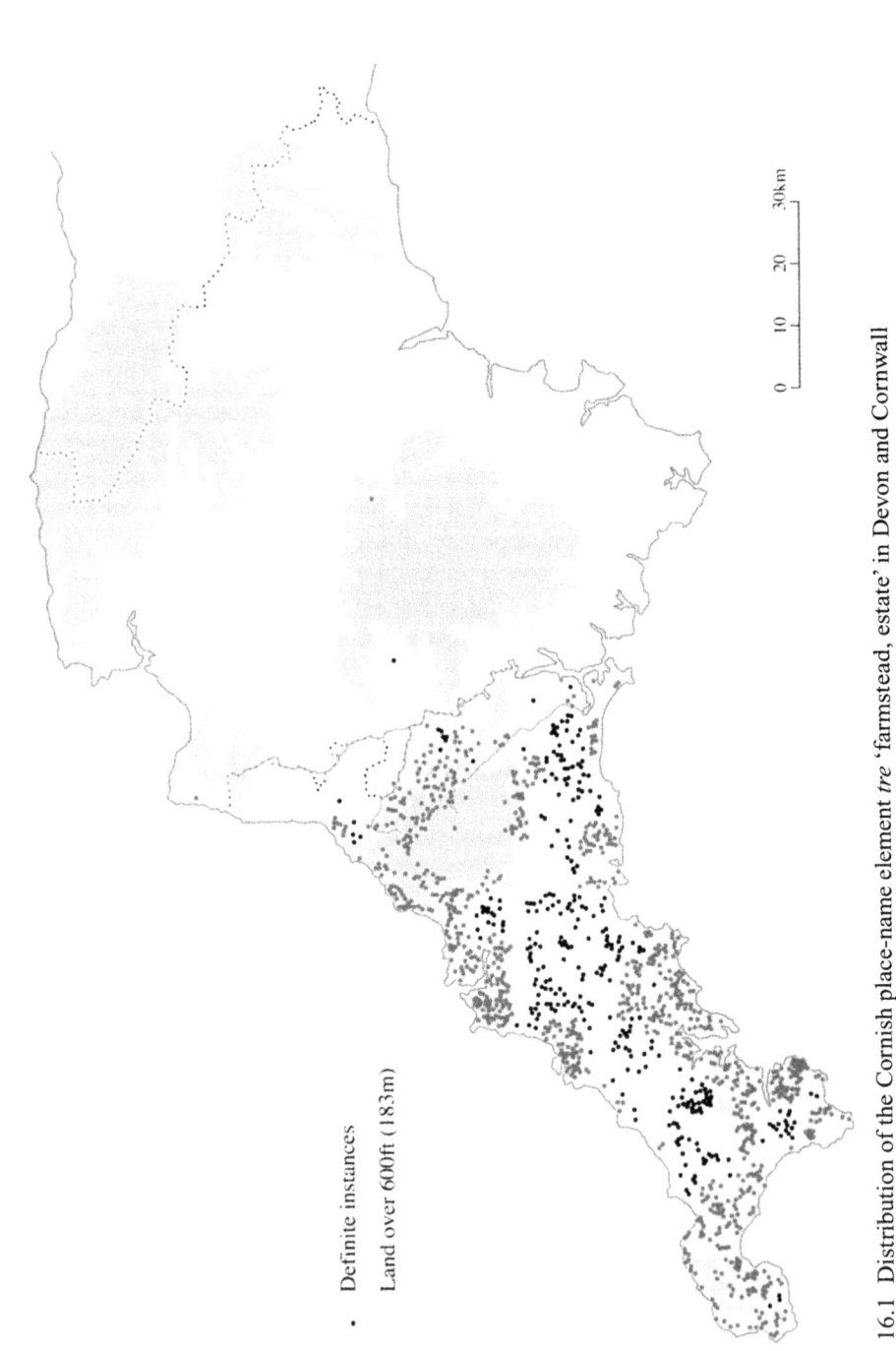

16.1 Distribution of the Cornish place-name element *tre* 'farmstead, estate' in Devon and Cornwall

where the last battle between Cornish and English was fought in 838. In the north, therefore, the limit of the distribution was formed not by the river Tamar but by a tributary river, the Ottery. (As the maps show, this tributary also came to form part of the county boundary, since two parishes west of the Tamar, though lying more naturally in Cornwall, were transferred into Devon. The transfer was seemingly made in the late eleventh century, and for the tenurial convenience of Tavistock Abbey in Devon, so the irregular boundary is not of significance for the period before 1066.[5]) In Devon, by contrast, it can be seen that the absence of *tre* is almost total: in this rather larger county there are just three known examples, two of them near to the boundary with Cornwall.

One might theoretically argue that this marked distribution could be due to *tre* not having been used before a certain date – which would need to be around the eighth or ninth century, if it were to explain the distribution. But that is not convincing, when we note that this Brittonic element was also used in Wales and southern Scotland, suggesting that its currency as a place-name element goes back to an earlier period of unity between the various Brittonic languages.[6] However, we could nevertheless allow that such a scheme might offer a partial explanation, in the case of this one element – if, for instance, its use was related to a system of landholding which arose independently in Cornwall, Wales and southern Scotland, under fringe-English influence. However, a similar picture emerges if we plot another habitative generic element, also shared with Wales, Cornish **bod* 'a dwelling' (Illus. 16.2); and similarly if we were to plot generic elements forming place-names based on natural features, such as Cornish *cuit* or *cos* 'a wood', *nans* 'valley' or *pen* 'head, top, end'.[7] In each case the names are again plentiful west of the Tamar, contrasting with an almost complete absence to the east of it. Moreover, that absence continues eastwards from Devon, all the way to the North Sea. There is a slight (and patchy) increase from east to west across England; but in the light of this stark contrast across the Cornish county boundary, the overall density of Brittonic place-names in Devon hardly appears significantly different from that in other counties further east, from Somerset and Dorset to Kent and Essex.[8]

Of course, this absence should not be exaggerated. Brittonic names are present in all counties of England, and they are highly significant; but they remain a tiny minority. The contrast between Cornwall and Devon typifies a general pattern of Brittonic place-names, both habitative and natural-feature ones. The point is not only the scarcity of Brittonic names across most of England, although that presents a major problem, but also that such Brittonic place-names as do occur further east are mostly of quite a different kind from those found where

---

[5] H. P. R. Finberg, 'The Making of a Boundary', in his *Lucerna* (London, 1964), pp. 161–80.

[6] M. Richards, 'Local Government in Cardiganshire, Medieval and Modern', *Ceredigion* 4 (1960–63), 272–82 (at pp. 273–5); W. F. H. Nicolaisen, *Scottish Place-Names: their Study and Significance* (London, 1976), pp. 166–70.

[7] Padel, *Cornish Place-Name Elements*, pp. 23–6 and map, p. 353 (**bod*), 66–8 (*cos*), 170–1 (*nans*), and 177–80 (*pen*).

[8] Compare Gelling, 'Why aren't we Speaking Welsh?', p. 55.

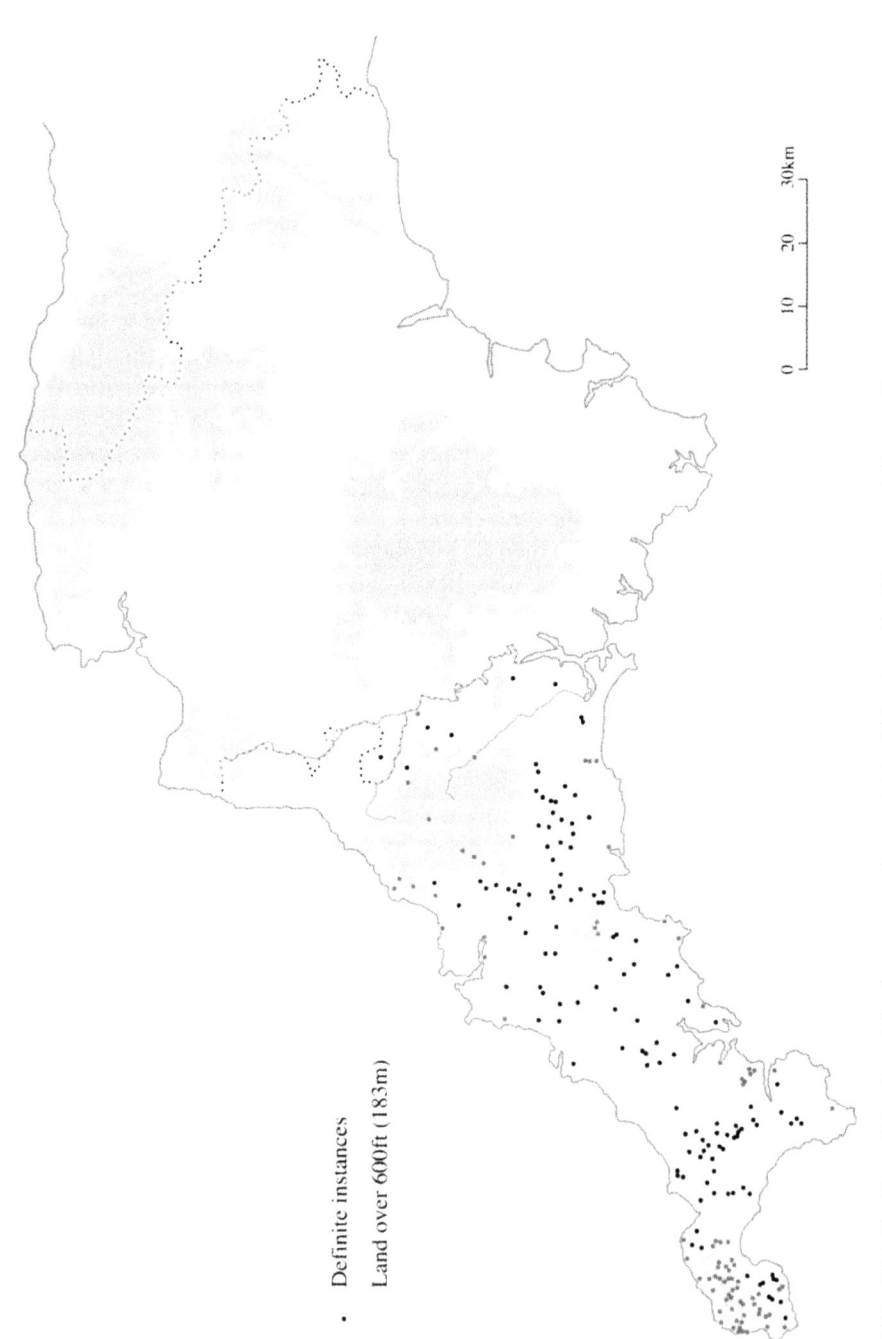

16.2 Distribution of the Cornish place-name element *bod* 'dwelling' in Devon and Cornwall

a Brittonic language continued to flourish. There is a handful of names such as Penge 'wood's end' (Surrey) and Pentridge 'boar's head' (Dorset), which conform nicely to the type normal in areas where Brittonic languages survived.[9] This handful confirms that the later type of Brittonic place-name did presumably exist before the Saxons came;[10] but apart from these few instances, the Brittonic names in most of England consist predominantly of single-element names for rivers or forests, single syllables derived from Romano-British town names, and the like. When Brittonic place-names do survive for habitations, they are generally major names – names of manors, or of towns based on Roman forts or settlements, such as Exeter.

These maps can further be taken to indicate where Cornish was still being spoken from about the ninth century to about the twelfth, before a further dieback of the language to mid-Cornwall in about the thirteenth century. We can interpret the situation by suggesting that the survival of the language in the western sector served to preserve the place-names there, or, conversely, that the eastern loss of the language offers the beginnings of an explanation for the loss of the place-names. By implication we are returned to the more basic question of why the Brittonic language disappeared so thoroughly, both in Devon and further east; and the Brittonic place-names merely provide a graphic representation of that greater problem.

A mirror image of this picture is shown by a map of a Saxon habitative generic such as *tūn* (Illus. 16.3), with a meaning probably quite close to that of Cornish *tre*. The two main areas in Cornwall where ordinary names in *tūn* occur are precisely those two areas on the county boundary where *tre* and **bod* are absent, namely the northernmost end of the county and the area towards the south-east. The element also extends in small numbers further into Cornwall, right down to the far west, but the picture is obscured slightly by two special types of *tūn*-name which occur thinly all over the county. It is not clear when *tūn* died out as an ordinary formative element in English, but the majority of personal names compounded with it are Old rather than Middle English ones.[11] (The few ordinary *tūn*-names in the western half of Cornwall had mostly been formed by the thirteenth century, two of them appearing in Domesday Book.) We may also note that within Devon ordinary *tūn*-names are considerably denser in the south than the north; and this greater southern density is reflected in the two areas where it is common within Cornwall.

The first of the two special types of *tūn*-name is the settlement name Newton. This compound must have continued to be given as a name after *tūn* had largely

---

[9] V. Watts, *The Cambridge Dictionary of English Place-Names* (Cambridge, 2004), pp. 466 (Penge) and 468 (Pentridge); Padel, *Cornish Place-Name Elements*, pp. xiv–xvi. As the map of Devon suggests, there are no examples of *Tre-* in middle or eastern England.

[10] Jackson, *LHEB*, pp. 225–7; Padel, *Cornish Place-Name Elements*, pp. xv–xvi.

[11] Of the examples in Devon where *tūn* is qualified by a personal name, a proportion of about 170 Old English personal names to 60 post-Conquest ones is indicated in J. E. B. Gover and others, *The Place-Names of Devon*, 2 vols., English Place-Name Society 8–9 (Cambridge, 1931–2), II, 672. The proportion in Cornwall appears to be more heavily weighted towards Old English.

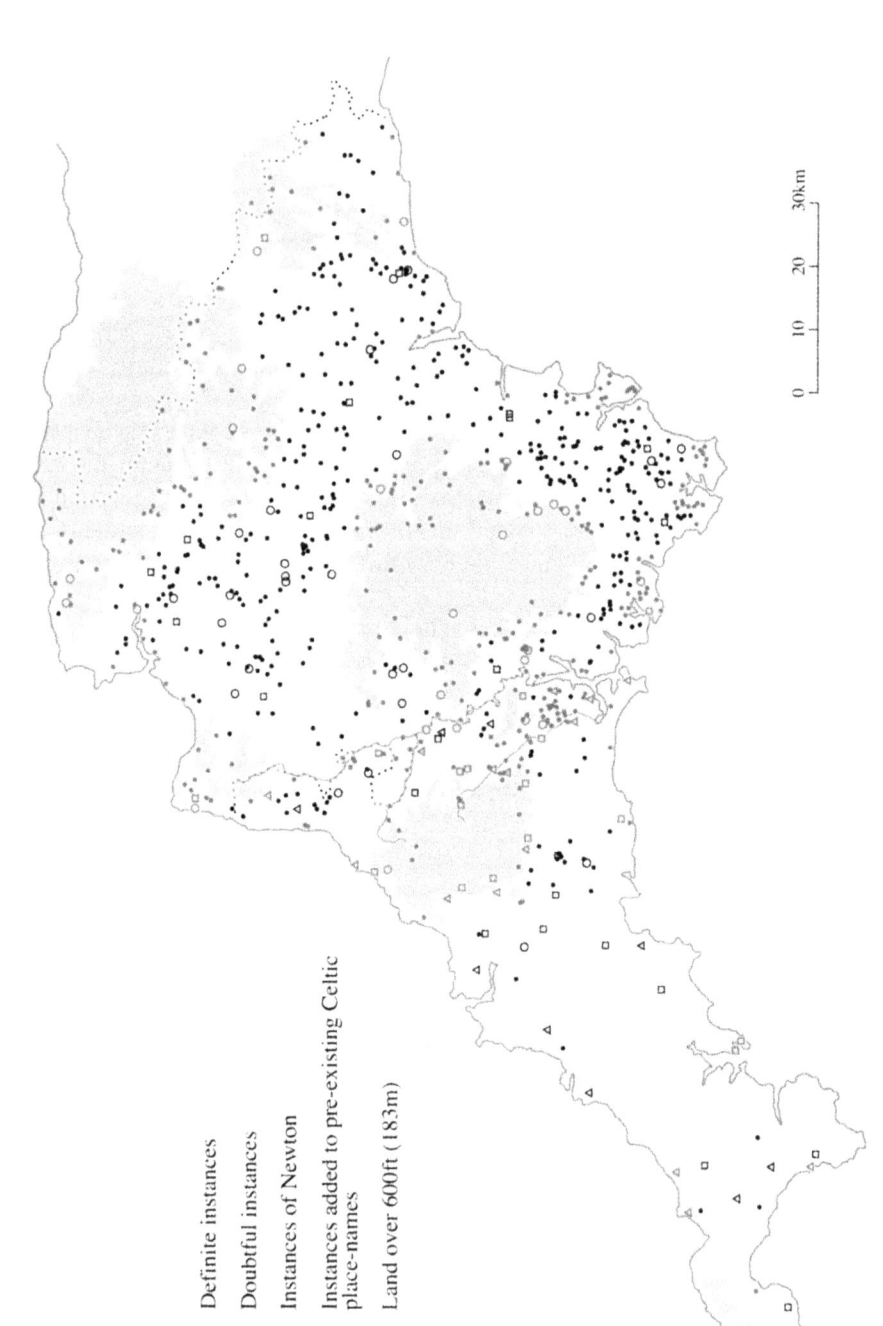

16.3 Distribution of the English place-name element *tūn* 'farmstead, estate' in Devon and Cornwall

gone out of use out as an ordinary formative element; hence the westerly distribution of Newton is proportionately greater than that of ordinary *tūn*-names, reflecting its continuing currency at a later period. The second special type is manorial names in which *tūn* was attached to a pre-existing Cornish-language place-name, such as Helston from earlier Cornish **Hen-lys* 'old court' plus Old English *tūn*. By the later eleventh century such names already extended right across the county, fairly evenly spread; their distribution reflects the Anglo-Saxon manorial administration, which apparently covered the whole county by the mid-tenth century.

Another English habitative generic element shows the same contrast between the two counties even more clearly. The word *cot* 'cottage' presumably designated, initially at least, a less important habitation than *tūn*, though by the time of Domesday Book some places containing it in their names had risen to the level of manors. The element is predominantly northern within Devon, perhaps complementing the southern frequency of *tūn*; and that northerly bias is again reflected in Cornwall, where it is much more common in the northern of the two Saxon areas (Illus. 16.4). Like *tūn*, *cot* also penetrates further down into Cornwall, though less deeply, fading out in the middle of the county. These sporadic western examples are mostly of a compound Chalcott, 'cold cottage', which probably continued to be given to places after *cot* had ceased to be used for forming other names, like Newton among the *tūn*-names. In the middle of the boundary zone, the *cot*-names cluster right up to the river Ottery, facing across to the *tre*-names on the other side of the river.

It seems probable that the complementary north-south distributions of *tūn* and *cot,* in both counties, imply some significant difference within the Anglo-Saxon takeover of Devon and parts of east Cornwall.[12] However, we are not concerned here with that dimension, but with the more fundamental east-west contrast between Brittonic and Saxon names. Two obvious questions arise from it. First, what was the process which caused the distributions to be so clear-cut and complementary? Second, why did that process, whatever it was, stop where it did, and not continue through Cornwall, down to the western end of the peninsula?

In these maps we are evidently looking at the tail-end of whatever remarkable process it was that brought about the thorough-going replacement of Brittonic language and place-names throughout England. By looking at the interface, at the western edge of the replacement, we may hope to gain a better understanding of the process, potentially throwing light on its occurrence further east in England, not merely in Devon. What we see in these complementary maps of elements is the process of Anglicization losing momentum, fading out westwards.

In considering possible explanations for the distributions, the first point to establish is the date of the situation which they represent. The maps of Cornish

---

[12] Toponymic aspects of the Saxon takeover of Devon, chiefly in the Exeter area, have received useful recent discussion by Duncan W. Probert, 'Church and Landscape: a Study in Social Transition in South-Western Britain, A.D. c. 400 to c. 1200' (unpublished PhD thesis, Birmingham, 2002), chapter 4.

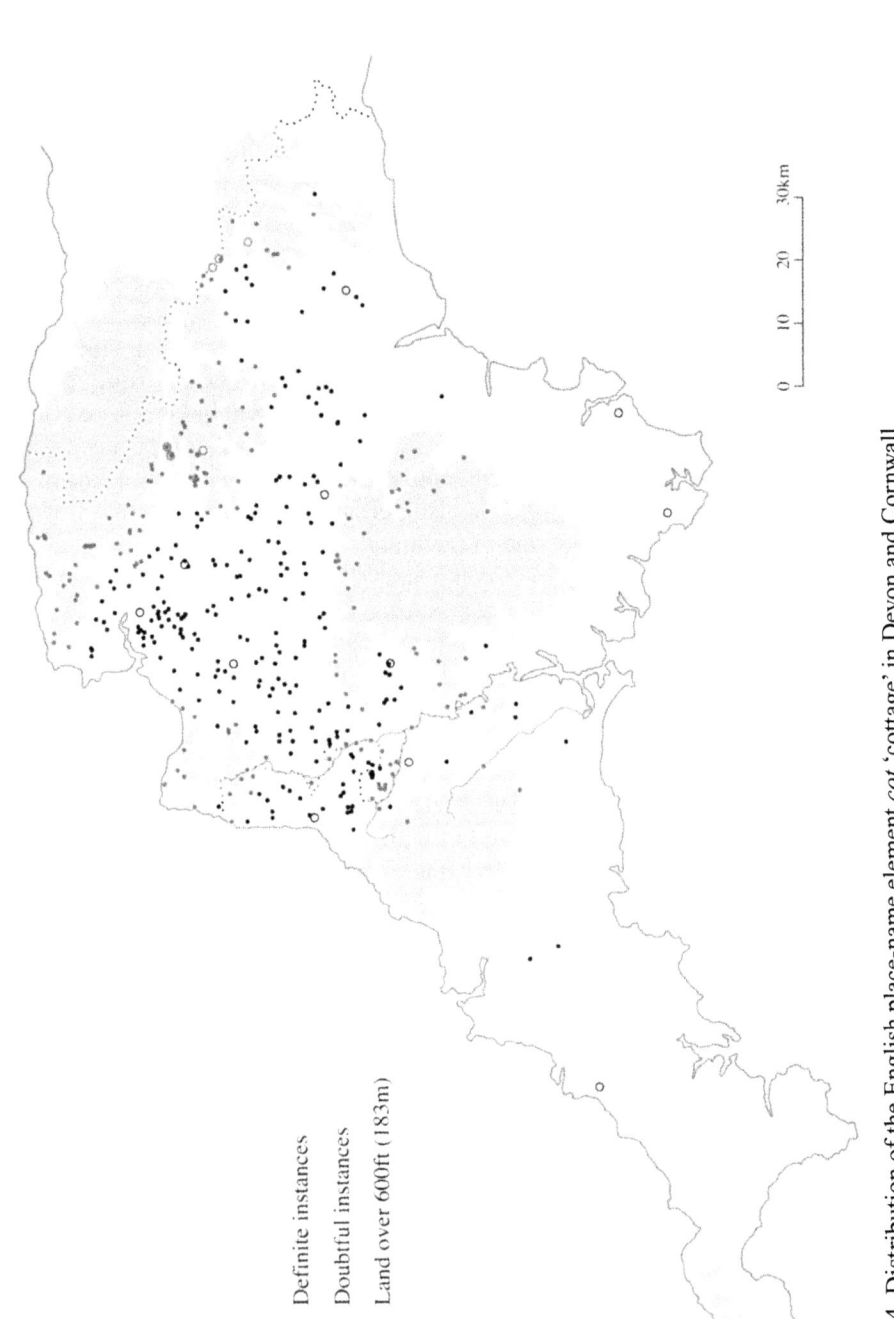

16.4 Distribution of the English place-name element *cot* 'cottage' in Devon and Cornwall

- Definite instances
- Doubtful instances
- Land over 600ft (183m)

and English elements show place-names which have, in most cases, medieval attestations sufficient to establish their derivations. The earliest source providing consistent coverage of place-names across the two counties is Domesday Book, which can safely be assumed to represent the toponymic situation in 1066 as well as 1086. At that date the place-names of Devon already showed their modern linguistic pattern.[13] In east Cornwall, if we plot the Domesday place-names according to their derivation from Cornish or Old English, irrespective of the particular elements which they contain, again we find the same complementarity already present, and in the same areas (Illus. 16.5). So it seems that the situation shown in the maps of individual habitative elements already existed, as a more general linguistic contrast, by the mid-eleventh century.

In fact, it seems probable that the situation had reached much this state by around 800, or 900 at the latest. The river Tamar can be seen emerging as the boundary between Wessex and Cornwall, between Saxons and *Wealas,* in the eighth to early ninth centuries, and it is during King Ecgbert's reign (815–39) that we first know of a Saxon king making grants of estates in eastern and central Cornwall.[14] By the later ninth century King Alfred held royal estates in precisely those two areas of Cornwall which show dense English place-names, though he also hunted further west into the county, around Bodmin Moor.[15] The location of his estates, as of King Ecgbert's grants, raises the interesting question of which came first, the English place-names (whatever they imply) or the English estates within the same areas. If we work back through the historical record, in either county, from the eleventh century to the ninth or (in Devon) the eighth century, the documents continue to show very much the same distribution of languages in the place-names which they record, whether major or minor ones.[16] As far as the evidence goes, therefore, the linguistic pattern seen in the maps appears to go back to the earliest written records in the region, in the eighth and ninth centuries.

To explain why the English replacement stopped where it did, we need to consider why the process of Anglicisation ran out of momentum at all. One might wonder whether there were perhaps political forces at work. It is remarkable how well the distributions coincide, in part, with the county boundary. In the twelfth century William of Malmesbury asserted that King Æthelstan (924–39) had established the Cornish county boundary at the river Tamar; yet the documentary evidence indicates that by Æthelstan's time the northernmost area, in terms of its place-names, would have belonged more naturally in Devon rather than Corn-

---

[13] For the Exeter area, Probert, 'Church and Landscape', pp. 314–19.
[14] See recently L. Olson, 'The Absorption of Cornwall into Anglo-Saxon England', in *Between Intrusions: Britain and Ireland between the Romans and the Normans*, edited by Pamela O'Neill (Sydney, 2004), pp. 94–102 (at p. 96).
[15] *Alfred the Great: Asser's Life of King Alfred and other Contemporary Documents*, trans. S. Keynes and M. Lapidge (Harmondsworth, 1983), pp. 89 and 175, and (on the estates) notes 18 and 56 (pp. 317 and 321).
[16] For the documents, see most recently Della Hooke, *Pre-Conquest Charter-Bounds of Devon and Cornwall* (Woodbridge, 1994); and for discussion Probert, 'Church and Landscape', pp. 290–314.

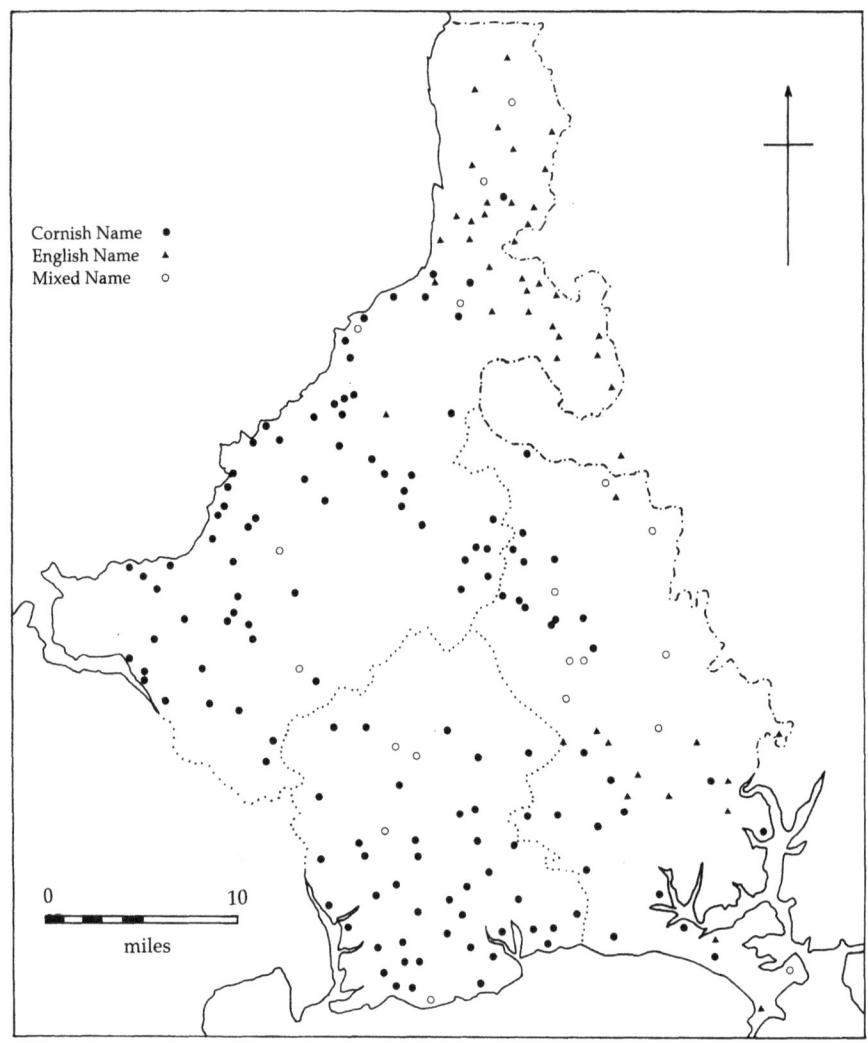

16.5 Cornish and Old English place-names in eastern Cornwall in Domesday Book

wall. Why was the northernmost section not included in Devon, following the river Ottery rather than the Tamar? The reason seems to have been Saxon retention of an ancient Cornish administrative district which extended from the Tamar westward to the Camel estuary, comprising the great Cornish hundred of Stratton which appears in Domesday Book.[17] Whether it was Æthelstan who established the county boundary or another king at about that period, it could have been that political act of fixing the boundary which hindered the Saxon encroachment from progressing any further – if, indeed, it still had any momentum left by that date.

[17] Padel, *Cornish Place-Name Elements*, pp. 64–5 and map, p. 351.

However, although political forces may offer a partial explanation for the place-name distributions, they are not the only possible one. Later, in the fourteenth to eighteenth centuries, evidence of various kinds shows the Cornish language dying out westwards across the county, not gradually but in apparent geographical steps, with periods of stability in between;[18] and these place-name distributions may display an earlier instance of the same phenomenon. It might be a sufficient explanation of the distributions to postulate that the survival of the Cornish language in a given area at a certain date somehow ensured the survival of Cornish place-names within that area, but only there.

The next question is, what does this extensive toponymic replacement mean on the ground? One may suggest three main hypotheses, offered here in increasingly cataclasmic order. First, there was little intrusion by Saxons into Devon, and no change in the native Brittonic-speaking population there, nor in their settlement-patterns; but for some reason the Britons there carried out, or adopted, or accepted, a wholesale renaming of all their settlements, including the minor ones, into Old English. Or, second, these English names represent, in many cases, new settlements created by a new Saxon population, which moved amicably in, side-by-side with any existing Brittonic settlements, which in turn then gradually died out (for some unknown but presumed amicable reason) along with their names. Or, third, the names were changed because of a widespread change in the ethnic and linguistic makeup of the population: the Saxon settlers may have occupied either new sites or a mixture of new and some older ones, but, if the latter, they largely renamed the older sites in their own language, the previous inhabitants either not being around or not being in a position to object. There could obviously be gradations between these possibilities and perhaps other ones not envisaged here.

The first option seems too improbable to merit serious consideration. We could reformulate it, more plausibly, by hypothesising that the renaming was carried out by a small ruling class and was adopted by, or forced upon, a native majority. Renaming of places can play an important role in political conquest, as seen in eastern Europe in the mid-twentieth century.[19] However, we have noted that where Brittonic names have survived at all in Devon and further east, they tend to belong to major places. If an Anglo-Saxon ruling minority were carrying out a policy of renaming places into English, one might have expected them to have concentrated on precisely those major names, and not to have bothered so much with individual farms and minor hamlets, since those places were (under this model) still occupied by the Brittonic-speaking natives. Under this reformulation we should therefore need to explain, first, why a few colonial administrators imposed a whole new system of names on a settled population, down to the level of the smallest farms; and, second, why they consistently did so in

---

[18] See most recently M. Spriggs, 'Where Cornish was Spoken and When: a Provisional Synthesis', *Cornish Studies*, 2nd series 11 (2003), 228–69; but the crucial evidence in east Cornwall, for the central- and late-medieval period, needs re-examination and more careful interpretation.

[19] I owe this point, and the parallel, to the kindness of Sigrid Padel.

Devon but not in most of Cornwall. The ethnic situation hypothesised under this reformulated first option would be similar to that which existed in all of England after the Norman Conquest, where an incoming French-speaking minority ruled an English majority; but that situation produced hardly any renaming of places. Reformulating the first option in that way still fails to produce a convincing explanation for the toponymic evidence.

The two remaining options both represent settlement by substantial numbers of incomers, through either infilling or replacement, again with social dominance probably on the side of the settlers. Extensive settlement of this kind seems necessary to explain the contrasting maps of Cornish and English place-names. However one examines the evidence, it is hard to conceive that such widespread and detailed renaming as apparently occurred in Devon can be due to anything other than a considerable influx, if not change, of population. Once one has formulated this unfashionable thought, it carries potential implications all the way back to Kent and Essex.

As a parallel, there are about 350 instances in Wales of place-names containing English *tūn*, predominantly in the fertile lands of the south, especially Glamorganshire and Pembrokeshire. Nobody questions there the idea that these place-names represent English settlement under Norman lordship, in the colonising sense, particularly since that settlement is documented in historical sources.[20] In this context, we could remember that in 1116 a Welsh chronicler observed that the Anglo-Normans settling in a part of west Wales were taking land which had previously been virtually empty,[21] and we may wonder whether the densities of British population in parts of lowland England were also very low, even where there is some evidence suggesting continuity of agricultural (or sometimes pastoral) exploitation.[22] This picture of English place-names in Wales arising from English colonisation in the twelfth and thirteenth centuries accords very well with what we need to envisage a few centuries earlier, say in the eighth and ninth centuries, in Devon and east Cornwall. Once one accepts that necessity, there then seems little reason to be shy of extending the same process further back and eastwards into the rest of England, at earlier dates.

It should be noted that I am not suggesting Old English *tun* as a particular marker of Anglo-Saxon colonisation, here or in Wales; it is merely a suitably common element which can be used to typify English place-names generally, including ones based on natural features. The crucial difference between the

---

[20] B. G. Charles, *Non-Celtic Place-Names in Wales* (London, 1938), pp. xxviii–xxx; R. R. Davies, *The First English Empire: Power and Identities in the British Isles 1093–1343* (Oxford, 2000), pp. 153–4.

[21] Davies, *First English Empire*, p. 153; the Norman settlers in Ireland appear to have found similarly low densities there (ibid., note 39).

[22] H. Härke, 'Briten und Angelsachsen im nachrömischen England: zum Nachweis der einheimischen Bevölkerung in den angelsächsischen Landnahmegebieten', *Studien zur Sachsenforschung* 11 (1998), 87–119 (at p. 106 and references); idem, 'Population Replacement or Acculturation? An Archaeological Perspective on Population and Migration in post-Roman Britain', in *The Celtic Englishes*, III, ed. H. L. C. Tristram (Heidelberg, 2003), 13–28, at p. 16.

distributions in England and Wales is that in Wales the colonising English names usually coexisted alongside native names, which are still there today, whereas in most parts of England there seems to have been near-total replacement. The reason for that difference seems likely to lie in the different relative numbers of native and settler populations.

We could also wonder, under the second or third options, whether the replacement of names in Devon was not an immediate process. Some of the English names could represent a process of infilling by Saxons of the second, third or later generations. However, the overall effect of that scheme would not be very different from straightforward colonisation, merely stretched out over a longer period. It would still imply that what the Saxons found was a landscape with plenty of space for expansion within it, and that many of the settlements indicated by the names were new foundations. Domesday Book shows that the Anglicization of place-names in Devon and north Cornwall was already complete by the mid-eleventh century – we do not know how much earlier, though the pre-Norman records suggest that it goes back to the eighth and ninth centuries. Whether we ascribe the process to one or two generations, or to three or more, does not make a great difference to the process itself, or to the required starting-point.

It may be illuminating to look at some possible parallels from more recent history. This is suggested here simply as a means of thinking in different ways about the various models, in contexts where we have fuller historical information about what actually happened, linguistically and ethnically. My first parallel is the slightly later Saxon conquest of Cornwall in the ninth and tenth centuries. It appears from the historical record that in most of the county this conquest did indeed entail what some archaeologists call 'élite dominance', that is to say a small number of rulers moving in to govern a larger group, which remained, for a while, ethnically and linguistically distinct.[23] However, if Cornwall shows the toponymic result of 'élite dominance' by the Saxons, then in Devon we seem to be dealing with something quite different, unless a plausible theory can be suggested to explain why the results differed so markedly on either side of the river Tamar.

Such an explanation might invoke the slightly different chronological horizons of the Saxon conquest in the two counties. The increasing use of written documents from the seventh and eighth centuries into the ninth and tenth could suggest the written medium as a possible cause of the dramatically greater survival of Brittonic place-names in Cornwall. However, although a small number of Cornish place-names are known to have existed in written form before Domesday Book, both in the few Anglo-Saxon charters and possibly also in hypothetical native sources,[24] there is no basis for supposing that they were consistently written down at such a micro-level as could account for the survival

---

[23] Most recently discussed by Olson, 'Absorption of Cornwall into Anglo-Saxon England', with references.

[24] O. J. Padel, 'The Charter of Lanlawren (Cornwall)', in *Latin Learning and English Lore (Studies in Anglo-Saxon Literature for Michael Lapidge)*, ed. K. O'Brien O'Keeffe and A. Orchard (Toronto, 2005), II, 74–85; Hooke, *Pre-Conquest Charter-Bounds of Devon and Cornwall*, p. 18.

of thousands of sub-manorial names in the county, whether based on *Tre-* or on other Cornish elements.

The Cornish side of these maps, showing survival of the native names beside few names in the language of the conquerors, is indeed comparable with situations where so-called élite dominance has occurred in other parts of the world more recently, including the Norman Conquest, as mentioned earlier, or British rule in India, where a few colonial settlers governed a stable population and the place-names survived largely unchanged. These two situations provide good parallels with Anglo-Saxon rule in Cornwall, but such a model does not come remotely near to explaining the linguistic evidence in Devon and the rest of England.

It may well be anyway that few investigators would still adopt such a model for the rest of England. A more popular model now might be what could be called a South African one, with enough Anglo-Saxon settlers to make a major contribution to the linguistic and toponymic situation (as in South Africa), while retaining and working with a substantial subject population from the older ethnic groups, living side by side perhaps in a kind of apartheid. We can recall the laws of Ine, showing separate *wergilds* for Saxons and *Wealas* in late-seventh-century Wessex.[25] This model, unlike the Indian-raj one, can be adjusted in terms of relative numbers of settlers and natives, so as to produce a more plausible explanation for the linguistic evidence in England. Provided that it were adjusted far enough in the numerical favour of the settlers, it might satisfy the linguistic requirements.

But a far more suitable model, in my view, would be what might be called a North American one, whereby a major replacement of population, language and place-names occurred over a large area in a comparatively short space of time. However the overall Anglicization of lowland England happened, the end result was, for its day, not unlike the remarkable European settlement of North America, which occurred over a comparable time-scale, though a much vaster area.[26]

It is worth emphasising what this model does not entail. We tend to think of the European settlement of North America as wipe-out, genocide on a grand scale; but even if that was the net result in large measure over the three centuries from 1600 to 1900, it was not consistently so on the ground. There was also much living side-by-side, trading, working together and intermarriage. One regularly meets North Americans who are proud of a Native American ancestor not far back. Archaeologically, the evidence for some continuity of population, and for the native adoption of the settlers' culture, could be compared with the material evidence for continuity that has been identified in England. The early

---

[25] *The Laws of the Earliest English Kings*, ed. F. L. Attenborough (Cambridge, 1922), pp. 42–7; but Härke has pointed out ('Briten und Angelsachsen', p. 91) that similar provisions mentioning *Wealas* are significantly absent from other Anglo-Saxon codes, both earlier and later.

[26] North American parallels have been drawn previously, albeit in different contexts: *The Anglo-Saxons from the Migration Period to the Eighth Century: an Ethnographic Perspective*, ed. John Hines (Woodbridge, 1997), pp. 63 (P. J. Fowler) and 163 (H. Härke).

Saxon king Cerdic bore a Brittonic name but was claimed as the founder of a royal Saxon dynasty, so he and one or two other early kings have been thought to suggest assimilation between Anglo-Saxon settlers and native British;[27] if so, then one may compare him with a Native American such as Pocohontas (though admittedly she was too early to found a presidential dynasty). There has been a tendency to portray an 'ethnic cleansing' model of the Anglo-Saxon takeover too simplistically, usually for the purpose of discrediting it. Once it is allowed that such a model also has room for intermarriage, trading, and other kinds of friendly cooperation and cultural intercourse, the reasons for rejecting it in early England become less cogent.

This model is attractive because, of the three crude colonial parallels outlined above (India, South Africa and North America), it provides easily the best match for the degree of linguistic and toponymic replacement that occurred in England, while still leaving room for the borrowing of some native place-names, as occurred in both Anglo-Saxon England and North America. It also leaves room for all kinds of coexistence on a local level, such as occurred in North America, and such as people are pleased to posit in England wherever they can find evidence suggesting it.

It is worth asking, in passing, why people are so keen to demonstrate continuity in England wherever possible. Many research programmes, particularly in archaeology departments, seem to be predicated on the assumption that there *was* British continuity, and that it is desirable to demonstrate as much of it as possible.[28] One factor may be that English academics are, for understandable reasons, as uncomfortable with ethnic cleansing in their history books, particularly of their own country, as everyone is with it in the newspapers. An additional reason may be a dissatisfaction with the simplistic models common among previous generations of archaeologists, whereby changes of material culture were generally assumed to coincide with changes of population, and potentially of language as well. These models have become discredited, so that some archaeologists are now excessively wary of positing large-scale population movements at all in prehistory, even though such movements are well documented within historic times, not only in the European expansions to other continents.

In the case of North America, many people would adduce the disparities between Europeans and Native Americans, in both material and social culture, to explain the remarkable completeness of the European conquest. Given the collapse of Roman-derived culture among the Britons in the fifth century, it is reasonable to wonder whether there was, by the middle of that century, a comparable disparity of material and social culture between Anglo-Saxons and native Britons in eastern England. Town life had declined greatly since Roman times,

---

[27] The linguistic problems of Cerdic have been discussed by D. Parsons, 'British *Caratīcos, Old English Cerdic', *Cambrian Medieval Celtic Studies* 33 (1997), 1–8, with references to discussion of other aspects; see also Härke, 'Briten und Angelsachsen', p. 96.

[28] Compare H. Härke, 'Archaeologists and Migrations: a Problem of Attitude?', *Current Anthropology* 39 (1998), 19–45, especially p. 20.

coinage had ceased to circulate, and most of the Britons seem not to have been making pottery.

To the extent that the Britons in eastern England may have adopted incoming Anglo-Saxon material culture or practices, as has been suggested to explain their apparent invisibility,[29] the parallel with the European takeover of North America would be reinforced. Disparities in social structures or organisation, such as existed in North America, could also have had important consequences, while leaving little archaeological trace. One might again compare, too, the Anglo-Norman conquest of parts of Wales and Ireland, where we have already noted the low density of the native population, and where the disparities in both technological culture and social structures were remarked upon, to similar effect, on both sides of the divide.[30]

These recent parallels may have all kinds of unsuitable aspects, caused by differences of date, scale or other factors. They have been suggested previously and perhaps rejected for good reason. Despite such reservations, the illumination which they potentially offer may be not only what they can suggest in terms of relative numbers of natives and settlers, which we may never know in early England, but in ways of considering the possible kinds of relations between the two groups, and possible kinds of native continuity. Probably most, if not all, of the indicators which have been claimed to demonstrate British continuity in England can also be observed in North America, even though the net result has been an effective replacement of the native population. Examining the western limit of the Saxon settlement serves to demonstrate the comparative absence of Brittonic place-names over most of England, in sharp contrast with those areas where a Brittonic language continued in use. It is difficult to explain that absence other than by positing a low density of native British population after the conquest and settlement by the Anglo-Saxons, whether caused by 'ethnic cleansing' or other factors – and perhaps also before their settlement, too. The toponymic evidence needs to be reconciled with such evidence as has been held to demonstrate a continuity of a substantial native population.[31]

---

[29] Catherine Hills, *Origins of the English* (London, 2003), p. 111; *The Anglo-Saxons*, ed. Hines, pp. 149–50 (H. Härke) and 168–9 (P. J. Fowler, C. Scull, H. Härke).
[30] Davies, *First English Empire*, pp. 101–2.
[31] I am most grateful to Dafydd Kidd and Drs Heinrich Härke and Catherine Hills for their generous and patient comments given while this article was in preparation; however, they are in no way to be associated with the suggestions made in it.

17

Mapping Early Medieval Language Change in South-West England

DUNCAN PROBERT

Context and methodology

THIS paper explores the potential for using evidence preserved in certain place-names to map the linguistic transition from a Brittonic to an Old English vernacular in south-west England.[1] The traditional account of the corresponding political transition is well known.[2] In the late sixth century the English reached the lower Severn, thereby isolating south-western Britons from their compatriots in the West Midlands and Wales. The takeover of what became Dorset and Somerset was complete by the late seventh century and, according to the *Anglo-Saxon Chronicle*, included battles at which the Britons were driven 'as far as the Parrett' and 'as far as the sea'.[3] During the late seventh and early eighth centuries the eastern part of British Dumnonia became English Devon. Cornwall remained independent for longer; but a Cornish bishop had submitted to Canterbury by 870, its last known king died in 875 and West Saxon kings were holding lands in Cornwall well before this.[4] By the time that Æthelstan formalized the river Tamar as the boundary between Devon and Cornwall in the early tenth century,[5] Cornwall had been incorporated into the emergent kingdom of England.

Despite some recognized problems with this account its basic chronology

---

[1] This paper was written during a Post-Doctoral Fellowship from the British Academy, whose support I gratefully acknowledge here; I am also grateful to Steven Bassett, Matt Edwards, Margaret Gelling, Oliver Padel, David Parsons, Jens Röhrkasten and Peter Schrijver for their constructive criticisms of earlier versions.

[2] E.g. William G. Hoskins, *The Westward Expansion of Wessex*, Leicester University Department of Local History Occasional Papers 13 (1960), 7–16; H. P. R. Finberg, 'Sherborne, Glastonbury, and the Expansion of Wessex', in *Lucerna: Studies of Some Problems in the Early History of England*, ed. H. P. R. Finberg (London, 1964), pp. 95–115.

[3] *Anglo-Saxon Chronicle* (*ASC*) 658, 682 : *Two of the Saxon Chronicles Parallel*, ed. Charles Plummer (Oxford, 1892–9) I, 32–3, 38–9.

[4] *Cartularium Saxonicum*, ed. W. de G. Birch, 3 vols. (London, 1885–93) II, no. 527; *Nennius: British History and the Welsh Annals*, ed. John Morris, Arthurian Period Sources 8 (Chichester, 1980), 85–91, *s.a.* 875; S 1296, 1451a, 1507.

[5] *William of Malmesbury: Gesta Regum Anglorum*, ed. and trans. R. A. B. Mynors, R. M. Thomson and M. Winterbottom (Oxford, 1998), pp. 216–17; Duncan Probert, 'Church and

is generally accepted.⁶ Yet it created an enduring image of steady West Saxon 'conquest and settlement' from which Britons conveniently disappear once an area comes under English control. There are, however, indications that the reality was less straightforward. Bede's account of Chad's consecration in the 660s suggests that two British bishops could (and would) travel safely to Winchester in order to assist.⁷ Conversely, Aldhelm's poem about a journey through Cornwall and Devon, written before 710, implies that a West Saxon ecclesiast could travel in lands then under nominal British control.⁸ Not all interactions between Britons and English were hostile in what English writers referred to nebulously as 'the western regions'.⁹ Furthermore, Bede notes that many of 'those Britons who were subject to the West Saxons' (probably referring to Dumnonia as a client kingdom in the mid-690s) had adopted the Catholic Easter, while the laws attributed to Ine provide for Britons living under West Saxon jurisdiction.¹⁰ Although the lower status accorded to Britons in Ine's laws might provide an incentive to adopt an 'English' identity,¹¹ it is apparent that an identifiably 'British' population still existed in areas now in West Saxon hands.

Nevertheless, nothing more is heard of these Britons after the early eighth century. Had they migrated elsewhere or been eliminated in an early medieval form of 'ethnic cleansing', or had they remained *in situ* and undergone rapid cultural assimilation? It has been suggested that localized 'clusters' of pre-English toponyms and those of the 'Walton' type may indicate the late survival of identifiably British communities.¹² Yet 'late' is a relative and imprecise term, while the presence or absence of such clusters may reflect the adequacy of early place-name records as much as putative British survival.

The English Place-Name Society (EPNS) survey in the 1930s, for example, argued that, because less than one per cent of modern Devon's place-names are of pre-English origin, the English conquest must have been so complete that 'no

---

Landscape: A Study in Social Transition in South-Western Britain, A.D. *c*.400 to *c*.1200', unpublished PhD thesis (University of Birmingham, 2002), pp. 66–71.
⁶ E.g. Barbara Yorke, *Wessex in the Early Middle Ages* (London and New York, 1995), pp. 52–60; Duncan Probert, 'New Light on Aldhelm's Letter to King Gerent of Dumnonia', in *Aldhelm West of Sherborne* [provisional title], ed. Katherine Barker (forthcoming).
⁷ *Bede's Ecclesiastical History of the English People*, ed. Bertram Colgrave and R. A. B. Mynors (Oxford, 1969), III.xxviii.
⁸ *Aldhelmi opera omnia*, ed. R. Ehwald, Monumenta Germaniae Historica (MGH), Auct. antiq. 15 (Berlin, 1919), 524–8; Michael Lapidge and James L. Rosier, *Aldhelm: The Poetic Works* (Cambridge, 1985), pp. 177–9; Probert, 'New Light on Aldhelm's Letter'.
⁹ *SS Bonifatii et Lullii epistolae*, ed. M. Tangl, MGH Epist. select. 1 (Berlin, 1916), 52–3; cf. *Aldhelmi opera*, ed. Ehwald, p. 480.
¹⁰ *HE*, V, 18; *The Laws of the Earliest English Kings*, ed. F. L. Attenborough (Cambridge, 1922), pp. 36–61, chs. 23.3, 24.2, 32–3, 54.2, 74; Probert, 'New Light on Aldhelm's Letter'.
¹¹ Bryan Ward-Perkins, 'Why Did the Anglo-Saxons Not Become More British?', *EHR* 115 (2000), 513–33, at pp. 523–4; Martin Grimmer, 'Britons and Saxons in Pre-Viking Wessex: Reflections on the Law Code of King Ine', *Parergon*, new series 19 (2002), 1–17.
¹² E.g. Kenneth Cameron, 'The Meaning & Significance of OE *walh* in English Place-Names', *Journal of the English Place-Name Society* 12 (1980), 1–34; cf. Margaret Gelling, 'Why Aren't We Speaking Welsh?', *ASSAH* 6 (1993), 51–6.

considerable native population remained'.[13] However, this argument discounted not only pre-English river names but also both simplex and compound place-names derived from them on the presumption that these were entirely English coinings. It also took little account of the processes of place-name formation and replacement over time. By contrast, the limited evidence from the Exeter area shows a steady decline in the proportion of place-names containing pre-English toponyms, falling from sixty percent of those recorded in the ninth century to forty percent in the tenth century and twenty-five percent by the time of Domesday Book.[14] It reminds us that even as successive centuries provide more recorded place-names with which to reconstruct the early toponymic landscape, so that landscape itself is changing through the ongoing replacement of earlier place-names and the formation of new ones, particularly during periods of demographic and agricultural expansion.

That having been said, it must also be admitted that the relative scarcity of pre-English toponyms in both modern and Domesday Devon is in stark contrast to their predominance in Cornwall. Oliver Padel has argued that the almost mutually exclusive distributions of certain Cornish and English habitative generics in the two counties reflect an early medieval linguistic boundary.[15] It is clear that the circumstances affecting place-name formation and replacement in Devon were markedly different from those obtaining in Cornwall. What is less clear is when and how this linguistic boundary developed. Does it represent a rapid replacement of Brittonic by Old English in Devon in the eighth century, for example, or does it owe more to the administrative policies of Æthelstan in the early tenth century? It certainly originated before the late eleventh century, when the place-names recorded in Domesday confirm its existence. That it retained an active linguistic significance at that time is suggested by the work of Ken George and others, who have mapped, albeit approximately, the post-Conquest resurgence and then westerly retreat of the Cornish language along the peninsula until its eventual extinction in (probably) the late eighteenth century.[16]

George used place-names whose recorded forms showed the presence or absence of known developments in the Cornish language to produce his map. In other words the emphasis is more on the linguistic evidence for the survival (or non-survival) of Cornish at particular times and places than on the quantity of surviving place-names. A similar approach may allow us to map the disappearance of Brittonic east of the Tamar despite the paucity of recorded pre-English

---

[13] J. E. B. Gover, A. Mawer and F. M. Stenton, *The Place-Names of Devon*, 2 vols., English Place-Name Society 8–9 (Cambridge, 1931–2) I, xix–xx.

[14] Probert, 'Church and Landscape', pp. 290–319; Duncan Probert, 'Pre-Conquest Place-Name Formation in Exeter's Hinterland' (forthcoming).

[15] O. J. Padel, 'Cornwall as a Border Area', *Nomina* 6 (1982), 18–22; Oliver Padel, 'Place-Names', *Historical Atlas of South-West England*, ed. Roger Kain and William Ravenhill (Exeter, 1999), pp. 88–94, and this volume.

[16] K. George, 'How Many People Spoke Cornish Traditionally?', *Cornish Studies* 14 (1986), 67–70; cf. Matthew Spriggs, 'The Cornish Language, Archaeology, and the Origins of English Theatre', *Traces of Ancestry: Studies in Honour of Colin Renfrew*, ed. Martin Jones (Cambridge, 2004), pp. 143–61, at pp. 145–50.

place-names. Three propositions underpin this approach. The first is that a place-name originates as a vernacular description of some feature of the natural or human landscape and remains part of contemporary language until it becomes an abstract label.[17] The second is that the processes and relative chronologies established by philologists are sufficiently reliable for us to reconstruct developments in the Brittonic and English languages.[18] The third is that although a borrowed word may develop as part of the receiving language, it does not reflect subsequent developments in the donor language.[19] If these propositions are correct, then pre-English place-names with the potential to have been affected by early medieval developments in Brittonic may indicate whether or not these had occurred when each place-name was adopted by Old English speakers.

Example 1: Old English borrowings of British /ū/ and Brittonic /ǖ/

An example of this involves a sequence of vowel changes in both Brittonic and Old English.[20] The final stage of these changes is apparent in the orthography of a grant to Glastonbury minster in 682. It mentions 'the hill called in the British tongue *Cructan*, by us *Crycbeorh*', referring to Creechbarrow Hill in west Somerset.[21] The Brittonic word underlying the first element of these place-names is *crūg, which signifies 'abrupt hill, mound or tumulus'.[22] From the late third until the early sixth century, the British vowel of this word was /ū/, for which Old English speakers could use their own /ū/ when they adopted place-names containing it. However, in all the emergent neo-Brittonic languages this /ū/ had become a raised /ǖ/ by about the mid-sixth century. As Old English had no direct equivalent for this Brittonic /ǖ/, subsequent borrowings had to substitute either OE /ū/ as before or else the slightly closer OE /ī/. Old English then developed a

---

[17] Frederick T. Wainwright, *Archaeology and Place-Names and History: An Essay on Problems of Co-ordination* (London, 1962), pp. 45–7.
[18] Much of what follows inevitably relies on the pioneering work of Jackson, *LHEB*, which has survived modern scrutiny largely intact (e.g. William Gillies, 'Foreword to 1994 Printing', *Language and History*, Jackson (Dublin, 1994), pp. iv(a–f), at p. iv(f); Patrick Sims-Williams, *The Celtic Inscriptions of Britain: Phonology and Chronology, c. 400 – 1200*, Publications of the Philological Society 37 (2003), 8, 21).
[19] Roibeard Ó Maolalaigh, 'Place-Names as a Resource for the Historical Linguist', in *The Uses of Place-Names*, ed. Simon Taylor, St John's House Papers 7 (Edinburgh, 1998), 12–53, at p. 15.
[20] For details see Jackson, *LHEB*, pp. 305–11, 315–17, 321, 600; A. Campbell, *Old English Grammar* (rev. edn, Oxford, 1968), pp. 15, 17–18, 71–2, 78–9, 106, 109; Sims-Williams, *Celtic Inscriptions*, pp. 105–6, 283, 293, 351–3.
[21] S 237; Heather Edwards, *The Charters of the Early West Saxon Kingdom*, BAR, BS 198 (Oxford, 1988), 15–17; Lesley Abrams, *Anglo-Saxon Glastonbury: Church and Endowment*, Studies in Anglo-Saxon History 8 (Woodbridge, 1996), 99–100.
[22] Margaret Gelling, *Place-Names in the Landscape: The Geographical Roots of Britain's Place-Names* (London, 1984), pp. 137–9; Margaret Gelling and Ann Cole, *The Landscape of Place-Names* (Stamford, 2000), pp. 159–63; cf. Oliver J. Padel, *Cornish Place-Name Elements*, EPNS 56/57 (Nottingham, 1985), 73–4.

/ȳ/ vowel through umlaut (probably by the later seventh century) that was much closer to, and a more obvious substitution for, the contemporary Brittonic /ü/.

All such borrowed place-names might be subject to later developments that affected OE /ū/, /ī/ and /ȳ/ in both Old and Middle English and their dialects.[23] This can render the etymologies of modern forms ambiguous. Although borrowings of British *crūg* or Brittonic *crūg* with OE /ū/ often produce modern forms such as 'Crook' or 'Crouch', for example, while borrowings with OE /ī/ or /ȳ/ often produce forms such as 'Crick' or 'Creech', this cannot be assumed to be the case without sufficient early spellings. Nevertheless, there are enough examples with recorded early forms to produce a distribution map (Illus. 17. 1).[24]

There are inevitable gaps where either no place-names affected by the relevant sound changes are recorded or else place-names derived from British *crūg* or Brittonic *crūg* lack early forms. However, the triangular symbols in Gloucestershire, north-west Wiltshire, east Dorset and most of Somerset and Devon should represent areas in which Brittonic was still spoken when OE /ī/ first became a potential substitution for the new Brittonic /ü/ in about the mid-sixth century. They do not indicate when Brittonic ceased to be spoken in these areas, of course, and the bilingual forms and orthography in the Creechbarrow charter of 682 imply its survival in west Somerset for at least another century and after the development of OE /ȳ/.

The round symbols in central and south Wiltshire, on the other hand, may represent borrowings made by Old English speakers before British /ū/ became Brittonic /ü/ in the mid-sixth century. But those in south Somerset, west Dorset and east and central Devon are very unlikely to have been borrowed at such an early date. Instead, they probably represent later borrowings in which OE /ū/ was substituted for Brittonic /ü/. Even so, they are most likely to have been borrowed before the late seventh century, by which time OE /ȳ/ would be a much closer substitution for Brittonic /ü/ than either OE /ū/ or OE /ī/.[25]

However, some apparent borrowings of Brittonic *crūg* with OE /ū/, extending from south Somerset into central Devon, are close to former Roman roads that probably survived as early medieval routeways. As an 'abrupt hill, mound or tumulus' might well function as a travellers' landmark,[26] perhaps some were

---

[23] Richard Jordan (trans. and revised Eugene Joseph Crook), *Handbook of Middle English Grammar: Phonology* (The Hague, 1974), pp. 34, 65–72, 84, 87, 239–40; Gover *et al.*, *Place-Names of Devon* I, xxxiv; J. E. B. Gover, Allen Mawer and F. M. Stenton, *The Place-Names of Wiltshire*, EPNS 16 (Cambridge, 1939), xx–xi; A. H. Smith, *The Place-Names of Gloucestershire*, 4 vols., EPNS 38–41 (Cambridge, 1965) IV, 69–71. For Gloucestershire: Gillis Kristensson, *A Survey of Middle English Dialects 1290–1350: The West Midland Counties*, Publications of the New Society of Letters at Lund 78 (Lund, 1987), 63–6, 79–99. For the rest of the study area: Gillis Kristensson, *A Survey of Middle English Dialects 1290–1350: The Southern Counties. I. Vowels (Except Diphthongs)*, Publications of the New Society of Letters at Lund 93 (Lund, 2001), 62–5, 91–120.

[24] There is insufficient space to detail the place-names and forms on which the maps presented here are based; these will be discussed elsewhere at a later date. Note that shires are mapped at their *c.*1850 extents.

[25] Cf. Jackson, *LHEB*, pp. 315–17.

[26] A. Cole, 'The Anglo-Saxon Traveller', *Nomina* 17 (1994), 7–18.

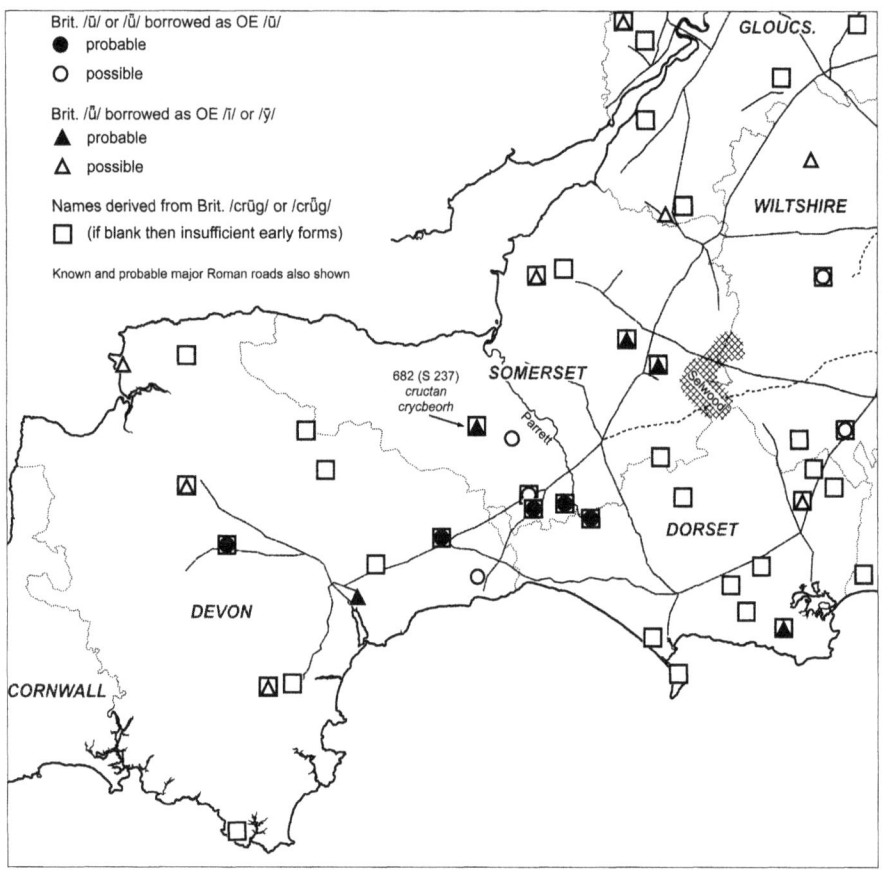

17.1 Borrowings of Brittonic /ū/ and /ŭ/ into Old English as preserved in place-names

adopted by Old English speakers using these routeways at a relatively early date. Alternatively, perhaps British *crūg had been adopted (with OE /ū/) into Old English as a toponym *crūc before Old English speakers reached the south-west;[27] if so, then some instances could represent new coinings by Old English speakers (using OE *crūc) rather than borrowings. But there are problems with both these hypotheses. In south Somerset and east Devon are two possible instances of Brittonic /ŭ/ borrowed with OE /ū/ that cannot derive from Brittonic *crūg or OE *crūc. They imply that a local substitution of OE /ū/ (rather than OE /ī/ or /ȳ/) for Brittonic /ŭ/ was not restricted to a particular toponym or to those occurring on major routeways. Furthermore, the instances of Brittonic *crūg borrowed with OE /ī/ or /ȳ/ (rather than OE /ū/) elsewhere in Devon, Somerset and east Dorset, which include some close to former Roman roads, do not suggest the widespread use of a hypothetical OE *crūc toponym. It perhaps remains possible that the

[27] Gelling and Cole, *Landscape of Place-Names*, pp. 143, 159; but cf. Eilert Ekwall, *Studies on English Place- and Personal Names* (Lund, 1931), p. 48 n. 2. On OE /c/ for Brit. /g/ see Jackson, *LHEB*, pp. 556–7; Campbell, *Grammar*, pp. 20–1.

substitution of Brittonic /ü/ by OE /ū/ in preference to OE /ī/ (or even OE /ȳ/) reflects the dialect of a particular group of Old English speakers; but if so, then the distribution does not correspond to that later evidenced for Middle English dialects.[28]

On balance, the round symbols in Somerset, Dorset and Devon seem best explained as representing genuine borrowings of Brittonic /ü/ using OE /ī/, although some of these (such as that in central Devon) may be 'travellers' landmark' borrowings. In chronological terms, and in both cases, the round symbols seem most likely to indicate the presence of Old English speakers before OE /ȳ/ developed to become a possible substitution for Brittonic /ü/, probably before the late seventh century. They may also represent areas in which Brittonic was effectively extinct by this time, although strictly we can only say that Brittonic no longer affected the local pronunciation of borrowed place-names by Old English speakers.

An unresolved problem, however, remains the potentially large temporal overlap between the data represented by the round and triangular symbols. We cannot usually determine, for example, if Brittonic /ü/ was borrowed as OE /ī/ in one place before or after it was borrowed as OE /ū/ in another. Similarly, although the cluster of round symbols around south Somerset may appear to provide tacit support for the *Chronicle*'s claim that the Britons were driven 'as far as the Parrett' after a battle near Selwood in 658,[29] the linguistic evidence suggests only that Old English became locally predominant at some point before the late seventh century. Rather than speculate further on the basis of just this one linguistic criterion, therefore, it seems preferable to consider the evidence that other examples provide.

Example 2: Old English borrowings of lenited British /m/

The second example of language change is relatively straightforward. Between the fifth and eleventh centuries an intervocal British /m/ in certain words gradually denasalized to become Brittonic /v/ through lenition.[30] When affected placenames were borrowed by Old English speakers the ambiguous intermediate Brittonic /μ/ sound would be substituted by OE /m/ in the early stages of its development and by OE /v/ (often spelt <f>) in the later ones. As there was no

---

[28] Kristensson, *Southern Counties I*, 65, 91, 116–20 and maps 7, 8; cf. Jackson, *LHEB*, pp. 316–17; Gelling, *Place-Names*, p. 139.

[29] *ASC* 658 : *Two Chronicles*, ed. Plummer I, 32–3. *Æt Peonnum* is usually identified as (Pen)Selwood, but cf. Katherine Barker, 'The Early History of Sherborne', in *The Early Church in Western Britain and Ireland*, ed. Susan M. Pearce, BAR, BS 102 (Oxford, 1982), 77–116, at pp. 110–11 n. 3.

[30] Jackson, *LHEB*, pp. 480–95, 560; Sims-Williams, *Celtic Inscriptions*, p. 48; cf. Probert, 'Church and Landscape', p. 287 n. 154. For the use of /μ/ to represent the intermediate stages, see Richard Coates and Andrew Breeze with a contribution by David Horovitz, *Celtic Voices English Places. Studies of the Celtic Impact on Place-Names in England* (Stamford, 2000), p. xi.

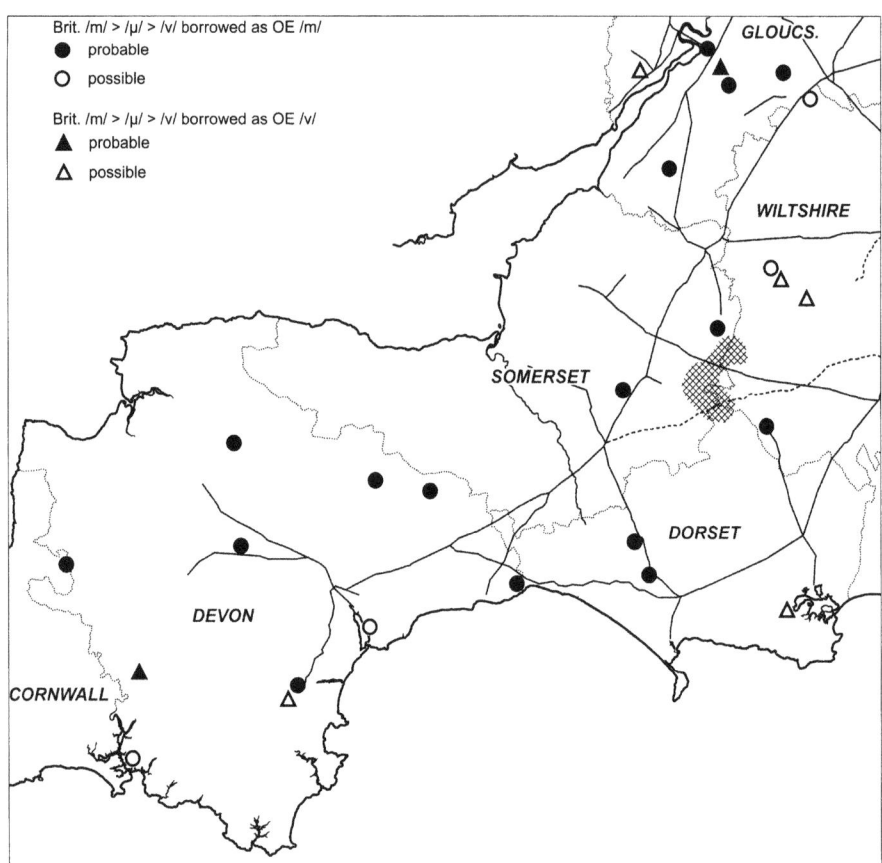

17.2 Borrowings of Brittonic /m/>/μ/>/v/ into Old English as preserved in place-names

equivalent change in Old or Middle English, such place-names should preserve how Old English speakers perceived the local pronunciation of Brittonic /μ/ at the time of borrowing (Illus. 17.2).

Despite the paucity of known examples in Somerset it is apparent that the round symbols predominate and occur as far west as the Tamar, which suggests that borrowings of Brittonic /μ/ as OE /m/ were possible well into the eighth century. The triangular symbols, on the other hand, represent Brittonic /μ/ perceived by Old English speakers as closer to OE /v/ than to OE /m/. That this was possible in or before the ninth century is shown by the <f> spellings of OE *Def(e)na* in the *Chronicle*, derived from the British name Dumnonia (discussed below).[31] However, we should allow for a period of ambiguity in which Brittonic /μ/ could be represented by either OE /m/ or OE /v/. It seems reasonable to suggest that this could occur during the eighth century, but the extent to which

[31] *ASC* 823 A, 851 A : *Two Chronicles*, ed. Plummer I, 60, 64. The spellings could be those obtaining at the dates of the annals or when the *ASC* was compiled in *c*.890; the contexts imply that they refer to the population of English Devon not that of British Dumnonia.

it may have begun in the seventh century or continued into the ninth century is debatable.

Where both OE /m/ and OE /v/ occur locally it seems likely that such borrowings were made when Brittonic /μ/ was perceived as ambiguous by Old English speakers. This is perhaps not unexpected in south Devon, where Brittonic almost certainly survived beyond the early eighth century and Old English speakers are unlikely to have arrived much before this. A similar explanation may underlie the possible borrowing with OE /v/ in Gloucestershire west of the Severn.[32] But what about those in Gloucestershire east of the Severn, west Wiltshire and south-east Dorset? That the instances of OE /v/ in east Gloucestershire and west Wiltshire are in close proximity to borrowings with OE /m/ suggests that they, too, were borrowed during the 'period of ambiguity' but does not provide a more precise indication of date. With regard to the possible example of OE /v/ in south-east Dorset, the evidential lack of nearby examples with OE /m/ renders the potential period of borrowing here open-ended.

To explain these 'eastern' borrowings of Brittonic /μ/ as OE /v/ within the traditional chronology for the political transition from British to English control, it has been suggested that the period of ambiguity began very early in the seventh century.[33] Yet all known examples further west until south Devon were borrowed using OE /m/ not OE /v/, which is remarkably consistent if Brittonic /μ/ was already perceived as ambiguous by Old English speakers in the early seventh century. Two alternative interpretations of the data seem preferable. The first is that Brittonic /μ/ remained sufficiently nasal to be heard only as OE /m/ until at least the late seventh century (if not later), so that all borrowings with OE /v/ indicate the correspondingly late survival of Brittonic in these eastern areas. If so, then the extinction of Brittonic speech in these areas was not concurrent with the political transition. The second is that as the west and south-west dialects of British diverged towards the 'Primitive' stages of the neo-Brittonic languages of Welsh and Cornish respectively, so the nasality of Brittonic /μ/ weakened faster in the former than in the latter.[34] If so, then some or all of the eastern instances of OE /v/ might reflect this linguistic divergence and represent borrowings made before the late seventh century, although not necessarily as early in that century as the attempt to parallel the political transition would require.

However, a comparison between the evidence for Brittonic /μ/ in Illus. 17.2 and that for British /ū/ and Brittonic /ǖ/ in Illus. 17.1 is inconclusive. In east Dorset, for example, borrowings of Brittonic /ǖ/ as either OE /ī/ or OE /ÿ/ imply the survival of Brittonic in either the mid-sixth or later seventh century respectively. The possible local borrowing of Brittonic /μ/ as OE /v/ in or after the early seventh century may help to refine these *termini post quos*, but it remains unclear as to which interpretation of Brittonic /μ/ is locally correct. Similarly, the

---

[32] Smith, *Place-Names of Gloucestershire* IV, 25–30, 42–3; Coates *et al.*, *Celtic Voices*, pp. 297–301, 378.
[33] Jackson, *LHEB*, pp. 490–3.
[34] See Jackson, *LHEB*, pp. 19–20 for west and south-west dialects of British (developing into what became Primitive Welsh and what became Primitive Cornish and Breton respectively) and pp. 481, 486 for intervocalic /m/ retaining nasality in Breton; cf. pp. 11–12.

borrowings of Brittonic /ü/ as OE /ū/ in the south Somerset area, which probably predate the late seventh century, lie within the area in which Brittonic /μ/ was borrowed only as OE /m/. This implies that Brittonic /ü/ was borrowed as OE /ū/ locally before Brittonic /μ/ became ambiguous to Old English speakers but does little to refine our dating for either. In short, further data are needed to triangulate these findings with any confidence.

Example 3: Brittonic 'pretonic reduction' and 'internal i-affection'

To introduce the final distribution map, it is useful to consider a name that does not appear on either Illus. 17.2 or 17.3 but was affected by linguistic changes depicted in both. It was noted above that OE *Def(e)na* (hence modern 'Devon') derived from the British name Dumnonia. British */Dŭmnoniā/ had become */Dŭμneniā/ through lenition of /m/ (discussed above) and the 'final i-affection' (whereby the vowel of the penultimate syllable was raised in anticipation of an /i/ in the final syllable) of /o/ to /ẹ/, which after the loss of final syllables in Brittonic would produce */Dŭμneṇ/ by the late sixth century.[35] This name was borrowed by Old English speakers who perceived Brittonic /μ/ as OE /v/, although precisely when (and where) depends on our interpretation of the distributions mapped in Illus. 1.2. Equally ambiguous, however, is how the /ŭ/ of Brittonic */Dŭμneṇ/ had developed to be borrowed as the OE /e/ implied by the OE *Def(e)na* spellings recorded in the ninth century.

There are two possible explanations. The first is by 'pretonic reduction' in the later sixth century in what became Welsh, whereby an unstressed British /ŭ/ (or /ĭ/) before a stressed syllable was reduced to Brittonic /a/, although this did not occur in what became Cornish (apart from a few exceptional cases).[36] The second proceeds from British /ŭ/ developing into Brittonic /ọ/ during the sixth century in what became Cornish, although it remained as /ŭ/ in what became Welsh.[37] Brittonic /ọ/ would become /ẹ/ through 'internal i-affection' (whereby an /i/ or /e/ modified the vowel of the preceding syllable), which probably occurred in the second half of the seventh century in Primitive Welsh and around the mid-eighth century in Primitive Cornish.[38] In other words two possibilities underlie OE *Def(e)na*: either it was borrowed in or after the later sixth century from a Primitive Welsh */Daμneṇ/ (through 'pretonic reduction'), or it was borrowed in or after the mid-eighth century from a Primitive Cornish */Dẹμneṇ/ (through 'internal i-affection').

---

[35] Jackson, *LHEB*, pp. 480–95, 560–1, 579–81, 587–9, 592–3, 595, 597–603, 618–33, 675; Peter Schrijver, *Studies in British Celtic Historical Phonology*, Leiden Studies in Indo-European 5 (Amsterdam and Atlanta, 1995), 23–4, 265–76, 461–2; Sims-Williams, *Celtic Inscriptions*, pp. 70–3, 109–15, 250, 352.

[36] Jackson, *LHEB*, pp. 656, 664–81; Schrijver, *British Celtic*, pp. 26–7, 161–8; Sims-Williams, *Celtic Inscriptions*, pp. 146–52, 254–5, 352.

[37] Jackson, *LHEB*, pp. 274–5; Sims-Williams, *Celtic Inscriptions*, pp. 100–2, 252, 284.

[38] Jackson, *LHEB*, pp. 579, 590–6, 604–18, 697; Schrijver, *British Celtic*, p. 259; Sims-Williams, *Celtic Inscriptions*, pp. 184–90, 204–7, 256, 286, 291.

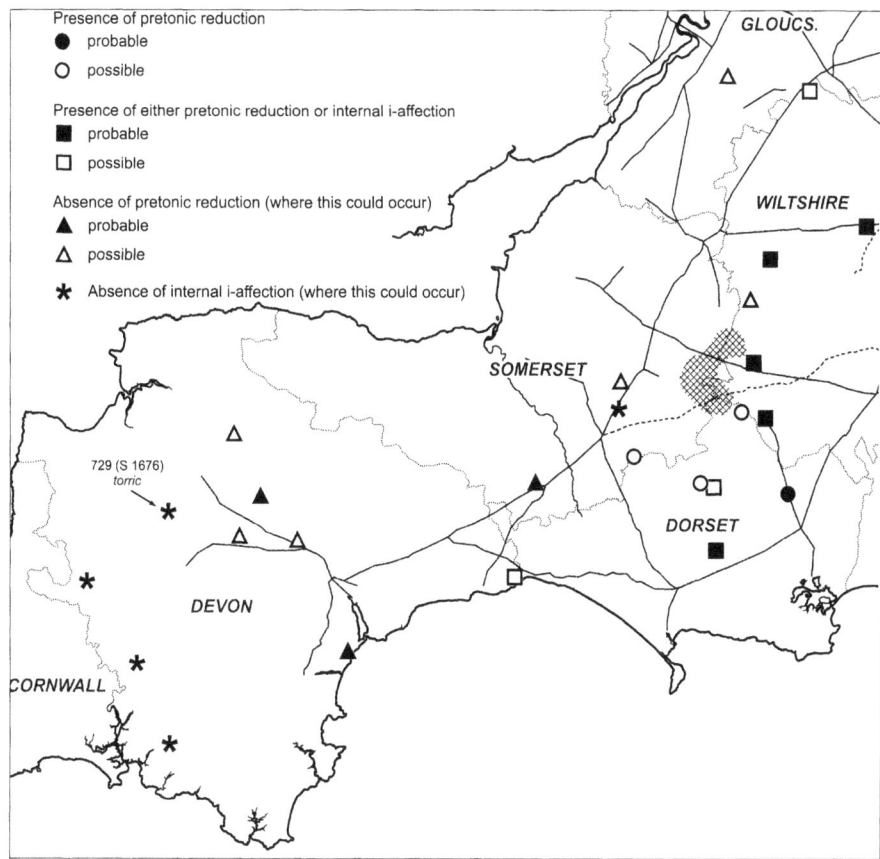

17.3 Evidence for Brittonic 'pretonic reduction' and 'internal i-affection' preserved in English place-names

Illus. 17.3 maps the evidence for Brittonic 'pretonic reduction' and 'internal i-affection' as fossilized in place-names adopted by Old English speakers. Again there are areas for which suitable evidence is scarce, notably in much of Somerset, east Devon, west Dorset and south Gloucestershire. Nevertheless, the round symbols around north Dorset represent Old English borrowings of Brittonic place-names in which pretonic reduction had occurred. They imply that the local Brittonic survived into the later sixth century and was developing towards Primitive Welsh rather than Primitive Cornish, although they do not indicate when Brittonic ceased to be spoken in this area.

By contrast the triangular symbols in Devon, Somerset, Gloucestershire and west Wiltshire represent Brittonic place-names in which pretonic reduction could occur but had not done so when they were adopted by Old English speakers. This was either because they were borrowed from what became Primitive Welsh before pretonic reduction in the later sixth century or because the local Brittonic was developing towards Primitive Cornish, in which pretonic reduction did not occur. Although the latter seems the more probable for all except perhaps the

Gloucestershire and Wiltshire examples, further discussion should be postponed until the remaining symbols in Illus. 17.3 have been considered.

The square symbols in Wiltshire, central Dorset and east Devon are ambiguous. They represent Brittonic place-names whose borrowed forms can be explained by either pretonic reduction or internal i-affection. However, that they are unlikely to be borrowings made after internal i-affection in Primitive Cornish is suggested by the distribution of asterisk symbols, all in west Devon except for one in east Somerset. These represent Brittonic place-names in which internal i-affection could occur but had not done so when they were adopted by Old English speakers. It is absent from the Brittonic river name in west Devon recorded as OE *Torric* in c.729, for example, or the spelling would have been OE **Terric*.[39] As internal i-affection had occurred in Primitive Welsh by the late seventh century, it is probable that the asterisk symbols showing its absence in west Devon were borrowings from Primitive Cornish, in which internal i-affection did not occur until around the mid-eighth century. The east Somerset example could theoretically represent a borrowing from either Primitive Welsh or Primitive Cornish, although its proximity to a triangular symbol perhaps renders the latter more likely.

This strongly suggests that the square symbols represent Old English borrowings from a local Brittonic that was developing towards Primitive Welsh. It remains uncertain as to which was the result of pretonic reduction in the later sixth century (and as such should be grouped with the round symbols in Illus. 17.3) and which was the result of internal i-affection in the later seventh century. In either case, however, all imply the local survival of Brittonic until at least the late sixth century. Given that the square and round symbols extend across most of the eastern part of Illus. 17.3, it therefore seems likely that the late sixth century is the effective *terminus post quem* for virtually all Old English borrowings of Brittonic place-names that lie further to the west on the three maps presented here.

Furthermore, if the round and square symbols represent Old English borrowings from what became Primitive Welsh while most asterisk and triangular symbols represent borrowings from what became Primitive Cornish, then Illus. 17.3 also provides an indication of a linguistic boundary. The distributions suggest that a west British dialect developing into Primitive Welsh was spoken in Wiltshire, parts of Dorset and possibly extended into east Devon, while a south-west dialect that became Primitive Cornish was spoken in west and central Devon and south Somerset. The boundary between them remains ambiguous because of evidential lacunae and because the triangular symbols in south Gloucestershire and west Wiltshire could represent borrowings from either Primitive Welsh or Primitive Cornish.

Even so it is worth comparing these distributions with those mapped in Illus. 17.2, for which an interpretation based on Brittonic dialects was one possibility. The two distribution patterns appear sufficiently different to suggest that devel-

---

[39] S 1676; Abrams, *Anglo-Saxon Glastonbury*, pp. 232–4; Eilert Ekwall, *English River-Names* (Oxford, 1928), pp. 413–14; Jackson, *LHEB*, p. 612.

opment of Brittonic /μ/ was not in fact affected by dialect. Admittedly, some data mapped in Illus. 17.3 coincide with evidential lacunae in Illus. 17.2 (e.g. in north Dorset) and vice versa (e.g. in east Devon and west Dorset) and may leave room for doubt. Nevertheless, the available data seem more likely to support the non-dialectal interpretation of the development of Brittonic /μ/ and hence that borrowings with OE /v/ indicate the local survival of Brittonic in or after the late seventh century.

Conclusions

In the mid-sixth century Brittonic was probably spoken throughout the mapped area except in parts of central and south Wiltshire. In eastern areas the local Brittonic was developing towards what became Primitive Welsh while in the west it became Primitive Cornish, although the linguistic boundary between these cannot yet be defined. By the mid-eighth century Old English speakers had reached the Tamar and south Devon, after which Brittonic speakers do not appear to influence the local Old English pronunciation of borrowed place-names. Between these spatial and temporal limits, however, the linguistic data preserved in borrowed Brittonic place-names need not support the idea of a steady West Saxon 'conquest and settlement' of the intervening territory. It is equally possible that some of these data indicate enclaves of Brittonic speakers that survived long after local political control had passed into English hands.

In the area of east Dorset, for example, the data mapped in Illus. 17.1 imply the local survival of Brittonic into the mid-sixth century and perhaps after the mid-seventh century if Brittonic / ū/ was borrowed as OE /ȳ/. The possible borrowing of Brittonic /μ/ as OE /v/ mapped in Illus. 17.2 could be as late as the eighth century. In Illus. 17.3 the presence of pretonic reduction implies a local Brittonic developing into Primitive Welsh that survived into the late sixth century, but the square symbol in central Dorset could represent internal i-affection and imply a borrowing in or after the later seventh century. Overall, these data are consistent with a local transition from British to English control during the seventh century. Yet they can also be used to argue either for the presence of some Old English speakers by the late sixth century or for the patchy survival of Brittonic into the early eighth century; indeed, it may be that these are not mutually exclusive interpretations.

This example illustrates both the potential and the ambiguities of this approach to the linguistic evidence preserved in certain place-names. Obviously, more work is needed to refine the data and interpretations presented here. It must also be emphasized that these interpretations are based on incomplete data. There is as yet no EPNS survey for Somerset,[40] that for Dorset is incomplete and those for

---

[40] For Somerset we remain dependent on Eilert Ekwall, *The Concise Oxford Dictionary of English Place-Names*, 4th edn (Oxford, 1960); Coates *et al.*, *Celtic Voices* (esp. pp. 330–4); *The Cambridge Dictionary of English Place-Names*, ed. Victor E. Watts (Cambridge, 2004).

Devon and Wiltshire are less thorough than more recent volumes. It is therefore probable that more examples, and additional forms for known examples, will be recovered. There are also other known developments in early medieval Brittonic that, although represented in only a few place-names borrowed into Old English, need to be incorporated, as do the linguistic data preserved in early Christian epigraphy.[41]

Once these linguistic data are mapped and interpreted their distributions can usefully be compared with those of the archaeological remnants of material culture. Although the latter need not reflect the same aspects of cultural transition as the linguistic data, both provide spatial and temporal contexts that facilitate further discussion. Within this framework the limited historical data can then be re-assessed. This multidisciplinary approach seems the most likely to advance our understanding of the transition from a British to an English linguistic, material and political culture in what became south-west England.

---

[41] Elisabeth Okasha, *Corpus of Early Christian Inscribed Stones of South-West Britain* (London and New York, 1993); Charles Thomas, *And Shall These Mute Stones Speak? Post-Roman Inscriptions in Western Britain* (Cardiff, 1994) (but cf. Probert, 'Church and Landscape', pp. 256–9 and n. 69); Sims-Williams, *Celtic Inscriptions*.

Index

Abingdon (Berkshire)   52
Aboriginal languages   176
adventus   5, 8, 10; *see* Anglo-Saxon Settlement
Aëtius, Roman general   117
Africa   197
Akerman, John   28, 30, 31, 34
Alamanni   61–2, 118, 119
Alaric, Visigothic king   119
Alba, kingdom of   117
Albanian   168, 209
Alberbury (Shropshire)   142
Aldhelm, abbot   76, 109, 232
Alfred, West Saxon/English king   19, 20, 76, 101, 114, 189, 223
Alveston (Warwickshire)   52
Angles   7, 79, 137, 172, 175, 192
Anglian   194
Anglicization   133, 139, 207, 221, 227–8
Anglo-Norman   197
Anglo-Norman England   117, 155
Anglo-Saxon Attitudes (by Angus Wilson)   16, 17
Anglo-Saxon Chronicle   23, 40, 107, 112, 137, 189, 231, 238
Anglo-Saxon England   1, 3, 9–11, 13, 15, 21, 47, 68–70, 82–4, 110, 115, 127, 130, 132–4, 143, 229
Anglo-Saxon (language) *see* Old English, Old Saxon
Anglo-Saxon graves   80–1, 87, 89, 95; *see also* burial rites, cemeteries
Anglo-Saxonism   29, 38, 41
Anglo-Saxons   6, 8, 12 ,14, 15, 17, 21, 23–4, 28–30, 37–9, 42, 44, 46, 52–4, 57–60, 68, 77, 79, 81, 86, 88, 90, 92, 95, 96, 100–1, 102, 113, 115–17, 120, 127–9, 137, 140, 165, 168, 170, 172, 173, 188, 201, 203, 214, 221, 225, 228–30
Anglo-Saxon Settlement   5–11, 69; *see also adventus*
Annales Cambriae (Welsh Annals)   120
Aquitaine, Aquitania   70, 182–4
Arabic   197
Archenfield (Herefordshire)   132–3, 136–9, 145, 150, 153, 161, 163
Argonne ware (pottery)   61

Armorica   6, 70, 117, 118; *see also* Brittany
Arnold, Chris   9
Arosæte (Warwickshire)   141
Arras, France   117
Arrow (Warwickshire)   141
Arthur, legendary king   2, 76
Ascoli, Graciadio   195
Asser, bishop of Sherborne   1, 76
Atiscross (Clwyd)   150
Augustine, saint and archbishop of Canterbury   76, 93
Ausonius, Roman poet   73
Australian English   176, 186, 190–1
Austrasia   84
Avon valley   95, 96
Æthelfrith, Northumbrian king   3, 189
Æthelhere, East Anglian king   92
Æthelstan, king of England   120, 223, 224, 231, 233

Baden-Württemberg, Germany   119
Badleybridge (Suffolk)   54
Balkans   117, 168
Balliol, Reginald, Domesday tenant in Cheshire   154
Bangor-is-y-coed (Wrexham)   94
Banham, Debby   16, 21
Banstead Down (Surrey)   54
Barham (Suffolk)   54
Barrington (Cambridgeshire)   52
Bartlow Hills (Ashdon, Essex)   35
Barton (Suffolk)   44
Basingstoke (Hampshire)   54
Basque   168, 182–4
Bassett, Steven   93, 106, 121
Bately, Janet   209
Bateman, Thomas   35
Bath (Somerset), pendant   168–70
Baudecet (Belgium), gold plate   169–70
Baugh, Albert   177
Bavaria, Baiuwaria, Germany   69, 70, 84, 116–19
Bawsey (Norfolk)   54
Bayonne, France   183
Bede, monk and author   2, 3, 7, 17, 21, 26, 36, 76, 78, 91, 98, 101, 139, 232
Bekesbourne (Kent)   54

Belgica 118
Belgium 169
Benedictine Reform 204
Benty Grange (Derbyshire) 53
Beowulf 186
Bergh Apton (Norfolk) 88
Beverley (Yorkshire) 44
Bifrons (Kent) 52–3
Birch (Herefordshire) 160, 163
Bistre (Clwyd) 132
Blair, John 122
Bleddyn ap Cynfyn 164
Bodmin Moor (Cornwall) 223
Boniface, saint and missionary 77
book-land 121
Book of Llandaff 161, 163
Bowcombe Down (Isle of Wight) 30
Braaten, Bjørn 124
Breach Down (Kent) 35
Breeze, Andrew 180, 186
Brent, John 32
Breton 145, 165–8, 212
Bretons 185
Brighthampton (Oxfordshire) 52
Bristol Channel 43, 51, 122
Britain 16, 19, 69–73, 75–7, 79, 82, 119, 125, 165, 173, 176, 194
'Britain AD' (television programme) 16
Britannia 7, 20, 43
British (the language), 12, 109, 197, 235–7, 239–40
British (the people) 86, 130, 142
British Church 93–4, 97, 100
British Highland Celtic 165–70
British Highland Zone 167–8
British Lowland Celtic 165–70
British Lowland Zone 168, 170–1
'British-ness' 13–15, 71–8, 92, 93, 114
British prehistory 3–4, 9, 13, 36, 39
Britons 1, 3, 5–7, 10, 12–15, 16, 21, 27–9, 31, 33–4, 36, 38–41, 58–60, 91, 92, 96, 97, 101, 101, 102–10, 112–14, 115–16, 123, 127–9, 172, 173, 181, 183, 189–91, 229, 230, 231, 232
Brittany 6–7; *see also* Armorica
Brittonic 6, 7, 14, 70, 74, 125–6, 145, 165, 172–3, 175, 177–8, 181, 184–8, 190–1, 197–9, 201, 203, 207–8, 211, 213, 215, 217–19, 221, 225, 227, 229, 231, 233–44; *see also* British (the language), Celtic, Late British
Bromfield (Shropshire) 95, 154
brooches 42–3, 46–7, 49, 51, 54, 58, 87–9
Broomfield (Barrow, Essex) 86
Broughton Lodge (Nottinghamshire) 52

Bruning, 1066 lord of Clifford 132
Buckland (Kent) 86
burial rites 28–9, 31–3, 35, 38, 40, 49; *see also* Anglo-Saxon graves, cemeteries
Bury St Edmunds (Suffolk) 44
Butler's Field (Lechlade, Gloucestershire) 87

Cable, Thomas 177
Cadbury Castle (Somerset) 44
Cadbury Congresbury (Somerset) 43
Cadien, tenant of Kilpeck in 1066 161–3
Caernarvon (Gwynedd) 52
Caerwent (Monmouthshire) 51, 52
Caesar, Julius 72
Caistor (Lincolnshire) 53
Caledonians 13
Camel, river 224
Camerton (Somerset) 54, 55
Campbell, James 9
Cannington (Somerset) 43
Canterbury (Kent) 231
Capheaton (Northumberland) 53
Carausius, count 31
Carpow (Perthshire) 89
Carroll, Lewis 16–17
Castell Collen (Radnorshire) 51
Castilian 182, 186
Catullus, poet 72
Celtic 7, 166, 167, 177, 189, 195; *see also* Breton, British, Brittonic, Cornish, Irish, Late British, Middle Welsh, Old Irish, Old Welsh, Pictish, Welsh
Celts 38, *see also* Britons, Bretons, Irish
cemeteries 9, 11, 13, 23–4, 27–41, 42, 58, 62, 85, 86, 90; *see also* Anglo-Saxon graves, burial rites
ceorl 105, 106
Cerdic, legendary West Saxon king 229
Chad, bishop of Lichfield 232
Chalcott (Cornwall) 221
Channel, the 71
Charles-Edwards, Thomas 106
Charlesworth, Dorothy 52
charters 227
Châteaubleu tile 169–70
Chavenage (Gloucestershire) 35
Cheshire 93, 95, 150, 151, 153
Chichester (Sussex) 47
Childeric, Merovingian king 118–19
Chisenbury Warren (Wiltshire) 59
Christianity 17, 68, 109, 116, 121
Churchstoke (Powys) 142
Cilternsæte, Chilterns 140
Claudian, Roman panegyrist 73
Clifford (Shropshire) 132

cloth   80–90
Clovis, Merovingian king   70, 118–19, 186
Clwyd   137
Cnut, king of England   120, 158
Coates, Richard   5, 9, 12, 192
Coddenham (Suffolk)   54
Colchester (Essex)   47
Collins, Roger   111
Cologne, Germany   61
Conderton (Worcestershire)   137
Constantine III, usurping emperor   74
Constantine Porphyrogenitos, emperor   42
contact linguistics   193–203
Coombe Down (Wiltshire)   59
Corbridge (Northumberland)   52, 89
Cornish (the language)   26, 120, 145, 165–8, 212, 215, 217, 219, 221, 233, 239–43
Cornwall   116, 119, 120, 122, 124, 130, 182, 186, 198, 215, 217, 219, 221, 223–4, 226–7, 231, 233
Costelin, Domesday landholder in Herefordshire   160
Cotswolds   36, 95, 96
Creechbarrow Hill (Somerset)   234, 235
creole   198–9
Crundale sword   53
Crystal, David   192
Cumbria   130; *see also* Lake District
Cuthbert, saint and bishop   17

Dafydd ab Owain Gwynedd   138
Danelaw   130, 214
Daniel, bishop of Winchester   77
Danube, river   77, 119
Dark, Petra   22
Dee, river   132
Deheubarth   158, 160
Derbyshire   98
Devon   108, 116, 120, 215, 217, 219, 221, 223, 225–7, 231, 233, 235–8, 240–4
Dickinson, Tania   47
Dixon, Philip   9
Domesday Book   1, 15, 23, 121, 132–7, 144, 145, 149, 150, 153, 157, 160, 163–4, 223, 224, 227, 233
Dorchester (Dorset)   141
Dornsæte (Dorset)   141
Dorset   108, 116, 217, 231, 235–9, 241–3
Douglas, James   28, 31, 34
Dumnonia   76, 107, 109, 231, 232, 238
Dunadd (Argyll)   56
Dungarth, king   120
Dunsæte (Somerset)   141–2
Dutch   125, 213
Dyfed   76

Eadric the wild, Domesday landholder in Shropshire   132, 135
Eadwine Psalter   80
East Angles   7, 92, 101
East Anglia   7, 85, 120
Eastry (Kent)   53
East Saxons   86
East Yorkshire   86
Ebrington (Gloucestershire)   44
'Eccles' place-names   99, 181
Ecgberht, West Saxon king   120, 223
Ecgfrith, Northumbrian king   78
Edward the Confessor, king of England   132, 133, 135
Edward the Elder, king of England   137
Edwin, in Welsh naming   149
Edwin ab Einion   158, 160
Edwin, earl of Mercia   132, 135
Effros, Bonnie   38
Ekwall, Eilert   178
elite dominance, or emulation, theory   11–13, 115, 116, 129, 217
empire collapse theory   57, 62, 65
Emscote (Warwickshire)   44
enamelling   43–6, 58, 60
England   3, 10, 17, 20, 40, 69–70, 96, 116, 121, 122, 124, 132, 164, 172, 183, 185, 204, 211, 215, 226–8, 231
Englefield (Clwyd)   132–4, 137, 138
English (the language)   15, 109, 120, 123, 126–7, 132–6, 138, 140, 173, 178–81, 186, 188, 190, 192, 194, 197–8, 204, 205, 207, 227, 231, 232, 243
English (the people)   26, 76, 78, 91, 100, 105, 108, 113
'English-ness'   2, 5, 78, 101
English Place-Name Society (EPNS)   232
Entwhistle, William   186
Eowa, king Penda's brother   100
Erbistock (Wrexham)   154
Ergyng   (Herefordshire)   137, 150, 161, 163
Essex   179, 217, 226
Estursete (Kent)   141
ethnicity   71
Evison, Martin   25
Evison, Vera   49
Ewen, Cecil   124
Exestan Hundred (Wrexham)   150, 154
Exeter (Devon)   120, 219, 233

Fairford (Gloucestershire)   36
Faussett, Bryan   28, 34, 44
Faversham (Kent)   30, 53, 54
Fécamp, pin type   42
feld place-names   137–40

Finnish 198
FitzOsbern, William, Domesday tenant 157, 159
FitzWarin, Fulk, Domesday tenant 155
Flemish 198
Flensburg, Schleswig-Holstein, Germany 7
Flintshire 94, 150, 153, 154
Förster, Max 177, 178
Fowler, Elizabeth 49
Fowler, Peter 22
France 61, 125
Francia 7, 10, 69
Franks 61–2, 79, 106, 116–18, 128
French 127, 130, 135, 168, 186, 197, 204, 207, 209, 226
Frilford (Oxfordshire) 32, 37
Frisia 84
Frisian 190, 194; *see also* Old Frisian
Frocester (Gloucestershire) 52

Gaelic 184
Gage, John 35
Gallia Cisalpina 195
Gallia Transalpina 195
Gallo-Roman 186
Gallo-Romans 61–2, 79, 106, 116, 128
Garonne, river 184
Garryduff (Co. Cork) 55
Gaul 6, 7, 10, 61, 68–73, 77, 79, 116, 117, 125, 166, 169, 170
Gaulish 169, 195, 197
Geake, Helen 88
Gelling, Margaret 99, 138, 141, 215
genetics 13, 24–5, 182
Geoffrey of Monmouth 26
George, Ken 233
Geraint, king of Dumnonia 107, 109
Gerald of Wales 138–9
Germanic (languages) 70, 116–19, 123, 127, 190, 191, 194, 197, 205, 207, 213; *see also* Anglian, Anglo-Saxon, Dutch, English, Frisian, Jutish, Kentish, Middle English, Old Frisian, Old Norse, Old Prussian, Old Saxon, Saxon, Scandinavian, West Saxon
Germans 27, 38, 61, 65, 71, 72, 77, 116
Germany 69, 76, 84,
Gerontius, British general 74, 76
Gildas, British author 2, 21, 36, 69, 74–8, 176
Gilton (Kent) 43, 44
Glamorganshire 226
Glaston (Rutland) 52
Glastonbury (Somerset) 43, 234
Gloucester 43, 97
Gloucestershire 150, 151, 153, 235, 239, 241, 242

Goltho (Lincolnshire) 121
Goodrich (Herefordshire) 163
Gorrochategui, Joaquín 184
graffiti 64
graves, *see* Anglo-Saxon graves, burial rites, cemeteries
Great Chesterford (Essex) 44
Great Saxham (Suffolk) 44
Greek 197, 209
Gregory of Tours 118
Grimmer, Martin 15
Gruffudd ap Maredudd 153, 157, 158, 160
Gruffudd ap Llywelyn 132, 160, 164
Guest, Edwin 40
Gwent 141–2
Gwynedd 92

Halhsæte (Alcester, Warwicksire) 141–2
Hampshire 108
hanging bowls 43, 46, 53–4, 58
Härke, Heinrich 15, 19–20
Harnham Hill (Wiltshire) 31
Harold, earl and king 132
Hebrides 185
Hedges, John 85
Helston (Cornwall) 221
Hengest, legendary English leader 76, 78
Henry II, king of England 155
Hereford 93, 133, 142
Herefordshire 93, 132, 134, 141, 142, 150, 151, 153, 157, 158, 160, 163
Herewald, bishop of Llandaff 161
Hertford, synod of 109
Higham, Nicholas 93, 123
Highdown (Sussex) 52
Hills, Catherine 9, 12, 15
Hingley, Richard 38
Hingston Down, battle of 215
Historia Brittonum 76, 78
Historia Ecclesiastica 78; *see also* Bede
'History of Britain' (television programme) 19
Hoare, Sir Richard Colt 35
Hobson-Jobson vocabulary 176
Hockwold-cum-Whitton (Norfolk) 44
Hodges, Richard 9–10, 115
Hoffmann, Marta 85
Hooke, Della 99
Hoxne (Suffolk) 46
Huddersfield (West Yorkshire) 138
Hugh, earl of Chester 154
Humberside 43, 49
Hummer, Hans 119
Huntcliffe ware 52
Hunterston Brooch 56

Hurst, Henry 168
Hwicce 92, 93, 96–8, 100
Hywel, king of Deheubarth 159

Iceland 69
Imma, Northumbrian thegn 109
India 72, 176, 188, 228–9
Indian English 176
Indo-European 166
Ine, West Saxon king 102, 104, 107, 112, 120, 127–8, 189, 228, 232
Ine's law code 102–14
Inker, Peter 46
inscribed stones 94–5
Iona 55
Ireland 38, 40, 52, 59, 76, 89, 117, 122, 198, 201, 213, 230
Irish 26, 100, 109, 126–7, 180, 186, 188
Italian 167, 209
Italy 69, 73, 83, 116, 117

Jackson, Kenneth 166, 187
Jones, Glanville 121
Jørgensen, Lise 84, 89
Jutish 194

Kastousky, Dieter 179, 180
Kaufman, Terence 193
Kemble (Gloucestershire) 31
Kemble, John 28, 29, 39
Kempton (Shropshire) 52
Kendrick, Thomas 17
Kent 30, 38, 86, 107, 211, 217, 226
Kentish 203
Kentishmen 137
Kilpeck (Herefordshire) 161, 163
Kingston Brooch 46
Kirkby Thore (Westmorland) 52
Klemola, Juhani 177

Lagore (Co. Meath) 40, 55
Laing, Lloyd 14
Lake District 182; *see also* Cumbria
Lakenheath (Suffolk) 44
Lambert, Pierre-Yves 187
Lamel Hill, York 33
Lancashire 139, 182
landscape history 7, 8, 11
Langobards 116, 117
Late Antiquity 4
Latin 5, 7, 12, 14, 68–70, 77, 127, 165–70, 172, 178, 182, 184, 189, 191, 195, 197, 207
law codes 69, 102–3, 106, 111, 114, 118, 127–8
Lechlade (Gloucestershire) 86

Leeds, E. T. 47
Leeds, Winifred 186–7
Leicestershire 98
Lex Salica 106
Lewis, C. P. 15
Lichfield (Staffordshire) 97, 100, 139
Lincolnshire 86
Lindisfarne Gospels 179
Linto Heath (Cambridgeshire) 35
Little Eriswell (Suffolk) 86
Llangarron (Herefordshire) 163
Llanwarne (Herefordshire) 161, 163
Lloyd, Sir John 144
Llwyd, Humphrey 157
Longley, David 54
looms 80–2
Lotharingians 130
Lowbury (Berkshire) 44
Low Countries, the 70
Lucy, Sam 25
Ludlow (Shropshire) 186
Lugdunensis II 6
Lullingstone (Kent) 53
Lye (West Midlands) 157, 158

Macclesfield (Cheshire) 139
Macfarlane, Alan 10
Maelor Gymraeg (Wrexham) 154, 155
Maesbury (Shropshire) 133–5, 139
Magonsæte 92, 95, 96, 98, 100
Majorian, Roman general and emperor 117
Makerfield (Lancashire) 139
Manchester conference 15, 20
Manchester Medieval Textiles Project 81, 85
manorialisation 121–2
Marwnad Cynddylan 99
Marchudd ap Cynan 164
Maredudd, king of Deheubarth 158, 159
Maserfelth, battle of 139–40
Mawfield (Herefordshire) 139
Mayer, Joseph 32
McMahon, April 174, 176
Meaney, Audrey 89
Mekrijarvi, Finland, conference 180, 187–8, 205, 207
Melverley (Shropshire) 132
Mercia 91, 98, 100, 107, 141, 186
Mercian 203
Mercians 7, 91, 92, 98, 100, 101, 139
Merewalh, king of the Magonsæte 92
Merfyn, king of Gwynedd 150
Merovingians 117; *see also by name*
Mersete Hundred (Shropshire) 132–6, 142
Middle Angles 7, 92, 100

Middle East 197
Middle English 204, 207, 211, 212, 213, 219, 235, 237, 238
Middle Welsh 212
Mildenhall (Suffolk) 54
Milfield (Northumberland) 86
millefiori 46
Milton Regis (Kent) 46
Minerva Park (Cambridgeshire) 89
Mitchell's Hill (Suffolk) 87
'Monarchy' (television programme) 16, 18–19
Monmouthshire 153
Morris, John 23
Morville (Shropshire) 139
Moselle, river 61–3
Mossé, Fernand 124
Mote of Mark (Dumfries and Galloway) 56
Mount Badon, siege of 2
Mount Sorrel (Leicestershire) 54
Mucking (Essex) 49, 86
Muids, pin type 42
multiple estates 121; *see also* 'shire'
Myres, J. N. L. 20, 23, 26

Needham Market (Suffolk) 54
Nennius, putative Welsh author 21
Netherlands, the 83, 84
Newgrange, Ireland 40, 47
Newton (Cornwall) 219–21
Newton (Shropshire) 135–6
Nickel, Gerhard 124
niello 46
Norman Conquest 4, 5, 133–4, 143, 203, 214, 226, 228
Norman-French 203; *see also* French
Normans 20, 122, 132–4, 193, 201, 204
North America 228–30
Northfleet (Kent) 37
Northumberland 86
Northumbria 1, 21, 78
Northumbrian 203
Northumbrians 7, 91, 139
Norwich (Norfolk) 120
Nottinghamshire 98

Offa, Mercian king 101, 141
Offa's Dyke 132, 134
Ohthere, author and traveller 209
Oldbury (Warwickshire) 35
Old English 3, 10, 11, 104, 115, 125, 135, 171, 177, 180, 183, 191, 198–201, 203–5, 207–9, 211, 213–14, 219, 221, 225, 231, 233–44
Old Frisian 125; *see also* Frisian

Old Irish *see* Irish
Old Norse 180, 184, 198, 205, 207, 211, 214
Old Prussian 197
Old Saxon 125
Old Welsh 208, 211
Orkney 55
Orosius, fifth-century writer 209
Oswald, saint and king 91, 100, 139–40
Oswestry (Shropshire) 134, 135, 139
Ottery, river 217, 221, 224
Owain , Welsh personal name in Domesday Book 150, 158, 159, 160
Oxborough (Norfolk) 88
Oxfordshire 179

Padel, Oliver 9, 233
paganism 16–17, 95, 100, 116, 118
palaeobotany 7, 8, 14
Pannonia 70
Parker, Matthew 26
Parrett, river 231, 237
Patrick, saint and missionary 69, 74, 76
Peada, Mercian king 92
Pecsæte (Peak District) 140
Pelagius, Romano-British heretic 68
Pelteret, David 120, 122
Pembrokeshire 226
Penda, Mercian king 91, 92, 100, 101, 139
Penge (Surrey) 219
'Pennine Wales' 182
Pentridge (Dorset) 219
Peterborough Chronicle 203; *see also Anglo-Saxon Chronicle*
Petersfinger (Wiltshire) 86
Peterstow (Herefordshire) 161
Peverell, William 155
Pictish (language) 109
Picts 75
pins 42
place-names 177–8, 181
Pokorny, Julius 178
Portchester (Hampshire) 47
Poussa, Patricia 123–4
Powlesland, Dominic 22
Preussler, Walther 123–4
Prittlewell (Essex) 16, 18
Probert, Duncan 15
Procopius 6
Pryor, Francis 18–20, 22, 25
psycholinguistics 199
punched decoration 46–7
Pyrenees 168, 183–4

Queenford Farm (Dorchester, Oxfordshire) 59, 62

INDEX 251

Raetia 118
Rahtz, Philip 51
Raunds (Northamptonshire) 121
Reynold de Bailleul 134
Reynolds, Susan 110
Rhine, river 61, 70, 118, 119
Rhineland 61, 70, 77, 84
Rhiwsete (Shropshire) 141–2
Rhydderch ab Iestyn 160
Rhys ap Tewdwr 158, 164
Rhys Sais 154–7, 159, 164
Richborough (Kent) 54
Risley (Kent) 53
river names 233
Roach-Smith, Charles 28–30, 32–3, 37
Roger de Lacy 160–1
Roger de Powis 155
Roger of Montgomery 157
Rogers, Penelope 85
Rollason, David 21
Rolleston, George 32–4, 37
Roman army 170
Roman artefacts 30–2, 38
Roman Britain 2, 10, 11, 15, 16, 21, 23, 29–30, 36–7, 42, 46, 55, 58–60, 69, 82, 89, 90, 108, 166–8
Roman roads 235–6
Romance (the language) 6, 10, 115, 116, 127, 166, 167, 169, 171, 184, 186, 195
Romanian 167
Romanity 71–3, 75, 76, 77, 79, 116
Romanization 4, 11, 34, 39, 71, 73, 119, 182
Romano-British metalworking 42–56
Romans 20, 22, 30, 33–5, 75, 183, 195
Roundway Down (Wiltshire) 55
Russia 63, 65–7, 117, 122, 207; *see also* Soviet Union, USSR
Rutilius Namatianus, Roman poet 73

sæte place-names 137, 140–2
Said, Edward 72
Saissil, Old Welsh personal name 145
Salian Franks 118
Salic Law 128
Sandwich (Kent) 31
Sardic (Sardinian) 167
Sarre (Kent) 46
Sawyer, Peter 4, 122
Saxon (language) 194, 204, 219, 221
Saxons 16, 20–2, 28, 30, 33–5, 37–8, 41, 75, 77–9, 105–7, 110, 112, 172, 175, 192, 219, 223, 225, 227–9
Scandinavia 10, 14, 82, 83, 85
Scandinavian 184, 213
Scandinavians 205, 207, 208

Scandinavianization 4
Schama, Simon 19, 23
Schleswig, Germany 7
Schrijver, Peter 124–5, 172, 187, 190, 191, 198
Scopwith (Lincolnshire) 44
Scotland 17, 20, 38, 184, 198, 217
Scots 26, 75
Selwood, battle of 237
Serjeantson, Mary 179
Severn, river 43, 49, 95, 132, 231, 239
Sewerby (Humberside) 88
'shire', multiple estate 121, 122
Shropshire 93, 95, 132–4, 139, 141–2, 151, 153–5, 157
Sibbertswold (Kent) 46
Silures 13
Sims-Williams, Patrick 93, 96, 166
Siward, Shropshire land-holder in 1066 135
Skaill (Orkney) 55
skeletons 33–4, 40
slaves 104, 106, 112, 172, 189, 190–1
Slavic 197, 209
Slavs 117
Snape (Suffolk) 31
social psychology 202–3
Somerset 108, 217, 231, 235–8, 240–3
Somerton (Somerset) 141
Somme, river 118
South Africa 228–9
South Saxons 107
Soviet Union 62, 65, 66; *see also* Russia, USSR
Spain 69, 70, 72, 182
Spanish 209
spinning 80
Spong Hill (Norfolk) 32
Staffordshire 98
Starkey, David 18, 20, 24
Staxton (North Yorkshire) 52
Stenton, Sir Frank 5–6, 20
Stephen, *Life of Wilfrid* 99, 100
Stilicho, Roman general 73
Stowting (Kent) 32
Stratford (Warwickshire) 52
Stratton (Cornish hundred) 224
Stukeley, William 39
Sumorsæte (Somerset) 141
Sutton Hoo (Suffolk) 16–18, 46, 53, 81, 86
Swallowcliffe Down (Wiltshire) 54–5
Switzerland 61, 70
systems collapse 67

Tacitus, Roman historian 13–14, 73, 138

Tamar, river   120, 215, 217, 223, 224, 231, 233, 238, 243
Tasmania   191
Tavistock Abbey (Devon)   217
Tegeingel (Englefield, Clwyd)   138; *see also* Englefield
Temesæte (Shropshire)   141–2
Tewdws ap Marchi   163
Theodore, archbishop of Canterbury   78, 98
Thomas, Mark   25
Thomason, Susan   193
Thornton, David E.   15
Thurnam, John   33
Tolkien, J. R.   186
Tournai, Belgium   118
Trak, Larry   182
Tribal Hidage   141
Trier, Germany   61
Tristram, Hildegard   13, 126
Turkey   63, 65
Tyesmere (Worcestershire)   98
Tyler, Damian   15

Upper Thames Valley   36, 47
USA   65
USSR   19, 62; *see also* Russia, Soviet Union
Utrecht Psalter   80

Vale of Pickering (North Yorkshire)   22
Varangians   122
Vascones   184
Vennemann, Theo   196
Verulamium (St. Albans, Hertfordshire)   49
Victorian England   18, 28–9, 38
Viennensis   69, 70, 77
Vikings   20, 24, 193
Vindolanda (Northumberland)   73
Virgil   69
Visigothic Spain   116, 117

Wacher, John   179
Walcot type place-names   190
Wales   1, 17, 20, 38, 92, 100, 116, 117, 120, 122, 124, 133, 138, 144, 150–1, 153, 160, 164, 182, 198, 217, 226–7, 230, 231
Wall (Staffordshire)   99
Wallingford (Oxfordshire)   60
Walloon   198
Walton type place-names   1, 190, 232
Ward-Perkins, Bryan   68, 112, 116, 185
Wareham (Dorset)   128
Warwickshire   95, 98
Wayland's Smithy (Berkshire)   36
weaving   80
Wednesbury (West Midlands)   98
Wednesfield (West Midlands)   98
Weeford (Staffordshire)   98
Welch, Martin   121
Wellington (Herefordshire)   158
Welsh Bicknor (Gloucestershire)   163
Welsh (language)   26, 126, 127, 130, 131, 165–8, 190, 197, 207, 239–43
Welsh (personal names)   145, 149, 150–1
Welsh (people)   76, 92, 132–8, 140, 142, 144, 145, 149, 153, 164
Wentsæte (Gwent)   141–2
wergild   104–6, 108, 127, 128, 228
Wessex   1, 107, 108, 110, 111, 122, 173, 207, 211, 223, 228
'Westwood' (Herefordshire)   132, 136
West Midlands   231
West Heslerton (North Yorkshire)   22, 25
West Saxon   203, 207
West Saxons   103, 113, 114, 119, 127, 128, 231, 232
West, Stanley   59
Whitby (North Yorkshire)   54, 109
White, David   207
White, Roger   47, 51, 88
Whithorn (Dumfries and Galloway)   76
Whittington (Shropshire)   134–6
Wijester, pin type   42
William the Conqueror   144, 203
William of Malmesbury   120, 223
Williams, Howard   15
Willingdon (Sussex)   53
Wilson, Angus   16–18
Wilson, Daniel   39
Wiltshire   108, 177, 182, 235, 239, 241–4
Winchester (Hampshire)   232
Winnall (Hampshire)   55
Wischer, Ilse   209
Witcombe Villa (Gloucestershire)   52
Wolfram, Herwig   118
Wood, Ian   118
Woodyates (Dorset)   46
Woolf, Alex   15
Worcester   97
Wordsworth, William   187
World Wars   2
Wormald, Patrick   108, 111
Wormelow hundred (Herefordshire)   132–3
Worsaae, Jens   39
Wrekin (Shropshire)   141
Wreocensæte (Shropshire)   93, 94, 95, 96, 98, 100, 141
Wrexham   150, 154
Wright, Thomas   28, 30–1, 34, 37, 39
Wroxeter (Shropshire)   47, 97, 141
Wulfhere, Mercian king   100

Wye, river 120, 132
Wylie, William 28, 36

Yale (Wrexham) 154

York 33, 54
Yorke, Barbara 173

Zandvoort, Reinard 205, 213–14

Lightning Source UK Ltd.
Milton Keynes UK
UKHW050135070223
416581UK00005B/348